MW00579268

Esther

Power, Fate, and Fragility in Exile

Erica Brown

אסתר

Esther

Power, Fate, and Fragility in Exile

OU Press
Maggid Books

Esther
Power, Fate, and Fragility in Exile

First Edition, 2020

Maggid Books
An imprint of Koren Publishers Jerusalem Ltd.

POB 8531, New Milford, CT 06776-8531, USA
& POB 4044, Jerusalem 9104001, Israel
www.maggidbooks.com

The publication of this book was made possible
through the generous support of *Torah Education in Israel.*

ISBN 978-1-59264-539-8, *hardcover*

A CIP catalogue record for this title is
available from the British Library

Printed and bound in the United States

In loving memory of Irving and Beatrice Stone,
who dedicated their lives to the
advancement of Jewish education.
We are proud and honored to continue in their legacy.

Their Children, Grandchildren, and Great-Grandchildren
Jerusalem, Israel
Cleveland, Ohio USA

To Manette and Louis Mayberg
"The righteous guide their friends…"
(Proverbs 12:26)

Thank you for your
guidance and friendship.

Contents

Preface

The Book of Esther, and its millennia of commentary, invites us to consider Jewish life in the diaspora as a tug-of-war between power and powerlessness. It encourages readers, across the globe, even those living in the State of Israel, to consider the tensions between authority and autonomy while exploring key questions of Jewish identity and influence. As such, it has inspired important conversations that I have tried to capture, many as old as the Talmud itself. A key example of an ongoing conversation appears in an obscure tractate in the Talmud. The third-century scholar Rava was troubled that on Purim we do not recite Hallel, a series of psalms of joy normally said on holidays. He used the first verse from Hallel, Psalms 113:1, to offer his explanation: "Give praise, O servants of the Lord." When the Jews left Egypt, they left slavery and were able to become God's servants in earnest, Rava believed. This was not true, however, after Purim. "We are still the servants of Ahasuerus," Rava observed of life in Babylonia, long after Ahasuerus died.[1]

Are those of us in the diaspora today, still, in some way, servants of Ahasuerus? This is the central question of this complex biblical book.

We may read the Book of Esther as an entertaining story, a theological challenge, a discussion of governance, leadership, and gender, or a social commentary on life in the diaspora. There were times when the

1. Arakhin 10b.

world of commentary around Esther flourished for the simple reason that Esther is the only biblical book to describe an integrated diaspora community under the threat of mass persecution, making it an obvious framework for interpreters to analyze their own historical and political situation within. One scholar goes as far as to say that the holiday itself allows the community of celebrants to experience exile: "Since Judaism's arena is the arena of history, and exile is an aspect of Jewish existence, Judaism must deal with it. Exile must be grasped existentially. Purim does that. It is the enacting of exile."[2]

To consider the enormity of exile's weight, we will approach the Book of Esther from many different perspectives. The Bible scholar David Clines observes that because the Hebrew Bible is such a rich text, those who write on it should favor biblical interpretation that is "poly-commentary, multi-voiced, indeterminate, divergent, suggestive and limitless."[3] All interpretation relies on making the text central and foundational whether the commentary is spiritual, intellectual, philological, archaeological, or historical. To understand and celebrate a text, we must invite many different readers and readings, each offering us a way of viewing the same lines through completely different lenses. In the pages ahead, you will find a medley of ancient and medieval commentaries sitting side by side with modern scholarship, punctuated by snippets on culture and whimsy: the mention of a painting, a stanza of a poem, the observation of a novelist. Some see Esther as a search for God in an unlikely place, while others regard it as a comedic farce. It is a story about peoplehood, a leadership manual that continues to instruct, a text that challenges its readers to step into the unknown and change reality for the good. We will explore these polymorphic voices from a posture of curiosity.

The Book of Esther asks its celebrants to turn the world upside down because that is what can be expected in exile: the unpredictable, the surprise turn, the change in fate. If Purim is a holiday to examine

---

2. Monford Harris, "Purim: The Celebration of Dis-Order," *Judaism* 26 (1977): 167.
3. David J. A. Clines, "Esther and the Future of the Commentary," in *The Book of Esther in Modern Research*, ed. Sidnie White Crawford and Leonard J. Greenspoon (London: T & T Clark International, 2003), 21.

exile, then Esther is its textbook and our guide. The punctures of divine providence throughout its ten chapters make it a story of simplicity wrapped in layers of mystery, as the author Dennis Covington observed, "Mystery…is not the absence of meaning, but the presence of more meaning than we can comprehend."[4]

4. Dennis Covington, *Salvation on Sand Mountain: Snake Handling and Redemption in Southern Appalachia* (Boston: Addison-Wesley Publishing Company, 1995), 203–4.

Introduction

Esther: An Overview

Satire, Drama, Fiction, History, or Theology?

Esther as Social Commentary

Esther: An Overview

The Book of Esther is much beloved in the biblical canon. It is a story of suspense and intrigue, royalty and beauty, great heroes and terrible villains. It has inspired countless plays, theatrical productions, and princess costumes. Beyond its cultural impact, the book ostensibly presents a radical proposition: Jews can be successful in the diaspora. In contrast to the prophet Jeremiah, who conceded that life outside the homeland must continue for the sake of survival and continuity, Esther represents the opportunity for Jewish strength and influence in exile. Jeremiah wanted his exiles to remain productive but hardly expected diasporic communities to thrive. He told those in his charge to "build houses and live in them, plant gardens and eat their fruit." He advised Jews to marry and seek the welfare of their host government (Jer. 29).

The Book of Esther, however, offers a vision of Jewish power in exile and a promise of more than just basic sustenance. Aaron Koller notes in *Esther in Ancient Jewish Thought* that when the events of the book took place, "not a person alive remembered a time when the Persians were not in control. As the reality became less traumatic and more 'normal,' the theological challenge it presented became more difficult."[1] The normalization of an exilic state softened the theological blow. This

1. Aaron Koller, *Esther in Ancient Jewish Thought* (New York: Cambridge University Press, 2014), 8.

new reality did not come without accompanying difficulties, spoken and unspoken, yet the Book of Esther presents an unapologetic narrative of Jewish pride in a land not their own. The Jews, like Esther herself, perceive themselves as a chosen people who find themselves in harm's way. They strategize for survival and, in so doing, create a platform for lasting impact. While this is the story the book tells, there is a deeper truth behind the carefully constructed façade of success; namely, success does not persist; sometimes it lasts for decades. Sometimes it lasts for centuries. It will not last forever. The fortunes of Jews living without true autonomy, independence, and self-governance can change instantly, as they so often have.

Adam Kirsch reminds us that the double bind of Esther has been true throughout history: "When the Jews are powerless, they are prey to the murderousness of their enemies, but if an individual Jew becomes powerful enough to defend his people, the fact of Jewish solidarity is another proof of dangerous Jewish difference."[2] It seems that there is no winning strategy for diasporic success. Nevertheless, as the events of the book unfold, Esther and Mordecai act with the understanding that they are living in a momentous epoch, a time worthy of record.

Who Wrote the Book of Esther?

"Mordecai recorded these events…" (Est. 9:20). Events are written down for a variety of reasons: to inform, to expose, to chastise, to record, to unify. When Mordecai recorded the dramatic events of the book, it seems most likely that some clarification was necessary following the unexpected victory in Shushan and beyond. The confusion of decrees and their reversals, and the fact that much took place in the royal palace away from the public eye, meant that Mordecai had to explain the decree against the Jews, its revocation, the role Haman played, and the battle and victory that ensued.

Mordecai knew he needed to record these events immediately; for those in Shushan, those across the empire, and those far beyond in both place and time. Rashi suggests that what Mordecai actually wrote

2. Adam Kirsch, *The People and the Books* (New York: W. W. Norton & Company, 2017), 44.

was not a brief letter to be delivered to all in the kingdom, but the Book of Esther as we know it today.[3] The Jews had a story for themselves and for posterity, and needed to tell it in their own way (although as the Book of Esther ends, we learn that its central characters and events were also recorded in the annals of Media and Persia).

Yet, nine verses after being told Mordecai recorded the events, we are puzzled. The text reads: "Then Queen Esther daughter of Abihail wrote a second letter of Purim for the purpose of confirming with full authority the aforementioned one of Mordecai the Jew" (Est. 9:29). Ibn Ezra steps in to clarify: Mordecai wrote the story, and a year later Esther confirmed the observance of Purim for eternity. One told the tale, and the other cemented the celebration.

The Talmud credits the writing of the book to the Men of the Great Assembly, a kind of group project, likely written at a distance from the story's actual time and place.[4] Modern Bible scholars are less sure who wrote Esther.[5] One of the difficulties of dating the book lies in identifying Ahasuerus in history. In the Septuagint version of Esther, Ahasuerus is referred to as Artaxerxes. Others believe he is the Persian king Xerxes, and the Hebraicized version of his name took us to Ahasuerus.[6] In the Talmud, we also have confusion around this central character: "Darius, Cyrus and Artaxerxes were all one: he was called Cyrus

3. Rashi on Est. 9:20.
4. Bava Batra 15a.
5. Michael V. Fox, along with many other scholars, dates the book to the Hellenistic period without hazarding a guess at actual authorship. The Greek translation of the book was brought to Egypt in 73 BCE, and he notes, "There is nothing to allow a more precise dating" (*Esther: Character and Ideology in the Book of Esther* [Grand Rapids, MI: William B. Eerdmans Publishing, 2001], 139). For more on Esther's historicity and the date of its composition, but not its likely author, see Jon D. Levenson, *Esther: A Commentary* (Louisville, KY: Westminster John Knox Press, 1997), 23–27.
6. Leonard J. Greenspoon suggests in his curiously titled article, "From Maidens and Chamberlains to Harems and Hot Tubs: Five Hundred Years of Esther in English," that the common use of Xerxes in Esther translations follows Herodotus' labeling, despite its phonetic distance from a more simple transliteration: "Translations that use this name instead of one or another form of the Semitic are engaging in the process of substituting a more familiar name or term for the less well known" (in *The Book of Esther in Modern Research*, 227).

because he was a worthy king; Artaxerxes after his realm; while Darius was his own name."[7] To minimize the confusion of names, the Talmud smooths out the problem by suggesting the names are descriptors, honorifics, or personal names. Thamar Gindin, a professor of ancient Persia and modern Iran at the Hebrew University, resolves the naming discrepancy: "In my opinion, the simplest solution for the discrepancy between the king's names in the different versions is that the translators had different versions before them, and because they had no prior knowledge of Old Persian, Persian phonology and contact linguistics, the name Ahasuerus sounded to them more similar to *Artaxerxes* or *Ardeshir* than *Xerxes* or *Khashayar*."[8]

Regardless of the book's authorship and dating, we are sure that its writer had a keen sense of irony, humor, and literary skill. The author of Esther could create a mood, heighten suspense, and deliver profound messaging through a relatively simple tale. The Book of Esther reveals the hand of a deeply religious scribe with a keen understanding of realpolitik. The author wove a layered story of intrigue that mined the depths of what a diasporic culture could look like at its most fragile and its most commanding. Thus, it does not surprise us to find a talmudic discussion crediting Esther's author with the divine inspiration to produce a master work to be read for centuries, if not millennia:

> R. Eliezer says: Esther was composed under the inspiration of the Holy Spirit, as it says, "And Haman said in his heart." R. Akiva says: Esther was composed under the inspiration of the Holy Spirit, as it says, "And Esther found favor in the eyes of all who looked upon her." R. Meir says: Esther was composed under the inspiration of the Holy Spirit, as it says, "And the thing became known to Mordecai." R. Yose b. Durmaskit said: Esther was composed under the inspiration of the Holy Spirit, as it says, "But on the spoil they laid not their hands."[9]

---

7. Rosh HaShana 3b.
8. Thamar E. Gindin, *The Book of Esther Unmasked* (Los Angeles: Zeresh Books, 2015), 29–30.
9. Megilla 7a.

In this fascinating discussion, each scholar agrees that divine inspiration created the book but disagrees about the verse that most evidently reveals that inspiration, connecting the source to comments about different characters. If "Haman said in his heart," but not aloud, an author must have known what Haman was really thinking. If Esther had a sense of grace that could be understood as divine favor, then perhaps she was given the inspiration for the composition. As evident by Mordecai's ability to stop the killing of the king, he clearly knew matters concealed from others; perhaps he authored the book. Or maybe God wrote it, endowing this book with the sacred properties generally reserved for the Pentateuch alone. After all, someone knew the enemy's heart, the heroine's grace, and the hero's intuition.

Even though God's name never appears in the book, and the accompanying holiday was a human, not biblical, construct, the Talmud gives Esther a rabbinic seal of approval, stating: "Reading the scroll of Esther is derived from a verse: 'The Jews confirmed, and they took upon themselves' (Est. 9:27). They confirmed above, and they took it upon themselves below."[10] Jews looked above, in the direction of heaven, received divine confirmation that their unexpected political and military triumph should be marked for the ages, and observed Purim as a staple of the Jewish holiday calendar. The reading of the scroll became a ritual centerpiece. Yet the popularity of Esther far exceeds its annual festivities. It is so central to the biblical canon that Maimonides, basing himself on rabbinic dictum, codified in law that Esther will continue to be read in the messianic era, even when other biblical books will fade in significance.

> All the books of the prophets and all the writings will no longer be valid in the days of the Messiah except for the scroll of Esther. It will remain together with the Pentateuch and the Oral Torah, which will never lose their validity. Even though all memory of troubles will be forgotten, as Isaiah states, "All former troubles will be forgotten; they will be hidden from my eyes" (65:16), the days of Purim will remain, as it is written in Esther: "These days of

10. Makkot 23b.

> Purim will not pass from the Jews, and their memory will never be forgotten by their descendants" (9:28).[11]

Certain texts are so fundamental to Jewish life that no matter the circumstance, they must be read. Out of all the prophetic works and later scriptures, only Esther will remain. Maimonides, living in Egypt at the time, and the sages in Babylonia before him, understood that Jews would always occupy a place outside the Land of Israel and would need the vision of hope the Book of Esther provided.

Maimonides points to a future for the scroll. He also offers a robust present when discussing how it is to be read annually. The text requires attentiveness, even a fierce vigilance when chanted. Almost nothing else matters when it is time to read the *Megilla.* Maimonides opens his legal discussion of Purim with this very thought:

> It is a positive commandment ordained by the Sages to read the scroll at the appointed time. It is well known that this was ordained by the prophets. Everyone is obligated in this reading: men, women, converts, and freed servants. Children should also be trained to read it. Even the priests should pause in their service in the Temple and come to hear the reading of the scroll. Similarly, Torah study should be postponed to hear the reading of the scroll. This applies to all other commandments in the Torah: the observance of all of them is superseded by the reading of the

11. Maimonides, *Mishneh Torah, Hilkhot Megilla VeḤanukka* 2:18. Maimonides bases his view on a passage in the first chapter of the Y. Megilla: "R. Yoḥanan said the books of the prophets and the writings will be invalid in the future, but the five biblical books will remain as they are written forever, as it says: 'A mighty sound that does not end' (Deut. 5:19). Reish Lakish added that the scroll of Esther and the laws will also remain. 'It is written here: "A mighty sound that does not end," and there it is written: "These days of Purim will not pass from the Jews and their memory will never be forgotten by their descendants" (Est. 9:28).'" The Ravad, ad loc., vociferously objected to this statement: "These are the words of a non-scholar: no biblical text will be removed from the canon; every work has something to teach. What was said was that even if other writings would no longer be read publicly, the scroll of Esther will continue to be read in public."

> scroll. There is nothing that takes priority over the reading of the scroll except the burial of a corpse that has no one to attend to it. A person who encounters a corpse should bury it and then read the scroll.[12]

To demonstrate the priority that Esther is given, all commandments are put aside when the story is read liturgically except in one urgent case that demands human dignity: the burial of an unattended corpse. Otherwise, we must listen to the scroll with rapt attention. Individuals of every age and status – from priest to servant – even those engaged in the holy occupations of study or performing other commandments, must drop everything for Esther. Nothing else matters but this story. Its message transcends time and place and will do so for eternity.

This intense emphasis on the preservation of one biblical book above most others begs the question: Why Esther? What is it about this story that makes it supersede in urgency narratives of the conquest of the Land of Israel, the appointment of judges and kings, the diatribes of our greatest prophets, such that it demands the undivided attention of all possible listeners?

This question can be answered in one of two ways. First, we must read the Book of Esther because its happy ending foreshadows all future Jewish redemption. It signals hope in the face of the impossible, which has come to characterize Jewish history; our hope encompasses everything from the providential and enduring belief that "relief and deliverance" will always be forthcoming for the people of Israel to faith in the coming Messiah. In preventing disaster, Mordecai and Esther give their fellow Jews the agency, courage, and optimism to stand up for the values they hold dear, even if all fate is ultimately divinely construed. It holds this hope because the Book of Esther is a magical story of good versus evil, of ostentatious power and wealth versus immense national vulnerability. It contains action and suspense, even if you've read the

---

12. Maimonides, *Mishneh Torah, Hilkhot Megilla VeḤanukka* 1:1. He may have based this reading on a passage in Arakhin 4a that states that even priests and Levites in the midst of active service must suspend their activities to hear the *Megilla.*

story dozens of times. The drama lies not in the outcomes we already know, but in the knowledge that these outcomes are terribly unlikely to be repeated in the future. This reversal of fortune sings with an evergreen message of optimism. We read the Book of Esther not only because of its happy ending but because Jewish readers throughout history have always needed happy endings, waited for them, and often been denied them. Finding one at the end of this book allows readers to hope for their own happy ending. There is solace in these pages.

The book's ten chapters certainly impart these worthy messages, but Esther is not the only biblical book to do so. One might argue that Maimonides insists on the book's supremacy because it is the most dramatic showcase of divine and human miracle making, but with so many wondrous, incredulous events dotting biblical pages, this is not an easy or obvious case to make.

Our second answer suggests reading the *Megilla* for the very opposite reason. It is not the happy ending that should drive its readership, but rather the cautionary warning: believing in such happy endings is natural but may eventually prove disastrous. The glimpse of momentary victory in the scroll is not part of a continuous narrative of success in exile, a narrative which has long held false hope. The "victory" in Esther is a mere historical blip, no more than a lukewarm bath of self-importance in exile. One glamorous victory and two royal robes was not enough to secure Jewish status when the Jews remained politically and spiritually dependent on the good graces of others.

The Book of Esther presents the move from exile to diaspora, from the painful loss of homeland to the eventual adjustment of Jews to their foreign surroundings and a desire to be successful on terms not their own.

Timothy Beal reads Esther as

> …a literature of identity crisis, brought about initially by exile and dispersion, and accentuated by an identity politics that frames this scattered people as the one problematic divergence, and then explores the possibilities of transformation produced by that crisis. Jewish identity in the diaspora is displaced, as Judah has

> been carried away, ungrounded, dispersed, and to some degree alienated from a God who remains, at best, hidden.[13]

Solomon Goiten has argued that Esther is the only authentic book about Jews in exile, not because of the absence of God, but because there is no mention of, or interest in, the Land of Israel at all.[14] This feature, more than any other, makes this book distinctive in the biblical canon. While we have other Jewish courtiers who served or lived in foreign households – like Joseph, Moses, and Daniel – their positions were more temporal than the situation described in Esther. In that sense, the book offers us a guide for success when political autonomy and self-government are no longer options. "The author sees the Jews' fate as depending on its leading individuals, whose lives both epitomize and entail the nations' fortunes. Just as a danger to highly placed individuals imperils the people, so does the leaders' personal success entail the people's welfare."[15] This assumes, of course, that a foreign potentate will identify a wise, heroic Jew who can curry favor with the powerful and secure positive outcomes for his or her people.

Esther is not alone in this objective. Sidnie White demonstrates that heroes of biblical diaspora stories understood how to live in two worlds and master each successfully.[16] Granted, this is no insurance policy, but a wise leader who can masterfully steer dual commitments as a representative in government is surely a help. Beauty cannot hurt either. While these points seem evident enough, they are not sufficient to describe what takes place on Esther's pages.

Timothy Laniak puts forward a compelling argument in his overview of Esther. He contends that the destruction of Jerusalem and the Temple occasioned "an identity crisis of unprecedented proportions"

---

13. Timothy K. Beal, *The Book of Hiding: Gender, Ethnicity, Annihilation, and Esther* (London: Routledge, 1997), 120.
14. Solomon Goitein, "Megillat Esther," in *Iyunim BaMikra* (Tel Aviv, 1957), 59–72.
15. Michael V. Fox, *Character and Ideology in the Book of Esther* (Grand Rapids, MI: William B. Eerdmans Publishing, 2001), 229.
16. Sidnie White, "Esther: A Feminine Model for Jewish Diaspora," in *Gender and Difference in Ancient Israel*, ed. Peggy L. Day (Minneapolis: Fortress Press, 1989), 161–77.

for those living in Judea. It deeply unsettled what Jewish life looked like, with its central institution in its most holy city gone. Whereas other biblical figures mourned their losses and continued to define themselves through these critical touchstones, Esther presented a viable, even attractive, alternative:

> Esther seemingly moves away from the traditional paradigms in unexpected and even disturbing ways. In Esther, answers to fundamental concerns are not found at the traditional center but out of the precarious periphery. It represents a perspective that qualifies and reframes the hopes of a community in crisis. While others call for a return to Jerusalem, to temple and Torah, and to the lineages of Israel's ancient leaders, Esther moves away from them. Or, at the very least, so it seems. Hope in Esther is found in the Jewish community itself. Esther invites its readers to re-engage a fundamental understanding of the covenant that stands behind their traditions.[17]

In Esther, the Jewish homeland and the Temple altar are supplanted by the Jewish community, what might be called Jewish peoplehood. In the books of Daniel and Nehemiah, Daniel prayed in the direction of Jerusalem at great risk to himself (Dan. 6:9), while Nehemiah requested leave from a Persian court to rebuild the walls of Jerusalem (Neh. 2:3–5). The God of Ezekiel promises to accompany His people into exile, "though I scattered them among the countries, yet I have become a sanctuary to them for a little while in the countries where they have gone" (Ezek. 11:16). Yet God's presence in exile did not constitute a permanent condition of exile. Ezekiel's dry bones will only come back to life when they return to their homeland: "I am going to open your graves and lift you out of the graves, O My people, and bring you to the Land of Israel" (Ezek. 37:12).

By contrast, Esther, Laniak notes, offers no such prayer, makes no such request. "Resolution takes place in Esther not through returning

17. Timothy S. Laniak, "Esther's 'Volkcentrism' and the Reframing of Post-Exilic Judaism," in *The Book of Esther in Modern Research*, 79.

to Palestine, but by remaining in Persia. Esther risks her life to save the Jews in Persia with no anticipation of anything better or safer at 'home.'"[18] Laniak believes that the Book of Esther proposes a way not only to survive "on the edges of our world, at the center of our enemy's universe," but to live a legitimate, prosperous, and purposeful life. The book becomes an affirmation of Jewish existence outside a homeland, helping Jews and gentiles prosper. He goes as far as to suggest that Esther even seems "flagrantly anti-Torah" in that her behaviors reflect none of the religious norms or behaviors of others in the diaspora, and yet she achieves immense success.[19]

Koller compares the Books of Daniel and Esther to suggest a strong dissonance of diasporic orientation: "The book of Daniel takes exile to be a thoroughly lamentable and hopefully brief episode in the history of the Jews. In Esther, on the other hand, diaspora life is simply a reality to be navigated."[20] There is a danger to the longevity, durability, and stability of a people when exile becomes normative.

Success or Failure?

But what if Laniak is profoundly mistaken, and this is not a story of Jewish success but of failure? The Book of Esther may be read as a didactic tale and a warning not to get too comfortable in the diaspora precisely because the miraculous turn of events is too unlikely to count on in the future. Accept it at risk. The Talmud, in a brief story, presents a complex understanding of the residual dangers of Shushan. Two rabbis, the legend goes, drank on Purim to the point of inebriation. In a ridiculous haze, one sage killed the other. Astonished and deeply remorseful, the sage begged God to spare his colleague and bring him back to life. God assented. When the next Purim approached, the once-violent sage once again asked his friend to drink with him on the holiday. But, by now, the

18. Laniak, "Esther's 'Volkcentrism,'" 80. Levenson makes a similar point in "The Scroll of Esther in Ecumenical Perspective," *Journal of Ecumenical Studies* 13 (1976): 440–52.
19. Laniak, "Esther's 'Volkcentrism,'" 83.
20. Koller, *Esther in Ancient Jewish Thought*, 85.

other rabbi had wisened: "Miracles do not happen every day."[21] He may have been spared once, but twice would be pushing his luck.

Alcohol in this talmudic passage and in the Book of Esther is symbolic of risk, an apt "sponsoring" beverage of this scroll and a metaphor to be explored in a later chapter. Like Esther's central villains, alcohol is fluid; it is essentially liquid irrationality and predictable in its unpredictability. Against this fragility, God has a message for those who live under the rule of others: "I am hidden because I Myself cannot watch the dangers you are putting yourselves in. I will not appear every time to catch you when you fall because of your own regrettable decisions." Instead of praying for her people to be saved in Shushan, where they might one day live peaceably but never with governmental control, Esther should have prayed for a return to Zion and the political self-determination that comes with redemption.

The randomness driving the plot of Esther is itself illustrative of the costs of exile. Exile first makes people deeply and distressingly conscious of their distinctiveness. With that knowledge comes the eventual desire to neutralize that distinctiveness through assimilation. Finally, what emerges are the strategies and mechanisms by which Jews change their identities and maneuver the polarities. This process is neither willful nor obvious. Jews in exile often believe they are protecting their allegiances while adapting in a survivalist mode to their surroundings, not realizing how extensively the contours of their Jewish identity have been reshaped. In his book *The Dawn*, Yoram Hazony explores the trials of an exile psyche that has not yet settled into the "comfort" and replacement mentality of diaspora living:

> In exile, the Jews must live in dispersion, their institutions weak, their concerns wandering far from Jewish things, and their politics alienated from every obvious source of cohesiveness, direction and strength. It is clear at the outset that under such conditions there is no possibility of freely seeking and implementing any Jewish ideal.... Thus exile, while never precluding entirely the possibility of Jewish power, nevertheless established a formidable

21. Megilla 7b.

> presumption against it – a presumption which has ominous theological echoes in the fact that even the most devout come to feel that the way has been lost, and begin to speak as though in winter, of God having "hidden his face" from his people.[22]

With Esther emerges not only a new way of living but a new way of being. An exile never forgets where he or she calls home. Yet over time, the exile becomes a resident of the diaspora, adjusting to foreign surroundings until they are not foreign, exchanging dreams of Jewish autonomy and spiritual achievement for external measures of success that soon become normative. By the book's end, Mordecai, the exile, exchanged his sackcloth and ashes for royal robes and a crown of honor, making it hard to imagine that even with the possibility of return, he would pack his belongings and opt for less ornate new frocks. Influence in the diaspora can make one forget that one is in exile, but the reader must remain wary of the momentous and sudden emergence of Jewish political power in the Book of Esther. Each year we must read its first five chapters and remember that its particularly happy ending was a highly improbable one.

Eliezer Berkovits understood exile as a force deeper than political dependence. He believed that exile and redemption – *galut* and *geula* – are inherent in the Jewish condition. Abraham was the very first exile; God asked him to leave his father's home and his homeland, founding a place of redemption out of the experience of leaving his place of origin. "Even before there was a Jewish people, there was already Exile and the promise of Redemption."[23] For Berkovits, national exile accompanies cosmic exile. The latter is derived from God's plan that the world fulfills its divine purpose. Human beings, with their own desires for power, possession, and domination, deny their divine purpose, becoming at odds with their spiritual reason for existing:

> As a result, God's own purpose finds itself in Exile in the history of mankind. So long as the divine plan remains unrealized in his-

22. Yoram Hazony, *The Dawn: Political Teachings on the Book of Esther* (Jerusalem: Shalem Press, 1995), 3–4.
23. Eliezer Berkovits, "Exile and Redemption," *Tradition* 14, no. 4 (Fall 1974): 10.

> tory, the history of mankind tells of the story of – what tradition calls – *Galut ha-Shekhinah*, the Exile of the Divine Presence. God Himself is, as it were, a refugee from the world of men.[24]

Given Berkovits's understanding of both national and cosmic exile, we might argue that the Book of Esther offers us a story of national exile but not of cosmic exile; dispersed across Persia's mighty empire, the Jews were unable to fulfill a divine plan and never seem to try. We, therefore, conclude the book not with declarations of Jewish victory, but with two prosaic messages about the Jewish presence after the celebrations end. Taxation returns. Mordecai is well liked by *almost* all of his coreligionists. These are hardly expressions of divine calling. Maximally what can be achieved in exile is meaningful survival, government protection, usefulness to that government, and a measure of popularity for enabling these factors to remain stable. Jewish accomplishment under such conditions is measured by the success of the reigning non-Jewish powers, not by adherence to God's plan.[25]

A Repeated Story of Identity Loss

This message of fragility does not begin with the Book of Esther. Abraham himself was unsure of his status in Canaan among the kings and ancient potentates he encountered. To protect his life, he hid his marital status on two different occasions, and did not trust the kindness of a powerful stranger when it came to burying his wife. Only after the death of Sarah, lacking a foothold in Canaan, did he utter the ringing words

24. Ibid., 11.

25. This reading of exile, while descriptive of the Jewish condition for millennia, is potentially symbolic of all the world's disenfranchised peoples. Susan Zaeske reads the Book of Esther as a "rhetoric of exile and empowerment that, for millennia, has notably shaped the discourse of marginalized peoples" including gender, race, and sexual orientation and claims that her reading will "contribute to efforts to move beyond a unitary, male-dominated history of rhetorical theory through the recovery and recognition of a work that does not announce itself as a rhetorical theory, but has operated as such" ("Unveiling Esther as a Pragmatic Radical Rhetoric," *Philosophy and Rhetoric* 33, no. 3 [2000]: 194).

that suggest the vulnerability of being *in* a place but not *of* a place: "I am a resident-alien among you" (Gen. 23:4).

Continuing the theme of geopolitical fragility, Jacob was exploited time after time by Laban, who became, in the Haggada, the very epitome of Pharaoh, the precursor to a crippling power imbalance. When Jacob left his home for Padan-Aram, he found himself trapped in his father-in-law's home, helpless and isolated. After twenty years of servitude, Jacob finally got the divine push to return to his homeland; he tried, subsequently, to obtain what he thought was rightfully his in a transparent financial arrangement with his father-in-law. But Jacob's success only irked the man who kept him in invisible chains: "Jacob also saw that Laban's manner toward him was not as it had been in the past" (Gen. 31:2). Jacob could enjoy his earnings only if they augmented the coffers of Laban but not his own. After leaving in the dark of night with his family and his goods, Jacob finally confronted the man who dogged him for so long, showcasing the fragility of a life consumed by tyranny:

> Now Jacob became incensed and took up his grievance with Laban. Jacob spoke up and said to Laban, "What is my crime, what is my guilt that you should pursue me?.... These twenty years I have spent in your service, your ewes and she-goats never miscarried, nor did I feast on rams from your flock. That which was torn by beasts I never brought to you; I myself made good the loss; you exacted it of me, whether snatched by day or snatched by night. Often, scorching heat ravaged me by day and frost by night; and sleep fled from my eyes. Of the twenty years that I spent in your household, I served you fourteen years for your two daughters, and six years for your flocks; and you changed my wages time and again. Had not the God of my father, the God of Abraham and the Fear of Isaac, been with me, you would have sent me away empty-handed. But God took notice of my plight and the toil of my hands, and He gave judgment last night." (Gen. 31:36–42)

God was the only power greater than Laban, the only authority that could force Jacob to leave his terrible situation in exile. Reading Jacob's cathartic confession, we are struck by his statement of personal integrity. Trust, too, is another cost of exile. It is only a matter of time before every Jacob faces every Laban, whose "manner toward him was not as it had been in the past."

To this heartfelt plea for absolution and liberty, Laban is predictably Laban, the prototypical voice of authoritarian voracity against the stranger: "Then Laban spoke up and said to Jacob, 'The daughters are my daughters, the children are my children, and the flocks are my flocks; all that you see is mine'" (Gen. 31:43). Ultimately, outside of his own land and jurisdiction, everything Jacob ever did would only contribute to someone else's prosperity. In exile, nothing ever truly belongs to the sojourner.

The story continues. Joseph's powers seemed expansive and unchecked, but his task, like Jacob's, was economic preservation and restoration of a people not his own. The text makes explicit that Joseph's successes did not ultimately benefit him or his people, other than ensuring temporal safety. Like everyone else, the Israelites lived under his harsh financial reforms: "Joseph gathered in all the money that was to be found in the land of Egypt and in the land of Canaan, as payment for the rations that were being procured, and Joseph brought the money into Pharaoh's palace" (Gen. 47:14). Joseph brought the money to Pharaoh. "So Joseph gained possession of all the farmland of Egypt for Pharaoh, every Egyptian having sold his field because the famine was too much for them; thus the land passed over to Pharaoh" (Gen. 47:20). He even brought the land acquisition – in an act that took advantage of starvation – into Pharaoh's treasury. The ultimate slap in the face occurs only a few chapters later when a newly appointed pharaoh changes the fate of the Jews in Egypt: "A new king arose over Egypt who did not know Joseph" (Ex. 1:8).

With the passage of time, there will be a new monarch – a new source of power – who cares little for the Jews as a people, valuing them only for personal and national gain. If the Jews are lucky, this precarious state will operate in their favor for a limited time, but permanent security is an illusion. Exiles know this, but residents of a diaspora rarely do, believing themselves to be special and unique.

Esther and Mordecai do manage to secure power in a land not their own, and they must have felt a sense of incredible, unbelievable, and undeniable achievement. Yet in the face of success, a passage of wisdom literature reminds us – to everything there is a time. "A time for weeping and a time for laughing, a time for wailing and a time for dancing" (Eccl. 3:4). What begins with tears, ends with laughter, and what ends in laughter reverts to tears. The exile moves from worry to wonder. Time passes, and wonder returns to worry.

The Book of Esther's intricate web of plot twists takes us from the cry of outrage to the outpouring of gratitude, where we like our stories to end. Yet the Book of Esther continues. Mordecai understood this implicitly when he told Esther that she could be part of our master narrative or not. Either way, the story would continue because relief and deliverance were guaranteed to occur in the great cycle of events. What was not guaranteed was the human force that would be responsible for relief and deliverance: "If you keep silent in this crisis, relief and deliverance will come to the Jews from another quarter, while you and your father's house will perish. And who knows, perhaps you have attained to royal position for just such a crisis" (Est. 4:14). The operative word here is almost forgettable: "this." Esther may have been uniquely positioned to avert *this* crisis, but in the long history of Jewish exile, another crisis is always pending. Relief and deliverance will come. Who will partner with God in bringing them is important but ultimately less significant than the fact that they will come.

Living with the knowledge that we will experience redemption also means living with the knowledge that we will experience persecution. The twentieth-century German philosopher Leo Strauss once wrote, "The Jewish people and their fate are the living witness for the absence of redemption. This, one could say, is the meaning of the chosen people; the Jews are chosen to prove the absence of redemption."[26] This sobering thought requires attention. We like our stories to prove that redemption happens, but so often they are better at proving that we are or were in desperate need of redemption. Esther is the biblical story that perhaps demonstrates this most because it takes place entirely in

26. From Strauss' essay, "Why We Remain Jews" (1962), reprinted in *Jewish Philosophy and the Crisis of Modernity: Essays and Lectures in Modern Jewish Thought*, ed. Kenneth Hart Green (New York: State University of New York Press, 1997), 327.

the diaspora, where our choices about self-governance were limited, and our ability to act was marked by Mordecai's request for Esther's silence. Yet it is the same Mordecai who tells Esther later that redemption comes through the opposite of silence. We are silent in spaces not our own. We speak, we laugh, and we shout with joy only in places where we feel a sense of ownership. We can be ourselves in a full-throated way. Exile makes us silent. Redemption lets us speak.[27]

Sequencing the Story

The fragility of fate in exile may explain another law related to the reading of the *Megilla*: it must be read in proper sequence.

> When a person reads the *Megilla* in improper sequence, he does not fulfill his obligation. If a person was reading, forgot a verse and read the following verse, went back and read the verse he forgot, and then read a third verse, he does not fulfill his obligation, because he read a verse in improper sequence. What should he do instead? He should begin from the second verse, the verse he forgot, and continue reading the *Megilla* in its proper order.[28]

Sequencing is critical in this story above others because the events are so unexpected. What turned out good could have turned out bad were we to shift verses or chapters only slightly. And unlike a completely happy outcome, what turns out positively for the Jews turns out terribly for those throughout Ahasuerus' enormous empire. The book records, including Haman and his sons, 75,811 deaths directly attributable to the decree against the Jews and its reversal. This toll of life may have provided temporary relief for the Jews but was likely to eventually backfire

27. Rabbi Joseph B. Soloveitchik notes the relationship of redemption and language in his essay "Redemption, Prayer, Talmud Torah" (*Tradition* 17, no. 2 [1978]), where he notes: "A history-making people is one that leads a speaking, story-telling, communing free existence, while a non-history-making, non-history-involved group leads a non-communing. and therefore a silent, unfree existence" (p. 55). This essay was originally presented at a faculty colloquium sponsored by B'nai Brith at the University of Pennsylvania in May 1973.
28. Maimonides, *Mishneh Torah, Hilkhot Megilla VeḤanukka* 2:1.

on the Jewish presence in Persia. Little demonstrates the fragility of the Jewish condition in exile more than this. Even "winning" is precarious.

The Book of Esther, with its uncertainty, chaos, and hope, does offer us the kind of magnificent story that both entertains and challenges while making its readers ponder at how one kind of life can become another. In the words of one Bible scholar,

> As the annual reading of the Esther Scroll comes to an end, I breathe a sigh of relief, but this expresses a prayer more than a certitude, for the resolution of the crisis is less believable than its onset. Still, the dramatic intensity of the tale propels us forward from the danger to the deliverance with such momentum that we find ourselves accepting the truth of the latter as well.[29]

Marveling at the outcome, we, too, breathe a sigh of relief each year as the book races to a deliverance that could not come soon enough.

In some way, Esther becomes both embodiment and metaphor for all Jews in exile. Orphaned in a foreign land, Esther found herself achieving the unimaginable, earning the love of the very people from whom she stood apart. Assimilating into the host culture and hiding her own background caused a crisis moment that helped her redefine her purpose. She could save her people only once she embraced her true identity. This identity proved a source of her strength. But the book does not end with her. She is displaced by someone who will have more power: Mordecai. The book records the bringing back of taxation, the local force of government's demands on its constituents. And then the story is over. As readers, we must ask, "What's next? Will life in Persia stay this way?"

This commentary is called *The Book of Esther: Power, Fate, and Fragility* because each of these states is represented in every chapter. The holiday's very name suggests the arbitrary nature of events in life and in the text. The powerful become vulnerable, the vulnerable become powerful. Vashti loses power, while Ahasuerus gains it, until he cedes authority to his ministers. Haman's power stands in contrast to Morde-

29. Fox, *Character and Ideology*, 12.

cai's vulnerability before Esther outmaneuvers him. Mordecai wields the power to save Ahasuerus from his plotting courtiers, but is powerless in the face of a decree to annihilate his people. All the characters' lives were impacted by a fate that seemed so random and accidental that we call the events of this book nothing short of miraculous. While God's name never appears explicitly, God's presence is stamped on virtually every word in the *Megilla*. Through a series of unfortunate and fortunate events, fate ensures that no character is absolved of the kind of life reversal that reminds us as readers of the fragility of the human condition. The tensile vulnerability suggests a world in constant flux, where one's ascent represents another's descent and vice versa. It is a world that can be naught but a fragile place.

Satire, Drama, Fiction, History, or Theology?

R. Akiva, according to a well-known midrash, was teaching when he noticed a group of students dozing. Every teacher recognizes this phenomenon. If one person falls asleep in a classroom, the onus is on the student. If many people fall asleep, the onus is on the teacher. To make the learning more engaging, more relevant, and more urgent, R. Akiva, a master pedagogue, believed that an odd question would be an apt motivator. "Why," he pondered, "did Esther rule over 127 provinces?" She must have been, he concluded, a descendant of Sarah, who died, according to Genesis, at the ripe age of 127. R. Akiva used a narrative and numeric wordplay to rouse his pupils, showing that a random prime number in the Hebrew Bible may not have been random. But he did not pick just any number from just any story. R. Akiva picked a tale that contained the kind of intrigue, mystery, revenge, opulence, and reversal of fortune that would simply not let a reader sleep: the Book of Esther.[1]

We read the Book of Esther with an initial sense of melancholy and fear as another historical saga of persecution in exile puts the Jewish people at peril. Yet, even when we've heard and reviewed its verses dozens of times, we are still enchanted by the Book of Esther's considerable charms.

1. Genesis Rabba 58:3.

Salman Rushdie, an author who famously lived in hiding to escape the power of a dangerous story, once said, "Even when things are at their worst, there's a little voice in your head saying, 'Good story!'" Esther is a good story, arguably a great one. Its compelling plot and characters have been the subject of numerous plays,[2] operas, and countless amateur re-enactments. It has been called a satire,[3] a comedy,[4] a parody,[5] a drama, a novel,[6]

---

2. Theodor Gaster observes that these plays became so coarse and inappropriate in nature that they were often stopped by local rabbinic authorities. See *Purim and Hanukkah in Custom and Tradition* (New York: Henry Schuman, 1950), 68–69. Chone Shmeruk, in his entry called "Purim-shpil," explains that many such performances used profanities or were overly erotic and thereby not in the religious spirit of the day (*Encyclopedia Judaica*, vol. 13 [1971], 1396–404). Scott M. Langston includes Annie Jonas Moses' play, *Esther: A Drama in Five Acts* (published in the 1870s), in his article, "Reading a Text Backwards: The Book of Esther and Nineteenth-Century Jewish American Interpretations," in *The Book of Esther in Modern Research*, 214. An appropriately moralistic play, Esther was a heroine for ambitious young women seeking fame and fortune.
3. Stephanie Dalley contends that ancient Mesopotamian satirical stories, in which all-powerful tyrants have their human frailties mocked, encouraged loyalty among constituents and reminded kings of their responsibility to the people. See Dalley's *Esther's Revenge at Susa: From Sennacherib to Ahasuerus* (London: Oxford University Press, 2007), 131–32.
4. Marc Zvi Brettler argues that "the factual errors, the literary symmetries, and the lighthearted style – point to the fact that Esther is not a historical account. Rather, it is more like comedy, burlesque, or farce. Probably the original social setting for this book was the annual party in celebration of the already existing holiday of Purim; the book, when read aloud, functioned as a justification for the upside-down festival" (*How to Read the Jewish Bible* [New York, Oxford University Press, 2005], 269). Adele Berlin argues that the book not only promotes the holiday but also the tone for the holiday: "The book is meant to be funny, and I want people to appreciate its comic nature and enjoy reading it" ("The Book of Esther: Writing a Commentary for a Jewish Audience," in *The Book of Esther in Modern Research*, 10).
5. Kenneth Craig believes Esther is a serio-comical genre, or *spoudogeloios*, translated wonderfully as the "serious-smiling" genre of literature. See *Reading Esther: A Case for a Literary Carnivalesque* (Louisville, KY: Westminster John Knox Press, 1995), 89.
6. Joyce G. Baldwin believes that Esther has many novelistic elements: "It restricts itself to a single event, which it tends to present as 'chance,' and the function of the Novelle is to reveal that, in reality, the event is due to fate. The outworking of the event reveals qualities of character in the persons concerned which were latent in them, and its action must take place in the world of reality.... It deals with a striking subject and in its structure has a turning point which moves the narrative in

a work of historical fiction,[7] a political treatise on how to live in the diaspora,[8] a postmodern text on gender,[9] a book of wisdom literature,[10] and an accurate historical account of events.[11] Stephanie Dalley believes Esther to be a story "with a solid ancestry in the cuneiform literature of Mesopotamia," likening it to ancient Near Eastern court stories in which "a man achieves high status at court, falls out of favour through no fault

---

an unexpected direction" (*Esther: An Introduction and Commentary*, Tyndale Old Testament Commentaries [Leicester, England: Inter-Varsity Press, 1984], 34). See also J. A. Loader, "Esther as a Novel with Different Levels of Meaning," *Zeitschrift fur die altestamentliche Wissenschaft* 90 (1978): 417–21 and Monique Siegel, "Book of Esther – a Novelle," *Dor le Dor* 14 (1985): 142–51.

7. Langston shares a sermon given by Reform Rabbi Kaufman Kohler in February of 1888 where he advised his listeners not to take Esther literally because "it has the character of fiction" ("Reading a Text Backwards," 210).
8. For example, see Yoram Hazony, *The Dawn*; Jules Gleicher, "Mordecai and the Exilarch: Some Thoughts on the Book of Esther," *Interpretation* 28 (2001): 187–200; Alexander Green, "Power, Deception, and Comedy: The Politics of Exile in the Book of Esther," *Jewish Political Studies Review* 23, nos. 1–2 (Spring 2011): 61–78; and Michael Eisenberg, *The Vanishing Jew: A Wake-Up Call from the Book of Esther* (Charleston: CreateSpace Independent Publishing Platform, 2017).
9. See Esther Fuchs, "Status and Role of Female Heroines in the Biblical Narrative," in *Women in the Hebrew Bible: A Reader*, ed. Alice Bach (London: Routledge, 2013); Beal, *The Book of Hiding*; and Timothy Laniak, *Shame and Honor in the Book of Esther* (Atlanta: Scholars Press, 1998).
10. Solomon Talmon, "'Wisdom' and the Book of Esther," *Vetus Testamentum* 13, no. 4 (1963): 419–55. Talmon believes that setting wisdom within a narrative context would help a book's lessons resonate more and offer more practical application for its readers.
11. C. F. Keil, *Commentary of the Old Testament*, vol. 3 (Grand Rapids MI: William B. Erdmans, reprinted 1971); Jacob Hoshander, *The Book of Esther in Light of History* (1923, reprinted Andesite Press, 1983); J. S. Wright, "Historicity in the Book of Esther," in *New Perspectives on the Old Testament*, ed. J. B. Payne (Waco, TX: Word, 1970); and R. Gordis, *Megillat Esther: The Masoretic Hebrew Text with Introduction, New Translation and Commentary* (New York: Ktav, 1974). Adele Berlin observes that "very few twentieth-century Bible scholars believed in the historicity of the book of Esther, but they certainly expended a lot of effort justifying their position" in "The Book of Esther and Ancient Storytelling," *JBL* 120, no. 1 (2001): 3. Among those she cites are Lewis Bayles Paton, *A Critical and Exegetical Commentary on the Book of Esther* (New York: Scribner, 1908), 64–77; Carey A. Moore, *Esther: A New Translation with Introduction and Notes* (Garden City, NY: Doubleday, 1971); and Fox, *Character and Ideology*.

of his own and is finally restored to grace."[12] Elias Bickerman included it as one biblical book among four in his *Four Strange Books of the Bible.*[13] The question of genre must preoccupy us as we approach interpretation, for genre largely determines how we reconstruct meaning and message.

Adele Berlin acknowledges the details that might lead one to regard Esther as history but advises readers to avoid this misleading assumption:

> To judge a story's historicity by its degree of realism is to mistake verisimilitude for historicity. Verisimilitude is the literary term for the illusion of reality. Just because a story sounds real does not mean that it is. Realistic fiction is just as fictional as nonrealistic fiction. Among the leading arguments for Esther's historicity are that its setting is authentic and that its knowledge of Persian custom is detailed and accurate.[14]

The realistic details offer the texture of a court story and may have led to the impression of a historical recording. Furthermore, the "verisimilitude" may have led to the misbelief that the book's message is not sacred in nature but the story is simply a romance or royalty tale. That this book has all of the elements of fiction was noted by more than one Jewish commentator. The medieval French exegete Rabbi Joseph ibn Kaspi (1279–1340) observes that the book could have been mistaken for a fictional story about a court with a king at its center. Ibn Kaspi felt

12. Dalley, *Esther's Revenge*, 130.
13. Elias Bickerman, *Four Strange Books of the Bible* (New York: Schocken Books, 1967), 171–240.
14. Berlin, "The Book of Esther and Ancient Storytelling," 4. Robert Gordis posits that there *was* a historical kernel to the story: "There is nothing intrinsically impossible or improbable in the central incident, when the accretions due to the storyteller's art are set aside" ("Religion, Wisdom and History in the Book of Esther," *JBL* 100, no. 3 [September 1981]: 388). He also posits in this article that Esther's Jewish author wrote this work as if he were a pagan chronicler. For this reason, he did not include any references to God or Jewish rituals, and the Jewish people are spoken of in the third person. Perhaps the author felt that this more dispassionate posture would make the story all that more convincing.

the need to reveal hidden meanings in the text, precisely because these are not obvious from a surface read:

> In general this book is one of the holy books, the details of which were composed and handed down to us in order to give us perfection of the soul. Nor is there any doubt that this book contains deep secrets and great hints regarding hidden matters of the Torah which are known to those who are better [scholars] than I. May the One who knows [such secrets] be blessed.[15]

Ibn Kaspi suggests that the Book of Esther may have been mistaken for something other than an inspired prophetic work. He assures the reader, however, that only an ignoramus would make such an error. While Ibn Kaspi mentions that the book is filled with exalted knowledge and hidden matters, he modestly claims he does not know what that knowledge is, assigning its explication to other, more competent scholars. He does state, however, in the same place, that the book teaches about divine providence and that the reader, through fasting and prayer, will merit redemption. Ibn Kaspi's cryptic remark may be an example of "pious statements [that] often mask more radical positions."[16] In explaining the esotericism, Robert Eisen claims that Ibn Kaspi regards the events in the book as actual historical occurrences, which Mordecai recorded in order to impart hidden wisdom: It only appears that God is the prime mover behind the causal links that lead to Jewish triumph. The hidden message, however, is that man propels history: "Kaspi views the Esther story as an allegory that shows how human beings can overcome unfavorable prophetic predictions that reflect the changeless will of God by explaining the unstated conditions of those predictions."[17]

---

15. Ibn Kaspi on Esther 1:1.
16. Robert Eisen, "Joseph Ibn Kaspi on the Secret Meaning of the Scroll of Esther," *Revue des etudes juives* (July–August 2001): 386. For more on Kaspi's esoteric style, Eisen cites H. Kasher, introduction to Kaspi's *Shulḥan Kesef* [Hebrew] (Jerusalem: 1996), 12–19.
17. Eisen, "Joseph Ibn Kaspi," 393.

Like Ibn Kaspi, the early-twelfth-century French exegete Rabbi Joseph Kara wrote, on Esther 10:2, that without a sacred lens, the book could easily be confused for court chronicles:

> *All his mighty and powerful acts*: This refers to the miracles and wonders that I believe are necessary to publicize. This book contains matters which may seem purely for amusement, such as the mighty and powerful acts of Ahasuerus and the complete account of the esteemed honor which the king bestowed on Mordecai. These seem to be mundane matters, not worth recording here. But this scroll was written in the holy tongue and was included in our canon. If you wish to amuse yourself with the mundane matters of Ahasuerus' powerful and mighty deeds and the account of Mordecai's advancement, they are written in the chronicles of the kings of Media and Persia.[18]

Later, in the sixteenth century, Rabbi Eliezer Ashkenazi suggests that the Book of Esther could have been mistaken for a love story. He had to distinguish the scroll from historical writing about human events. Esther's lack of typical religious details, starting with its omission of God's name, meant that it could just as easily be read as a record of royal events:

> It was not evident that the miracle enjoyed by our ancestors in the days of Ahasuerus was occasioned by God, blessed be He, since it is human nature that love is all-consuming. Ahasuerus loved Esther passionately; it was not at all remarkable that he should have done all of this for her love. It has already been said that "love changes the norm," all the more so the love of women, especially for those who desire and are nourished by their need for love. And if it was said of the one greater in his wisdom than all before him [Solomon], "His wives turned away his heart," then

18. Barry Walfish, *Esther in Medieval Garb* (Albany: State University of New York Press, 1993), 85.

> how much more would one who appears to act madly do all this for the love of a woman?[19]

Love is a compelling driver of plot. Since the scroll could have been mistaken for a simple love story between a king and a maiden, the narrative provides many supporting details to demonstrate that this is not the crux of the story:

> One should not, God forbid, think that this salvation was accidental or random or that it was necessary to write it because of Ahasuerus' love of women.... Rather, we must explain that this text is only necessary in detail to publicize it [the miracle] and that it was from Him [God], may He be blessed, and not an accidental or random act... although it is told through narrative...any one enlightened will understand this with wonder and know that it is from God.[20]

Simple or Not?

To some, the Book of Esther may seem an entertaining story, but one hardly worthy of deep analysis. Its stock characters do not surprise or intrigue us, and the plot is well known. "The problem," Michael Fox writes in his academic study of the Book of Esther, "is in the book's simplicity; it is more difficult to analyze simplicity than to respond to it."[21] Having said that, he believes that these simple characters are powerful:

> Their surface clarity and vividness make them fascinating and meaningful to children, but these qualities are the products of a sharp and subtle craft that makes the characters intriguing to adults as well, and worthy of repeated scrutiny. These characters become vehicles in conveying a surprisingly sophisticated – in

19. Eliezer Ashkenazi, *Yosef Lekaḥ* 1:1. He also mentions a similar theme in his comments on 5:4. Translation is my own. "Love changes the norm" is a citation from Sanhedrin 105b, comparing verses about Abraham (Gen. 22:3) and Balaam (Num. 22:21). The citation about Solomon is from I Kings 11:4.
20. Ashkenazi , *Yosef Lekaḥ*, 1:1.
21. Fox, *Character and Ideology*, 1.

> some ways strikingly modern – view of person, nation and religion.[22]

Jewish readers tend to focus on the hero and heroine of this story, Esther's legal ramifications for Purim rituals, and the self-congratulatory sense of the underdog in a state of triumph. But the Book of Esther also lives within its historical and legendary context. The fairy-tale quality of this story seems a Jewish version of Scheherezade's *One Thousand and One Nights*, a collection of tales likely first communicated orally between the sixth and ninth centuries in Iran, Saudia Arabia, and India. In Middle Persian, Scheherezade means "noble lineage" and contains fantastical tales premised on a central plot. King Shahryar's wife betrayed him with another man. In an act of paranoia and hedonism, he was brought a new virgin each day, slept with her, and then had her decapitated. This odd method of romance assured that no wife would ever be unfaithful to him again. He went through a thousand such disposable brides and a thousand hedonistic nights until he was introduced to a noble's daughter who captured his heart, leaving him unable to part with her. She nourished something deeper within him that went beyond physical pleasure alone.

Esther, it seems, had the same effect. Ahasuerus, no different from old King Shahryar, saw women as mere objects of temporal desire. He rid himself of his first wife and then he, too, went through a parade of young and innocent women, condemning them to captivity in a second harem after deflowering them, until Esther's grace captivated him. So delighted was he with his new prize that he soon forgot his first wife. The anger he felt when he realized Vashti was permanently removed from Shushan dissipated, and the momentary ecstasy of pleasure without responsibility blissfully returned. He even put a remission on taxes in his sprawling empire so that all the people of his land could celebrate the change that Esther brought to their king. No one, let alone the king of Persia, was allowed to stay unhappy for long. Ahasuerus called yet another feast to mark the occasion. Esther would change the king's life in more ways than one. Her uncle saved Ahasuerus' life, she relieved the king of Haman's megalomaniac grip on the empire, and the two restored stability and

22. Ibid.

taxation to his provinces, all the while rescuing their own people from annihilation. Esther was more than just a pretty face.

Since the story is entertaining in its own merit, its spiritual lessons may be lost to the reader, provoking a larger question: Was Esther anything more than a Jewish version of a Persian court tale enmeshed in similar cultural norms? So distressing was this problem and others about the religious characterization of the book that, as Alexander Green points out, both the Talmud and medieval commentators "attempted to solve some of these conundrums by reinterpreting the characters through subtle textual interpretations. They transformed the characters into pious Jews in order to show how the narrative is another example of God's surprise intervention in history to save the Jewish people."[23] Ibn Kaspi's and Ashkenazi's readings typify such an understanding. Interpreters went to great lengths to repurpose the surface reading of the text and spiritualize it.

One might even question the canonization of the book; God's name is nowhere apparent in its ten chapters. It is the only biblical book to take place entirely in exile with no real intimation that Jews should be in their homeland,[24] and its similarity to Persian romantic tales was unmistakable. Nevertheless, R. Akiva, who used the story to rouse his students, fiercely defended its canonization,[25] even if the Talmud itself records opinions that the book may have been too secular:

> Levi bar Shmuel and R. Huna bar Ḥiyya were mending mantles for the sacred scrolls of the school of R. Yehuda. When they reached the scroll of Esther they said: This scroll of Esther does not require a mantle, as it is not as significant as the other sacred

23. Green, "Power, Deception, and Comedy," 61–62.
24. The obvious exception is Esther 2:5–6, where Mordecai is introduced as an *ish Yehudi*, a Jewish man, and an exile, as if he were the only Jewish man in Shushan, implying, in some sense, that his true location was not ultimately where he currently resided.
25. Megilla 7a. See Michael J. Broyde, "Defilement of the Hands, Canonization of the Bible, and the Special Status of Esther, Ecclesiastes, and Song of Songs," *Judaism* (Winter 1995): 65–79; and Solomon Zeitlin, "An Historical Study of the Canonization of the Hebrew Scriptures," *Proceedings of the American Academy for Jewish Research* 3 (1931–1932): 121–58.

> scrolls. R. Yehuda said to them: A statement of that sort also seems to express irreverence...[26]

This desacralization may help us understand why there was no scroll of Esther found among the Dead Sea Scrolls.[27] Bible scholar James Kugel notes of the Dead Sea Scrolls found at Qumran that "excerpts of every book of the Hebrew bible is represented among these fragments except for the Book of Esther."[28] Kugel ponders whether or not this was an intentional omission. Later, however, Mordecai and Esther make an appearance on a wall painting at the Dura Europos Synagogue (ca. 250 CE) in what is today modern-day Syria. We will never know why the book is missing from Qumran, but in the pages ahead we will consider not only a chapter-by-chapter reading of the book with a line-by-line interpretation, but also its place in the world of exegesis and the controversies surrounding its religious significance.

Reading Backward and Forward

The Book of Esther consciously includes parallels to other books of the Bible. Jonathan Grossman posits that biblical references and allusions punctuate the Book of Esther and are used in a sophisticated manner to provide additional meaning to the literal reading:

---

26. Sanhedrin 100a. Rashi, ad loc., explains that they took it upon themselves to arrive at this conclusion and did not consult R. Yehuda; in this lay the irreverence, suggesting that it was not irreverent to assume the Book of Esther was less holy than other books. Rabbi Samuel Eidels, ad loc., however, argues that the irreverent act was the discussion itself, not the lack of consultation with R. Yehuda.
27. See Carey A. Moore, *Esther: A New Translation with Introduction and Notes*, xxi–xxii. Moore there suggests that Esther does not appear in the Dead Sea Scrolls because it was intentionally excluded by the Qumran community for theological reasons. Moore also summarizes the general opposition to the Book of Esther among Christians and Jews.
28. James L. Kugel, *The Great Shift: Encountering God in Biblical Times* (Boston: Houghton Mifflin Harcourt, 2017), 315. There is a theory that the scrolls found at Qumran were part of a *geniza*. Because God's name did not appear in Esther, it may have not been discarded as carefully as other sacred literature and therefore is not found at Qumran. See Millar Burrow, *More Light on the Dead Sea Scrolls* (London: Secker and Warburg, 1958), 15–19, 174–76.

> The author of the book of Esther makes special use of allusions that he inserts throughout the story, and whose purpose is to hint to the reader about a different biblical narrative which he is being asked to keep in mind as a background to his reading. The better-known allusions in the book are those that refer the reader to the stories of Joseph in Egypt, Saul's war against Amalek, the end of David's life, the Book of Daniel.... It seems in light of the multiplicity of instances in which this occurs in the book of Esther, it should be regarded as an intentional literary phenomenon which does indeed present an obstacle to the reader in maintaining a steady reading of the analogies between the narratives.[29]

Hints to other biblical narratives amplify central themes in Esther and connect the book to others. In this vein, the narratives of Moses also share similarities with the Book of Esther.

Gilles Gerleman, for example, compares the Moses/Passover story with the Esther/Purim story.[30] He observes that both stories take place in a royal court, involve an annihilation threat to an entire people, exhibit a desire for revenge, and culminate in a holiday. Each hero has an important support companion in the figures of Aaron and Mordecai. He suggests that because Esther is a later story, the recorded details try to surpass the earlier redemption narrative of the Exodus.

---

29. Jonathan Grossman, "'Dynamic Analogies' in the Book of Esther," *Vetus Testamentum* 59 (2009): 395. On the comparison with I Samuel, see W. McKane, "A Note on Esther IX and I Samuel XV," *JTS* 12 (1961): 260–61. See also M. Garsiel, *The First Book of Samuel: A Literary Study of Comparative Structures, Analogies and Parallels* (Ramat Gan: Revivim Publishing House, 1985), 25; and J. Magonet, "The Liberal and the Lady: Esther Revisited," *Judaism* 29 (1980): 167–76. For other examples of this literary phenomenon, see P. R. Noble, "Esau, Tamar, and Joseph: Criteria for Identifying Inner-Biblical Allusion," *Vetus Testamentum* 52 (2002): 219–52. On this technique more generally, see Y. Zakovitch, *An Introduction to Inner-Biblical Interpretation* (Even Yehuda: Kadima, 1992), 44–49 and Joshua Berman, "Establishing Narrative Analogy in Biblical Literature: Methodological Considerations," *Beit Mikra* 53, no. 1 (2008): 31–46.
30. Gilles Gerleman, *Esther, BKAT* 21 (Neukirchner Verlag: 1973). See also Humphreys, "A Lifestyle for Diaspora: A Study of the Tales of Esther and Daniel," *Catholic Bible Quarterly* 92 (1973): 211–23.

For example, the Jews of Egypt were enslaved. Esther's Jews were consigned to death. Where the Jews of Egypt were told repeatedly to take the goods of their enemies (Ex. 12:35–36), Esther's Jews refused any loot whatsoever (Est. 9:10, 15–16). Both redemptions take place in the Hebrew month of Nisan.[31] This comparison suggests that later writers structured their respective understandings of the Jewish master narrative within an earlier codified story of the underdog's travails and triumphs, adding period detail and color.

There are significant ways in which the Exodus and Esther stories differ, however. Many chapters at the end of Genesis are devoted to explaining how Jacob's sons got to Egypt, suggesting the importance of the past as an explanation or a context for the present. The emphasis on child-bearing and the protection of infants in Exodus 1 stresses a future for the Israelites. Esther, Koller notes, has "a radical focus on the present."[32] There is no explanation of how the Jews got to Persia, and the only one described as having children in the scroll, ironically, is Haman, whose sons are killed by the story's end. "Mordechai and Esther, even Xerxes, have no descendants, and there is therefore no hint of a promise for the future."[33] Koller believes that this and other details of the Book of Esther link it to the Exodus in a way that demonstrates that the scroll is "indeed a pale shadow of what 'redemption' used to mean."[34]

Because the allusions to other narratives are not always consistent, and one character can be represented by multiple characters in another text, these parallels can seem slippery, causing the reader "to feel unequipped to assess fully the situations that he reads about and the characters he encounters, and thus contribute to the sense of the capriciousness and instability that the author is trying to convey."[35] It is for this reason that Grossman calls such allusions "dynamic analogies." Reading a text with many allusions to parallel biblical narratives slows down the reader, allowing for a rich, multilayered study experience. The

31. See Levenson, *Esther*, 73.
32. Koller, *Esther in Ancient Jewish Thought*, 93
33. Ibid.
34. Ibid.
35. Grossman, "'Dynamic Analogies,'" 394.

author assumed enough biblical fluency to encode the Book of Esther with sufficient intertextual cross-references to deepen the narrative and its meaning.

Christian Readings of Esther

Theological troubles plagued the book for centuries, particularly among Christian religious leaders. Firstly, as Lewis Bayles Paton notes, the Book of Esther was roundly ignored: "Not a single Christian commentary was written on this book during the first seven centuries of our era."[36] Martin Luther objected to its inclusion in the Old Testament with an almost viscerally negative reaction: "I am so hostile to this book [2 Maccabees] and Esther that I could wish that they did not exist at all, for they Judaize too greatly and have much pagan impropriety."[37] C. H. Cornill did not hide his distaste for Esther: "All the worst and most unpleasing features of Judaism are here displayed without disguise."[38] Christian scholars point to its overtly nationalistic elements, its sour attitude toward gentiles, and its primal emotions of anger and revenge. B. W. Anderson writes, "The story unveils the dark passions of the human heart: envy, hatred, fear, anger, vindictiveness, pride."[39] Anderson went so far as advising Christian ministers to stay away from Esther texts when giving sermons.[40] The rancor and malice directed toward Esther is difficult to digest for any Jewish reader.[41] As David Clines notes, the "catalogue of anti-Semitic sentiments that have been voiced under the guise of interpretation of Esther makes depressing reading."[42] Despite this, Esther in the medieval

36. Paton, *Critical and Exegetical Commentary on Esther*, 101.
37. Quoting *Table Talk, xxiv*, in William D. Barrick, "Old Testament Introduction," *Syllabus OT* 796 (Summer 2012): 22.
38. C. H. Cornill, *Introduction to the Canonical Books of the Old Testament*, trans. G. Box (New York: Williams and Norgate, 1907), 257.
39. Bernard W. Anderson, "The Place of the Book of Esther in the Christian Bible," *Journal of Religion* 30 (1950): 39.
40. Ibid., 42.
41. For a review of this literature and a reassessment, see Frederic W. Bush, "The Book of Esther: *Opus non gratum* in the Christian Canon," *Bulletin for Biblical Research* 8 (1998): 39–54.
42. Clines, Review of W. Hermann, *Esther im Streit der Meinungen Society for Old Testament Study Book List* 78 (1988): 10.

period served as a pre-figuration for the Virgin Mary in Christian iconography: "As Mary intercedes on behalf of Christians with God, Esther intercedes on behalf of the Jews with Ahasuerus."[43]

Many modern commentators joined in the ranks of this negative attitude to the book, noting Esther's distinct lack of spiritual qualities, be it the sexualization of the plot, the merriment, the treatment of non-Jews, or the undercurrent of revenge that dominates the last chapters.[44] A Jewish professor of Bible and Hellenistic literature commented that he would "not be grieved if the Book of Esther were somehow dropped out of Scripture"[45] and another ventured that both Purim and the scroll were not worthy of their nation.[46] Such sentiments seem to miss the point entirely. It is the very similarity of detail with a love story or novel and then the sudden shift of perspective and outcome that makes the book not only compelling and distinct but also profoundly spiritual. No matter what others think (including some Jewish thinkers), the Book of Esther found a proud home in the Hebrew Bible.

Different Versions of Esther

Adding to the confusion of genre, treatment, and message is the fact that the Book of Esther is not one book but several. While traditional Jews know the Masoretic Text (MT) of Esther in Hebrew, it was translated into Greek as part of the Septuagint (referred to in scholarly literature as LXX), spreading the reading population of the book but also adding some significant changes in the form of six additions, likely

---

43. Ori Z. Soltes, "Images and the Book of Esther: From Manuscript Illumination to Midrash," in *The Book of Esther in Modern Research*, 140.
44. See Anderson, "The Place of the Book of Esther in the Christian Bible," 32–43; Robert Pfeiffer, *Introduction to the Old Testament* (New York: Harper and Brothers, 1941), 747; and L. E. Browne, *Esther: Peake's Commentary on the Bible* (London: Thomas Nelson and Sons, 1962), 383. Otto Eissfeldt wrote, "Christianity… has neither occasion nor justification for holding on to it" (*The Old Testament* [New York: Harper and Row, 1965], 511–12).
45. Samuel Sandmel, *The Enjoyment of Scripture* (New York: Oxford University, 1972), 44.
46. Shalom ben Chorin, *Kritik des Estherbuches: Eine theologische Steitschrift* (Jerusalem, 1938), 5, cited in Anderson, "The Place of the Book of Esther in the Christian Bible," *Journal of Religion* 30 (1950): 34.

added by a later redactor. These were removed in the fourth century by Jerome in the Vulgate without clear indications of where each passage once appeared. The text was rendered even more befuddling in the late medieval period when chapters were assigned to the Vulgate, and all the chapters of Esther, the Jerome version and the additions he collected and excised, were numbered consecutively. Later scholars reconstructed the likely order of the original document, and much ink has been spilled comparing and contrasting details: where Haman is from tribally, when Mordecai discovered the plot against Ahasuerus, and important dates throughout the scroll.

These additions add 107 verses to the original Hebrew text of 167 verses and are designated as sections A–F. But even these different additions were not written at the same time or in the same place, although all were likely written during the second century BCE.[47] The most notable change, according to Carey Moore, is that God's name, which makes no appearance in the MT version, appears over fifty times in these additions.[48] To add to this already complicated development, there is a second Greek version of the Book of Esther called either the Alpha Text (AT) or the Lucianic Text (L) or simply the second Greek text. The AT is slightly shorter than the LXX but also contains some details not present in either the MT or the LXX.[49]

The additions added to the MT, rendered in the Oxford Apocrypha as "The Rest of the Chapters of the Book of Esther," begin with a fantastical dream Mordecai had, rendering it closer to the Book of Daniel or Joseph, two other courtier tales that involve dreams, than to the traditional Book of Esther. These chapters are short and God saturated.

47. See Clines, *The Esther Scroll*, 70; Craig, *Reading Esther*, 27; and Moore, *Daniel, Esther and Jeremiah*, 13.

48. See Carey A. Moore, "A Greek Witness to a Different Hebrew Text of Esther," *Zeitschrift fur die Alttestamentliche Wissenschaft* 79 (1967): 351–58. This article also appears in Moore's *Studies in the Book of Esther* (New York: Ktav, 1982), 521–28. The citation above is from p. xxiv.

49. For a discussion of these texts and their relationship to each other, see Kristin De Troyer, "Esther in Text – and Literary – Critical Paradise," in *The Book of Esther in Modern Research*, 31–49; and Michael Fox, "Three Esthers," in *The Book of Esther in Modern Research*, 50–60; and Moore's "On the Origins of the LXX Additions to the Book of Esther, *Journal of Biblical Literature* 92 (1973): 382–93.

Mordecai's dream portends a change of fate: "And my nation is this Israel, which cried to God, and were saved; for the Lord hath delivered us from all those evils, and God hath wrought signs and great wonders, which has not been done among the Gentiles."[50] The additions also introduce new eunuchs, who make no appearance in the original text, and protests against evil treatment without any Jewish identity cover-up. The most dramatic difference is Esther's plea. She changed her garments and made herself vulnerable, not before the king but before the King of kings:

> And laid away her glorious apparel and put on the garments of anguish and mourning: and instead of precious ointments, she covered her head with ashes and dung, and she humbled her body greatly, and all the places of her joy she filled with torn hair. And she prayed unto the Lord God of Israel saying, O my Lord, thou only art our King: help me, desolate woman, which have no helper but thee: For my danger is in mine hand. From my youth up I have heard in the tribe of my family, that thou, O Lord, tookest Israel from among all people, and our fathers from all their predecessors, for a perpetual inheritance, and thou hast performed whatsoever thou didst promise them. And now we have sinned before thee: therefore hast thou given us into the hands of our enemies. Because we worshipped their gods: O Lord, thou art righteous .... Remember, O Lord, make thyself known in time of our affliction, and give me boldness, O King of the nations, and Lord of all power.[51]

Sixteen verses of prayer are insufficient. The next chapter tells us that she ended her prayer on the third day. Here, the narrator reduces the beauty queen to a shriveled supplicant, trading in her perfume for the smell of dung and putting away her ermine cape for burlap. Esther ripped out her hair to get God's attention, showing in word and deed that there was only ever one authority over her. Esther interpreted what happened to her and her people as a consequence of Israelite sin. This sense of causation appears nowhere in the MT text, but we can see how

50. *Esther, The Apocrypha: Authorized Version* (London: Oxford University Press), 102.
51. Ibid., 104–5.

the author/s of these additional passages may have lifted the themes from the Book of Daniel:

> I turned my face to the Lord God, devoting myself to prayer and supplication, in fasting, in sackcloth and ashes. I prayed to the Lord my God, making confession thus: "O Lord, great and awesome God, who stays faithful to His covenant with those who love Him and keep His commandments! We have sinned; we have gone astray; we have acted wickedly; we have been rebellious and have deviated from Your commandments and Your rules, and have not obeyed Your servants the prophets who spoke in Your name to our kings, our officers, our fathers, and all the people of the land. With You, O Lord, is the right, and the shame is on us to this very day, on the men of Judah and the inhabitants of Jerusalem, all Israel, near and far, in all the lands where You have banished them, for the trespass they committed against You. The shame, O Lord, is on us, on our kings, our officers, and our fathers, because we have sinned against You." (Dan. 9:3–8)

Much of traditional and academic exegesis on Esther focuses on the absence of God in the *Megilla,* a subject to which we will devote an entire chapter. What we find in the additions to the MT is that the "problem of God" for some in the world of antiquity did not exist at all. God is highly present. Both Mordecai and Esther prayed to their Deity; Esther, in fact, changed her clothing before appearing before the king, indicating that she perhaps wore different clothing in the presence of her own people, suggesting a more authentic life among her own. These additions may have been conveniently placed to overcome the assumed secular, material, or political nature of events and the discomfort they caused to the reader. Pointing to Israelite sin and guilt is another familiar Christian trope.

To add greater complication, there are two Aramaic translations of Esther: *Targum Rishon* and *Targum Sheni*[52] and a host of midrashim

52. For more on these *Targumim,* see Bernard Grossfeld, *The Two Targums of Esther: Translated, with Apparatus and Notes* (Collegeville, MN: Liturgical Press, 1991).

or midrashic collections.[53] Some believe Esther is not one story but two. Elias Bickerman, in *Four Strange Books of the Bible,* contends that there are two main characters because these are two conjoined stories:

> It has two heroes because it has two plots. In the first, Esther, a Jewess, becomes a Persian queen, but the enmity of Haman, the king's vizier, endangers her position and her life. She succeeds in saving herself and her people and in bringing Haman to the gallows. In the second, Mordecai, a Jewish courtier, is hated by the vizier Haman. The latter prepares the gallows for his enemy but by accident the king discovers Mordecai's past services and orders Haman to honor his rival. In other words, the book has two heroes and two plots, but the villain is the same in both.[54]

Such a reading significantly diminishes the tight literary weaving of coincidences that are really miracles in court clothing.

The language used in the book can also be challenging: "The Hebrew book of Esther contains more Akkadian and Aramaic loanwords in proportion to its length than any other book in the Ḥebrew Bible. Many words, phrases, and customs can be traced back to the Assyrian period, and in a few cases we can show that they fell out of use before the Persian period."[55] In isolated places, for example, the text uses two words as a way to translate the term into a more acceptable idiom, such as in 3:7 or 9:24 where *pur* is translated into the Hebrew *goral.*[56]

Esther as Theology

In addition to the above curiosities, one obvious problem persists. It is impossible to sustain a religious life in exile without God. Thus, God's

---

53. Among these – that will be cited throughout this commentary – are Esther Rabba, *Abba Guryon, Panim Aḥerim, Lekaḥ Tov, Midrash Megillat Esther,* and *Aggadat Esther.* Other midrashic works that contain sections on Esther include *Pirkei DeRabbi Eliezer, Seder Olam, Midrash Shoḥer Tov,* and *Yalkut Shimoni.* A full list appears in Walfish, *Esther in Medieval Garb,* 363–448.
54. Bickerman, 172.
55. Dalley, *Esther's Revenge,* 165.
56. Ibid., 167.

name going unmentioned in the Book of Esther seems an unfathomable theological omission.[57] Meir Steinberg observes that absences of information and detail are not uncommon in the Hebrew Bible; the attempt to fill in the gaps occasions a good deal of Bible commentary:

> A gap is a lack of information about the world – an event, motive, causal link, character trait, plot structure, law of probability – contrived by a temporal displacement. Like the objects displaced, the forms of displacement may vary. What happened (or existed) at a certain temporal point in the world may be communicated in the discourse at a point earlier or later, or for that matter not at all.[58]

But the absence of God in a biblical book is an entirely different matter. There is something religiously elemental and even terrifying in a sacred text shorn of its Holy Center, as if the world could topple at any moment. Indeed, in Esther it does. Theologically this state of affairs was untenable; thus, the search for God in Esther preoccupied many ancient and medieval commentators and has stimulated a variety of discussions in modern scholarship. As mentioned earlier, the two *Targumim* of Esther and the Apocryphal text supplement this absence by adding God into the cast of characters.

It was difficult to believe that all of the book's many connected events were to be regarded simply as coincidences and that none of its characters, especially Mordecai the Jew, would attribute its dramatic events to the King of kings. Esther may have fasted, but she did not pray, at least according to the MT text, to the God who had brought salvation

57. Many are of the traditional view that Esther is the only biblical book with no mention of God. However, God's name is not mentioned in the Song of Songs either. For observations on this, see Renita Weems, "Song of Songs," in *The Women's Bible*, ed. C. Newsom and S. Ringe (Louisville, KY: Westminster John Knox Press, 1992), 156; and Robert Gordis, *The Song of Songs* (New York: Jewish Theological Seminary, 1961), 2–4. For a fuller treatment, see David Blumenthal, "Where God Is Not: The Book of Esther and Song of Songs," accessed at http://www.js.emory.edu/BLUMENTHAL/EstherSong.html.

58. Meir Sternberg, "The Relevance of Absence," in *The Poetics of Biblical Narrative: Ideological Literature and the Drama of Reading* (Bloomington, IN: Indiana University Press, 1987), 235.

to her people time and again. In this scenario, God's hidden face is intentional, as the Talmud suggests: "Where does one find an allusion to Esther in the Torah? In the verse 'I [God] shall surely hide My face from them (Deut. 31:18).'"[59] This wordplay on the name Esther and the Hebrew word for "hidden," *astir*, that appears in the verse cited in Deuteronomy, share the same root and sound enough alike to make God's hiddenness an act of intention rather than coincidence.

Rabbinic sages and medieval exegetes searched for implicit references to God in the work. Saadia Gaon (882–942), in the introduction to his commentary on Esther, claims that there is information in the work that only God could have known. He explains that had God's name been used, it would have been erased and replaced by the names of pagan gods by Persian chronicle writers. In order to circumvent this problem, no name of God was used in the book at all.[60] Ironically, the author secularized the book to keep it religiously viable; the identification of God as the cause of events was to be the work of exegetes on Esther.

One oblique reference demonstrates an almost spiritual desperation to find God: Mordecai's plea to Esther in chapter 4: "On the contrary, if you keep silent in this crisis, relief and deliverance will come to the Jews from another quarter, while you and your father's house will perish" (4:14). "Another quarter" is rendered in Hebrew as *makom aḥer*. *Makom*, a name for God that situates God as the Ultimate Place, would render the verse's meaning: God will bring salvation whether or not Esther is involved. Ibn Ezra rejects this reading and implies that people with high levels of spiritual perfection would immediately recognize God's role in the work without attaching it to what he considered to be an inaccurate wordplay:

59. See Ḥullin 139b. The principle that such allusions should exist was stated by R. Yoḥanan in Taanit 9a: "R. Yoḥanan sat down and wondered aloud about this verse, saying: 'Is there anything that is written in the Writings that is not alluded to in the Torah?'"

60. See Yehuda Ratzaby, "MiFeirush Rav Se'adya LiMegillat Esther," in *Sefer Yovel LiKhevod...Yosef Dov HaLevi Soloveitchik*, ed. Shaul Yisraeli, Nahum Lamm, and Yitzhak Refael (Jerusalem: 1983–1984), 763.

> And behold, there is no mention of God's name in the scroll, yet it is a sacred text. Many have explained that it is found in the term *makom*, "place," yet this is not correct, since there is no such use of the term *makom* as a name of God in all of Scripture[61]... and what I consider correct is that there are many references to Mordecai...and this is the reason that there are many Persian writers who chronicle the events of their kings – they were idol worshippers and they would have included their gods in place of His revered name...therefore, Mordecai did not mention the name of God in the *Megilla*.[62]

Ibn Ezra offers a simple, literal reading of 4:14, suggesting that if Esther did not redeem her people someone else would. He mentions earlier commentators, without naming them, who say the word *makom* is an allusion to God, and that while that may be their view, this is not a name ever used to refer to God in the Hebrew Scriptures. Furthermore, if this reading were so, why use the word *aḥer* in connection with it?[63]

Although Ibn Ezra does not cite it, Deuteronomy records a distinction between God and place, using the very word *makom*: "But look to the site (*makom*) that the Lord your God will choose amid all your tribes as His habitation, to establish His name there. There you are to go" (12:5). Ibn Ezra, addressing the question of God's absence, does mention Saadia Gaon's view by name. Some scholars have made a similar argument,[64] while others believe that *makom* is not a reference to God at all.[65]

---

61. The word *makom* appears twice in Esther, in 4:3 and 8:17.
62. Abraham ibn Ezra, in his brief introduction to *Ḥamesh Megillot, Mikraot Gedolot* (Vilna, 1889), 651.
63. Peter R. Ackroyd makes a similar case, going as far as to suggest that in conjunction this expression may infer another god. "Two Hebrew Notes," *Annual of the Swedish Theological Institute* (1967); see pp. 82–86.
64. L. H. Brockington, *Ezra, Nehemiah and Esther*, Century Bible New Series (London: Thomas Nelson & Sons, 1969).
65. J. M. Brown, "Rabbinic Interpretations in the Characters and Plot of the Book of Esther (as Reflected in Midrash Esther Rabba)," *HUC-JIR* (1976): 52.

A number of traditional commentators believe that God's overt absence is a fault of the Israelites themselves and not a matter of the text being co-opted for pagan use. Ashkenazi, cited earlier, offers a parable suggesting that because of Israel's sin, God only appears in a hidden fashion, both in name and in action:

> To what may this be compared? To the son of a king who sinned greatly against his father, and he [the father] threw him out. But a lion grabbed him [the son]. The father, out of compassion for his son, sent others to save him from the lion. The father, however, did not try to save him lest the son think that his father's anger had abated. Such is God's behavior, blessed be His name, while we are in exile. His face is hidden from us so that He must find subtle ways to rescue us from our enemies – so much so, that it is not evident that the salvation actually came from Him, blessed be He.[66]

In this delicate balance, God moves from anger to tenderness, unable to fully consign the Jews to exile without protection, but unable, out of justice, to redeem them directly lest they fail to see the causality of their actions and their consequences. Ashkenazi makes divine providence the crux of his Esther commentary following a long tradition of exegetes who pursued the same theme: Rabbi Joseph Kara (born ca. 1060–70) in the early eleventh century, Gersonides (1288–1344) and Rabbi Joseph ibn Kaspi (1279–1340) in the fourteenth century, and Rabbi Isaac Arama (1420–1494) and Rabbi Zechariah ben Saruk of the fifteenth century. "All these exegetes to one degree or another believe that God's hidden hand guided events in the Esther story."[67]

God's absence may signal a radical adjustment to a life outside of the Land of Israel and away from the Temple and its worship. André LaCocque describes an incremental process. An emerging identity at a distance from its natural center can find its foundational values and even shift its understanding of God:

66. Ashkenazi, *Yosef Lekaḥ* 1:1.

67. Eisen, "Joseph Ibn Kaspi on the Secret Meaning of the Scroll of Esther," 400.

> The more they [the Jews] feel the absence of the Land, of priests, prophets and kings, as well as of altar and sacrifices, of the sacred festivals' ground, the more they develop an exile mentality. It can be expected, therefore, that their understanding of their relationship with God will undergo a profound revision: since God does not reveal himself directly in a foreign land, he is thought of as indirectly providential. Consequently, the accent is now on peripeteia, on some felicitous turn of fortune, on serendipity. And, because divine providence is experienced within the course of events, narrative emphasis also shifts from charismatic personalities to plot.[68]

In other words, God's absence in the Book of Esther may be explained, as LaCocque suggests, as a reflection of a slow turn of perception of God as a force less active outside of Israel where God "lived." This turn represents another sacrifice or cost of exile: the loss of intimacy with God that is supplanted by the perception of life on the margins of God's favor.

Whether or not Esther is read as a theological search for God in exile, it is clear that this theme spoke profoundly to those who wrote on Esther in the midst of or in the aftermath of persecution and tragedy. Given the checkered nature of Jewish history, this implies that virtually every generation had its Haman, a figure so callous and brutal that the search for God's love and redeeming hand became all the more urgent. It is not clear, though, that every generation had its Esther.

Far from Simple

This supposedly simple book is far from simple. It is an artful tale told in a manner that is theologically complex. Not only is Esther's genre heavily debated; its actual text outside of the MT serviced different agendas, begging the question: Which depiction is the most accurate of Esther and her story? The clear heroes and villains of the story, far from making the narrative flat and unengaging, showcase the people and events that are more difficult to grasp. We are unsure how to characterize the

68. André LaCocque, *Esther Regina: A Bakhtinian Reading* (Evanston, IL: Northwestern University Press, 2000), 10.

king. We do not know if Vashti was deserving of the hideous spots the rabbis in a midrash gave her. We are uncertain about Esther's hesitations and Mordecai's attempts to silence her. We do not know what to make of Esther's marriage to a gentile or how to manage the heartache of Persian civilian deaths in Jewish self-defense. Even the deaths of Haman's sons, who were previously unmentioned, seem an unfair condemnation of those guilty by mere association. Its final and lingering question remains as complex today as it was through the ages: Can religious life be sustained for Jews in exile?

Esther as Social Commentary

If it please Your Majesty, let a royal edict be issued by you, and let it be written into the laws of Persia and Media, so that it cannot be abrogated, that Vashti shall never enter the presence of King Ahasuerus. And let Your Majesty bestow her royal state upon another who is more worthy than she. Then will the judgment executed by Your Majesty resound throughout your realm, vast though it is; and all wives will treat their husbands with respect, high and low alike." The proposal was approved by the king and the ministers, and the king did as Memucan proposed. Dispatches were sent to all the provinces of the king, to every province in its own script and to every nation in its own language, that every man should wield authority in his home and speak the language of his own people. (Est. 1:19–22)

On the thirteenth day of the first month, the king's scribes were summoned, and a decree was issued, as Haman directed, to the king's satraps, to the governors of every province, and to the officials of every people, to every province in its own script and to every people in its own language. The orders were issued in the name of King Ahasuerus and sealed with the king's signet. Accordingly, written instructions were dispatched by couriers to all the

> king's provinces to destroy, massacre, and exterminate all the Jews, young and old, children and women, on a single day, on the thirteenth day of the twelfth month – that is, the month of Adar – and to plunder their possessions. The text of the document was to the effect that a law should be proclaimed in every single province; it was to be publicly displayed to all the peoples, so that they might be ready for that day. The couriers went out posthaste on the royal mission, and the decree was proclaimed in the fortress Shushan. The king and Haman sat down to feast, but the city of Shushan was dumbfounded. (Est. 3:12–15)

> So the king's scribes were summoned at that time, on the twenty-third day of the third month, that is, the month of Sivan; and letters were written, at Mordecai's dictation, to the Jews and to the satraps, the governors and the officials of the one hundred and twenty-seven provinces from India to Ethiopia: to every province in its own script and to every people in its own language, and to the Jews in their own script and language. He had them written in the name of King Ahasuerus and sealed with the king's signet. Letters were dispatched by mounted couriers, riding steeds used in the king's service, bred of the royal stud, to this effect. (Est. 8:9–11)

> The couriers, mounted on royal steeds, went out in urgent haste at the king's command; and the decree was proclaimed in the fortress Shushan. (Est. 8:14)

A considerable amount of effort has been invested in recording the mechanisms of Persia's highly bureaucratic structures in the Book of Esther, as illustrated by the above passages. The pomp and circumstance, the constant ministerial counsel, and the way laws were formulated, rigidly kept, and disseminated throughout the kingdom all contribute to a sense of the bulkiness of governance. It is enough to make one wonder if Mordecai's sartorial robes of power are a privilege, a burden, or a sham and if Jews in such a diaspora community should aspire to contribute to a systemically flawed, inefficient, and meaningless bureaucracy. One of the recurrent themes of the Book of Esther is the dysfunctional nature of government. Jon Levenson contends that what pervades the Book of Esther is "a deep skepticism about the whole Persian imperial regime":[1]

> This is evident primarily in the portrayal of King Ahasuerus and the way his court functions. He is portrayed as a man of inordinate official power but no moral strength. His regime is enormously bureaucratic, yet he lacks all personal complexity. It is this disparity between the office and the man, between what he decrees and what actually happens, that imparts to the book many of its funniest scenes. But underneath the humor is a belief that the imperial administration is overblown, pompous, over-bureaucratic, and, for all its trappings of power, unable to control events. On its surface, the narrative of the book of Esther approaches the category of a farce on occasion, but the more serious category of satire always lurks behind the crude, visual humor to remind the attentive reader of the larger issues.[2]

Levenson was not the first to observe the tragicomic nature of leadership in the book. Esther's backdrop of the ancient Persian government has long invited interpreters to draw comparisons to their own political and societal contexts, dressing the story up as a social commentary on their respective times with the function of government at the heart of interpretation. Esther is an excellent textual stage from which to discuss the relationship of a Jewish community to its gentile ruler or monarch or to their own statesmen employed in royal courts. This theme acquired greater seriousness by virtue of the fact that incompetent or malicious rulers could determine the fate of negligible minorities in their lands.

To illustrate, the Book of Esther was a seminal text and springboard for sixteenth-century commentators to ruminate on the great physical and scholarly upheavals experienced in the wake of the Spanish Inquisition and the exile of Jews from the Iberian Peninsula to major Jewish centers in Europe, Asia, and Africa.[3] During the 1500s, the Jewish

1. Levenson, *Esther*, 12.
2. Ibid.
3. Political insecurity clearly began before the Expulsion, as Jews increasingly experi-

diasporic community experienced seismic movement and subsequent reorganization; this, in turn, before the formal writing of history, became a subject worthy of reflection in comments on a foundational text. Because God's name makes no appearance in Esther and the entire book is based solely in the diaspora, it became a natural locus for social commentary on human agency, the state of leadership, and the conditions of exile: "Among some of the writers and their descendants, feelings of bereavement and loss are particularly marked."[4] In *Meḥir Yayin* (Cremona, 1559), a philosophical commentary on Esther, Rabbi Moses Isserles (1530–1572) remarks several times that his commentary was written "in the exile in which we have been exiled,"[5] in a "place of neither fig nor vine."[6] Although Esther describes several wine parties, Rabbi Isserles, basing himself on Isaiah 35:10, writes in the first-person plural that the days of Purim cannot be celebrated with enough wine and merriment to remove the pain and anguish of exile.[7] In another example, Zechariah ben Saruk, exegete and exile, includes his own personal experience in his introduction to Esther. Ben Saruk, according to Walfish,

> gives full vent to his sorrow and frustration at the loss of his home and property and the tremendous disruption in his life that the expulsion has caused. In typical Scholastic fashion, he begins by naming three conditions that an author needs in order to be

enced alienation and persecution from the Catholic monarchs of Spain; see Yitzhak Baer, *A History of the Jews in Christian Spain*, vol. 2 (Philadelphia: Jewish Publication Society, 1992; first edition, 1966), 300–424. Even after leaving the Iberian Peninsula, Jewish fate was uncertain. For a general view of the issue in specific locales, see Bernard Lewis, *The Jews of Islam* (Princeton: Princeton University Press, 1984), 107–92; primary documents collected in Norman Stillman, *The Jews of Arab Lands* (Philadelphia: Jewish Publication Society, 1979), 255–323; and Robert Bonfil, *Jewish Life in Renaissance Italy* (Berkeley: University of California Press, 1994), 19–78.

4. Joseph R. Hacker, *The Ottoman-Jewish Encounter: A Social and Cultural History of the Jews in the Ottoman Empire* (Jerusalem: Hebrew University Press, 2013), 115.
5. This is a play on Est. 2:5, where Mordecai is introduced as an exile.
6. Introduction to *Meḥir Yayin*, ii. The combination of a fig and grapevine is a common symbol for the Land of Israel in prophetic texts, as in II Kings 5:5, Is. 34:4, and Jer. 5:17.
7. Ibid., 4.

> able to write: wisdom, books, and peace of mind. Because of the Expulsion Zechariah claims he has forgotten what he learnt, has aged a great deal; he has lost his books; and since being forced to leave his home for a new, hostile place, he has no peace of mind.[8]

Expulsion and political uncertainty also had a marked influence on family structures, Jewish communal institutions, and personal religious faith. These, too, shaped commentaries on Esther from the period.

> The generation of the exiles left the Iberian Peninsula in an atmosphere of grief and crisis, a crisis of faith and a crisis of values. The Expulsion itself dealt a desperate blow to the family unit, to the group image and to the exiles' economic power.... The crisis of values reinforced demands for a radical reform in the conceptual sphere, for criticism and for the rejection of the cultural values and spirit of the educated elite. Some even questioned the very object and possibility of future Jewish existence and were skeptical of the Prophets' promises.[9]

More specifically, the high regard Spanish Jews accorded the courtier class was not necessarily shared by the Jews in their new host countries. This confrontation of views about gentile leadership also contributed to an increased interest in interpreting the Book of Esther:

> In pre-Expulsion Spain the class of leaders-courtiers did not encounter basic criticism of its existence and its benefit to Jewish society...in the Ottoman Empire this stratum was subjected to criticism so severe that it rejected the entire concept of the courtier, considering it as a stumbling block and an enemy.[10]

---

8. Walfish, *Esther in Medieval Garb*, 7.
9. Ibid., 125. See also Joseph R. Hacker, "HaYeiush Min HaGeula VeHaTikva HaMeshiḥit BeKhitvei Shelomo LeVeit HaLevi MiSalonika," *Tarbiz* 39 (1970): 195–213, and H. H. Ben Sasson, "Dor Golei Sefarad Al Atzmo," *Zion* 26 (1961): 23–64.
10. Hacker, "HaYeiush," 131.

The rise of Mordecai and Esther, the fall of Haman, court structures and rivalries, the monarchy, and the interior of the palace were all of interest to those concerned with the royal court and Jewish participation in it.[11] The fact that Esther was read twice a year over the liturgical calendar meant that these themes invited annual reflection.[12]

Jewish success in the diaspora is a compelling image in any period where rights were arbitrarily given to Jews and often randomly rescinded, but there may have been greater sensitivity to these vulnerabilities among post-Expulsion refugees. Levenson believes that the book's influence lies in its presentation of Jewish courtier leadership and what he calls the "fantasy" of Jewish power:

> Mordecai is an exile from Judah who, by adhering to his ancestral traditions in defiance of the king's command and at the risk of life itself, saves the lives of his people and becomes the second to the king and the beloved advocate of the Jews. Esther is not only an exile, but an orphan and a person who must disguise her ethnicity. Yet through good luck of mysterious origin, great personal courage, obedience to her foster father, and rare eloquence, she too rises to royal estate and effects the deliverance of her threatened nation. Those transformations from refugee to prime minister and from orphan to queen recall prophetic visions of restoration after exile (e.g., Isaiah 54) and suggest that Mordecai and Esther, for all their particular character, are also allegorizations of Israel's national destiny.[13]

---

11. For more on Jewish success in the Spanish royal court, see Eliyahu Ashtor, *The Jews of Moslem Spain*, vol. 1 (Philadelphia: Jewish Publication Society, 1992), 155–263.
12. See Hacker, *The Ottoman-Jewish Encounter*, 111–13. In addition to assuming that books read the most often would encourage the most commentary, Hacker also adds that "almost everyone was writing on the same biblical books." He attributes this to the literary heritage of Spanish and Portuguese refugees: "An examination of the entirety of the intellectual creation of the Jews of the Ottoman Empire during the sixteenth and seventeenth centuries reveals the existence of consistent patterns of intellectual activity from the Iberian Peninsula."
13. Levenson, *Esther*, 16.

This fantasy of power persisted even through the dictates of an alternative reality. In perhaps one of the most fascinating aspects of Esther as a social commentary during this period, historian Yosef Hayim Yerushalmi contends that Spanish Jews steadfastly held on to a positive royal image despite changing historical realities. Paradoxically, the ruthlessness of particular kings and queens in the fifteenth century did not greatly diminish respect for the monarchy. Yerushalmi analyzes attitudes to the court from the historical chronicles of Solomon ibn Verga (second half of the fifteenth century), the *Shebet Yehudah* (1554). Ibn Verga himself had been the victim of the cruelty of Manuel I (1469–1521), the king of Portugal:

> He was one of the many Spanish exiles of 1492 who had later crossed into Portugal, only to be swept up five years later in the forced baptism of all the Jews of the realm. Living the dual life of a crypto-Jew when the pogrom occurred, Ibn Verga would seem to have had every reason to revile rather than extol the king [whom he referred to as *melekh ḥasid*] who had compelled him and so many other Jews to abandon the religion of their fathers.[14]

Ibn Verga uses the encomium *melekh ḥasid* to refer to the king and uses other adjectives of piety, like "just," "righteous," and "lover of Jews" to apply to kings whose surface behaviors did not seem to warrant these praiseworthy descriptions. Instead, the general populace, the queen, or a particular minister were singled out and blamed in the king's stead. As an example, in Ibn Verga's writing, he claimed that

> generally the kings of Spain and France, the nobles and savants, and all the distinguished persons of the land, used to love the Jews and hatred fell among the populace who were jealous of the Jews.[15]

By blaming the masses, Jews could remain loyal and committed to the king until the violence ceased; the king and the Jews could then resort

14. Yosef Hayim Yerushalmi, *The Lisbon Massacre of 1506 and the Royal Image in the Shebet Yehudah* (Cincinnati: Hebrew Union College, 1976), 3.

15. Ibid., 48, citing the *Shebet Yehudah*, ch. 40, discussing the Disputation of Tortosa.

to their normal relations. "In Ibn Verga's eyes, kings and royal officials were always ardent protectors of the Jews against the attacks of the rabble. When the Jews are not saved, it is not for lack of royal will, but because of the obstinacy and power of the *vulgus*."[16] The same interpretation of events was offered to justify the behavior of Ferdinand and Isabella:

> In Spain there was a priest who greatly hated the Jews...and he was confessor to the queen. He incited the queen to force the Jews to convert, and if not, that they perish by the sword. And the queen pleaded with the king and begged this of him.[17]

In this reading, Isabella, who took the characterization of Vashti in *Shebet Yehudah*, provoked Ferdinand to force the Jews to convert. She, not he, incited the violence. Yerushalmi claims that Ibn Verga was not the only one to write this way about the king and the public; his views were "far from unusual or eccentric."[18] Jews should always behave, he believed, in gentile society in ways that protect the relationship between them and their ruler. Many commentators during the sixteenth century deliberately ignored or reframed negative actions of Ahasuerus positively, even at times blaming the Jews rather than the king, to maintain a positive view of the monarchy.

> Jews at large must... conduct themselves in their daily lives as to reduce potential frictions with the rest of the population. They should, on the whole, display a low profile, avoid ostentation in dress and refrain from flaunting their luxuries in any way.... Though popular hatred can perhaps not be eradicated, it need not be inflamed.[19]

The king was not to be found wanting. At worst, he was faulted for being malleable to public demands or to the manipulation of the queen. There-

16. Yerushalmi, *Lisbon Massacre*, 39.
17. Yerushalmi's translation of *Shebet Yehudah, Lisbon Massacre*, 50.
18. Ibid., 52.
19. Ibid., 51.

fore, the Jews needed to secure their position with the king and in the kingdom by behaving as model citizens and not attracting attention to their differences.

It is no surprise, therefore, from a social commentary perspective, that in this century of transition more Esther commentaries were produced than in any other century prior.[20] The Book of Esther was a natural locus for deliberations on Jewish power and its absence in this new diaspora. It also affirmed that Jews, even those facing persecution, could hopefully use their faith and their political prowess to engender protection under gentile rulers. As a result, between 1492 and 1600, over thirty Esther commentaries were written.[21] In the four hundred years preceding the sixteenth century, only twenty-eight commentators on the Book of Esther have been identified, including "virtually every

20. Barry Walfish (*Esther in Medieval Garb*, 5) claims that there was a "veritable explosion of commentaries" on Esther in this period. In his own words, "In the sixteenth century nearly as many major Esther commentaries were produced as in all the preceding centuries" (237 fn 14). He repeats this contention elsewhere as well: "Commentaries on Esther of a homiletical nature proliferated in this period, with as many commentaries appearing in the sixteenth century as in all the preceding centuries" ("Kosher Adultery? The Mordecai-Esther-Ahasuerus Triangle in Talmudic, Medieval and Sixteenth-Century Exegesis," in *The Book of Esther in Modern Research*, 125).

21. These include commentaries by Aaron Abayuv (*Shemen HaMor*), Isaac Adarbi (*Commentary to Esther*), Shlomo HaLevi Alkabetz (*Manot HaLevi*), Moses Almosnino (*Yedei Moshe*), Isaac Arama (*Commentary to Esther*), Meir Arama (*Commentary to Esther*), Joseph ben Gershon Concio (*Divrei Esther*), Solomon ben Zemah Duran (*Tiferet Yisrael, Megillat Sefer*), Elisha Galiko (*Commentary to Esther*), Isaac Gershon (*Shelom Esther*), Hayim ben Abraham (*Ateret Zahav*), Joseph Hayyon (*Commentary to Esther*), Moses Isserles (*Meḥir Yayin*), Judah ben Bezalel Loewe (*Ohr Ḥadash*), Isaac Luria (Fragments in Hayim Vital's *Sefer HaLikkutim* and *Shaar HaPesukim*), Shemtov Melamed (*Maamar Mordecai*), Menahem ben Daniel Modena (*Commentary to Esther*), Abraham Saba (*Eshkol HaKofer*), Zechariah ben Saruk (*Commentary to Esther*), Samuel de Uceda (*Commentary to Esther*), Samuel Valerio (*Yad HaMelekh*), Joseph ibn Verga (*Commentary to Esther*), Joseph ibn Yahya (*Commentary to Esther*), Abraham ben Isaac Zahalon (*Yesha Elokim*), and Yom Tov ben Moses Zahalon (*Lekaḥ Tov*). Ashkenazi's teacher in Salonika, Joseph Taitatzak (*Leḥem Setarim*), and his fellow student in Salonika, Moses Alsheikh (*Masat Moshe*), also wrote Esther commentaries during this period. For a review of over twenty commentaries on Esther from the sixteenth century, see Yosef Kohen, "Megillat Esther BaAspaklarya Shel Ḥakhmei Tzefat BaMe'a Ha-16," *She'arim* 4 (March 1966).

identified medieval commentary on the Book of Esther as well as several anonymous ones."[22]

Esther Models Being Jewish in Secret

Crypto-Jews, referred to as Marranos or conversos, also read Esther into their situation; she was a heroine who, like them, veiled her true Jewish identity while functioning in larger society, never compromising on her authentic convictions.[23] Judith Neulander, in exploring the Book of Esther across three Western faiths, describes *ayuno*, a three-day fast broken at night with meatless meals, observing the legend that Esther ate no meat while living in the palace.[24] In another intriguing example of the Book of Esther co-opted as social commentary, Vashti, in a late eighteenth-century illustrated Haggada from Alsace, bears a striking likeness to Marie Antionette: "The fall of one queen is seen as an echo of the fall of the other, albeit under very different circumstances and with very different consequences."[25] Despite the differences, Ori Soltes remarks that the aftermath of the French Revolution that brought about the death of the French queen also led to the Emancipation decree that catalyzed citizenship rights for the Jews, suggesting obliquely that the downfall of a despised queen may have led to greater societal openness.

Jumping across centuries and continents, Esther had a role as social commentary in America as well. Scott Langston, for example,

---

22. Walfish, *Esther in Medieval Garb*, 2.
23. See Cecil Roth, *A History of the Marranos* (Philadelphia: Jewish Publication Society, 1947), 26, for a brief discussion of Esther as the archetypal Marrano who hid her true faith in order to save her people. In the seventeenth century, Abraham Cardoso in a letter supporting Shabbetai Tzvi, mentions the role that Esther played for Peninsular Marranos: "Similar to this is that which happened to Esther, for through her a great deliverance was accomplished in Israel. And certainly most of the ignorant must have loathed her for having been married to a gentile idolater, which is a stringent prohibition of the Torah, but the sages who knew this secret and recognized the truth of the matter, did not regard her as a sinner" (as cited in Yosef Hayim Yerushalmi, *From Spanish Court to Italian Ghetto* [New York: Columbia University Press, 1971], 320).
24. Judith S. Neulander, "The Ecumenical Esther: Queen and Saint in Three Western Belief Systems," in *The Book of Esther in Modern Research*, 187.
25. Soltes, "Images and the Book of Esther," 149–50.

writes that an American Reform rabbi of the late nineteenth century, Isaac L. Leucht, used Esther to describe two American Jewish responses to diasporic living: despair that led to a replacement of their God with the gods of those around them or faith that was the provenance of a "small minority" who remained true to their God.[26] In either response, the Land of Israel is not perceived as central to Jewish identity, making the Book of Esther an apt platform to discuss the role of the Jew in the diaspora. Leucht described himself in a 1904 article in the New Orleans *Daily Picayune* as "an anti-Zionist of the most pronounced type" who believes "that a Jew must work out his destiny in the community in which he lives..."[27] Thus, Langston observes, "the book of Esther offered fertile ground for the consideration of Jewish identity in America." Leucht was not, however, trying to minimize overt expressions of Jewish identity in America, according to Langston: "Rather, he envisioned a fluid process of alternating between identities of self and other."[28] This could only, in his view, be accomplished in the diaspora. Leucht also read into the character of Haman "a critique of American Protestant discrimination against and hatred toward a multitude of non-Protestants, including Jews."[29]

Moving to contemporary times, Adele Berlin, having written commentaries on Esther in both English and Hebrew, makes this observation about their respective audiences:

> American Jews read this diaspora story as diaspora Jews, while Israelis read it from a different social location – as Jews living in the land of Israel and in the modern State of Israel. The Israeli

26. See Scott M. Langston, "Reading a Text Backwards," in *The Book of Esther in Modern Research*, 200–216. Leucht also believed that Esther was not mentioned in other biblical texts because of prophetic embarrassment that the Persian Jewish community housed itself willingly in a foreign country. This is difficult to appreciate given that the prophets expressed outrage at any number of Jewish failings.
27. For more on Leucht's anti-Zionist views, see Langston: "A Jew must work out his destiny in the community in which he lives, suffering, as he goes along, through the ordination of Providence, as an example which will later bring about the reign of love and benevolence" (p. 204). Esther, taking place solely in the diaspora and mentioning no God, was an important book Leucht used to support his views.
28. Langston, "Reading a Text Backwards," 205.
29. Ibid., 208.

> reader tends to see the characters in terms of his or her own modern stereotypes of a diaspora Jew: someone who prefers to hide his identity, who wants to assimilate into the majority population and who behaves in a passive manner even when faced with a threat. My evidence is anecdotal, but my impression is that American Jews, and I would assume other diaspora Jews, like the book more than Israelis do because they see themselves in it to a greater extent.[30]

Where you live likely influences how you read; historical circumstances have influenced the way Esther has been understood through the ages. Its lively cast of characters and royal backdrop invite readers and scholars to enter its world and bring to it their own.

The Carnival of Esther

Some have called Esther a literary carnivalesque, basing themselves on the work of the Russian scholar Mikhail Mikhailovich Bakhtin.[31] Bakhtin investigates the genre of novel or novella written during the Middle Ages and Renaissance that uses the carnival motif to upend power hierarchies and status in the form of the fair or the feast. The carnival was, he believed,

> a peculiar second world within the official medieval order and was ruled by a special type of relationship, a free, familiar, marketplace relationship. Officially the palaces, churches, institutions, and private homes were dominated by hierarchy and etiquette, but in the

30. Adele Berlin, "The Book of Esther: Writing a Commentary for a Jewish Audience," 9.
31. See, for example, Kenneth Craig, *Reading Esther.* Barbara Green critiqued his study, saying that although Craig had made a "formal case for Esther's suitability to be read as a carnival," he did not actually demonstrate the implications of such a reading in *Mikhail Bakhtin and Biblical Scholarship: An Introduction* (Atlanta: Society of Biblical Literature, 2000), 146. Subsequently, André LaCocque took up Green's challenge in *Esther Regina: A Bakhtinian Reading,* 11. See also Ahuva Belkin, "Zmeris Purim – the Third Phase of Jewish Carnivalistic Folk Literature," in *Politics of Yiddish: Studies in Language, Literature and Society,* ed. Dov-Ber Kerler (Lanham, MD: AltaMira Press, 1998), 149–56.

> marketplace a special kind of speech was heard, almost a language of its own, quite unlike the language of Church, palace, courts, and institutions. It was also unlike the tongue of official literature or of the ruling classes.... The festive marketplace combined many genres and forms, all filled with the same unofficial spirit.[32]

For Bakhtin, the carnival was a way for the masses to overcome the constraints placed by those who had authority over them.[33] At carnival time, antinomian behavior becomes normative, if only temporarily. The poor dress as the rich and vice versa, often masked so that their identities are hidden. Under the cover of disguise, it becomes safe and entertaining to challenge and to poke fun at those with power. Laughter itself becomes a powerful tool to gain the sensation of empowerment, as Kenneth Craig notes:

> Laughing at another's discourse is a means of deflating authority, of drawing near what had been distant, of unmasking what had functioned as a veil. The carnival world is permeated with collective gaiety that destroys every form of authority, and communal laughter is fundamentally opposed to all hierarchies. This laughter is a subversive force, one which liberates victims from the restrictions of a prevailing order.[34]

Laughter may not effect social change, but it can shift the attitude one has toward traditional hierarchies of authority. "Carnival extends a kind of general hegemony over people, places, even time," observes Craig, synopsizing Bakhtin.[35] "While carnival lasts, there is no other life outside of it. During carnival time life is subject only to...the laws of its own freedom."[36]

---

32. Mikhail Bakhtin, *Rabelais and His World*, trans. Helene Iswolsky (Bloomington, IN: Indiana University Press, 1984), 154.
33. Ibid., 167.
34. Craig, *Reading Esther*, 156.
35. Ibid., 30.
36. Bakhtin, *Rabelais and His World*, 7.

Although Bakhtin did not write on Esther, later scholars adapted his research as an overlay on the book. We can read Bakhtin's theory playing out in the emphasis the author of Esther places on individual freedoms and proclivities Ahasuerus offered, like drinking, that are minimal in light of the higher freedoms he did not offer. Wine was given "to comply with each person's wishes" (1:8). Edicts were declared to protect the dignity of each man in his home (1:20), but justice and fairness in the more global sense of governance was not offered.

The official feast at the beginning of the Book of Esther showcases the weight of the law, the limits of law, the bending of it, and the complexities of Persian bureaucracy. All stress a universe subjected to authority that ends with an unofficial carnival-like atmosphere as the Jews successfully overturned officialdom in their favor. Craig enlists an example to prove this point by looking at who arranges the story's banquets. The official, royal call to feast happens five times: three decreed by the king, one by Vashti, and then the drinking to mark the decree to annihilate the Jews. After 3:15, however, the other banquets will be arranged by those without real power. This response from those disempowered provides a fascinating and empowering reaction. As the holiday evolved over time, Purim carnivals, dressing up in costume, costume balls, and poking fun at authority in *Purimshpiels* became associated practices and rituals.

Another aspect of carnivalesque literature is the hovering presence of death. The death of authority and its replacement by the birth of new hierarchies is presaged by human death and subsequent renewal or rebirth. The Jews experience this in the collective, Esther as an individual. Every chapter contains some hint that death is an ever-present threat, be it the banishment and possible death of Vashti at the beginning, the conspiracy of Bigthan and Teresh and their subsequent execution, the decree against the Jews, Esther's fear of dying, or Haman's actual death and those of his sons and the people of the empire who tried to kill the Jews but were rebuffed. Craig suggests that the carnival is a place where mortality drives celebration:

> Death offers the greatest challenge to celebration, but it also becomes the necessitating force, the driving force *for* celebration.

> Always ambiguous, death is what is most celebrated against.... Triumph over death requires a recognition of its power as an inevitability, but a larger sense of life emerges when the community affirms itself against individual mortality.[37]

Alternatively, the carnival may be viewed as a postponement of death; celebration is the ultimate distraction. When one is heady with pleasure and laughter, death becomes a momentary afterthought. The celebrations that mark the end of Esther blossom with relief, but, as the carnival reminds us, this relief is always short-lived.

LaCocque reads the Book of Esther not as an upending of social class per se, but what he calls a comparable social situation: "the relationship of a minority population to a hostile majority."[38] The carnival, he posits, is a "strategy for negotiating the interface between official and unofficial" life.[39] As such, the negotiation, to be interesting, must challenge the dominant paradigm. LaCocque suggests that the story's victory comes in the form of implicit sedition:

> Jewish subversion not only overcame a crowd of anti-Semites but, more decisively, it overcame the machinery of the state itself. The oppressed have captured their enemy's fortress and turned its power against their tormentors. Therefore, what the Jewish authorities originally and paradoxically ordered becomes something the people choose to celebrate.

In this view, it is not only how the subversion is celebrated but that it is celebrated; the "carnival" or ending feast highlights more than the defeat of personal enemies. It celebrates a more radical systemic change in both the leadership and the structure of government. In this sense, Mordecai and Esther achieved and modeled a true victory over bias of any kind. Eliminating those who hate is not sufficient. More who hate will breed. Only a shift in law and leadership will bring lasting transformation.

37. Craig, *Reading Esther*, 121.
38. LaCocque, *Esther Regina: A Bakhtinian Reading*, 5.
39. Ibid., 5.

Jewish subversion in Craig's study uses Bakhtinian thought to reframe the Book of Esther. Queen Esther becomes the unlikely lynchpin who bridges these two unrelated cultures:

> Official culture bears down on unofficial culture as we observe a shift from gender violence to ethnic violence: One woman is banished; all women become subject to their husbands; all virgins are summoned only to be followed by the news that all Jews will die because of the evil plan of one demonic man. This is the fate for all in the unofficial realm who suffer under official laws of the land. These scenes of gender and ethnic violence end with a description of the king and Haman sitting down to drink as the "city of Susa is thrown into confusion." How can non-official, powerless culture respond? Esther holds the key.[40]

When the carnival is held is also significant. Bakhtin makes a point of showing that the carnival marked some kind of change or transformation symbolizing a move from darkness to light:

> The feast is always essentially related to time.... Moreover, through all the stages of historic development feasts were linked to moments of crisis, of breaking points in the cycle of nature in the life of society.... Moments of death and revival, of change and renewal always led to a festive perception of the world.[41]

In other words, the carnival would have less meaning as a literary trope if it implied only lighthearted fun, culminating with a return to the bleak, unjust universe of sameness. Instead, it offered moments of social absurdity that foreshadowed the possibility of something greater on the horizon for those victimized or on the lowest rungs of society. Having tasted the possibility of power and freedom, it becomes harder to return to a pre-existing condition of powerlessness.

---

40. Craig, *Reading Esther*, 59.

41. Bakhtin, *Rabelais and His World*, 68.

In the Book of Esther, the move from darkness to light, emblematic of the celebratory feast, is quite literal:

> Mordecai left the king's presence in royal robes of blue and white, with a magnificent crown of gold and a mantle of fine linen and purple wool. And the city of Shushan rang with joyous cries. The Jews enjoyed light and gladness, happiness and honor. And in every province and in every city, when the king's command and decree arrived, there was gladness and joy among the Jews, a feast and a holiday. And many of the people of the land professed to be Jews, for the fear of the Jews had fallen upon them. (8:15–17)

In this sense, the carnivalesque atmosphere at the end of Esther introduces an actual change in the kingdom, as the reader is notified a chapter later:

> And so, on the thirteenth day of the twelfth month – that is, the month of Adar – when the king's command and decree were to be executed, the very day on which the enemies of the Jews had expected to get them in their power, the opposite happened, and the Jews got their enemies in their power. (9:1)

The carnival is a place where upending the norm *is* the norm. In this sense, while there are many possible genre categories within which to place the Book of Esther, it will always retain its carnival-like features. The powerless will gain power. The fasting will give way to feasting. The darkness will become light.

Chapter One

In the King's Palace

Alcohol: The Lubrication of Kings and Fools

Vashti's Ignoble Exit

In the King's Palace

> It happened in the days of Ahasuerus – that Ahasuerus who reigned over a hundred and twenty-seven provinces from India to Ethiopia. In those days, when King Ahasuerus occupied the royal throne in the fortress Shushan, in the third year of his reign, he gave a banquet for all the officials and courtiers – the administration of Persia and Media, the nobles and the governors of the provinces in his service. For no fewer than a hundred and eighty days he displayed the vast riches of his kingdom and the splendid glory of his majesty. At the end of this period, the king gave a banquet for seven days in the court of the king's palace garden for all the people who lived in the fortress Shushan, high and low alike. [There were hangings of] white cotton and blue wool, caught up by cords of fine linen and purple wool to silver rods and alabaster columns; and there were couches of gold and silver on a pavement of marble, alabaster, mother-of-pearl, and mosaics. (Est. 1:1–6)

Imagine, for a moment, a resident of Shushan receiving an embossed invitation to King Ahasuerus' palace on hard stock, counting the days until this grand affair. On entering the hall, the visitor stood gobsmacked. He had never seen anything like it. His eyes were first drawn to the ceiling and then worked their way down to the floor, trying hard to remember every visual delight to repeat to friends and relatives later. The text magically takes the reader into this precise moment of voyeurism by creating a visual sweep: "White cotton and blue wool, caught up by cords of fine linen and purple wool to silver rods and alabaster columns; and there were couches of gold and silver on a pavement of marble, alabaster, mother-of-pearl, and mosaics" (Est. 1:6). From ceiling to floor, the palace's magnificence points to something both grand and unnerving. There is power in these walls, a power so awe-inspiring and pervasive that when the king allows Haman's evil machinations to prevail, every Jew viscerally understood the danger. The joy of acceptance, of being invited to such a feast, of the near reverence it created, literally bled into another type of trepidation; the fear of ostracism and death. The palace symbolized the reach of Persia's power and influence.

That the palace and its chief resident signaled danger is amplified in a rabbinic reading of the scroll's very first words: *Vayehi bimei*, "And it came to pass." This expression portended trouble for the talmudic Sages: "This matter is a tradition from the members of the Great Assembly: Anywhere that the word *vayehi* is stated, it is a term signifying nothing other than grief."[1] This is, however, only true for the beginning of the story. Whenever *vayehi* opens a story, it implies that tragedy is near, but a happy ending will come, even if it takes place far into the future. It opens the Tower of Babel narrative, the story of Hannah's infertility, the tensions between Saul and David, and the opening tragedies in the Book of Ruth: the famine, political unrest, the move to Moab, the death of a patriarch, the marriages of Naomi's sons to gentile women, and then the death of those very sons. These words, "And it came to pass," are one way the biblical text prepares us for the immediate heaviness of human loss while asking us to stay with the story until the sadness curves into something redemptive and promising. We are not sure, however, what could bode poorly when a book starts in a palace and opens with a party. Immersing ourselves in the palace design, we begin to construct an image that will help reveal its perils.

We have documents that reconstruct the palace complex in Susa (Shushan), originally built in the sixth century BCE by Darius I and continued by his son Xerxes, Artaxerxes, and then Darius II. Each subsequent monarch sought to augment the royal home and center of

1. *Megilla* 10b. See also Gen. 14:1–2, Is. 7:1, Jer. 1:3, Ruth 1:2.

government, which stood as a daunting royal structure until Alexander the Great captured and plundered it in 330 BCE. What interests us, millennia later, is how this complex looked and the place it occupied in the mental landscape of the Jews who lived in the capital city and perhaps worked in its grand halls of power. The palace dominated the physical landscape as well, since the land that housed it was literally raised fifty feet above ground to elevate the palace above other buildings; the complex sprawled across 250 acres.[2]

Buildings of this grandeur are meant to validate the importance of their occupants and humble their visitors.

It was impossible to take in all the majesty at once. The residential facilities included many rooms to house courtiers, harems, and the king's private chambers. There were also non-residential areas; an audience hall (*apadana*) and a large decorated gate, presumably the location where Mordecai was most often found. This was no ordinary gate, but a massive structure that either invited in or kept out visitors and employees of the royal household. It was likely a place where many congregated, making Haman's ire at seeing Mordecai beside the gate all the more believable. Haman was unprepared to be humiliated at such a busy public location. Ahasuerus' party led people through gates they thought were previously inaccessible since this compound was set apart from other buildings in the area.

Looking at archaeologists' renderings of the palace, we can almost imagine Hegai shuttling a young and frightened Esther between the women's apartments and the king's chamber and later a more mature and confident Esther at the end of the great hall preparing a banquet for the king and his chief minister before outing Haman. The enormity of the site enables readers to understand the importance of the story. It seems extraordinary that such a minority as the Jews could have, for a brief window in time, occupied an influential place in the goings-on of a royal seat of power that extended across this far-flung empire. And just as astonishing is that a king with such immense holdings of status and money would have paid attention to the fate of this people at all.

2. See Jean Perrot, *The Palace of Darius at Susa: The Great Royal Residence of Achaemenid Persia* (London: I. B. Taurus, 2013).

The Jews would soon disappear from Persian annals – even while the palace walls were still standing. They would relocate, as diaspora communities do, and ultimately outlive a nation whose authority and presence seemed limitless.

What Palace Excavations Revealed

There is little ancient description of the palace compound other than scattered statements about the luxury materials, often imports, used in its building and the fact that it was an important stop on trade routes. The ruins were only rediscovered in 1851 and excavated in pieces during the next century. From 1969 to 1979, the French archaeologist Jean Perrot did the field research that gave the world the palace's expansive dimensions as the once-royal seat of the Persian Empire. What archaeology lends the story is arguably one of its central messages: the Jewish triumph loomed large for a relatively unknown minority. Note that the Jews were not even recognized by the king when Haman initially suggested their annihilation. Haman, in fact, made no mention of their name. In the scheme of Persian history, the Jews were so minor as to be only a brief detail in a foreign potentate's annals.

Austin Henry Layard, the excavator of Nineveh and Nimrud, originally dismissed Susa's significance, writing in 1841, "The ruins are of no importance, and there is only one inscription in cuneiform, which I was unable to copy as it was with difficulty that I escaped, [having been] robbed and fleeced… in this savage and desert land. Other than the similarity between the name and the tomb of the prophets, there is nothing to indicate that a great city lies here."[3] How wrong Layard turned out to be. Decades later, other archaeologists uncovered the enormous pillars that flanked the great hall, the intricate, glazed tiles of the palace with its imposing lion and griffin imagery in bold golds, blues, and greens, and a variety of cuneiform inscriptions with the names of various Persian kings.[4]

---

3. E. Bore, "Letter sur quelques antiquites de la Perse," *JA* 13 (1842): 334–35, as cited by Nicole Chevalier, "The Discoverers of the Palace of Susa", in *The Palace of Darius*, 54.
4. In June of 1988, the president of France dedicated two rooms in the Louvre to the

Much of Susa's riches had yet to be uncovered, but in 1886 the Persian government put a stop to all the investigations. The work upset the surrounding population. It was also disconcerting to watch cart-loads of one's history be taken only to be displayed in another country. Reparations were given only for the gold and silver found in the rubble. No price was put on the history. By the time permission was once again granted in 1912, an enormous area of the palace had been cleared and identified, stretching six hundred by three hundred feet and revealing the outline of a great hall.

Work continued after the First World War, and the stop-start nature of excavations continued across the twentieth century. It was on the occasion of the 2,500th anniversary of the Persian monarchy in 1969 that interest in the site began with renewed zeal, resulting in a decade of new excavations and research. This yielded the following observation about the centerpiece of Jean Perrot's findings from Susa's last noted archaeologist: "[It is] a residential palace which had no equal in its time in oriental architecture."[5]

Perrot also implies that the remains at Susa suggest a "real possibility of a link between the lines from 'the scroll of Esther' and Susian archeological reality as it appears today, with the location described and internal layout of the royal apartments at the heart of the Residence; the discovery of the monumental Gate allows us to answer several questions relative to the comings and goings of Mordecai and his contacts with Esther, his pupil."[6] While Perrot does not claim enough links to establish the historicity of the Book of Esther, he imagines that one might be able to reconstruct the journey from the women's quarters behind the king's apartment and the inner court with some degree of accuracy from the book's description.

---

discoveries from Susa. A third opened three years later. The chief archaeologists who stocked these rooms with Persia's ancient treasures, Marcel Dieulafoy and his wife Jane, had not anticipated, however, how the difference in climate in Paris would affect their desert findings. The glaze of the magnificent tiles began to crumble, only to be restored by baking them with whale blubber.

5. Perrot, foreword to *The Palace of Darius at Susa*, xii.
6. Ibid., 475.

A View from Medieval Sources

It was not only archaeologists who were intrigued by the palace structure. Barry Dov Walfish in *Esther in Medieval Garb* points out that while many medieval commentators were fascinated by what happened inside the palace, only one was interested in its architecture: Rabbi Shemariah ben Elijah of Crete (1275–1355). In great detail, he explains the way the court and garden were configured based on the text and possibly his understanding of the palaces of Moorish kings in Seville and Granada. The relationship of the grounds, the residences, and the royal chambers for meetings were, in the hot climate, connected and often open to nature and the skies. These rooms formed an intricate balance of interconnected public, private, and semi-private spaces:

> *Bitan* [conventionally translated as "garden"]: This is a very large house which can sleep thousands of people.... The garden was surrounded by a wall and there was a large courtyard and, similarly, the garden was open to the courtyard. In my opinion, they would eat in the courtyard and stroll in the garden and sleep in the palace.... The king planted the garden close to the palace, so that he would be able to take a stroll in the garden at his pleasure and feast his eyes on various trees and plants. In order to prevent people from seeing him as he went in and out of the palace garden, he surrounded it with a wall and surrounded the wall with a court.[7]

The *bitan*, or garden, creates, according to this reading, the illusion of the outdoors in an indoor space, allowing access to nature while maintaining the privacy and the security of the royal family. A. L. Oppenheim translates *bitan* as a pavilion, "a small luxury structure, an independent architectural unit for the use of the king or the heir apparent... an open structure, probably colonnaded open hall."[8] The *bitan* is more than an architectural detail, since that alone is generally not of interest to the

---

7. Walfish, *Esther in Medieval Garb*, 102.
8. A. L. Oppenheim, "On Royal Gardens in Mesopotamia," *Journal of Near Eastern Studies* 24 (1965): 330.

biblical writer. Throughout Esther there is an interplay of indoor and outdoor spaces, places that trap and conceal and those that are open to public view. The inside/outside physical details support and draw attention to the insider/outsider status of the exile, and specifically the Jew in exile. Ahasuerus, on several occasions to be discussed in later chapters, left spaces in fury or confusion to bring his troubles to other spaces. These interconnected royal spaces allowed the king to enter and exit at will, a pattern that builds suspense and intrigue as the narrative develops. Yet the outside is no real outside in terms of the palace; it is only the illusion of outside. For this reason, Esther had to be informed of the decree against her people. Trapped in the palace confines along with the rest of the king's harem, Esther and all of the other contestants would remain cut off from their families and the world beyond its walls. Careful readers of the *Megilla* pay close attention to the staging of the scroll and the interrelationship of space to story.

Our understanding of royal residences is obviously shaped by societal forces. The Spanish palace is unlike the German castle and unlike the sprawling English great house. Even among Esther's interpreters who took no interest in what Ahasuerus' palace looked like, the oddity of starting the narrative with Ahasuerus' palace was startling. We have no other biblical book that begins with the inside of a foreign potentate's home. In point of fact, there are very few buildings in the Hebrew Bible generally and none, with the exception of the Tabernacle, the Temple, and Solomon's palace, that are described with this degree of opulence and detail. Where particular individuals lived and the interiority of their homes is of little consequence generally in the Hebrew Bible.[9] This makes the palace description as our introduction to the story deeply troubling. Why should this book take what appears to be too great an interest in the grandiosity and excessiveness of Ahasuerus' living conditions?

Classical medieval commentators, far from ignoring the palace splendor, appear just as intrigued as the residents of the king's empire might have been. Susa is not only important for readers of Esther but

9. For more on this economy of ordinary detail, see Eric Aurbach's seminal article, "Odysseus' Scar," in *Mimesis: The Representation of Reality in Western Literature* (Princeton: Princeton University Press, 2013), 3–23.

also for those of the Book of Daniel: "I looked into the vision; so while I was looking, I was at Susa, the citadel, which is in the province of Elam. I was looking into the vision, and I was near the river Ulai" (8:1–2). Daniel felt it necessary to describe where he was when he was overcome with a vision. Today, the Mosque of the Prophet Daniel at Shush-i Daniel suggests the significance of this prophet to the Muslims as well. Susa, a capital city that Jews are unlikely to visit today, was a place, not unlike Spain in its golden age or the United States or Britain today, where Jewish statesmen made a name for themselves in the government or royal court. As the Book of Esther begins, we step into the palace just as they did long ago.

The Palace as Setting for a Court Tale

Opening with a step into the royal palace immerses the reader in court life quite literally. Sandra Beth Berg suggests that the scroll's use of language and not only imagery communicates this preoccupation with royalty: "The Book of Esther clearly is concerned with the concept of kingship (*malkhut*), and the story itself is presented as a court tale. The importance of this motif is indicated by the frequency of the root *mlk* which occurs over 250 times in the 167 verses of Esther."[10] Naturally, midrashim and commentators are quick to point out that this introduction signals just how far a diaspora people had ventured physically and spiritually from their homeland and the religious ethos present in the Land of Israel. But for now, we stand with others staring at the opulence, wondering where else in the Hebrew Bible attention is given to man-made structures.

Buildings in the Bible

"Unless the Lord builds the house," says the psalmist, "they labor in vain those who build it; unless the Lord guards the city, the watchman stays awake in vain" (Ps. 127:1). This pithy guidance suggests that the spiritual foundations of a structure must be sound and are of greater importance

---

10. Sandra Beth Berg, *The Book of Esther: Motifs, Themes and Structure* (Missoula, MT: Scholars Press, 1979), 59.

than the physical structure. Buildings created to glorify humans, instead of the divine, will always remain unstable and unprotected. Our first biblical building – if we discount the floating residence of Noah's ark – suffers this exact problem. The Tower of Babel narrative in Genesis 11 is recorded primarily to communicate something about those living in the aftermath of the Great Flood. This new population gathered together in Shinar to build a ziggurat-like structure with which to achieve human prominence and safety in numbers after a devastating flood.[11] "They said to one another, 'Come, let us make bricks and burn them hard.' Brick served them as stone, and bitumen served them as mortar. And they said, 'Come, let us build us a city, and a tower with its top in the sky, to make a name for ourselves; else we shall be scattered all over the world'" (Gen. 11:3–4). The external building materials are conveyed in detail to communicate that advances in the construction process – oven-burned bricks and adhesive – allowed people to build tower-like structures previously unimaginable.[12] The building was a symbol of hubris and could not long stand. Its ruination would serve as a witness to human folly.

The rest of Genesis offers us no other glimpse into man-made structures (with the exception of an occasional tent flap) until chapter 39 where Potiphar's house becomes a place of Joseph's rising success and his related seduction. When Joseph states these alarming words – "No one is greater in this house than I am" (39:9) – to Potiphar's wife, it seems an invitation to strip this young and aloof steward of all of his authoritative muscle. His reference to the literal house precipitates yet another incarceration. As steward over this courtier's house, Joseph brought shine to all he did. Yet the same house, empty of almost all of its occupants,

11. See Theodore Hiebert, "The Tower of Babel and the Origin of the World's Cultures," *Journal of Biblical Literature* 12, no. 1 (Spring 2007): 29–58 and John H. Walton, "The Mesopotamian Background of the Tower of Babel Account and Its Implications," *Bulletin for Biblical Research* 5 (1995): 155–75.
12. Nahum Sarna observes that "Scripture has gone out of its way to remark upon the materials used in the construction of the Tower of Babel." He attributes this to the importance of bricks in Mesopotamia during this period that allowed for innovation in the construction and expansion of buildings (*Understanding Genesis: The Heritage of Biblical Israel* [New York: Schocken Books, 1970], 71–72). These details are, therefore, etiological in nature.

became a danger zone for Joseph when Potiphar's wife tried to ensnare and seduce him: "One day he went into the house to attend to his duties, and none of the household servants were inside" (39:11). Here, the physical structure serves as more than a background for Joseph's activities; it traps him. It also hints at his hubris and her abuse of status. The chamber was empty of people but full of temptation and tension.

Traveling from Genesis to Exodus, it is noteworthy that no building or monument marks the location of the giving of the Torah at Sinai. The law lives within its people, not in a brick-and-mortar edifice in a distant wilderness no one would inhabit. The Decalogue's words cannot be situated, bounded in space. They must remain timeless.

Our next building of significance combines the temporality of wilderness with the spirituality of consistent ritual: the *Mishkan* or portable Temple. Described in the last third of the Book of Exodus, the name signifies the God who dwells within the Israelite camp, not within the *Mishkan*'s makeshift walls: "Then have them make a sanctuary for Me, and I will dwell among them" (Ex. 25:8). Of note is the placement of this portable sanctuary in the heart of the camp, flanked by the priestly families of the Levite tribe. It was to be constructed the same way each time and only by the Levites in its charge, thus cementing its role as an anchor throughout the chaos of wilderness life, its requisite holiness created by its separation from common Israelites. Only the priests could place offerings upon its altar or move it, lest the place itself become a substitute for the God who is ephemeral:

> You shall put the Levites in charge of the Tabernacle of the Pact, all its furnishings and everything that pertains to it; they shall carry the Tabernacle and all its furnishings, and they shall tend it, and they shall camp around the Tabernacle. When the Tabernacle is to set out, the Levites shall take it down, and when the Tabernacle is to be pitched, the Levites shall set it up; any outsider who encroaches shall be put to death. (Num. 1:50–51)

The *Mishkan* was the center of the camp, and the Ark of the Covenant was the central object inside the *Mishkan*. The Ark was also carried before the Israelites when they traveled, serving as a stabilizing influence and as an inspiration to advance, particularly at times of military skirmish.[13]

Centuries later, the ark became the catalyst for another building when King David quipped to Nathan that it seemed wrong for him to live in a palace while the ark, a sacred object, was not properly sheltered: "Here I am living in a house of cedar, while the ark of God remains in a tent (lit., 'behind a curtain'; II Sam. 7:2)." Radak on Esther 7:2 observes that it was not only the ark that concerned David but all of the accoutrements and vessels of the Tabernacle that were in a simple tent. The *Mishkan* was adequate during the desert years, but wholly inappropriate, perhaps even disrespectful, now that the Israelites had settled. Oddly, it was David who initiated the conversation, rather than Nathan the prophet. David personally felt the dissonance between the way he lived and the way God lived, so to speak. Nathan directed David to follow his intuition without the prophet consulting God. Yet that very evening, God appeared to Nathan almost echoing David's very words:

> Go and say to My servant David: Thus said the Lord: Are you the one to build a house for Me to dwell in? From the day that I brought the people of Israel out of Egypt to this day I have not dwelt in a house, but have moved about in Tent and Tabernacle. As I moved about wherever the Israelites went, did I ever reproach any of the tribal leaders whom I appointed to care for My people Israel: Why have you not built Me a house of cedar? (II Sam. 7:6–8)

While the *Metzudat David* suggests that God never asked tribal leaders to build a temple because God was waiting for a very specific builder, that is not the literal meaning of the verse. Here it sounds as if God had not wanted any proper building to house the ark. He never required this of the people, preferring instead the basic construction methods of the Tabernacle, lest the people privilege grandiosity over simplicity in worship. Worship is an act of vulnerability; prayer changes when simple

13. See Num. 10:33: "The Ark of the Covenant traveled before them."

outdoor altars are replaced by grand altars in even grander buildings, like the Temple. A few verses later, the conversation with Nathan shifts to what God did value in a structure: "I will establish a home for My people Israel and will plant them firm, so that they shall dwell secure and shall tremble no more" (II Sam. 7:10). Israel needed a home for its security. God needed no such home.

Nevertheless, God sanctioned the building of the First Temple in this exchange but wanted David's seed and not David himself to construct it. Later, in the Chronicles' reiteration of the earlier text, David elaborated to those before him why he was not a suitable candidate: "But God said to me, 'You will not build a house for My name, for you are a man of battles and have shed blood'" (I Chr. 28:3). We have no reason to doubt David's understanding, but this reason is not mentioned in the earlier account in II Samuel. David was only told that God would be with him in all of his military ventures and that his heir was to build the Temple: "When your days are done and you lie with your fathers, I will raise up your offspring after you, one of your own issue, and I will establish his kingship. He shall build a house for My name, and I will establish his royal throne forever" (II Sam. 7:12–13).

Built during the fourth year of Solomon's reign, approximately in the mid-tenth century BCE, Solomon spared no expense in creating a magnificent structure. We are informed in I Kings 9:10 that it took twenty years to build both the Temple and the palace. We are also told that it took thirteen years to build Solomon's palace (I Kings 7:1), meaning that the Temple took considerably less time. Because we have the cubit measurements of both the First Temple and Solomon's palace, we know that his home was slightly larger than God's. The point is well taken, and the palace's opulence is communicated with every cedar-paneled room. The chief architect, Hiram, was foreign. Most of the building materials were foreign. Even many of the design elements were foreign, unlike the design of the Temple. The chapter detailing the building begs the reader to feel outrage about Solomon's imported notions of grandeur: "Solomon also constructed a palace like that portico for the daughter of Pharaoh, whom he had married" (I Kings 7:8). Recreating images of Egyptian royalty to please a foreign wife could only spell future trouble for what was supposed to be the Jewish center of government. Designing the palace to include Egyptian elements was, in effect, inviting the look of exile into Solomon's own Jewish kingdom.

Not unlike our first chapter of Esther, King Solomon also had an enviable collection of beverage dispensers: "All King Solomon's drinking cups were of gold, and all the utensils of the Lebanon Forest House were of pure gold; silver did not count for anything in Solomon's days" (I Kings 10:21). It is not surprising that Solomon's wealth and excess became his undoing, making God's initial hesitation of being housed anywhere a warning. Buildings cannot effectuate goodness; they are merely containers, structures for activities that may inspire piety or may vitiate it for those who think that the building is enough or that the perfunctory placing of sacrifices on empty altars cleanses the soul.[14]

One might argue that acquiescence matters little. God acted on David's initial suggestion with emendations. But in the scheme of human foibles, God preferred no human king[15] and no elaborate man-made house for the Ark. The risks are great in each. The Decalogue was given sparingly at Sinai, and its laws were to be followed with a simple and complete faith. The tablets were stone, products of the immediate surroundings, not fancy imports. The words and God's voice loomed large in the narrative. Nothing else.

Permission to Build

Subtle references to the Temple pepper the Book of Esther and create an important contrast to Ahasuerus' palace. If the king is indeed Xerxes, as in the Greek rendition, then he was the son of Darius I Hystaspes, whose reign coincided with the restoration of the Second Temple in 516 BCE.[16]

---

14. The message is subtly reiterated in a largely unstudied exchange that took place immediately after this prayer and response. Solomon gave Hiram twenty towns in exchange for the luxury materials Hiram provided, but when Hiram went to inspect the towns himself, he was disappointed: "'My brother,' he said, 'what kind of towns have you given me?'" (I Kings 9:13). This suggests that despite Solomon's visible success, he did not share the best of what he had, even with those who transformed his riches into opulent buildings.
15. The ambivalence about kingship in Deut. 17 stimulated a centuries-long discussion about the difficult relationship of power and the monarchy.
16. See Hag. 2:1–9, Zech. 7:1, 8:9.

In 539 BCE, just as the Persian Empire was emerging as a power, Cyrus permitted Jews to return to Jerusalem from Babylon. It took too many years to begin the Temple reconstruction, the prophet Haggai chastised. There were also many Jews who elected to stay in Persia, no longer carrying with them the dream of homeland and spiritual center. Positioning the palace as a replacement for the Temple in Esther's opening may have been a dig at those who placed the wrong building and the wrong ruler at the center of their lives.

Each time a building is described and discussed in the Hebrew Bible, it signals overweening pride and hazard. Ahasuerus' palace may be the most obvious and glaring example of this problem, yet it is in the more subtle examples, even in Israel's most sacred house, that we find ambivalence, hesitation, and genuine concern. Later, in rabbinic literature, when R. Yoḥanan b. Zakkai shifted the framework of religious practice from Temple ritual to study, from priest to sage, it may have been not only an attempt to salvage Judaism from the nihilism that came with the Temple's destruction, but also a way to save the people from themselves, adjuring them to allow God to dwell within them and not within buildings. The change of focus may have minimized the edifice complex and returned the people to a more personal intimacy with God.

We find faint echoes of this in a talmudic passage where the Sage Abaye explains his own shift in perspective. He used to study and pray in one place: the synagogue. But then he heard a teaching passed down through two other Sages before him: "Since the day the Temple was destroyed, the Holy One, blessed be He, has only one place in His world: only the four cubits of Jewish law alone."[17] From that point onward, Abaye prayed only where he studied. God, in this metaphor, occupied the bounded majesty of the Temple but contracted, after its destruction, into the very limited space afforded by a person in front of a holy book studying law. And in some way, this transference took Abaye away from the Temple but brought him ultimately back to Sinai.

Given the questionable nature of most biblical buildings as illusory and failed testaments to human power, beginning the Book of Esther with Ahasuerus' palace is a signal to its readers that something was amiss

17. Berakhot 8a.

for the Jewish population of Susa. Yitzhak Berger compares words used to describe both the Temple and practices within it and Ahasuerus' palace, language parallels that signal a deeper root issue in exile, namely that acts and objects used to support purity were used in the Book of Esther as a "repugnant violation of the sacred."[18] Berger contends not that the Temple was replaced by the Persian court but rather the king's palace functions as a faux sanctuary that "*threatens* to displace God, leaving the exiled Jews – already distanced from God's abode – to confront an existential *and religious* danger."[19] The ancient Persian palace became the center of human activity and power and the location of what could have been the end of all the Jews of the empire.

18. Yitzhak Berger, "Mordechai and Flowing Myrrh: On the Presence of God in the Book of Esther," *Tradition* 49:3 (Fall, 2016): 23.
19. Ibid, 21. Italics in original.

Alcohol: The Lubrication of Kings and Fools

> Royal wine was served in abundance, as befits a king, in golden beakers, beakers of varied design. And the rule for the drinking was, "No restrictions!" For the king had given orders to every palace steward to comply with each man's wishes. (Est. 1:7–8)

In *A History of the World in 6 Glasses,* Tom Standage opens his chapter on wine with an opulent royal banquet, that of King Ashurnasirpal II of Assyria in approximately 870 BCE. It bears more than a slight resemblance to Ahasuerus' party in chapter 1:

> The feasting went on for ten days. The official record attests that the celebration was attended by 69,574 people: 47,074 men and women from across the empire, 16,000 of the new inhabitants of Nimrud, 5,000 foreign dignitaries from other states, and 1,500 palace officials. The aim was to demonstrate the king's power and wealth, both to his own people and to foreign representatives.[1]

---

1. Tom Standage, *A History of the World in 6 Glasses* (New York: Walker and Company, 2005), 44.

Beer was the usual beverage of the empire, but on this occasion, wine had pride of place. Standage includes a photograph of a carved stone relief depicting Ashurnasirpal holding what is likely a shallow golden bowl level to his face, about to drink a much more unusual and expensive beverage to show his prominence: wine.

In the ancient world and arguably in the modern one as well, expensive wine served in lavish, distinctive vessels is the hallmark of a festive royal meal. In addition to Ahasuerus' feast, we have a similar display in a gentile royal court in the Book of Daniel. King Belshazzar held a grand celebration for his thousand nobles, and in the presence of the thousand he imbibed:

> Under the influence of the wine, Belshazzar ordered the gold and silver vessels that his father Nebuchadnezzar had taken out of the Temple in Jerusalem to be brought so that the king and his nobles, his consorts and his concubines, could drink from them. They drank wine and praised gods of gold and silver, bronze, iron, wood, and stone. (Dan. 5:1–4)

Wine feasts occasioned unusual demonstrations of power. Drinking out of "conquered cups" enhanced the association between alcohol and dominance at such festivities. It would also seem from this description that taking out the Temple's goblets was not an ordinary event but a decision Belshazzar only reached under the influence of alcohol, suggesting that these cups were extraordinarily beautiful and rare bounty.

This party was a mix of men and women, unlike Ahasuerus' lengthy, separate affair. Nevertheless, the two texts were certainly joined in the rabbinic mind. In aggadic literature, Belshazzar was the father of Vashti, who arranged the marriage (as will be discussed in the next chapter); the cups used for Ahasuerus' party were also Temple vessels, a detail not mentioned in the actual text of Esther but a melded association of the two books, mixing kings and parties while assuming that the best serving utensils were of Jewish origin in both.[2]

---

2. Megilla 11a–b, 12b, 19a. Oblique references to the Temple and Ahasuerus' exploitation of it are not only in drinking vessels but also in the royal wardrobe: "The verse

The wine was likely not homegrown. Wine drunk in Mesopotamia, the cradle of civilization that was controlled by the Sumerians, then the Akkadians, and which then transferred hands several times between the Babylonians and Assyrians and finally the Persians, had probably been transported from afar. In the above example of the court of Ashurnasirpal II, most in the empire had likely never tasted it before. "Serving wines from distant regions within his empire... underlined the extent of his power."[3]

This sounds not unlike Ahasuerus' magnanimity: "Royal wine was served in abundance, as befits a king, in golden beakers, beakers of varied design. And the rule for the drinking was, 'No restrictions!' For the king had given orders to every palace steward to comply with each man's wishes" (Est. 1:7–8). The palace stewards mentioned here were to optimize the comfort of every drinker and are reminiscent of other Nimrud banquet scenes Standage describes where partygoers drink wine

> from shallow bowls, seated on wooden couches and flanked by attendants, some of whom hold jugs of wine, while others hold fans, or perhaps flyswatters to keep insects away from the precious liquid. Sometimes large storage vessels are also depicted, from which the attendants refill serving jugs.[4]

This offers a likely picture of what happened at Ahasuerus' banquet while also inducting us into a world where food and drink are constantly plied with the consequences gently ignored or encouraged. Berg notes that the term *mishteh* – a wine festal – indicates the kind of food and drink served on special occasions and appears twenty times in the Book of Esther, even though it appears only twenty-four additional times throughout the rest of the Hebrew Bible.[5]

---

states: 'When he showed the riches of his glorious (*kevod*) kingdom and the honor of his majestic (*tiferet*) greatness' (Est. 1:4). R. Yosei bar Ḥanina said: This teaches that Ahasuerus wore the priestly vestments" (Megilla 12b).

3. Standage, *History of the World in 6 Glasses*, 46.
4. Ibid.
5. Berg, *The Book of Esther*, 31.

This particular *mishteh* was exceptional by any royal standards in duration and opulence and in the generosity of its host. Rashi, in his commentary on 1:7, describes what sounds like a fraternity hazing in his explication of the command "No restrictions": "Because there are feasts in which they coerce those seated to drink [the contents] of a large vessel, and some can only drink it with difficulty. But here it was 'with no coercion.'" The attendants may have been close at hand to keep everyone inebriated, but only of their own choosing, obviously a diversion from usual custom. Josephus points this out in his *Antiquities*: "He [Ahasuerus] also gave order to the servants, that they should not force them to drink by bringing them wine continually, as is the practice of the Persians, but to permit every one of the guests to enjoy himself according to his own inclination."[6]

Forcing people to drink in order to induce group insobriety and the frivolity that would follow demonstrates the power of a ruler to coerce undesirable physical states of individuals, crossing the boundary of expected personal privacy. Ahasuerus stopped short of this, but the very suggestion implies that his feasts regularly featured this expectation, highlighting yet another peril of a place so unlike home for the Jews in Persia. This, too, according to Rashi, who cites the Talmud, was addressed. Rashi explains that complying to "each man's wishes means that every person was served wine native to his own country."[7] This detail suggests Ahasuerus' desperate need to be accepted and praised by all, while also, as Standage suggests, demonstrating the ruler's wealth. Having wine native to each land gently whispers another inducement for the Jews in exile: the illusion of home through the taste buds. Do not be fooled. Drinking a native beverage in a foreign land offers the comfort and sentimental tastes of home but without any of its protections.

Were the Jews at the Banquet?

It is unclear in what way the Jews participated in Ahasuerus' banquet, since they are not mentioned outright. This itself may suggest they were

6. Flavius Josephus, *Antiquities of the Jews*, 11, 6, trans. William Whiston (London: Wordsworth Classics, 2006), 467.

7. Megilla 12a.

no different from anyone else in the kingdom. Gawkers all to Ahasuerus' wealth, those who went to the party may have enjoyed the visual intake or the sense of self-importance that came with the invitation. It ended badly, however, because of the inebriation. Alcohol, in the narrative, becomes the very symbol of exile itself. It causes loss of self-control, loss of memory, loss of dignity. It is no surprise that in order to recreate the story annually, we are commanded to drink until we, too, confound the line between those who are good and those who are bad. This is not an optimal state but designed to put us into the narrative and understand its perils. If in a drunken state a villain is confused for a hero, the reverse may also be the case.

The king's rule-less invitation to drink "as each and every man might wish" is usually regarded as an edict to make Ahasuerus look like a good and generous king, whose rule is characterized by the extension of personal liberties. And yet the word *dat*, "law," appears in variations in the scroll twenty times. The king himself was hamstrung by his own laws, undermining the free spirit that easy access to alcohol should generate. Moshe David Simon contends that Esther is replete with dramatic ironies, and this one is one of the first and most glaring.[8] As we enter the book and virtually attend the party with the king's guests, we are struck by its sumptuousness, by the invitation to engage in the hyperbolic royal feast, by the possibility of losing control.

The First Drink

Alcohol is first introduced very early in biblical literature in the postdiluvial narrative of Noah, who left his ark, planted a vineyard, and got drunk from the fruit of his labors: "Noah, the tiller of the soil, was the first to plant a vineyard. He drank of the wine and became drunk and uncovered himself within his tent" (Gen. 9:20–21). What ensues is the morally difficult and ambiguous story of Noah's physical exposure and his son Ham's disrespect. In the Talmud, Ubar the Galilean observes that in the Noah narrative and the subsequent drama in his tent, the Hebrew letters *vav* followed by a *yod* appear thirteen times, making the sound

8. Moshe David Simon, "'Many Thoughts in the Heart of Man…': Irony and Theology in the Book of Esther," *Tradition* 31, no. 4 (1997): 5–6.

"woe" in its Hebrew equivalent.[9] It is an audial suggestion of a person holding his head in the throbs of alcohol's aftereffects; the first incident of inebriation in the Hebrew Bible becomes an occasion of lament. The biblical text is rather matter-of-fact about Noah's stupor. He lived an additional 350 years after the incident: "Noah lived after the Flood 350 years. And all the days of Noah came to 950; then he died" (Gen. 9:28–29). A lengthy midrash on the story, however, suggests alcohol's increasingly embarrassing effects and the incremental cost to good judgment with every glass.

> When Noah began planting, Satan came and stationed himself before him and asked, "What are you planting?" Noah: "A vineyard." Satan: "What is its nature?" Noah: "Its fruit, whether fresh or dried, is sweet and from it one makes wine, which gladdens a man's heart." Satan: "Will you agree to let both of us plant it together?" Noah: "Very well." What did Satan do? He brought a ewe lamb and slaughtered it over a vine. After that, he brought a lion, which he likewise slaughtered. Then a monkey, which he also slaughtered over it. Finally, he slaughtered a pig over the vine. And with the blood that dripped from them, he watered the vineyard. The charade was Satan's way of saying that when a man drinks one cup of wine, he acts like a ewe lamb, humble and meek. When he drinks two he becomes like a lion and proceeds to brag mightily, saying, "Who is like me?" When he drinks three or four cups he immediately becomes like a monkey, hopping about giggling and uttering obscenities in public, without realizing what he is doing. Finally, when he becomes blind drunk, he is like a pig, wallowing in mire and coming to rest in refuse. All of the above befell Noah.[10]

---

9. Sanhedrin 70a. R. Ḥanan on the previous talmudic page contends that wine was created only to comfort mourners and sinners, with Rashi noting on this passage that wine "rewards" sinners for the little good they have done. The notion of comfort here is not insignificant given the enormity of Noah's task and the apocalyptic landscape he confronted when he left the ark. It is little wonder he planted a vineyard.
10. *Tanḥuma, Noaḥ* 13, as recorded in *The Book of Legends/Sefer Ha-Aggadah*, ed. Hayyim Nahman Bialik and Yehoshua Hana Ravnitzky (New York: Schocken Books, 1992), 29.

Increasing alcohol intake changes perception, inhibition, and action. All these may have befallen Noah. They certainly befell Ahasuerus.

The King's Hangover

Alcohol in the first chapter of Esther brought people together under the banner of entertainment and induced the poor judgment that propelled the story forward. In chapter 1 specifically, who Vashti was and what happened to her makes little sense without the destructive cocktail of alcohol and authority that guided Ahasuerus' poor decision making. Drinking is introduced before Vashti is introduced, making it the propaedeutic for the events to come. Drinking is a consistent preoccupation throughout the Book of Esther, used as the means to celebrate Haman's wicked plotting and an instrument in Esther's salvific strategy. Alcohol, paradoxically, is the symbol of both generosity and callousness and boosts the alignment of male insecurity and dominance.

Talmudic exegesis on a verse from Proverbs considers Ahasuerus' own animal-like behavior from excessive eating and drinking to be not only a sign of his personality but, in this midrash, a hallmark of his very nationality:

> "A roaring lion and a prowling bear is a wicked man ruling a helpless people" (Prov. 28:15). "A hungry bear"; this is Ahasuerus, as it is written about him: "And behold, another beast, a second one, like a bear" (Dan. 7:5). And R. Yosef taught that those who are referred to as a bear in the verse are the Persians. They are compared to a bear, as they eat and drink in large quantities like a bear; and they are coated with flesh like a bear; and they grow their hair long like a bear; and they never rest like a bear, whose manner it is to move about from place to place.[11]

The lion of the Proverbs verse is calculating, dangerous, angry, and tensile. The bear is large and restless, like the Persian Empire itself. In this metaphor, its ruler and citizens are primitives: hirsute, uncouth, stalking, beastly. The presence of the bear makes all frightened and vigilant.

11. Megilla 11a.

Like a mythic large animal, Ahasuerus behaved with neither restraint nor reason. Other verses from Proverbs make the connection to alcohol, lions, and royalty explicit: "Wine is a mocker, strong drink a brawler, and whoever is led astray by it is not wise. The dread wrath of a king is like the growling of a lion; he who provokes him to anger forfeits his life" (20:1–2). This captures Vashti's demise perfectly. She provoked the beast, and he devoured her. The drinking's apogee in chapter 1, the king's dismissal of Vashti with a peacock-like display of male bravado, alerts us to the danger for the Jews of Persia when the safety of enforced lines is crossed.

Ahasuerus' advisors understood this. Haman understood this. Esther understood this. But while alcohol was the free-flowing lubrication of fools in the story, it was also a concern in rabbinic literature. According to one midrash, Jews were apparently at Ahasuerus' party in great number: "Haman said to Ahasuerus, 'The God [of the Jews] detests immorality. Prepare harlots, make a feast, and order them all to come eat, drink, and do as they please.' Mordecai, who understood the situation, pronounced, 'Do not partake of the feast of Ahasuerus.'"[12] The invitation to drink was regarded as an invitation to lose inhibition, to lose moral reasoning, to lose faith itself in the coma of alcoholic indulgence where good judgment slips away.

Ahasuerus wanted every man to do as he pleased, but as a man, he could not get his wife to do as he pleased. This was so infuriating to him that he was easily persuaded both to punish the woman who stood in his way and to ensure that no man in his kingdom would be similarly rejected. The reader understands the farce of this because women are not like alcohol, to be picked up at whim, tossed back, then discarded. Although Ahasuerus will do just that with Vashti, he will wake up to the sober reality that Vashti was gone to his great personal loss. The alcohol drained from him without his regrets. The same cannot be said of his former wife.

> This irony of simple incongruity, the juxtaposition of the king's law with "no restrictions" and "to do as each and every man might

12. Esther Rabba 7:18.

> wish," forces the reader to question the previous description of the mighty Ahasuerus. In this verse, the true nature of Ahasuerus' kingdom is revealed. The king's "law" (*dat*), through which the king allegedly rules the empire, is in fact a farce. Its primary concern is that there be no restrictions and that every man do as he pleases.... Ahasuerus claims to be the ruler of the known world, yet the first order he gives, a simple request of his own wife that she appear before him and his guests, is brazenly disobeyed.[13]

The king's ministers attempt to resolve his sadness by making women the same "objects" of desire as a stiff drink, parading virgins before him so that he might have whichever he desires, just like the goblets of free-flowing wine. Yet his instinct is for the woman who ultimately defies objectification: Esther, a woman of beauty but, more distinctively, a woman of unparalleled grace. It is this inner beauty that entangles Ahasuerus and obfuscates his notion of the woman as powerless. Later, this very woman would upend the very rules that dominated the king's life, and he would let her.

A stunning display of sobriety's wagging finger is found in the first book of Samuel. David and his guerrilla army lacked supplies. They were hungry and stopped at the estate of a clearly wealthy man, Nabal, hoping for provisions:

> Nabal answered David's servants, "Who is David? Who is the son of Jesse? There are many slaves nowadays who run away from their masters. Should I then take my bread and my water, and the meat that I slaughtered for my own shearers, and give them to men who come from I don't know where?" (I Sam. 25:10–11)

Nabal had no intention of feeding this ragtag army and its fearless leader. Only Nabal's wife Abigail understood David's emerging power and influence. "Abigail quickly got together two hundred loaves of bread, two jars of wine, five dressed sheep, five seahs of parched corn, one hundred cakes of raisin, and two hundred cakes of pressed figs. She loaded them

13. Simon, "'Many Thoughts in the Heart of Man...,'" 6.

on donkeys, and she told her young men, 'Go on ahead of me, and I'll follow you'; but she did not tell her husband Nabal" (I Sam. 25:18–19). Abigail acted with speed and stealth to get David what he requested. She returned home to a drunk spouse who was too intoxicated to understand the consequences of his actions.

> When Abigail came home to Nabal, he was having a feast in his house, a feast fit for a king; Nabal was in a merry mood and very drunk, so she did not tell him anything at all until daybreak. The next morning, when Nabal had slept off the wine, his wife told him everything that had happened; and his courage died within him, and he became like a stone. About ten days later the Lord struck Nabal, and he died. (I Sam. 25:36–38)

Abigail knew better than to speak to her husband when he was inebriated, waiting until the awful dawn when the destruction of the previous night's festivities was laid bare in the cold light of day. Rabbi Joseph B. Soloveitchik uses this story to communicate the price of sin:

> This has been the way of sin since the beginning of time. It overtakes man while indulging in a night of iniquity. Mist and fog conceal the inner light of the soul of a man who is immersed in the blinding, obsessive night of his passions and is plunged within the oblivion of his lust. At the very hour when "Nabal's heart was merry within him," he was in such a state of intoxication that he did not notice the flashing blade of the sword hanging over his very door.[14]

A drunk person has closed ears. Abigail understood this. She kept the news of David's ire to herself until her husband had sobered. As Rabbi Soloveitchik explains, "There is a time when moral criticism is effective and a time when any discussion with the inebriate sinner is impossible

---

14. Joseph B. Soloveitchik, *On Repentance*, ed. Pinchas Peli (Jerusalem: Maggid, 2017), 10.

and nothing anyone says can penetrate his hearing or enter his heart."[15] But what Abigail kept inside her through a long night spilled out in the morning. "A state of intoxication always ends in a sobering up and it is an inflexible law of nature that night is followed by dawn."[16] Day follows the night. Awareness follows intoxication. "An Abigail follows every sinner."[17]

Despite the problems sobriety presents in both biblical narratives, they are not alike. The sword did not hang over Ahasuerus' door. It hung over Vashti's. Where David had power, and Nabal had wealth, Ahasuerus had both. And, when the time came, Vashti ultimately had neither. Chapter 2 opens with the passage of time and the abatement of the king's anger: "Sometime afterward, when the anger of King Ahasuerus subsided, he thought of Vashti and what she had done and what had been decreed against her" (Est. 2:1). Disconnected from what William James called "strong" or "coarser" emotions,[18] the king pondered Vashti's fate, describing what happened to her rather than what he did to her. Alcohol has the crushing effect of making those who drink it impervious to good judgment until sobriety sets in to confirm idiocy. The hangover is less painful than the realization of misconduct. Rashi on 2:1 tells us in simple language what it was the king remembered and what it was he felt: "He remembered her beauty and felt sad." But unlike his memory of her, he did not remember doing anything to her. A decree was placed upon her, as if it were the act of someone else, an enemy perhaps, the enemy within. Mistakes were made, he may have thought, but not by me, distancing the actor from the action.

Did Ahasuerus realize, when sober, that he had been manipulated, or did the king conveniently separate himself from what happened to Vashti? The flurry of anxious courtiers who appear next would seem to imply the former; their suggestion of the pageant creates the impression of moving Ahasuerus forward into distraction lest his advisors suffer punishment for what they encouraged the king to do. But the text points to the king's own lack of accountability.

---

15. Ibid.
16. Ibid, 10–11.
17. Ibid, 11.
18. William James, "What Is an Emotion?" *Mind* 9, no. 34 (1884): 188–205.

The text is also a foreshadow. We will confront this passivity turned quickly to intensity again when Haman manipulates the king to initiate his decree and again, when the king loses control upon seeing Haman prostrated on Esther's couch. The anger will subside but not before another life is lost. The word *keshokh*, "abated," is found only five times in the Hebrew Bible. Two of them appear in Esther, in 2:1 and in 7:10, linking incidents of the king's rage into a portrait of a man out of control. Wealth and power gave Ahasuerus the ability to exhibit rage unchecked. Alcohol fomented the rage that resulted in death.

Jewish Drinking

As mentioned earlier, the Jews drank their fill in rabbinic tradition and enjoyed themselves at the party, like all the other citizens of Persia. Herein lay the problem. Exile was not to be a place for such merriment. The freedom and autonomy offered at the party were the trinkets of exile, the paltry seductions that enticed Persia's Jews. Concern about Jews in exile losing their way at a party surfaces in an enigmatic and engaging passage of Talmud found in a tractate devoted to analyzing the intricacies of idol worship. It describes Jews who participate in a feast, even one with kosher food, drink, and rabbinic supervision, as being engaged in idol worship in purity. Can there be pure idol worship? The paradoxical nature of the expression draws us in to the contradictions of exile:

> R. Yishmael says: Jews who are outside of the Land of Israel engage in idol worship in purity. How? A gentile prepared a feast for his son and invited all the Jews in his town; even though they eat of their own and drink their own and have their own attendant who stands before them, the verse describes them as if they ate of the offerings of the dead [idols], as it is stated: "And sacrifice to their gods, and they call you, and you eat of their sacrifice" (Ex. 34:15). But say [that the verse means] only once they eat [from the sacrifice]? Rava said: If that were true, the verse could have said [only], "And you eat of their sacrifice." What does "And they call you" mean? From the time of the call…[19]

19. Avoda Zara 8a.

Whatever activities took place at the festivities do not vitiate the fact that Jews were invited to the affair and actually showed up. The simple fact that they could participate and did, even on their own terms, does not mean they were guilty of worshipping idols but suggests their proximity to idol worship; the margins of assimilation became fuzzy. Accepting an invitation places one dangerously close to pernicious influences. The invitation to join merges into an invitation to participate, then snakes into an invitation to get closer and closer to the party's hosts and their intentions. Participants at such a banquet may even convince themselves that they are totally pure and innocent, free of any corrupting foreign influences, as the Talmud suggests. It is here that Rava adds the aspect of being called before actually eating. They did not eat at the party. Their sin began when they responded yes to the invitation.

The vulnerable dance of exile, symbolized by alcohol, is memorialized in the ritual of Purim to drink until one does not know the difference between Haman and Mordecai, surely an absurd task. Rabbi Binyamin Lau mines this absurdity to discover the genius of the demand:

> This dimension of Purim is so confusing and confounding that it is itself emblematic of the inability to distinguish between a blessing and a curse. Instead of devoting ourselves to dealing with serious questions and a Jewish self-accounting, we spend our time mocking the significance and magnitude of life. The wine helps us forget, divert our attention, and pollute our hearts. This is obviously tragic, because every drunken night is followed by a morning hangover. At the end of the night, the sun rises and with it man awakens to his day. To his job, and to his life. He regains awareness of everything he tried to escape.[20]

Wine helps us forget but is not helpful when we need to remember. The command to drink so that one cannot distinguish between Mordecai and Haman, blessing and curse, is itself a profound manifestation of an exile on its way to becoming a diaspora – a hazy, distorted reality that can morph into a state of mind. In the diaspora, there is always the

20. Binyamin Lau, introduction to Eisenberg, *The Vanishing Jew*, 8.

anxiety of forgetting who one is, who one is meant to be, where one is meant to live, what one is meant to do, and who one is meant to serve. It is akin to drinking that starts off pleasantly and becomes gradually better before getting much, much worse.

Rabbi Yehudah Leib Alter (1847–1905), the *Sefat Emet*, explains the demand to be so drunk on Purim so as not to know the difference between hero and villain. He believes this mandate speaks to Purim's most profound meaning:

> One is obligated to become so drunk on Purim that one cannot tell the difference between "Blessed be Mordecai!" and "Cursed be Haman!" We thereby show that this day has nothing at all to do with our merit. It is called Purim because of the casting of lots; the fate was entirely natural and appropriate; the forces of evil having been strengthened by our own sins. God saved us out of love alone.[21]

God's love saved us when we could not save ourselves. The Jews of Persia acted in ways that resembled drunkenness, forgetting where they came from or what it is that Jews ultimately desired for themselves as a nation. Safety is a basic need, but it is not a mission. Because the Jews may have forgotten their way, God saved them out of love and not merit, contends the *Sefat Emet*. It is this that merges the festiveness of Purim with the sobriety of Yom Kippur:

> It is taught that Purim is like the Day of Atonement, called *Yom Ki-Purim*. On Yom Kippur we reach beyond the natural state by negating our bodies, by abstaining from food and drink. This brings us to a certain freedom, one where transgressions are forgiven. On Purim we get to the same place by means of drinking

21. *Sefat Emet* 2:179. Translated and explained by Arthur Green in *The Language of Truth: The Torah Commentary of the Sefat Emet* (Philadelphia: Jewish Publication Society, 1998), 384. Green observes here that this idea is common to Hasidic thinking and "expresses the hope that on Yom Kippur God will become so intoxicated by 'drinking' the prayers of Israel that He will no longer be able to distinguish between the righteous and the wicked, and thus have to save us all."

> and merrymaking, all with the help of God, not because of our own deeds.[22]

On the surface the two holidays could not be more different. Abstention takes the place of feasting. Refraining from anointing contrasts with twelve months in myrrh and oil. No shoes or non-supportive shoes are juxtaposed with elaborate and ornate clothing. Yet the *Sefat Emet* challenges us to see that the end goal of both observances is the same: submission to God's love and forgiveness. God, in the background or foreground, offers support when change seems impossible. It is upon us to sober up to reality.

22. Green, *The Language of Truth*, 384.

Vashti: An Ignoble Exit

Queen Vashti gave a banquet for women, in the royal palace of King Ahasuerus. On the seventh day, when the king was merry with wine, he ordered Mehuman, Bizzetha, Harbonah, Bigtha, Abagtha, Zethar, and Carcas, the seven eunuchs in attendance on King Ahasuerus, to bring Queen Vashti before the king wearing a royal diadem, to display her beauty to the peoples and the officials; for she was a beautiful woman. But Queen Vashti refused to come at the king's command conveyed by the eunuchs. The king was greatly incensed, and his fury burned within him. (Est. 1:10–12)

Then the king consulted the sages learned in procedure. (For it was the royal practice [to turn] to all who were versed in law and precedent. His closest advisors were Carshena, Shethar, Admatha, Tarshish, Meres, Marsena, and Memucan, the seven ministers of Persia and Media who had access to the royal presence and occupied the first place in the kingdom.) "What," [he asked,] "shall be done, according to law, to Queen Vashti for failing to obey the command of King Ahasuerus conveyed by the eunuchs?" Thereupon Memucan declared in the presence of the king and the ministers: "Queen Vashti has committed an offense not only against Your Majesty but also against all the officials and against all the peoples in all the provinces of King Ahasuerus. For the queen's behavior will make all wives despise their husbands, as they reflect

> that King Ahasuerus himself ordered Queen Vashti to be brought before him, but she would not come. This very day the ladies of Persia and Media, who have heard of the queen's behavior, will cite it to all Your Majesty's officials, and there will be no end of scorn and provocation!" (Est. 1:13–18)
>
> "If it please Your Majesty, let a royal edict be issued by you, and let it be written into the laws of Persia and Media, so that it cannot be abrogated, that Vashti shall never enter the presence of King Ahasuerus. And let Your Majesty bestow her royal state upon another who is more worthy than she. Then will the judgment executed by Your Majesty resound throughout your realm, vast though it is; and all wives will treat their husbands with respect, high and low alike." The proposal was approved by the king and the ministers, and the king did as Memucan proposed. Dispatches were sent to all the provinces of the king, to every province in its own script and to every nation in its own language, that every man should wield authority in his home and speak the language of his own people. (Est. 1:19–22)

Vashti is identified in the Talmud as "the granddaughter of Nebuchadnezzar, the wicked."[1] With this family introduction, one senses immediately that rabbinic literature considered Vashti irredeemable; evil was embedded in her very DNA. In *Yalkut Shimoni,* a late collection of midrash, it was Vashti who prevented Ahasuerus from building the Temple.[2] This was not her only act to undermine Jewish life. She was put to death on the Sabbath because, as queen, she forced Jewish women to take off their clothes and work on their day of rest, inflicting the indignity on them that was later inflicted on her.[3]

Others suggest that Ahasuerus and Vashti were made for each other and were equally immoral.[4] *Yalkut Shimoni* asks how the two

1. Megilla 10b.
2. *Yalkut Shimoni, Esther* 1049.
3. Megilla 12b.
4. Ibid.

met and brings the reader into a far from romantic scene. Vashti's father Belshazzar was killed when the Persians conquered Babylon. The night of the murder, Darius ascended the throne. Chaos ensued. In the confusion, Vashti, a young woman among those innocently enjoying a royal banquet, did not realize that her father had been murdered. She ran to his chamber and suddenly realized her father was dead. Vashti was distraught. Darius had compassion on her and betrothed his son Ahasuerus to her.[5] It is an odd way to meet one's spouse but an interesting way for the ancient Sages to meld the political strains of both Babylon and Persia, making Vashti a hybrid enemy. The midrash also suggests that this was not a marriage born of unrequited love between aristocratic equals but one born of a father's compassion that ended in the callousness of a son. That Ahasuerus chose Esther of his own free will, in contrast to this midrash which suggests the torment of his first marriage, explains the pure delight Ahasuerus found in her.

While this midrash on royal matchmaking puts two of noble birth together, the text of Esther suggests distance. Vashti's party for women and her refusal to respond to the king's summons may indicate that the two lived at a remove from each other and were ultimately ill-suited. A hasty marriage on a tragic night led to a hasty dismissal on a night of merriment. Others view the separate parties as natural manifestations of a gender-separate society with different proclivities. Vashti's party was for women only, as indicated by the separate chamber for women where she hosted her compatriots: "In addition, Queen Vashti gave a banquet for women, in the royal palace of King Ahasuerus" (Est. 1:9). A Sage, R. Abun, in Esther Rabba believed that women would rather have "well-appointed rooms and elegant clothes, than eat fattened calves."[6] In other words, the food and drink at Ahasuerus' party was less enticing than the opportunity to impress and to be impressed at a women's gathering. It is not puzzling that Vashti held a separate party, away from the louche goings-on and debauchery of Ahasuerus and his band of courtiers. What is puzzling is the Hebrew word *gam*, "in addition," or, "also," found at the beginning of the verse. The two-letter addition suggests that this verse is

5. *Yalkut Shimoni, Esther* 1049.
6. Esther Rabba 3:10.

connected to the one before it. The "also" may suggest that Vashti was no different from her husband. She, too, indulged herself without restraint and invited the women in her presence to do the same. Alternatively, the *gam* may implicate Ahasuerus. His desire to indulge without coercion and engage in whatever each man wished for was a gender-specific request. *In addition* to his desire for all men to enjoy, he *also* wished to enjoy himself, but the object of his enjoyment was not in the room. Punch-drunk with the flush of power, what he wished for was a public display of his wife's beauty. He had no hesitation in compromising her dignity and intended the same freedom he demanded of his guests to apply to himself. In wanting his wife and coercing her to attend to him, Ahasuerus broke the thin margin of propriety between male and female decorum that characterized these feasts, thereby highlighting the imbalance of power.[7] All did not genuinely have the freedom to do as they wished at the party. Some had power; others were powerless. Vashti was once powerful but found herself without any semblance of authority.

The license that this all-male free-for-all offered created an atmosphere conducive to loss of control and good judgment. This show of hedonistic glee that resulted in an abuse of power is reminiscent of an earlier story told in both the books of Kings and Chronicles where royal men were encouraged to act badly by other men in a display of force. Rehoboam, son of Solomon and heir to the throne, was asked to lessen the harsh labor his father imposed on thousands in the building of the Temple and his palace. "Your father made our yoke heavy. Now lighten the harsh labor and the heavy yoke which your father laid on us, and we will serve you" (I Kings 12:4). When Rehoboam consulted his father's advisors, they considered the matter and told him to lighten the load.

7. Some scholars note that men and women did go to royal drinking parties together, as evidenced in one verse in the Book of Daniel where men and women participated equally at a banquet: "Under the influence of the wine, Belshazzar ordered the gold and silver vessels that his father Nebuchadnezzar had taken out of the Temple at Jerusalem to be brought so that the king and his nobles, his consorts and his concubines, could drink from them" (Dan. 5:2). There is a clear separation of men and women throughout the Book of Esther, and even in Daniel, there is no indication that men and women drank together, only that both could enjoy wine in the Temple's vessels.

He then sought the counsel of his peers, who, with the sexual undercurrent of the young and immature, recommended that Rehoboam act with even greater violence. "My little finger is thicker than my father's loins. My father imposed a heavy yoke on you, and I will add to your yoke; my father flogged you with whips, but I will flog you with scorpions" (I Kings 12:10–11). Naturally, the strategy that enhanced Rehoboam's authority was more appealing than one abounding in justice. Privileging power over influence, the youthful king's swagger in the presence of the other male peacocks got the best of him. His poor decision resulted in insurrection and death.

In our Esther story, we will see Ahasuerus compelled time and again by the counsel of men who used their power for evil. In the case of Vashti, Ahasuerus' ministers pressured him because of his subjugation of one woman to subjugate all women in his empire, whether by banishing them from the palace or by consigning them to it for life. This state of male freedom and female captivity affected not only the palace but was to be enforced in every home. What happened in the palace did not stay in the palace. It spread to all corners of the kingdom.

Modern Readings of Vashti

The name Vashti is both familiar and unfamiliar to us. We know the name from the holiday rendition of the scroll, but we are told little about her. Even her name, according to scholar Joyce Baldwin, is not familiar:

> The name Vashti is puzzling because, according to Herodotus, the queen's name was Amestris, daughter of Otanes, who had supported Darius in his bid for the throne in 522 BC, but it is possible that he had other queens, whose names do not happen to have come to light, or that she had alternative names. The name Vashti, which is spelt in seven different ways in as many versions, has been associated with Persian words meaning "best" or "the beloved," "the desired one," a lovely name by which to be known.[8]

8. Baldwin, *Esther*, 59–60.

If indeed her name meant "the best" or "the desired one," it suggests the first reversal in the book: the desired becomes undesirable. The best becomes bested. The Persian etymology of the name means "beautiful," though Dalley suggests that it could also be related to the Akkadian word *basti*, meaning "dignity." The difference between these two meanings may be the difference between a woman who displays her beauty freely and one who protects her integrity by keeping her beauty a private matter.

Modern and traditional understandings of Vashti's character differ greatly. Whereas ancient Jewish commentators vilify her as a disobedient wife, pocked with pimples and too much moxie, modern writers see in Vashti a precursor of women's liberation. Vashti was regarded as a heroine by pioneers of the suffrage movement Elizabeth Cady Stanton and Lucinda B. Chandler. To them, Vashti was an ancient iconoclast, a symbol of conviction in the face of exploitation, in contrast to Esther's passivity:

> Vashti had exercised heroic courage in asserting womanly dignity and the inherent human right never recognized by kingship, to choose whether to please and to obey the king. Esther, so as to save her people from destruction, risked her life.... Women as queenly, as noble and self-sacrificing as was Esther, as self-representing and as brave as was Vashti, are hampered in their creative office by the unjust statutes of men.[9]

Those who regard Vashti as an early radical read Esther as a book ahead of its time: "The Book of Esther is a magnificent short story. Yet it also has a hidden agenda. Between the lines it transmits a code, a norm of behavior for women. This code and this norm is delivered completely from a male point of view."[10] These interpreters sought role models of

9. Elizabeth Cady Stanton and Lucinda B. Chandler, "The Book of Esther," in *The Woman's Bible*, ed. Elizabeth Cady Stanton, reprint (Mineola, NY: Dover Publications, 2003), 92. See also Susan Zaeske, "Unveiling Esther as a Pragmatic Radical Rhetoric," *Philosophy and Rhetoric* 33 (2000): 215–16.
10. De Troyer, "An Oriental Beauty Parlor: An Analysis of Est. 2:8–18 in the Hebrew, the Septuagint and the Second Greek Text," in *A Feminist Companion to Esther, Judith and Susanna*, ed. Athalya Brenner (Sheffield: Sheffield Academic Press, 1995), 55. More

bravery and self-awareness. Vashti became a female paragon of self-determination:

> Vashti stands out as a sublime representative of self-centered womanhood. Rising to the heights of self-consciousness and of self-respect, she takes her soul into her own keeping, and though her position both as wife and as queen are jeopardized, she is true to the Divine aspirations of her nature.[11]

"Divine aspirations of her nature" seem a bit rich when characterizing a woman who we know only through her refusal to appear before the king and his comrades, but these were heady days for the early suffragettes who needed their mascots and found one in Vashti. They neglect to mention here that Vashti was killed (or banished) for this subversion, her story an instantiation of good intentions destroyed by her failure to be pragmatic.

Vashti as Warning

Vashti pleaded with Ahasuerus not to force her to attend his party. According to one midrash she suffered leprosy and did not want to be seen in that compromising state.[12] Having terrible spots that marred her beauty and made her unsightly in front of the king's officers was an easier excuse than one midrash's approach of reasoning with the king: "'If they consider me beautiful, they will take advantage of me and will kill you,' begged Vashti in front of her husband. 'If they do not consider me beautiful, I will bring indignity to you.'"[13] Her words fell with a thud onto alabaster floors. Two scholars suggest that in ancient Persia there was a law of modesty that Vashti was not prepared to breach.[14]

---

generally, see Esther Fuchs, "Status and the Role of Female Heroines in the Biblical Narrative," in *Women in the Hebrew Bible: A Reader*, ed. Alice Bach (Abingdon, UK: Routledge, 1998), 77–84.

11. Stanton and Chandler, "Book of Esther," 88.
12. Megilla 12b.
13. Esther Rabba 3:14.
14. Richard J. Coggins and S. Paul Re'emi, *Israel among the Nations: A Commentary on the Books of Nahum and Obadiah* (Grand Rapids, MI: William B. Eerdmans Publishing, 1985), 117.

In another midrashic treatment, when the king still insisted on her appearance, Vashti asserted her dominance by reminding Ahasuerus of his humble origins as a stable boy in her father's household, where he developed low tastes and promiscuity that he brought to the palace by insisting Vashti, a woman of noble birth, show herself off in front of his courtiers (according, to some, wearing only her crown and nothing else).[15] Ahasuerus, celebrating his third year on a throne he inherited through marriage, was most insecure in front of his wife, who knew the full truth of his crass and vulgar bygone days. His demotion of Vashti was a statement about the distance he had come from his poor beginnings; as king he finally had the authority to rid himself of an undesirable past by ridding himself of the one person who reminded him of it. These midrashim create an elaborate context for Vashti's punishment and demonstrate how invested the Sages were in the story, trying to explain rash impulses that really needed no explication. Impulsivity by its very nature need not be rationalized, only described.

One matter requires no interpretation. Vashti moved from person to object in the king's drunken stupor. But one need not sink so low as to suggest he wanted her to appear naked before him and his courtiers. Having her appear fully clothed and with a crown was his display of the authority of his crown over hers. His crown at this point was taller. This would teach his unbending wife a lesson, though he hardly intended it to be her last. That came from the male jeers and the triangulating ministers.

Vashti's change in status is presaged by a shift from addressing her as Queen Vashti (1:9, 11, 12, 15, 16, 17) to simply the queen (1:17, 18) and then to Vashti with no honorific at all (1:19). She moved from one who embodied royalty to one who occupied a royal position to one who had neither title nor favor. After that, she is never mentioned again. The language shift in the mouth of a trusted advisor prepared the king to demote her from his emotional concern before physically banishing her. Instead of relieving his anger and mending the marital breach, Ahasuerus was advised to minimize her significance to both him and the empire. As a woman of too much independence, Vashti made the

15. Song of Songs Rabba 3:5.

king look foolish. She offset the balance of authority that his ministers believed should ideally exist in every Persian household.

Vashti's appearance and sudden disappearance may have been an important literary device to create a compelling transition to Esther's appearance, suggesting that the king, or, more likely, those who advised him, sought a different kind of consort:

> The Vashti episode is prefixed to the story to demonstrate that humility and indirection were necessary to Esther's success. Vashti's fate showed that the king may react badly to strong-willed women who do not temper their strength with subtlety. What would a direct and bold demand have achieved, besides giving Esther a self-satisfied feeling of moral virtue as *she* was deposed in turn?[16]

Someone of no royal bearing would make a far better, more malleable, and less haughty consort than Vashti. By advising Esther to withhold her background, Mordecai may have understood what the king was really seeking in Vashti's replacement: beauty twinned with powerlessness. Therefore, Mordecai advised Esther to keep her royal lineage their shared secret. It may have seemed to Mordecai from the hearsay at the king's gate that Ahasuerus wanted a woman who was intimidated by him, who would never openly humiliate him. Initially he found that woman in Esther, a young orphan who refused to assert herself and appear before the king unsummoned. Little did Ahasuerus (or Esther, for that matter) know the courage to challenge him that was lodged within her grace.

The text recounts the aftermath of the Vashti debacle. Her story turns into Ahasuerus' next challenge. Vashti did not die in the Book of Esther; she suffered a fate perhaps worse than death: invisibility. Because she questioned her husband, he quieted her and potentially any other woman in his kingdom with a voice of resistance:

---

16. Fox, *Character and Ideology*, 201. See also Esther Fuchs on this subject in "Status and Role of Female Heroines in the Biblical Narrative," *Mankind Quarterly* 23 (1982): 156.

> In Memucan's frantic misinterpretation, Vashti's act signals a universal crisis, a rebellion against the sexual and social order, a violation of the harmony of every home and marriage. As he sees it, female contempt is always lurking just below the surface, waiting to pop up whenever the opportunity arises. And he is right, but only because insecure men like him make it so, for if a man's "honor" depends on his ability to dominate his wife, then any failure to enforce obedience is tantamount to male disgrace.[17]

Even among those who regard Vashti's leave-taking as the ultimate sacrifice for a cause before its time, her invisibility did not create a standard for women as much as a cautionary tale, one that Esther was the wiser for knowing. Alice Laffey believes of Esther that "rather than defend Vashti's decision and protest the injustice of her banishment, Esther uses Vashti's rejection for her own benefit."[18] It is hard to make sense of this reading because Esther was not introduced in the story early enough to protest. Were Laffey observing that Esther could have protested or offered reflections to the king on Vashti's treatment when she appeared on the scene, this would be out of line with any characterization of her thus far. This did not, however, quiet feminist scholars of the book from comparing the two women and how they lived within a profoundly patriarchal society. "In contrast to Vashti, who refused to be men's sexual object and her husband's toy, Esther is the stereotypical woman in a man's world."[19] Esther was not using the ghost of Vashti for her own gains as much as protecting herself from the king's mercurial temper. Only later, after Haman's decree was pronounced, was Esther called upon to effect change. She had to use a more circuitous route to achieve it than the more direct, confrontational approach of Vashti (of course, since all is done through intermediaries, it was not exactly direct but as confrontational as one could be in the Persian Empire).

17. Fox, *Character and Ideology*, 21.

18. Alice L. Laffey, *An Introduction to the Old Testament: A Feminist Perspective* (Philadelphia: Fortress Press, 1988), 156.

19. Ibid., 216.

> Esther upholds the patriarchal norms of ancient Jewish society in several ways. First of all, she is married (even if it is to a Gentile), a proper role for a young woman. Her primary characteristic is her beauty; as the object of man's gaze and the king's possession her beauty adds to his honor. In this she is identical to Vashti. Further, she is obedient. She obeys Mordecai; she obeys Hegai; she also obeys the social system in which she is located. Esther does not try to alter the patriarchal structure of her society; rather she works from within the system to gain her ends.[20]

Esther is condemned for holding up those norms rather than bucking them, as her unfortunate predecessor did.[21]

Whether in modern or ancient readings, commentaries that focus on Vashti's character rather than her behavior are troubling to the reader. We do not know what kind of woman Vashti was; any attempt to characterize her personality is mere speculation. As is typical for the Bible, we know characters by what they do, not by what they think or feel.

A Change in Law

In Esther 1:12, when Queen Vashti refused to come to the king's party, the presence of others turned the subversion into a public, legal spectacle. Ahasuerus' counselors emphasized the possible threat of embarrassment in front of all 127 provinces that the king ruled over if he did not take public action against her. Fearing that Ahasuerus would set a bad model for male subordination, his ministers suggested deposing the queen, and Ahasuerus agreed.

One of the oddities of the chapter is that missives were sent in all the languages of the empire. We can only assume, given the vast reach of Persia at the time, that this involved many languages indeed. This gesture may be regarded as an act of generosity or insecurity on the king's part, an almost feverish need to promote male power in every

20. Sidnie White Crawford, "Esther and Judith: Contrasts in Character," in *The Book of Esther in Modern Research*, 71–72.
21. See Samuel E. Meier, *Speaking of Speaking: Marking of Direct Discourse in the Hebrew Bible* (Netherlands: Brill, 1992).

known language. There may also be, in the writer or editor's thinking, a hint at one of the costs of exile: the mingling of languages represents the loss of one's native language. Sacrificed on the altar of assimilation, language is not only a means of communication; it becomes a holder for thought and culture. The nuance of words captures aspects of a people not entirely translatable. With this in mind, we might read the notion that the message was delivered "to every nation in their own language (*ve'el am vaam kilshono*)" (1:22) in light of exhortations in Nehemiah not to marry foreign women: "Also at that time, I saw Jews had married Ashdodite, Ammonite, and Moabite women; a good number of their children spoke the language of Ashdod and the language of those various peoples (*vekhileshon am vaam*) and did not know how to speak Judean" (13:23–24). It is this failure to speak in Hebrew that stirred Nehemiah to chastise those guilty of this rabid intermingling. The two were interconnected in the mind of this scribe. For Ahasuerus to effect genuine societal change, his constituents had to be reached in a language they understood.

As noted earlier, there was resistance in the sixteenth century to assign any blame to the king. Only the queen, the royal entourage, or the *vulgus* bore responsibility for the wrongdoing. How could a wise and good-hearted king degrade his wife? Walfish contends that the "generally high opinion that the medieval commentators had of Ahasuerus and of the position of the king in general is also seen in their treatment of the Vashti affair":[22]

> All in all, there is complete unanimity among the exegetes all through the Middle Ages that, considering the circumstances, Ahasuerus's punishment of Vashti was justified. An additional consideration for some is that this was all part of God's plan to save the Jews and that Vashti had to be eliminated in order to make it possible for Esther to be chosen queen.[23]

22. Walfish, *Esther in Medieval Garb*, 195.
23. Ibid., 196.

Walfish does not go into much detail to bolster this assertion, yet Rabbi Isaac Arama, in his introduction to Esther, states that "through the providence of God they transformed Vashti from a powerful woman to a wicked one and replaced her with Esther the righteous."[24] Without Vashti's deposition, the salvation of the Jews would never have occurred through Esther. Arama writes that the king did not want to find Vashti guilty, but because of his public position he was obligated to consult advisors. In Arama's interpretation, had Vashti been tried in a regular court, she would have been vindicated. The other concerns brought to bear in a royal case, such as maintaining a certain public appearance, are extra-legal. It is in this capacity that advisors were used, and Vashti's fate was ultimately determined. Since her crime, according to Arama, was in public, her sin was against all of the officials and the provinces and not only against her husband. Arama provides a subtle defense of the king: Ahasuerus did not want this outcome; it was foisted upon him because of the public nature of the refusal. In addition, his advisors were not called upon to try Vashti but to determine the effect her behavior would have on the general public. Her punishment would serve as a deterrent.

In the same century, Ashkenazi diminishes the king's harsh treatment of Vashti by implicating her. Ashkenazi deems her arrogant in wanting her own party (1:9) and implies that because of her lineage, she may have had difficulty in obeying her husband's word:

> Why does the verse say the Queen Vashti and not "Vashti the queen, refused..."? It is as if it said that before she was a queen in name she was called Vashti since generally a woman is called a queen because her husband is a king. However, when a woman is called a queen because she is the daughter of a king, then her title precedes her name. And this is what it means when it says, "And the king was very angry and his indignation burned within him." He was angry because she ignored his word and indignation burned within him because of her haughtiness and malice in

24. Arama, cited in ibid., 228.

> saying that she was a royal even without being his wife...his anger was over the present and his indignation was over the future.[25]

According to Ashkenazi, Vashti used her parental home and royal background to exert her independence, thus aggravating the king's insecurity, making her not entirely blameless.

The second tactic Ashkenazi uses to mitigate blame on the king is the suggestion that the idea was Memucan's, identified in rabbinic writings as Haman.[26] The king desired a positive outcome for Vashti but was put in an uncomfortable position by his minister, who urged him to judge her quickly and avoid the formal process of law. Ashkenazi's third tactic is to suggest a change of law was taking place. The king's great innovation, according to Ashkenazi, was to dismiss the advice of any cabinet ministers and determine the outcome himself. It was Memucan who advised him in this course.[27]

> This is the new law: "That it shall be written in the laws of Persia and Media," namely that the king does not need the knowers of time.... Behold Haman, in his desire to oust and demote Vashti and bring about her [subsequent] death tried to show the king a way to make judgments immediately regarding Vashti and that this would elevate his position above all other kings. All the other kings who preceded him did not have the personal authority to make spontaneous judgments. They could only do so through the knowers of times, as it says, "Such is the way of the king..." And yet he would have the personal authority to make spontaneous judgments.[28]

Memucan tried to institute legal changes that would give the king executive privilege to make laws without the bureaucratic legislative process. He recommended expanding executive powers. With this change in

25. Ashkenazi, *Yosef Lekaḥ* 1:12.
26. Megilla 12b.
27. Ashkenazi, *Yosef Lekaḥ* 1:17.
28. Ibid. 1:19.

Persian law, Ashkenazi claims, the king was able to execute Bigthan and Teresh immediately, agree to Haman's proposal without consultation, later hang him, and then enable the Jews to defend themselves. Ashkenazi also uses this reasoning to explain Haman's elevation in position, which only highlighted his downfall. Haman, i.e., Memucan, created the very power that would eventually destroy him.

Because of these legal changes, Esther later manages, if not to shift the law, then to skirt around it in ways Vashti could not. Baldwin contends that the king's softening of law in the presence of Esther may suggest a deeper narrative shift to Esther as initiator as a result of her vulnerability as opposed to Vashti's show of strength: "The inference is not so much that human intervention shapes events as that human admission of weakness and need brings about a reversal which, in the light of the world's power struggles, has far-reaching implications for history. The expected course of events could suddenly be reversed in favour of the oppressed."[29] Berg regards this change in Ahasuerus as a possible signal to Esther that there were indeed opportunities to advance her cause: "Previous administrative responses toward lawbreakers, e.g., Vashti and Mordecai, suggest that Esther's infraction will not be tolerated. But Esther's unlawful act produces an unusual exception to the law. She wins Ahasuerus' favor, symbolized by the extension of the scepter. In addition, Ahasuerus promises Esther that her petition will be granted."[30]

This reading of a shift in law is compelling not only because it explains so many events and their consequences, but also because it is counter to the prevailing view of Persian law as inflexible, with the king trapped by his own law and cabinet. Fox understands this view of law in keeping with a more traditional reading where Vashti must be "banished by means of an irrevocable Persian law.... The notion that the Persians and Medes could not repeal their own laws, even ad hoc decrees, is an essential presupposition in the biblical book of Esther. It is found elsewhere only in Daniel (6:8, 12, 15). It is not attested in Persian or Greek sources and it seems an impossible rule for running an empire."[31] Moore

29. Baldwin, *Esther*, 31.

30. Berg, *The Book of Esther*, 77.

31. Fox, *Character and Ideology*, 22.

confirms this and finds the irrevocability of the laws of the Persian and Medes "improbable details" in the Esther story, while confirming that other details of the story ring true.[32] Wesley J. Fuerst in *The Cambridge Bible Commentary* also concurs that "Persian law and the strictness with which it was enforced became legendary," but admits that the irrevocability of decrees is a feature in the Hebrew Bible only in the books of Esther and Daniel.[33]

> Variant readings and editions in the early Jewish texts attempt to explain her disobedience. Either she was required to appear naked, or she had some disfigurement, both of which eventualities would have made her refusal understandable in Jewish eyes, or she was openly flouting her husband's authority, considering that his authority had proper limits. The omission of a reason strengthens the tension of the story by implying that Vashti had no rights in relation to her husband, and therefore reasons were irrelevant.[34]

Baldwin suggests that the writer may have had sympathy for Vashti.[35] Another scholar dismisses Vashti altogether and believes, as do others, that she was merely a literary device for introducing the protagonist Esther.[36]

> Some commentators find these qualities morally unappealing or offensive as an image of the feminine. Such reproaches might appear completely extraneous and anachronistic, except that the author himself seems almost to anticipate them by building rebuttals into the story. The Vashti episode is prefixed to the story

32. C. A. Moore, "Archeology and the Book of Esther," *The Biblical Archeologist* 78 (1975): 68. See also, Levenson, *Esther*, 52.
33. Wesley J. Fuerst, *The Cambridge Bible Commentary: The Books of Ruth, Esther, Ecclesiastes, the Song of Songs, Lamentations* (Cambridge: Cambridge University Press, 1975), 50.
34. Baldwin, *Esther*, 60–61.
35. Ibid., 61.
36. Dorothea Harvey, "Book of Esther," in *The Interpreter's Dictionary of the Bible*, vol. 2, ed. George Buttrick (Nashville: Abingdon, 1962), 747.

> to demonstrate that fate showed that the king may react badly to strong-willed women who do not temper their strength with subtlety. What would a direct and bold demand have achieved, besides giving Esther a self-satisfied feeling of moral virtue as she was deposed in turn?[37]

Vashti taught Esther by example how not to behave as a royal consort. Proving a point then losing a life hardly seemed worth it. By the time Esther was willing to forgo her life, it would be for a cause greater than self-protection.

Vashti as Symbol

Influenced by midrashic texts that vilify Vashti, we may find ourselves unable to have compassion on her plight and recognize the foreshadowing this incident provides for its protagonists. Influenced by modern readings that make Vashti into the patron saint of equal rights, we may fail to see her story within its proper textual context. Vashti serves in the immediate story as a flashpoint for the reader to understand the inner roil of the king. Her death foreshadows the fragility that Jews faced later in the story.

Ironically, it is Vashti who became a microcosm for the macrocosm of the Jewish condition in exile as the scroll begins. In Ahasuerus' Persia, banishment can happen on a whim, the collateral damage of an inebriated monarch sloshed with swagger. If Ahasuerus was prepared to do this to his own wife, a decision he would later regret, surely exterminating a nation he knew nothing of could not be very difficult. He may regret that, too, since it would throw the residents of his empire into turmoil, first in celebration of hate and then with the insecure wonderings of who would be next. The costs of his behavior for the Jews in his empire were apparent only later. The warning happened at the very beginning. The rabbis of the midrash imagine Mordecai at the king's gate, perhaps not even entering the palace walls, and adjuring each Jew at the party awed by the grandeur: "Do not partake of the feast of Ahasuerus," as

37. Fox, *Character and Ideology*, 201.

mentioned earlier.[38] It is a warning for them. It was also incongruously a warning for both Vashti *and* Ahasuerus.

The juxtaposition in chapter 1 of a grand celebration and then a royal banishment created dialectic and confusing tensions that trail the Book of Esther. Intense joviality with peers descended into the breakdown of the intimacy of a marriage. Excessive celebration in the royal palace resulted in an occasion that could have led to a reversal of power in the home of commoners. Stability was met with instability, as the personal fate of one was projected onto the entire kingdom. Rash and impulsive emotions were translated into law, as a hapless queen disappeared into ignominy. Predictably, a decree was necessary to stabilize the situation. Ahasuerus could not champion his authority and largesse throughout the kingdom if his own wife was disobedient. One senses immediately that Vashti's very life lay in peril. Although Ahasuerus instituted the liberal policy of "no restrictions" when it came to drinking, and palace stewards were directed "to comply with each man's wishes," the same sense of self-determination and enjoyment was not the policy for the one who shared the king's bed.

> The social order is precarious, threatened by anxieties and discords. Yet, at the start, society is in a sort of stasis, a state of repose celebrated in and symbolized by the king's banquets. The first conflict that breaks out is trite and silly, but it is portentous. Vashti's defiance of the rules disturbs stability, but the stasis, such as it is, is restored – at least to the satisfaction of those who felt disturbed.[39]

The Vashti incident signals the tremendous insecurity of political figures in a landscape dominated by hierarchies. Ahasuerus' sense of grandiosity could be challenged by a slight to his honor, throwing his entire empire into chaos. It is hardly surprising that when a similar but numerically greater challenge to the king's authority is raised two chapters later, the king would do just as he did before: display willingness to eliminate the problem by eliminating the people.

38. Esther Rabba 7:18.

39. Fox, *Character and Ideology*, 249.

Chapter Two

Ahasuerus: Foolish, Evil, or Wise?

Mordecai and Esther: The Exile and the Orphan

A Strange Beauty Contest

Ahasuerus: Foolish, Evil, or Wise?

> But Queen Vashti refused to come at the king's command conveyed by the eunuchs. The king was greatly incensed, and his fury burned within him. (Est. 1:12)

> Some time afterward, when the anger of King Ahasuerus subsided, he thought of Vashti and what she had done and what had been decreed against her. (Est. 2:1)

> The king, in his fury, left the wine feast for the palace garden, while Haman remained to plead with Queen Esther for his life; for he saw that the king had resolved to destroy him. (Est. 7:7)

James Kugel offers this characterization of the king: "Ahasuerus is a pompous windbag, whose main concern in life is the endless stream of all-night drunken revels that he enjoys in the company of various members of his immense harem."[1] In the Talmud, however, the famous Sages Rav and Shmuel had a disagreement about Ahasuerus regarding personality and actions. (In fact, the two disagreed about most things.)

---

1. James Kugel, *How to Read the Bible: A Guide to Scripture Then and Now* (New York: Free Press, 2007), 645.

One said that making the banquet showed that Ahasuerus was "a clever king."[2] The other said, based on his party, that he was a foolish king: "The one who said he was a clever king maintains that he acted well when he first brought close those who were distant, as he could appear to the residents of his city whenever he wished. And the other who said he was foolish maintains that he should have invited the residents of his city first, so that if those others rebelled against him, those who lived close would have stood with him."[3] As readers of the scroll, we might imagine that Rav and Shmuel argued about every single incident involving the king, because there is a multiplicity of ways to interpret each of the king's actions. In this instance, they argued about who the king needed to impress versus who the king needed as a support network.

In creating a portrait of the king, it is wise to understand the complex emotional topography of the man who could make or break Jewish existence. We know that opinions of Ahasuerus are divided because Rav and Shmuel continued their fierce debate:

> Ahasuerus. Rav said: The name should be viewed as a contraction: The brother of the head (*aḥiv shel rosh*) and of the same character as the head (*ben gilo shel rosh*). Rav explains: The brother of the head, i.e., the brother of the wicked Nebuchadnezzar, who is called "head," as it is stated: "You are the head of gold" (Dan. 2:38). Of the same character as the head, for he, Nebuchadnezzar, killed the Jews, and he, Ahasuerus, sought to kill them. He destroyed the Temple, and he sought to destroy the foundations for the Temple laid by Zerubbabel, as it is stated: "And in the reign of Ahasuerus, in the beginning of his reign, they wrote to him an accusation against the inhabitants of Judah and Jerusalem" (Ezra 4:6), and he ordered that the construction of the Temple cease.[4]

Rav took the beginning and end of the king's name and created a wordplay in Hebrew, tying together "brother" and "head" to show that this

2. Megilla 12a.
3. Ibid.
4. Megilla 11a.

king was a conceptual brother to Nebuchadnezzar. In other words, he was beyond redemption. He, like Nebuchadnezzar, not only killed the Jews, he prevented the Temple from being rebuilt. This is an enormous leap outside of the book because no Jews actually died in the *Megilla,* and we have no evidence that Ahasuerus had anything to do with the Temple. Yet, his willingness to rid his empire of the Jews in principle was all the proof this Sage needed.

Other Sages engaged in other wordplays to explain the king's name: he was a source of darkness, woe, or poverty. And this general wickedness did not cease, even if the status of the Jews had shifted by the end of the book:

> And Shmuel said: The name Ahasuerus should be understood in the sense of black (*shaḥor*), as the face of the Jewish people was blackened in his days like the bottom of a pot. And R. Yoḥanan said a different explanation: Everyone who recalled him said: "Woe upon his head" (*aḥ lerosho*). And R. Ḥanina said: The name alludes to the fact that everyone became poor (*rash*) in his days, as it is stated: "And the king Ahasuerus laid a tribute upon the land" (Est. 10:1). The Talmud continues: "This is (*hu*) Ahasuerus" (Est. 1:1); the term *hu,* "this is," comes to teach that he remained as he was in his wickedness from beginning to end.[5]

Poverty and woe were a consistent feature of life under King Ahasuerus. These observations are all part of a larger issue of how to read the character of the king. Fox offers us his estimation, saying it is hard to imagine Ahasuerus "having any thoughts not obvious to everyone."[6] Ahasuerus was not a deep thinker. He may not have even been a thinker at all, governed only by primitive and base instincts. Fox articulates this very sentiment: "His most dangerous flaw is his failure to think."[7] Even when he does have independent thoughts, like his sudden desire to reward Mordecai in chapter 6 or his desire to kill Haman in chapter

5. Ibid. 11a.
6. Fox, *Character and Ideology,* 171.
7. Ibid.

7, the king's ideas are never fully thought through with consequences attached. There was no guiding strategy or regard for the future. This worked to the advantage of some and the disadvantage of others, depending on how well one could manipulate the king to private or collective ends. This incapacity to do what is right in favor of "whatever is pleasing" (3:11) worked for the Jews ultimately, but impulsivity itself became a sign of exile's dangers. Rash actions may serve an audience well for a time with the caveat that the pendulum will likely swing back to idiocy.

Volatility is always worrying in a person, much more so in a monarch. Ibn Ezra[8] describes Ahasuerus' anger as a fire, a flammable sort of emotion that breeds heat and destruction. As discussed in the previous chapter, Ahasuerus' first jolt of anger was at Vashti's dissent, which quickly turned a private marital spat into a public conversation. It would be comedic if it were not so tragic. "'Therefore the king was very wrathful' (1:12). Why did his anger burn in him so fiercely? Rava said: Vashti responded to him: 'You son of a stableman. My father drank wine against a thousand and did not become inebriated, and that man has become senseless from his wine.' Because of this, immediately 'his anger burned in him.'"[9] Ahasuerus was told he could not hold his drink. This was enough to set off even more intense negative emotions. One expects that the king's ministers were put in position to manage his temper and curb his anger. Not so. Ahasuerus' anger was taken seriously by his ministers who, instead of calming him down, leveraged the king's emotional states, arguably for their own gain.

The text in the first chapter foreshadows another private anger that simmered into a public decision. Haman's anger at Mordecai became his anger at all Jews. By the time this occurred in chapter 3, the absurdity of private emotions translating into public policy is no surprise to the reader. We are prepared because we witnessed this torrid reaction earlier. The king, thus, had influence over his ministers, enabling and even granting license for them to express their worst instincts. In *The Legends of the Jews*, Louis Ginzberg alerts us to tales that suggest that "Ahasuerus

8. Esther 1:12.
9. Megilla 12b.

had long been acquainted with Haman's hatred of the Jews."[10] Ahasuerus, while bad, did not compare with Haman, who was evil incarnate, posing a far greater and immediate threat to the Jews:

> The Jews at the time of Ahasuerus were like the dove about to enter her nest wherein a snake lies coiled. Yet she cannot withdraw, because a falcon bides without to swoop down upon her. In Shushan, the Jews were in the clutches of Haman, and in other lands they were at the mercy of many murderous enemies to their race, ready to do the bidding of Haman to destroy and to slay them and cause them to perish.[11]

Initially, the portrait is of a snake and a falcon, both dangerous to the dove, the symbol of peace. The comparison then grows in intensity, extending to all and to everywhere. All prey on the innocent dove. The image is not far-fetched given that personal emotions of those at the top trickled down in the Book of Esther to the masses, fury upon fury, hate upon hate. The key distinction between Ahasuerus and Haman is that where Ahasuerus was a man of a full range of emotion – joy, joviality, and magnanimity – Haman had no range. He was bitter, spiteful, acerbic, and cruel from the story's beginning to its end.

The King's Generosity

The intensity of Ahasuerus' fury was matched only by the intensity of his generosity, which should not be ignored when studying the Book of Esther. Fox observes that the king "tried to buy honor by ostentatious generosity."[12] While, on one level, this seems quite obvious, perhaps it is itself an ungenerous reading of the king's character. His lavish party can be understood as a successful attempt to buy his way into popularity. Yet this does not explain away his lavishness; he was generous to Esther on many occasions when he had nothing to profit from it, other than

10. Louis Ginzberg, *The Legends of the Jews* (CreateSpace Independent Publishing Platform, 2015), 497.
11. Ibid., 489.
12. Fox, *Character and Ideology*, 172.

an intensification of his affection. The king remitted taxes after Esther won the sordid contest for his love, an act that surely depleted his own treasury. He was unstinting even at personal expense to himself or his kingdom. In fact, textually, there are more references to his generosity than to his fury.

> At Esther's coronation, he gives gifts and ordains tax relief. Demonstrative generosity accompanies his munificent grant to Haman, whom he tells (insincerely) to keep the money and to "do as you please" with the people. The same impulse inspires him twice to offer half his kingdom to Esther.[13]

Anger and generosity together create a portrait of passion over temperance. This uneasy combination can be unpredictable and threatening; even when the impulse is loving, it may become something else in a flash.

Ahasuerus and the Temple

Rabbinic literature abounds with criticism of Ahasuerus and his mistreatment of Temple-related matters, as referred to obliquely by Rav in the talmudic passage above. The opening banquet on the third year, in one midrash, refers to the third annual celebration marking the date Ahasuerus canceled the rebuilding of the Temple.[14] The party was not to celebrate his third year in office as much as it was a way to gloat publicly over obstructing the Temple's construction. While we do not expect the midrash to be a literal rendition of the text, this initially seems odd. Persecuting the Jews without reason would seem to be evil enough. Why add raucous and expensive celebrations into the mix? Yet elaboration on the story keeps pointing in a similar direction.

The drinking cups used at the banquet – "in golden beakers, beakers of varied design" (Est. 1:7) – were purloined, according to one midrash, from the ransacking of the Temple.[15] This midrash uses imagery

13. Ibid.
14. Esther Rabba 1:15.
15. Ibid. 2:11.

from Daniel about Belshazzar and applies it to the more famous royal drinking party in Esther.

> Under the influence of wine, Belshazzar commanded that they bring in the vessels of gold and silver that his father Nebuchadnezzar had taken out of the Temple in Jerusalem, so that the king and his lords, his wives and his concubines, might drink from them. So they brought in the vessels of gold and silver that had been taken out of the Temple, the House of God in Jerusalem, and the king and his lords, his wives and his concubines, drank from them. They drank the wine and praised the gods of gold, silver, bronze, iron, wood, and stone. (Dan. 5: 2–4)

Note the repetition in the verses to stress that there was more than simply drinking at this party. The vessels represented miniature military trophies to celebrate victory. Observe the contrast between goblets made of exquisite materials to worship one God with the same goblets used to worship gods of the same materials used in the making of the vessels, a jab at idol worship, to be sure. The irony was not lost on the author of Daniel and may have influenced the writer of Esther, depending on when these books were originally penned. Cups used for one purpose can easily be repurposed by victors. In this case, since the party was not only for royals, Jews could technically have drunk in Persia from cups reserved for sacrifices or priests alone in Jerusalem. The potential for profanation was profound indeed.

It was not only what Ahasuerus drank that spoke of the Temple's glory. According to the Talmud, the king dressed as a high priest at the banquet: "'When he showed the riches of his glorious kingdom and the honor of his majestic greatness' (Est. 1:4). R. Yosei bar Ḥanina said: 'This teaches that Ahasuerus wore the priestly vestments.'"[16] In yet another midrash, when Esther made her request at the wine party she commissioned, the king offered her up to half the kingdom, with one proviso: the portion of the kingdom containing the Temple was not to

16. Megilla 12a.

be given to her.[17] This piece of desirable territory was not up for grabs. Perhaps the limited offer demonstrates the king's military prowess and authority over a tiny, subjugated people. Alternatively, Ahasuerus may have wanted the Temple as the holy site; it would bring good fortune to its owner. The midrash is reminiscent of an opinion in Genesis Rabba as to what Cain and Abel were arguing about that created the pretext for Cain to kill Abel: According to R. Yehoshua Siknin in the name of R. Levi, one said, "'The Temple must be built in my area,' while the other claimed, 'It must be built in mine.'"[18] Long before there were any Jews, any discussion of the Land of Israel or a spiritual center called the Temple, Cain and Abel were already arguing over who would own the land where the Temple would be built because the holy site conferred special status or good fortune.

Why all this concern and association with the Temple? Some scholars believe it makes Ahasuerus appear more villainous and conniving:

> Painting Ahasuerus as the person responsible for stopping the Temple from being rebuilt reinserts Israel and God into the story and adds theological weight to it by making him an enemy of God. Moreover, it anchors the story within the context of the exile and the events leading up to the rebuilding of the Temple.[19]

It may have also served as a theological distraction of sorts, assigning the blame for the protracted reconstruction of the Temple to a foreign king instead of on the Jews themselves. Alternatively, building on the angst of exile and the Lethe of forgetfulness occasioned by living outside one's homeland, the repeated mention of the Temple in rabbinic literature may actually have been a warning to all Jews that they risked losing

17. Ibid. 15b.
18. Genesis Rabba 18:4 on Gen. 4:8: "And Cain spoke unto Abel his brother.... And it came to pass, when they were in the field, that Cain rose up against Abel his brother, and slew him."
19. Malka Z. Simkovich, Zev Farber, and David Steinberg, "Ahasuerus and Vashti: The Story Megillat Esther Does Not Tell You," http://thetorah.com/ahasuerus-and-vashti-the-story-megillat-esther-does-not-tell-you/.

their essential Jewish identity without a Temple. The very thought that the Jewish people could exist without one was unacceptable to the rabbis. Mordecai's clothing reminds us of the priests of yore, but instead of service at an altar, a hereditary position not his for the taking, Mordecai became the high priest of politics instead. The Jews were overjoyed at this eventual development instead of seeing it as a capitulation to exile. Blaming Ahasuerus was far easier than blaming themselves for what had happened to them since the Temple was destroyed. Holy Jerusalem was bereft of its crowds and its pilgrimages, while the Jews of Shushan found themselves far from home and unable to determine their own future.

Mordecai and Esther: The Exile and the Orphan

> There was a certain Jew in Shushan the capital, whose name was Mordecai the son of Jair the son of Shimei the son of Kish, a Benjaminite. [Kish] had been exiled from Jerusalem in the group that was carried into exile along with King Jeconiah of Judah, which had been driven into exile by King Nebuchadnezzar of Babylon. He was foster father to Hadassah – that is, Esther – his uncle's daughter, for she had neither father nor mother. The maiden was shapely and beautiful; and when her father and mother died, Mordecai adopted her as his own daughter. (Est. 2:5–7)

> Esther did not reveal her people or her kindred, for Mordecai had told her not to reveal it. Every single day Mordecai would walk about in front of the court of the harem, to learn how Esther was faring and what was happening to her. (Est. 2:10–11)

Our two central Jewish characters are heroic in distinctive ways, yet the two are aligned as leaders in their community, as active salvific forces, as influencers in the court. Both stood out even though they resisted being the center of attention. As a pair, they demonstrate the collaborative spirit of Ecclesiastes: "Two are better than one in that they have greater benefit from their work. For should they fall, one can raise up the other, but woe to the one who is alone and falls with no companion to raise him" (Eccl. 4:9–10). They are able to be effective precisely because they served in necessary and complementary roles. Mordecai and Esther did something of virtue and significance but only with the assistance of each other; one commanded and the other obeyed and vice versa. Craig suggests that Mordecai and Esther together, almost as a unit, offer a contrast in personality and character to Ahasuerus and Haman:

> In contrast to the story's fools, Esther and Mordecai emerge as exemplary literary opposites: they are rational, sensible, and courageous. They knew when to speak and when to sit silent. For her part, Esther is portrayed as contemplative, one who considers her actions' possible consequences before she acts. Both she and Mordecai have the ability to secure friendships, or at least to win the confidence and respect of those whom they meet at court.[1]

Ahasuerus' and Haman's narcissistic, angry, and self-interested personalities contrast with Mordecai and Esther's thoughtful, judicious and intelligent leadership. Sharing the positive dispositions between two characters suggests to the reader that these attributes belong not only to one extraordinary figure but can be shared, can even be part of a culture, a people. Everyone – men and women both – can aspire to live up to the legacy Mordecai and Esther crafted. The way each is introduced sets the tone and expectation for what follows. The verse that initially describes Mordecai states: "There was a certain Jew in Shushan the capital, whose name was Mordecai the son of Jair the son of Shimei the son of Kish, a Benjaminite" (Est. 2:5). By calling Mordecai the Jew, when he was clearly not the only Jew, we are left to wonder if he was the only unabashedly proud, unapologetic Jew in Shushan, unafraid of embracing his lineage and claiming his ancestry rather than blending in with the Persian throngs. One Sage in the Talmud questions the virtue of listing Mordecai's ancestors. It would have been sufficient merely to write that Mordecai was from the tribe of Benjamin.[2] The other names signify,

1. Craig, *Reading Esther*, 146.
2. Megilla 12b.

in this view, characteristics of Mordecai through wordplays: "He was called 'the son of Jair' because he was the son who enlightened (*he'ir*) the eyes of all of the Jewish people with his prayers; 'the son of Shimei' because he was the son whose prayers God heard (*shama*); 'the son of Kish' because he knocked (*hikish*) on the gates of mercy and they were opened to him."[3] All of these names suggest ways in which Mordecai was a spiritual role model and on intimate terms with God, religious details notably absent from the text.

The only matter of confusion in the talmudic passage is the name *Yehudi*, a possible reference to the tribe of Judah although we know Mordecai was a Benjaminite. Here R. Naḥman offers a creative solution: "Mordecai was crowned with honorary names."[4] Although not literally from the tribe of Judah, he was considered an honorary member of the tribe traditionally associated with royalty and leadership. This answer did not cohere for Rabba bar bar Ḥana, who explained instead that "Mordecai's father was from the tribe of Benjamin, and his mother was from the tribe of Judah. Therefore, he was both a *Yemini*, a Benjaminite, and a *Yehudi*, from the tribe of Judah."[5] Another suggestion is that given this parental divide, the different families fought over who should take tribal credit for Mordecai, each wanting to align itself with this hero. To this, R. Yoḥanan shared his view: "Mordecai came from the tribe of Benjamin. Why, then, was he referred to as a *Yehudi*? On account of the fact that he repudiated idol worship, for anyone who repudiates idolatry is called *Yehudi*."[6] The fact that Mordecai did not bow down to Haman was regarded in this talmudic passage as a frontal attack on pagan worship; Mordecai, following the midrashic legacy of Abraham, was an iconoclast who stood up and stood out with conviction.

Aggadot aside, we know little from the text about Mordecai. Jack Sasson observes that Mordecai's character is not fully developed until later in the book, "with fragments of his personality scattered in the

3. Ibid.
4. Ibid.
5. Megilla 12b–13a.
6. Ibid. 13a.

early chapters."[7] He is introduced, like other biblical characters, in the framework of family and place, but we get no glimpse into his character or looks, the way we do with the king or Esther. "Only after Haman's fall," according to Sasson, are these pieces "integrated into a full version to represent the writer's perfect image of a partisan Jew in position of mastery":[8]

> From the moment he first appears, Mordecai is a courtier, and his battles are with his colleagues at the royal court. The writer does not judge Mordecai when he brings his brethren to the brink of disaster either because of rancor (he had just saved the king and felt that he deserved better than to be forgotten) or because of insubordination and misplaced pride (it is the king, after all, who determines how to treat Haman). The storyteller is deadpan as he reports Mordecai's quick forsaking of his mourning garb when Haman calls for him with royal attire and chariot. Mordecai has come to represent the Jew who will not be bowed by circumstances and who will seize unforeseen opportunity.[9]

Sasson questions Mordecai's judgment and even paints a portrait of opportunism and spiritual compromise. Yet, if this is true, those who people the scroll make no note of it.

Mordecai bears an unusual name, possibly associated with the god Marduk. Dalley adds that the "ai" on the end of Marduk is a diminutive to make the name of a god mortal. Moore contends that this name appears in treasury tablets from Persepolis from the fifth century BCE; Mordecai served as an accountant and was from Susa, but it is not clear if this was a common name; the two are not likely the same.[10] Mordecai is introduced as part of a genealogical line that connected him to King Saul. Shimei and Kish appear in several other places in the Hebrew

---

7. Jack M. Sasson, "Esther," in *The Literary Guide to the Bible,* ed. Robert Alter and Frank Kermode (Cambridge, MA: Belknap Press, 1987), 338.
8. Ibid.
9. Ibid.
10. Moore, "Archeology and the Book of Esther," 73f.

Bible.[11] Berg suggests that the Shimei of II Samuel was also embroiled in a dispute over the monarchic succession, connecting the two as family in name and in deed.[12]

Connections between Saul and Mordecai go deeper than family associations. The two are introduced in a similar way, as relatives of Shimei and Kish. Both also achieve unexpected promotion to royal governance. There are important contrasts, however, in addition to similarities. Berger observes that Saul remained silent when he should have exerted his authority (I Sam. 10:27). This contrasts with Mordecai's challenge that Esther not remain silent (4:14).[13] Although in both narratives, two banquets take place in tight sequence (I Sam. 20:27), Saul's intent was to do evil against an Israelite insider, David, while Mordecai and Esther's intent is to use the scene of a banquet to "do evil" toward an Israelite enemy, Haman.[14] In comparing the two, the most glaring difference, as Koller notes, is that Saul disobeyed God by taking Amalekite spoils when told explicitly not to (I Sam. 15:9–14), in contrast to Esther and Mordecai, who admonish the people not to take spoils (9:15), even when they were told they could (8:11). Koller believes that much of the story redeems Saul's line, while at the same time showcasing his errors: "Clearly Mordecai and Esther are depicted as completing the work begun – and left unfinished – by Saul, and thus clearly they are seen as rectifying his faults and righting his wrongs."[15]

Introducing Esther

Esther's introduction gives us critical and unusual information about her and her relationship to Mordecai: "He was foster father to Hadassah – that is, Esther – his uncle's daughter, for she had neither father nor mother. The maiden was shapely and beautiful; and when her father and mother died, Mordecai adopted her as his own daughter" (Est. 2:7). Esther's looks are critical to the introduction given that the beginning of

11. See Ex. 6:17; II Sam. 19:21; I Kings 1:8, 4:18; Ezra 10:23; I Chr. 3:10–19, 4:24–26, 6:2, 8:21, 23:7; II Chr. 29:14, 31:12–13.
12. Berg, *The Book of Esther*, 64–65.
13. Berger, "Esther and Benjamite Royalty," 632–35.
14. Ibid., 636–37.
15. Koller, *Esther in Ancient Jewish Thought*, 88.

chapter 2 tells us that the king was looking for a beautiful maiden. Esther was doubly qualified, the text informs us, by having both the right looks for the position and the right proportions. One cannot help but contrast Mordecai's status as an exile with Esther's noticeable appearance. He would never fit in, nor did he want to, whereas Esther's looks created access to a society closed to others, highlighting the superficiality of Persian society where surface looks alone were enough to make a marriage.

Esther is quixotically introduced as an orphan twice after connecting her to Mordecai. The first instance is indirect, through her relationship to an adoptive father, and then the text states more directly that she had no parents, suggesting that the family arrangement explains her unusually close relationship to Mordecai. She was bereft of parents; thus, as her custodian, Mordecai would have been an important authority figure. Ashkenazi clarifies the relationship between Esther and her uncle, Mordecai. After defining an *omen*, a foster parent, as someone who taught and guided Esther, Ashkenazi claims that the order of Esther 2:7, namely, its mention that Esther is an orphan before the mention of her beauty, is intentional:

> [The clause] that Mordecai took her [as a daughter] precedes her beauty to demonstrate his caution. If a man becomes a guardian when a girl is young and raises her as a daughter, then he has no desire for her the way that the evil inclination might overpower him if she were adopted as an older and attractive girl and he had neither seen her when she was young nor nurtured her as an infant.... That is why the text says that he took her as a daughter; he distanced himself [sexually] as one would a daughter. The Sages, of blessed memory, interpreted "as a daughter" to mean as a wife. This is a midrash, but the literal meaning of the verse is as we earlier explained it.[16]

This reading sidesteps any imagined impropriety in this family arrangement while also dismissing the rabbinic reading of marriage.

16. Ashkenazi, *Yosef Lekaḥ* 2:7.

In explaining her background, one midrash contends that Esther's father died while her mother was pregnant and that her mother died during childbirth.[17] This makes her tragic situation that much more calamitous. Esther was born into grave loss, a loss that, regarding her mother, was on Esther's account. One wonders why a midrash would add torment to her already precarious family situation unless it was trying to understand what eventually moved her to throw her lot in with the Jews even at the risk of her life. In the midrashic mindset, perhaps she was weighed down by guilt, responsibility, and a desire to do something worthwhile and redemptive with her life to justify her existence. It may very well explain her willingness to make the ultimate sacrifice when called upon to do so. Mordecai, according to one midrash, nursed her when he could find no wet nurse to feed the infant, no doubt a play on the Hebrew word *omen,* shifting his role as steward to a nursing father, a term Moses used in Numbers 11:12.[18] Alternatively, Mordecai's wife, a woman who makes no appearance in the text, nursed her.[19]

The fact that Esther had no parents surfaces as a leadership provocation in a midrash on Psalms 27. There, David struggled with the fact that not only did he have no parents, but his parents forsook him: "Though my father and mother abandon me, the Lord will take me in" (Ps. 27:10). At base, it reminds the reader of an existential wound, the loss of one's foundations, that will never heal. Alternatively, one might interpret this bold statement as praise of God; should David's parents ever abandon him, God would always be a refuge, anchor, and support. The Book of Lamentations primes us for the same sentiment of loss, comparing loss of city and Temple to loss of home: "We have become orphans, fatherless; our mothers are like widows" (Lam. 5:3).

> R. Berekhia said in the name of R. Levi: The Holy One, blessed be He, said to Israel, "You wept and said before Me, 'We have become fatherless orphans...'" They lamented over the destruction of the Temple and the exile, complaining that they could no

17. Esther Rabba 6:5, Megilla 13a.
18. Genesis Rabba 30:8.
19. *Midrash Tehillim,* Ps. 22:23.

> longer rely, Heaven forbid, on their heavenly Father, their Protector, to rescue them in exile. Therefore, the Holy One, blessed be He, said, "By your lives, I promise that the redeemer who I will ultimately raise up on your behalf in Media will not have a father and mother either. I will save you from Haman's conspiracy, and in so doing, teach you that I am indeed the Father of orphans."[20]

Orphanhood, this midrash contends, is no excuse for a breach of faith in God, since God is the primary parent. Esther had no parents, yet she took a leadership role in saving her people. Some may argue that it was precisely because she did not have parents that she was able to take such risks and act as bravely as she did.

Well-known ancient stories like Oedipus, Heracles, Romulus, and Remus describe the fate of abandoned orphans. Cyrus himself fits in this genre. His grandfather Astyages, king of the Medes, apparently dreamed that his grandson would usurp the throne and had his servant murder Cyrus to relieve the king of the threat. The servant disobeyed and left Cyrus on a mountain, where he was raised by a shepherd and his wife. Ten years later his true identity was revealed.[21]

Some midrashim highlight Esther's own royal lineage. Laniak argues that other biblical stories situated in the Second Temple period focus on a singular, male leader to inspire and redeem the people. This is true for Jeremiah and Ezekiel (Jer. 22:30 and Ezek. 34:23, 37:24), for Ezra (3:2), Nehemiah (12:1), Zechariah (4:6), and Haggai (1:1). The figure may have been someone specific, like Zerubbabel, or more generalized male leadership, like that of the priests. Esther had no such pedigree or at least, unlike Mordecai, was not introduced with one. Both Mordecai and Haman were introduced by way of their royal ancestors' ancient conflict; Esther was not directly part of these associations. "The savior of the Jews in Esther is an orphaned, Jewish, female exile.... She met

20. Lamentations Rabba 5:3.

21. Nahum Sarna, in contrasting these ancient stories with the birth of Moses, suggests that his story does not have the conventional characteristics of these far-fetched tales. There was no divine pronouncement of his birth or future achievements. He cites no paternal hostility, nor was the child born to nobility. His birth mother made every attempt to retain contact, nursing him herself.

no traditional criteria for leadership. And yet Israel's ancient traditions are rich with examples of unlikely leaders. Had not the biblical tradition trained its hearers to expect the unexpected and the unorthodox?"[22] Esther, he contends, was able to accomplish what she did because she was an outsider, "a bridge between two patriarchal worlds with no inherited status in either."[23] He adds another observation about Esther in comparing her with other biblical women who led when men failed to, like Deborah and Yael: "The story celebrates the dramatic leadership of a marginal female figure during a time of crisis, but its denouement signals a return to the patriarchal norms it has qualified.... Esther's role makes a counterpoint, but it does not comprehensively challenge the paradigm."[24] In other words, the text reverts to, and closes with, Mordecai's leadership, in effect suggesting that Esther led until Mordecai surpassed her. Mordecai may have received special robes by the end of the book, but let us not forget that Esther was still queen. Laniak concludes from Esther's role that "the hope of salvation is found in any Jew."[25] Later, he observes that while male biblical leadership was necessary for the community at this period in history, it alone does not "exhaust the prospects for deliverance."[26]

Esther was beautiful by any standard, a fact we assume because the text tells us so, suggesting that her beauty was acknowledged before it was confirmed and validated in a pageant constructed by outsiders. First she gained the favor of Hegai (2:9) and then all who encountered her: "Esther won the admiration of all who saw her" (2:15). We assume this excluded those competing with her but included those who controlled the harem. This detail should be unimportant in light of the fact that the king was the only one Esther need impress. Yet a king who craved universal approval would likely be moved to select a woman already selected in the eyes of others. Ahasuerus was also highly malleable, especially in the charged environment of eunuchs who wielded influence in the

22. Laniak, "Esther's 'Volkcentrism,'" 87.
23. Ibid.
24. Ibid., 87–88.
25. Ibid., 88.
26. Ibid., 90.

royal household; the seal of approval by a courtier would make Esther that much more attractive.

Esther's charm lay not only in her beauty but also in her obedience, a trait lauded and valued in the wake of Vashti's disobedience. Beauty in this sense is more than skin-deep. It is the aptitude for grace associated with Esther that encouraged affection, a demure magnetism that emerged from the capacity to put the concerns of others before her own. Mordecai commanded Esther to be pliant, to be silent, to follow his orders. And so she did. Later Esther would follow the king's orders.

> This portrayal of an obedient Esther serves several functions in the story...it sharply contrasts with Vashti's disobedience in chapter one. It further prepares the audience for Esther's response to Mordecai in Esther 4:16, itself underscored by Esther 4:17: Mordecai did "everything which Esther commanded him." Finally, Esther's obedience contrasts with her later disobedience to the king's law (Esther 5:1–5). The latter provides for continued dramatic suspense and raises the question of whether Esther will obey Mordecai's instruction to intercede with the king (cf. 4:8–17).[27]

Is there a limit to obedience to uncle or king for Esther, particularly in the difficult instance where obeying one means disobeying the other? It seems that obedience to Mordecai won the day, as expected if the story is ultimately about Jewish identity and leadership in the diaspora. Crawford notes how the combination of beauty and obedience worked in Esther's favor:

> Esther upholds the patriarchal norms of ancient Jewish society in several ways. . . . Her primary characteristic is beauty; as the object of men's gaze and the king's possession, her beauty adds to his honor. In this she is identical to Vashti. Further, she is obedient. She obeys Mordecai, she obeys Hegai; she also obeys the social system in which she is located. Esther does not try to alter the patriarchal structure of her society; rather she works from within

27. Berg, *The Book of Esther*, 73.

> the system to gain her ends. And the system is centered on the power of the man over his household.[28]

Given this description, Crawford then has to explain Esther's seeming disobedience. She does: "It may be objected that Esther is disobedient in her central action in the book, her unsummoned appearance in the throne room. It is true that she is disobedient to the law, but she is not personally disobedient. She does not defy Ahasuerus; rather, she relies on their personal relationship to override the impersonal decree."[29] Where the king and his court imposed and upheld law, Esther relies on the virtue of personal relationships as a compelling means to challenge the system and the status quo.

The book may also be named after Esther because she is the very symbol of the Jews in exile. Orphaned but beautiful, she relies on outside affirmation of her worth even as she is subject to injustice and threats of death. Instead of cowing to external pressures, she ultimately finds her place and has her influence only when defending and owning her identity. It is interesting to note that although Esther has two names, she is never called by her Jewish name, Hadassah, while both Daniel and Joseph are given foreign names but the text never uses them. This, too, speaks to an understanding of diaspora living that is becoming an increasingly permanent state for its exiles.[30]

Mordecai and Esther as Gods?

Scholars have long pointed to the similarity of the names Mordecai and Esther to the names of the Semitic gods Marduk and Ishtar.[31] Esther was introduced with two names, the second being Hadassah, which means myrtle; the Talmud suggests this reflects her beautiful skin color.[32] The name Esther is generally regarded as Persian, with the meaning of either a star or in praise of the goddess Ishtar. Having a Persian name allowed

28. Crawford, "Esther and Judith," in *The Book of Esther in Modern Research*, 72.
29. Ibid.
30. Koller, *Esther in Ancient Jewish Thought*, 76.
31. See Dalley, *Esther's Revenge*, 175–76.
32. Megilla 13a.

Esther to pass as a citizen of the empire. Likely born and bred in Shushan, Esther was not a foreigner, nor did she regard herself as one. Yet her dual names may suggest a conflicted identity in contrast to Mordecai's one name that is then linked to many generations of Jews before him. Dalley remarks that Hadassah is identical to a parallel Akkadian word meaning "bride."[33] The fact that Esther has two names seems to support the notion that one name may have been used in general society while her Hebrew name was used in Jewish company. This confirms the ancient teaching of Bar Kappara that we did not lose our names through assimilation in Egypt; names were both a tool and symbol for preserving one's identity in exile.[34]

As in Roman and Greek mythology, ancient Near Eastern gods were often associated with many attributes and domains. Ishtar was a goddess of healing, jest, and fate. In keeping with the carnivalesque literary genre suggested earlier, Ishtar, according to Dalley, was a jester among gods: "Making people laugh, belittling them and puffing them up, is your business, Ishtar."[35] Esther is not a funny character, but her role highlights many of the absurdities in the book. Dalley also notes that Ishtar was listed as a controller of destiny with the Divine Fates in the *Addressbook of the Gods of Ashur*: "Fates were determined by casting lots, but the deity determined how they would fall, and the results were written on the tablet of destinies, sealed with the seal of destinies."[36] This, too, would associate Esther's name with a living predictor of fate, ultimately superseding the arbitrary lots associated with Haman.

Haman's name may have derived from the name for the god of Susa; this suggests that the characters in the Book of Esther were regarded almost as proto-gods, fighting over the future of Persia and the future of the Jewish people, as if the tale were taking place on two planes: the human and the divine. On a human level, this is a story of heroes and villains in a fight to the death. On the divine level, it is the story of

---

33. Dalley, *Esther's Revenge*, 169.
34. Leviticus Rabba 32:5.
35. Dalley provides a translation on p. 133 from W. Romer, "Der Spassmacher im alten Zweistromland," *Persica*, 7:53
36. Dalley, *Esther's Revenge*, 138.

one God defeating a malevolent pagan god through human intercessors. "Having identified Mordecai with Marduk, and Esther with Ishtar, we can see that the implications for readers in Assyria would be clear: the great gods had taken control of destiny in Esther 8:8 and were then in a position to defeat the wicked enemy, the forces of chaos."[37] Hadassah must become Esther in order to tackle the host forces of Persia, while among her people, she would continue to be Hadassah, if not literally then in terms of the way she regarded herself and the way she was regarded by her nation.

The Book of Mordecai?

There are some who question whether the book should be named after Esther or Mordecai, essentially asking: Who was the bigger hero?[38] The book may begin with Esther, but it ends with Mordecai. One scholar goes as far as to suggest that Mordecai was the brain and Esther merely the follower, a woman identified for her looks rather than her leadership.[39] From a hierarchal perspective, this is a troubling view. The queen trumps any ministers, even those with significant positions. Throughout the book, the king went out of his way to bestow generosity on Esther in the spirit of intimacy.

Craig is astonished that Moore could even suggest that Mordecai is the greater of the two:

> It is Esther who becomes queen in this Persian court, who outmaneuvers Haman.... It is Esther who not only saves her life by bringing Haman to the gallows, but also the lives of her own people. Esther gains power despite the fact that she, a woman, would have found herself virtually powerless in patriarchal Persia.... If Mordecai is the major character, why did someone name the story for Esther?[40]

37. Ibid., 176.
38. See Bickerman, *Four Strange Books*, 171; and David M. Gunn and Danna Nolan Fewell, *Narrative in the Hebrew Bible* (London: Oxford University Press, 1993), 76, 79–81.
39. Moore, *Esther*, lii.
40. Craig, *Reading Esther*, 26.

Another contemporary scholar regards Esther as more representative of a model of Jewish life in the diaspora than Mordecai because, winning a contest for the king's favor, it is she who is the real symbol of diaspora success:

> The Jews in the Diaspora...are in the position of the weak, as a subordinate population under the dominant Persian government. They must adjust to their lack of immediate political and economic power and learn to work within the system to gain what power they can. In the book of Esther, their role model for this adjustment is Esther. Not only is she a woman, a member of a perpetually subordinate population, but she is an orphan, a powerless member of Jewish society. Therefore, her position in society is constantly precarious, as was the position of the Jews in the Diaspora. With no native power of her own owing to her sex or position in society, Esther must learn to make her way among the powerful and to cooperate with others in order to make herself secure.[41]

Esther was able to surpass the many and significant hurdles in her path to leadership, overcoming natural disadvantages in ways alien to Mordecai.

Perhaps it is best to sidestep this competition altogether and state that it is no competition at all. By having both characters exemplify loyalty, intelligence, courage, and influence, the text promotes a combination of leadership exhibited by both Mordecai *and* Esther. His was extraordinary leadership; hers, perhaps more so because of all the potential obstacles in her path created by Persian culture toward women as objects rather than persons. Both were critical to the outcome. Their strengths complemented each other. Mordecai told Esther what to do, and she did the same. In many biblical books, we find one dominant hero – chieftain, priest, king, or prophet; here it is the partnership that saves the day. This, too, may be a message for those who lead in exile. Identify allies in the cause and the work. They are necessary in

---

41. Sidnie Ann White, "Esther," in *The Women's Bible Commentary*, ed. Carol A. Newsom and Sharon H. Ringe (Louisville, KY: Westminster John Knox Press, 1992), 124–29.

surmounting the challenges presented in a host culture where one can become friend or foe from one day to the next. Diaspora Jews must identify their partners as they create a more meaningful and impactful voice in foreign lands. Leadership may come from unexpected places and at unexpected times.

A Strange Beauty Contest

When each girl's turn came to go to King Ahasuerus at the end of the twelve months' treatment prescribed for women (for that was the period spent on beautifying them: six months with oil of myrrh and six months with perfumes and women's cosmetics, and it was after that that the girl would go to the king), whatever she asked for would be given her to take with her from the harem to the king's palace. She would go in the evening and leave in the morning for a second harem in the charge of Shaashgaz, the king's eunuch, guardian of the concubines. She would not go again to the king unless the king wanted her, when she would be summoned by name. (Est. 2:12–14)

When the turn came for Esther daughter of Abihail – the uncle of Mordecai, who had adopted her as his own daughter – to go to the king, she did not ask for anything but what Hegai, the king's eunuch, guardian of the women, advised. Yet Esther won the admiration of all who saw her. Esther was taken to King Ahasuerus, in his royal palace, in the tenth month, which is the month of Tevet, in the seventh year of his reign. The king loved Esther more than all the other women, and she won his grace and favor more than all the virgins. So he set a royal diadem on her head and made her queen instead of Vashti. The king gave a great banquet for all his officials and courtiers, "the banquet of Esther." He proclaimed a

> remission of taxes for the provinces and distributed gifts as befits a king. (Est. 2:15–18)

> When the virgins were assembled a second time, Mordecai sat in the palace gate. (Est. 2:19)

The king's beauty contest takes an absurdly long time. "When each girl's turn came to go to King Ahasuerus at the end of the twelve months' treatment prescribed for women (for that was the period spent on beautifying them: six months with oil of myrrh and six months with perfumes and women's cosmetics, and it was after that that the girl would go to the king), whatever she asked for would be given her to take with her from the harem to the king's palace" (2:12–13). Yet, it is difficult to gauge the passage of time because of pacing in the Book of Esther. Pacing in Esther will be discussed later, but at this juncture it is important to note that there are events that happen quickly – like the deposition of Vashti and Haman and the decision to annihilate the Jews. These acts do not allow justice to be served properly, or the consequences of each momentous decision to be processed. Other events seem to take a painfully long time and suck the reader into the inefficiencies of government, like the enactment that all husbands must rule in their own homes or the way in which the decree was communicated through Persia's postal system. Mordecai discovered a conspiracy and quickly brought it to Esther's attention. Ahasuerus was slow to acknowledge his contribution, the decision trapped in dusty pages of Persian annals. When Ahasuerus suddenly realized the mistake, he acted swiftly to reward Mordecai. This constant change of pacing connects events but also communicates the lack of constancy and stability one can expect in ancient Persia.

The reader does not know how long it took to gather women from Ahasuerus' empire of 127 provinces – possibly months or longer. We do know if each woman beautified herself for twelve months from the time of her arrival at the palace or if there was a general twelve-month period allotted in which to do so before the contest officially began. She was also allowed to bring with her any objects that would enhance her chances of winning, "whatever she asked for would be given her to take with her from the harem to the king's palace" (2:12). This has clear sexual connotations, what Alter calls "another fantastic detail of the fairy-tale plot":

> Each of these beautiful virgins spends a full year steeping herself in fragrant oil, perfumes, and unguents, so that when she comes to the bed of the king, her body will in every one of its cells be in a state of erotic attractiveness.[1]

The treatment of women has moved from the generalized requirement for wives to honor their husbands in chapter 1 to downright sexual abuse of them by chapter 2.

Some of the medieval exegetes tone down sexualized readings of what a woman could take with her upon visiting the king. Rashi on 2:12 interprets this to mean "any entertainment or type of music." Ibn Ezra on 2:12 explains that if any contestant needed something to enhance her chances but was not given it, she would become nervous and not be at her performative best. While Ibn Ezra offers us a glimpse into the possible inner state of these young women, it is Ibn Yahya on the verse who sensitizes us to what each really wanted: "She would ask the king for her life, such that even if she asked for something significant, it would be given to her." Every maiden who appeared was fighting for her very life. Every maiden had heard Vashti's story. Every maiden understood that all she had was one night of personal persuasion to win the king's heart or spend her life in the jail of a second harem: "She would go in the evening and leave in the morning for a second harem in the charge of Shaashgaz, the king's eunuch, guardian of the concubines. She would not go again to the king unless the king wanted her, when she would be summoned by name" (Est. 2:14). Every maiden wanted to make a lasting impression on a king overwhelmed by his glut of sexual interactions. The repeated sexual encounters of chapter 2 take on the ugly sheen of the king's many nights of drinking at his banquet in chapter 1, offering the reader a drumbeat of excess.

---

1. Robert Alter, *Strong as Death Is Love: The Song of Songs, Ruth, Esther, Jonah, Daniel* (New York: W. W. Norton & Company, 2015), 96.

Some later commentators who sought a positive view of the king had to justify, in some way, this clearly immoral contest. Ashkenazi on Esther 2:13, in defending the indefensible, observes that

> the king, because of his love of justice, allowed every woman any request when they came to the king.... On the way to the king's chambers from the women's harem [literally, "house"], she would pass stalls with cosmetics, perfumes and sellers of women's jewelry and trinkets and any request of the woman was granted... in this way, the gift induced her to come to the king's chambers with her consent, and she would not be considered raped...this bespeaks the praise of Esther that when she beheld the gift, since it would mean that she was not being raped [and was, therefore, going willingly], she avoided it and did not ask for a thing...[2]

Love of justice? This passage is not only a praise of Esther, who did not try to maximize her chances of being chosen, it is also an explicit praise of Ahasuerus, who is depicted as a lover of justice, even though the justice of inducing women into consent is blatantly immoral. Ahasuerus, according to this interpretation, was not raping these women, who were permanently condemned to harem life with the loss of virginity, but actually helping them win a place in his heart.

Many of us grew up imagining this ancient contest the way beauty pageants are currently conducted, with women paraded on a stage in swimsuits and evening gowns in front of a panel of judges. Because of this naive image, we do not pay careful enough attention to the absolute depravity of what the text tells us explicitly: these women were doused in perfumes and oils, heavily accessorized to be sexually compelling, deflowered, and then locked in a second harem by Shaashgaz, unlikely to be called for again and unable to go home.

The competition must have been brutal. Each woman must have experienced true terror. From the king's perspective, however, nothing could have been more amusing or distracting. Distracting the king from his momentary anger against Vashti is one thing. Having him be

2. Ashkenazi, *Yosef Lekaḥ* 2:13.

entangled in months, if not years, of sexual dalliance might derail him entirely from governance. One wonders if the court ministers advised this explicitly to keep him and his volatility away from the throne.

The Hidden Esther

Esther's victory in the beauty contest was unquestioned in the text but did raise some ethical questions among commentators. Many modern scholars question her pious reputation due to her participation in the selection process:

> The actual competition, to take place after a year of beauty treatments, is a sex contest, with the winner being whoever can most please the king during the night with him. Nothing but attractiveness to the king and sexual skills will, in this legendary account, determine who will become queen of Persia. In reality, political and familial factors would undoubtedly have played a major role in the selection. According to Herodotus, the queen of Persia had to come from one of seven noble families. In this story, the women are not even given the dignity of having political or familial significance, not even of having the importance as potential mothers of the heir to the throne. They are merely diversions for the king, truly sex objects.[3]

Not only are the women not given identities, but Esther, the only woman actually identified in chapter 2, is introduced as extremely attractive and an orphan; information that is repeated for emphasis. This would make her appear even more vulnerable and easily exploitable in the sexual arena. Fox comments that the sparseness of her introduction is "somewhat peculiar after the prolix description of the banquet hall."[4]

The Debate About Esther's Innocence

Despite – or because of – the obvious sexual nature of the contest, attempts were made to secure Esther's innocence, beginning in the

3. Fox, *Character and Ideology*, 28.
4. Ibid., 30.

Talmud, which depicts Esther fiercely resisting her summons: "Esther means 'hidden one,' since she remained hidden in her chambers."[5] Many medieval commentaries confirm this view, even though it is not apparent in the text. It is even suggested in some artistic portrayals of Esther. In the Renaissance period, for example, Esther is depicted in postures similar to the Virgin Mary. Cristelle L. Baskins comments on the depiction offered by Filippino Lippi, "Esther kneels obediently in front of Ahasuerus and, although the pendant sleeves partially obscure the position of her arms, Esther's submissive crossing of her breast foreshadows the Annunciation."[6] Even with this characterization, artists were often unsure of how to depict Esther given the sexual nature of the tale:

> Esther elicits contradictory readings of the female body; she both secures a typological parallel with the Virgin Mary, and simultaneously threatens typological coherence through a corporeal unruliness or autonomy portrayed as alien female sexuality. Esther's clandestine Jewish identity and flagrant sexuality as harem favorite and enchantress able to bend the royal will of her husband Ahasuerus, to overturn false decrees and to obtain revenge on the Persians generates anxieties of contagion that cannot be dispelled by a typological relation between Esther and the Virgin, nor naturalized with reference to the practice of apostate conversion and marriage.... The emphasis in the biblical text on the heroine's beauty and sexual potency undermines the retrospective juxtaposition of the Virgin Mary's conception and Esther's childlessness; the associations of the rape exceed prophetic history.[7]

Clearly, the ambiguity attached to Esther's behavior has been interpreted in different ways.

---

5. Megilla 13a.
6. Cristelle L. Baskins, "Typology, Sexuality, and the Renaissance Esther," in *Sexuality and Gender in Early Modern Europe: Institutions, Texts, Images*, ed. James Grantham Turner (Cambridge: Cambridge University Press), 44.
7. Ibid., 37–38.

Moore observed in *The Anchor Bible* that "it is not difficult to guess why many Christians were uncertain as to Esther's divine inspiration. The simple fact that some Jews were opposed to it would have been adequate reason for the tradition among some Christians that Esther was not canonical.... Moreover, apart from fasting, no distinctively religious practices or concepts seem to be in the canonical version."[8] One could take his remark a step further and conclude that details in the story are distinctly hedonistic and sexually permissive. Moore's own observations are that it has been found to be "excessively nationalistic and bloodthirsty but also somewhat anti-Gentile."[9] Paton's comments are even more caustic: "There is not one noble character in the book."[10] Other modern commentators are not as scathing but arrive at similar conclusions. Fuerst observes that

> there are varied judgments on Esther's morality at this point. Submitting to the pagan preparations and to the arms of the king, as well as concealing her Jewish identity, are unquestionably different from the strictness of Ezra or the stern, self-conscious piety and purity of Judith. Perhaps all that can and should be said is that many and various ways are the ways and rewards of God's children; it is essential to remember that the tradition, while enjoying the story of Esther, did not regard her or Mordecai as ethical or religious examples, and such diverse communities as Qumran and the Christian fathers gave little attention to the book.[11]

Here, Fuerst believes that Esther was seen as a figure of amusement and interest and not as a character of any religious dimension, even by traditional readers. It is no coincidence then that the same writer would see Esther as an avid participant in the king's contest:

8. Moore, *Esther: Anchor Bible*, vol. 7B (New York, Doubleday, 1971), xxxi–xxxii.
9. Ibid.
10. Paton, *International Critical Commentary*, 96.
11. Fuerst, *Cambridge Bible Commentary*, 50.

> Esther's pliability, or, as we may think, her cunning and willingness to subject her own desires to the advice of Hegai, are illustrated here. The Hebrew for "charmed all who saw her" is literally, "she gained favor in the eyes of all who saw her." The reader will keep in mind that at this point Esther's efforts are not spent to gain anything noble for her people, but to win the contest. And win she does![12]

This uncomfortable reading turns Esther into an opportunist who was willing to compromise her morals for the sake of besting others and securing an elevated place in Persian rather than Jewish society. One cannot even justify her acts at this stage for the sake of the greater Jewish good because Haman's decree had not yet been proposed.

Esther's participation takes a beating even after the contest victory. In commenting on the feast Ahasuerus made for Esther after choosing her, Moore writes that Esther, who partook of the delicacies, could not have adhered to Jewish dietary restrictions: "That Esther was able to conceal her Jewishness, that is, her adherence to the Jewish religion, clearly indicates that she did not observe all of the Jewish dietary laws."[13] This is contrary to the talmudic view of Esther 2:18 at the feast: "'And he changed her and her maidens'; [this means] he gave her Jewish food to eat."[14] Max Haller believes the Book of Esther reflects badly not only on Esther but on her entire people. The book showcases the "bad, even repulsive, features of this national character – above all the unrestrained vindictiveness, which with true Oriental savagery allows its imagination to swim and revel in the blood of the opponent."[15]

Rather than blame the king, Esther becomes the object of derision among these modern thinkers. Along with questions about Esther's ethical, sexual, and spiritual behavior comes a more recent critique from feminist writers. Esther, in some eyes, is submissive, deceptive, and a

---

12. Ibid., 55.
13. Moore, *Esther: Anchor Bible*, 22.
14. Megilla 13a.
15. Max Haller, "Esther," in *Die Schriften des Alten Testaments*, 2.III (Gottingen: Vandenhoeck & Ruprecht, 2nd ed., 1925), 328–29, as cited in Fox, "Three Esthers," 51.

woman whose good looks alone are the key to her success. She lacks religious depth, and her minor acts of heroism come essentially from her male guardian, Mordecai. This feeds into the view that essentially female characters in the Bible are able to wield power only through feminine wiles. "Celebrated or denigrated, the characters of deceptive women, which constitute the majority of female characters in the Bible, serve as an effective ideological tool that perpetuates the suspicion and distrust of women, and that validates women's subordination through discriminatory literary techniques."[16] Fox points out, however, in defense of Esther, "To describe a woman living a restrictive life in an Oriental court in which she gains goals through stratagems, rhetoric, manipulation, and ostensive pliancy is not to imply an ideology affirming this as the ideal female situation. That would be the case only if the author identified fully with the attitudes of all the males in the book and considered their society as exemplary."[17]

In contrast to these harsh criticisms, traditional commentators depict Esther as chaste, pious, and a leader who never acted out of self-interest. As with Mordecai, Ashkenazi presents the dilemmas of allegiance she faced and resolved and inserts moments of piety not evident from a literal reading.[18] As a repeated trope, for example, Ashkenazi staunchly defends Esther's role in the king's selection process and emphasizes Esther's attempts to hide herself:

> "And she was taken" means that she was taken with complete force. Esther qualified as one with both beauty and grace and was in Shushan [where the first collection of women was made] but was not taken until after the gathering of many maidens from other provinces who were brought to Shushan. This demonstrates the extent of her efforts to remain hidden. That is why

16. Esther Fuchs, "Who Is Hiding the Truth? Deceptive Women and Biblical Androcentrism," in *Feminist Perspectives on Biblical Scholarship*, ed. A. Y. Collins (Chico, CA: 1985), 143.
17. Fox, *Character and Ideology*, 207.
18. For more on one of the sexually compromising aspects of the text, see Barry D. Walfish, "Kosher Adultery?" 111–36.

> they called her Esther, because of the great efforts she made to secrete herself.[19]

This thought is continued in Ashkenazi's comments later in the chapter:

> Esther and Mordecai tried with all of their means to prevent Esther from being taken to the king. She hid and concealed herself so that she would not be captive to one who was not even from the Israelite nation. And when she was taken, she was taken with great force and anguish without anyone to rescue her, to the point where all the concealment and hiddenness prompted great fear and trembling in Mordecai lest the king, God forbid, become very angry.[20]

Not only was Esther forced to join the king's contest, but she hid herself until the last possible moment, endangering her health, according to Ashkenazi. When she was at last found, she submitted only with protest. Her attempts at concealment were so great that, consequently, Mordecai became frightened about the king's possible anger at Esther's resistance.

Her foreign name, Esther, was understood by the rabbis as a Hebrew form of the infinitive, *lehastir*, "to hide."[21] While her name may symbolically indicate the concealment of her identity in the king's palace, several midrashim mention that she acquired this name because she concealed herself physically to avoid being taken to the king's palace for this contest.[22] This reading of the story has also been corroborated by many modern scholars who see the descriptions of luxury and excess in the book not as an appeal for Esther or the Israelites but as a contrast, even comic at times, to Jewish values.[23]

---

19. Ashkenazi, *Yosef Lekaḥ* 2:8.
20. Ibid. 2:11.
21. For more on the meaning of her name, particularly the Persian or Greek "Esther," see A. S. Yehuda, "The Meaning of the Name Esther," *JRAS* (1946): 174–78.
22. See *Midrash Panim Aḥerim* in *Sifre de Aggadeta*, ed. S. Buber (Vilna: 1886), 63; *Yalkut Shimoni, Esther* 1053; and *Aggadat Esther* 2:2.
23. For more on the role of humor in the Bible, see the following essays in *On Humour and the Comic in the Hebrew Bible*, Bible and Literature Series (Sheffield: Sheffield

> Rather than see the party, the harem and royal power as a seductive lure for the Jew in the Diaspora, the book subtly laughs at these institutions and displays of false power. Esther is not seduced by pretensions of power but acts wisely and seeks means within her power to avoid being part of the court atmosphere in which the reader is meant to find humor.[24]

Nevertheless, it does not seem funny to us as readers. The entire chapter is riddled with moral dilemmas.

Marrying Out?

One of the questions some avoid and others confront with vigor is the nature of Esther's relationship with Ahasuerus and how she, a Jew, could have married and had relations with a man who was effectively a pagan. King or not, perhaps she should have refused, even at the point of death. Levenson suggests that since no language of marriage was used in chapter 2, the author of Esther may have wished to minimize the alarming nature of this relationship.[25] Suggesting that Esther and Ahasuerus were unmarried would have helped the rabbinic Sages who believed that Esther and Mordecai were actually married,[26] moving the "sin" from one of marrying out of the faith to an act of adultery. Walfish alerts us to the

---

Academic Press, 1990): F. Landy, "Humour as a Tool for Biblical Exegesis," 99–116; A. Brenner, "On the Semantic Field of Humor, Laughter and the Comic in the Old Testament," 39–58; Yehuda T. Radday, "On Missing the Humour in the Bible: An Introduction," 21–38.

24. Theodor H. Gaster, "Esther 1:22," *JBL* 69, no. 4 (December 1950): 381.
25. Levenson, *Esther*, 62.
26. Megilla 13a. One of the well-known ironies of this controversial discussion is that the Sages' version of the narrative had Esther married to Mordecai to avoid the problem of any potential intimacy between an uncle and niece living in the same quarters. To avoid any suspicions of impropriety, the Sages created greater impropriety by making Esther a potential adulteress. They sought a way out of this problem by suggesting that Esther is "only land" – a passive recipient of the king's sexual advances and not an initiator of any of their liaisons. See Sanhedrin 74a–b and *Tosafot*, ad loc. R. Abba makes a distinction in this categorization between those who cohabit for the sake of pleasure and those who do so to challenge Judaism's fundamental principles. Had Esther gone willingly to Ahasuerus, she would have been forbidden to Mordecai (Megilla 15a).

fact that the Septuagint also translates *bat*, "daughter," as *bayit*, "wife."[27] Ibn Yahya expands upon the talmudic reading:

> And as our Sages, of blessed memory [said]: Do not read "for a daughter" but rather "for a wife," which is to say, because she was an orphan with no father and mother, and there was no one to watch her and take pity on her, Mordecai agreed to take her for his wife. For he had the right of redemption and there was no redeemer beside him[28]especially since she was perfect and beautiful.[29]

Ibn Yahya tries hard – some might argue a bit too hard – to straddle the conflicting positions by suggesting that Mordecai married Esther purely out of compassion; yet, he undermines this very reading by suggesting that she was perfect and beautiful, thus indicating that marrying her would hardly be an act of compassion. Esther was more of a prize than a charity case. Had Ahasuerus never officially married Esther, this would downgrade the problem but not eliminate it altogether. Rashi, in both his commentary on Esther 4:16 and on the talmudic passage that advances this notion of Esther and Mordecai's marriage, suggests that when Esther cried out, "If I perish, I perish," she meant that when she was taken to the king's chambers, she would be lost (the literal translation of *avadeti*) to Mordecai, unable in Jewish law to sleep with him again.[30]

The Talmud offers a disturbing visual to convey the great lengths Esther went to in order to preserve her marriage while under the duress of her situation: "She would stand up from the bosom of Ahasuerus,

27. The linguistic "house" as "wife" appears in Mishna Yoma 1:1 as an explication of Lev. 16:6 and is used this way in Megilla 13a. Walfish discusses the verb *l-k-ḥ* in 2:7, which is commonly translated as "adopt," and its use as a term of marriage throughout the Hebrew Bible, from Gen. 25:20 all the way through II Chr. 11:20 and many other examples in between ("Kosher Adultery?" 114). Fox suggests that we may read this as an interesting combination of adopting and marrying, which was part of an ancient Near Eastern practice, whereby a man adopts a girl on condition that he may marry her when she reaches puberty. See Fox, *Character and Ideology*, 30, 275–76.
28. Language adapted from Ruth 4.
29. Ibn Yahya on 2:1, as translated by Walfish in "Kosher Adultery?" 126 fn 45.
30. Megilla 13b.

immerse herself, and sit down in the bosom of Mordecai."[31] This reading, passed down from one sage to another, highlighted immersion in a ritual bath that would shower this pagan from her skin and prepare her to confront her true love and protector. But, to the modern reader, it simply reinforces the incongruity of her situation, sexualizing her in either domain. The rabbis also understood that they had to smooth out another problem with this reading, namely, that the king would have accepted non-virgins in his contest. The king should not have been interested in such women, but the Sages described him as a man of such voracious and indiscriminating appetites that he would have made little distinction. In 2:17, the word *nashim*, "women," is used as is the term *betulot*, "virgins," leading R. Ḥelbo, ad loc., to the conclusion that the king "brought married women before him as well."

Rashi discusses Esther's focus on the greater good, and her courage in the face of this odd arrangement, commenting on the verse "Every single day Mordecai would walk about in front of the court of the harem, to learn how Esther was faring and what was happening to her" (Est. 2:11). Rashi explains that "Mordecai [said to himself], 'This righteous woman has been taken to a gentile's bed only in order to rise and save Israel.' He [Mordecai] therefore repeatedly went around to find out what would be her fate."[32] What exactly was Mordecai trying to find out in 2:11? He knew that Esther was destined to do something remarkable for her people, so he paced about waiting for her to actualize her leadership. Rashi, in essence, justifies her sleeping with the king as a wrongdoing "for the sake of Heaven," or the greater collective good.[33]

The Second Harem

Herodotus, ancient historian of the fifth century BCE, had unkind words about the way Persians treated their wives: "A man's wives would go to his bed in rotation."[34] While we cannot support or deny the veracity of this

31. Ibid.
32. Rashi bases himself on Esther Rabba 6:6.
33. For more on *gedola aveira lishmah*, see Nazir 23a–b and Horayot 10b.
34. *Herodotus*, vol. 3, trans. A. D. Godley (Cambridge, MA: Harvard University Press, 1924), 69.

observation, it certainly would explain events of the second chapter, particularly the troubling second harem. The Talmud shares its understanding of Ahasuerus' objectification of women that was triggered by drink:

> When the nations of the world eat and drink, they begin only with words of licentiousness. So, too, the feast of that wicked man. Some said, "The Median women are beautiful." Others said, "The Persian women are beautiful." Ahasuerus said to them, "The vessel that I use is neither Median nor Persian, but rather Chaldean. Do you wish to see her?" They said to him, "Yes, provided that she is naked."[35]

We can imagine the scene. Men discussing women as decorative ornaments, disposable playthings from different, even exotic, places. Perhaps because of this, the very same page of Talmud contrasts this contest to another selection of virgins. King David's ministers wanted to provide a virgin for his bed in the king's old age (to warm him [I Kings 1]) and the ministers of Ahasuerus sought a prize virgin for him. One difference the Talmud identified was the parents' reaction in each case:

> "In everything, a prudent man acts with knowledge" (Prov. 13:16). This refers to David, as it is written, "And his servants said to him, 'Let there be sought for my lord the king a young virgin'" (I Kings 1:2). Whoever had a daughter brought her to him. "But a fool unfolds his folly" (Prov. 13:16). This is Ahasuerus, as it is written, "And let the king appoint officers." Whoever had a daughter hid her from him.[36]

The Sages had a problem on their hands. How could they point to the immorality of a Persian king when a Jewish king had his own selection process of virgins also conceived and conducted by his ministers? The biblical text makes explicit that David, whose early years displayed foolish and immoral judgments in the sexual arena, repented and did not

35. Megilla 12b.
36. Ibid.

sleep with the woman chosen: "The girl was exceedingly beautiful. She became the king's attendant and waited upon him; but the king was not intimate with her" (I Kings 1:4). Interestingly, this verse is not cited in the Talmud to explain David's behavior. Instead the talmudic passage narrows in on the feelings of parents, who were happy to bring their daughters to David but hid them anxiously from Ahasuerus, a detail not mentioned in either original text.

Elizabeth Groves concludes her comprehensive analysis of 2:14 with an empathic observation related to the nature of the search and the future that awaited these young women:

> It is questionable whether any luxury or prestige they may have enjoyed there made up for their loss.... In addition to the loss which the girls experienced, of their virginity and of any future sexual pleasure with the king or any other man, one cannot escape the sense of bereavement of their families, who would never see the grandchildren that might have been theirs. The blessings of children, grandchildren and subsequent generations of descendants was of enormous importance in ancient cultures. The king's sexual indulgence represented a 'theft' of sorts, which affected the girls' families even into future generations.[37]

The opulence of the royal life was no compensation for the immense loss each young woman and each family experienced as a result of this vacuous pageant.

Another Contest?

Caught up in the pageantry of Esther's triumph, it is easy to pass over a brief and anti-climactic verse: "When the virgins were assembled a second time, Mordecai sat in the palace gate" (Est. 2:19). In the next chapter, we will explore Mordecai's role in this verse, but for now our attention remains on the first half. The need to gather virgins a second time is confusing. The contest was over. Esther had already been cho-

37. Elizabeth Groves, "Double Take: Another Look at the Second Gathering of Virgins in Esther 2.19a," in *The Book of Esther in Modern Research*, 103.

sen, and Vashti was replaced. Why bother with this detail? This verse is so unclear that it inspired one scholar's observation that Esther 2:19 is "highly problematic, so difficult to explain that scholars pull their hair out over it, and some eventually give up in despair and dismiss it entirely."[38] Moore notes that it "is one of the most difficult verses in all of Esther."[39]

A number of modern commentators attempted their own interpretations with varying degrees of success. One contemporary writer with a background in theater, who has performed a play based on the Book of Esther, suggests that this narrative turn is included to wake up the audience to the immorality of events:

> When I dramatize Esther, I deliver the line, "At a second gathering of virgins," looking at the king's throne, with the cold anger and disgust of the Persian populace who had now been robbed of their daughters twice.... Its brevity does not allow the audience to dwell on the shock, merely to sit up in surprise and do a double-take. "Hold on – what? A second gathering of virgins? But... wait a minute... why?" And then the narration quickly moves on. The clause serves to shake the audience awake.[40]

Robert Gordis suggests that the primary purpose of the second gathering of virgins was to make Esther stand out at her coronation as the "obvious winner beyond compare, as a way to highlight Esther's gentle beauty, which had won the king's love."[41] His reading fails to convince; she was obviously beautiful, a fact established because she was chosen as queen. Once chosen, there should have been no need for others. Moore suggests that this second gathering was of the women who arrived late in Shushan, after Esther was already coronated, hoping for a chance to compete.[42] Groves challenges this reading because the preparation time was at least twelve months, long enough, we assume, for all of the maidens

38. Ibid., 91. Groves, after looking at a variety of commentaries, concludes that they "almost unanimously confirmed this view" (p. 91).
39. Moore, *Esther: A New Translation*, 29.
40. Groves, "Double Take," 109.
41. Gordis, *Megillat Esther*, 30.
42. Moore, *Esther: A New Translation*, 30.

who wished to participate to get there, especially given the desire of the officials to please the king and move quickly with their plan.[43] Separately, it would seem an odd and unnecessary detail to include in a story so masterfully crafted – like a hasty mention of the "leftovers."

Fox believes these women were the ones gathered to the second house or harem overseen by Shaashgaz. In other words, these were the same women who had slept with the king and lost to Esther. When Esther was chosen, these women were then gathered together, escorted, and stewarded by a second royal eunuch to a place in the harem where they were likely to live out their lives in the palace with only the slimmest chance of ever being summoned to sleep with the king again.[44] The fact that they were called virgins but were not virgins may have been a minor slip.[45] However, one reading suggests that it was indeed a second harem. If the women were the same as those in the first harem, the text would have used the definite article with the word "virgins," rendering it *habetulot* in Hebrew, referring to the very same maidens who appeared earlier in the story.[46]

Levenson notes that the second gathering makes no appearance in the Greek versions of Esther, and suggests that it may be an "instance of textual garbling."[47] He also posits that this second gathering may have been the way Esther's ladies-in-waiting were chosen; these were the women who appear in chapter 4 and were commanded to fast with her.[48] This is plausible, since many secondary characters appear in the book; receiving a coterie of ladies-in-waiting upon her coronation would make Esther a royal woman of note. This explanation still begs the question: Was this detail necessary enough to merit inclusion in the book?

According to Amos Hacham, the second gathering may have been a chance for these women to appear at a women's banquet in Esther's honor, as a highly imaginative consolation prize.[49] He cites a biblical

43. Groves, "Double Take," 96.
44. Fox, *Character and Ideology*, 38; see also 276–77.
45. Ibid.
46. See Groves, "Double Take," 95 and footnotes 8 and 9 there.
47. Levenson, *Esther*, 63.
48. Ibid.
49. Amos Hacham, *Daat Mikra: Esther* (Jerusalem: Mossad HaRav Kook, 1973), 19.

prooftext from Song of Songs 3:11, where maidens were gathered to gaze upon King Solomon on his wedding day. Alternatively, he suggests that while the king may have rejected other women as queen, these women were gathered to select those who would serve the queen, a recycling of purpose, as it were, as reflected in Psalms: "The royal princess, her dress embroidered with golden mountings, is led inside to the king; maidens in her train, her companions, are presented to you. They are led in with joy and gladness; they enter the palace of the king" (Ps. 45:15–16).

Groves mentions the possibility that these women may have been gathered for a women's banquet in Esther's honor, much the way Vashti held a separate party the chapter before.[50] She is not convinced by this answer and instead offers a more compelling reading of the verse as a

> signal, a reminder, to the audience that Esther's position of influence over King Ahasuerus was tenuous. In combination with other hints imbedded in the text, 2.19a serves to make the audience uncomfortably aware that Ahasuerus did not regard Esther with the boundless esteem that would be necessary to outweigh his rage at her direct defiance of Persian law. The odds of her surviving the trip to his throne room, much less of obtaining the large favor she intended to ask, were heavily stacked against her.[51]

In other words, this verse primed Esther and the reader to understand that one wrong move on her part would bring the same fate as Vashti's, but this time a whole stable of beautiful women were prepared and ready to take her place instantaneously. "Should there be any wavering in the king's mind, it would take nothing for the appealing prospect of sampling a new batch of sweet young things to push him over the edge into a judgment against Esther."[52] Winning meant little in a contest that could take place again and again. It certainly builds suspense for the attentive reader, hoping Esther would overcome the odds and not only win but sustain her position.

---

50. Groves, "Double Take," 96.
51. Ibid., 92.
52. Ibid., 108.

Commitment Issues

While some of these readings cohere with the overall texture of the story, no writer captures the role of the second harem better than the nineteenth-century scholar Paulus Cassel, who mentions the struggles others have with a verse which seems straightforward to him and also of great importance to the story:

> Ahashverosh indeed loved Esther, but of the tyrannical Persian lust for women he had not given up a particle. The temptation to continually acquire new wives was as strong with him as ever, and he could not subdue his sensual infirmities and love of extravagance. He did not issue a decree to recall and annul his former one for the seeking out of women, although his heart had found satisfaction in Esther. The narrator intentionally brings out the contrast. "Look," says he, "just now the king has shown that he loved Esther above all women, and yet other women are so soon sought!".... Scarcely had the feast of Esther taken place, when they began to collect virgins; and so apparently the power of the new queen had already begun to decline.[53]

Ahasuerus never expected one woman, even his momentary favorite, to get in the way of long-entrenched habits of debauchery common to his position and status. And why would he? If Vashti could be replaced then so could Esther, if not out of malice then out of boredom. Which is worse matters little. Ahasuerus made explicit in law and personal behavior that women were powerless, and if they dared exhibit any subversive behaviors, they could be eliminated without recourse. No woman expected to be treated any differently. Only one outright refused.

Groves believes that the rapacity of Ahasuerus' lust combined with his preternatural need for submission, authority, and honor can explain both the fate of Vashti in the beginning of the book and Haman's undoing later: "Haman's audacity in falling on Esther's couch was an irreparable affront *to the king* [her italics]. What happened to women

53. Paulus Cassel, *An Explanatory Commentary on Esther* (Edinburgh: T & T Clark, 1988), 77–78.

mattered only in so far as it honored or shamed the men to whom they belonged."[54] In this regard, chapter 2 sets the groundwork for chapter 7. By bringing us into the harem, so to speak, the author has exposed us to a rapacious sexual hunger and a systematic objectification of women so that later when one such royal property, Queen Esther, is compromised, it is a direct insult to the king's authority.

Esther's real strength was that she refused to be only an object of desire. She took nothing with her but her charm, and it worked: "She won his grace and favor" (Est. 2:17). Beauty alone is deceitful. Beauty in combination with elegance and guidance subverted the dominant paradigm and ultimately gave Esther a voice in an otherwise voiceless role.

54. Groves, "Double Take," 100.

Chapter Three

Ignoring Mordecai, Promoting Haman

Mordecai's Dangerous Decision

Haman's Rage and Revenge

Ignoring Mordecai, Promoting Haman

> At that time, when Mordecai was sitting in the palace gate, Bigthan and Teresh, two of the king's eunuchs who guarded the threshold, became angry, and plotted to do away with King Ahasuerus. Mordecai learned of it and told it to Queen Esther, and Esther reported it to the king in Mordecai's name. The matter was investigated and found to be so, and the two were hanged on the gallows. This was recorded in the book of annals at the instance of the king. (Est. 2:21–23)

> Some time afterward, King Ahasuerus promoted Haman son of Hammedatha the Agagite; he advanced him and seated him higher than any of his fellow officials. (Est. 3:1)

The end of chapter 2 and the beginning of chapter 3 should be read as one continuous and related block of verses that introduce the inevitable tension between Mordecai and Haman. On a surface level, the tension is related to the promotion that Mordecai should have received but went instead to Haman. On a deeper level, this mistake highlights the injustice inherent in Ahasuerus' kingdom. Bible readers often make a mental stop when a chapter ends, naturally disconnecting the relationship between one chapter's last verse and the following chapter's first verse. Scrolls have no lines and chapters, just slight space indicators. If we ignore chapter divisions, we can see more clearly the juxtaposition of Mordecai's loyalty unrewarded and Haman's promotion unexplained.

Chapter 1 prepares readers for Ahasuerus' over-reliance on the advice of others, and chapter 2 offers readers an insight into Ahasuerus' appetites that distract him from good decision making. Therefore, the king's future rash decisions at the hand of Haman offer no real surprise.

Mordecai and the Second Harem

Mordecai first appears at the king's gate at the end of chapter 2, right before Esther was told not to reveal her nationality: "When the virgins were assembled a second time, Mordecai sat in the palace gate. Esther still did not reveal her kindred or her people, as Mordecai had instructed her; for Esther obeyed Mordecai's bidding, as she had done when she was under his tutelage" (Est. 2:19–20). By the time Mordecai appeared at the king's gate, Esther had already been chosen, feted, and publicly declared queen, with a tax remission given across the empire.

This link between the second gathering of women and Mordecai's presence is puzzling. Fox suggests that the time when the women who slept with the king were moved to the second harem under Shaashgaz coincided with the time that Mordecai joined government service and was appointed to guard the king's gate.[1]

According to Hacham the connection between the second harem and Mordecai's placement may not be as elusive as assumed. If the gathering of a second harem was an affirmation on the king's part of his consort choice, then even among the remaining maidens with whom the king had not yet slept, Esther surfaced again as the clear winner. Mordecai then appeared for this second round of contestants to give his ward a competitive advantage by telling her *not* to reveal her religious/ethnic background. He may have also been there, lurking in the background, to protect his niece and secure whatever benefits he could for her so that she stayed in place despite this second competition. If Fox is correct, then both Esther and Mordecai achieved royal placement at about the same time, offering geographic proximity and tightening their ability

1. Fox, *Character and Ideology*, 38.

to communicate, even if they had to do so via an intermediary. Fox contends that Mordecai's constant presence in the palace gave him the opportunity to communicate with Esther and to uncover the assassination plot.[2] By contrast, Paton believes Mordecai was merely an "idler" at the gate, without an official role. In this reading, Mordecai's meddling presence exposed him to the assassination plot but provided him no official mechanism to forestall it. He therefore had to communicate it to Esther in order to save Ahasuerus' life.

Joseph Kara created a coherent narrative context for this odd amalgamation of information, connecting the second harem, Mordecai's gate placement, and Esther's concealment of her identity:

> When Ahasuerus saw that even after he made her queen she refused to reveal her people or her kindred, he thought that perhaps she came from a family of slaves or one of lowly birth and was not worthy of the throne. He said to himself, "I will gather virgins a second time. Perhaps I will find among them one of royal lineage even prettier than this one, and I will remove Esther and make her queen instead." Therefore, it says "and when virgins were assembled a second time, Mordecai was sitting in the palace gate." This means that even though Esther saw what Ahasuerus was doing and that her position was in danger, nevertheless, she "did not reveal her kindred or her people." [Furthermore,] even though she saw that Mordecai was so important in the king's eyes that he appointed him to sit at the king's gate, as is the rule for officers who serve the throne and guard the king, and it would be an honor for her, not a shame, if she would tell the king how they were related, for Mordecai was descended from the house of Saul, and Esther, his niece, was worthy of the throne [still she refused].[3]

In this interpretation, Esther had a decision to make about her position: Would she compromise her chance of remaining queen because she

2. Ibid., 39.
3. Joseph Kara on Esther 3:90, as translated by Walfish, *Esther in Medieval Garb*, 66.

withheld her identity at the advice of her uncle or not? She chose to be loyal to her uncle rather than satisfy the desire of her new husband, even though her revelation would have made her potentially more attractive to the king. This interpretation is unlike those that suggest the revelation would have made her a less compelling contestant, eliciting a larger identity question of whether or not one's Jewishness was conceived of as an asset or a deterrent. Different exegetes in different eras had various opinions based on their respective historical and cultural contexts.

Threat at the King's Gate

If Mordecai was at the king's gate to find out about Esther's condition, he may have worried why the king assembled a second harem after already choosing a wife. The harem, which shunted women away, neatly contrasts with Mordecai's place at the gate. They could not get out, and he could not get in. By chance, Mordecai overheard information related to the king's future. The irony is that the very ones who were guarding the door provided not protection but threat. Craig renders their title in English "threshold guards,"[4] making particularly pronounced the fact that in this in-between space, they were undermining the very function they were supposed to perform. Like Mordecai, Bigthan's and Teresh's presence at the king's gate gave them crucial access to the king's whereabouts and activities, but instead of doing their jobs to prevent others from accessing Ahasuerus, they used their own access to threaten the king's life. Greenstein suggests that the Persians who were supposed to support the king rarely fulfilled their roles. While he does not single out Bigthan and Teresh, they follow the pattern he identifies:

> In each instance, an ethnic Persian had disappointed the king – first, his wife, Vashti, then his viceroy Haman. When the king overcame his exaggerated rage – as related in the parallel verses – he elevated Jewish counterparts who pleased him, Esther and Mordekhai. This dynamic is not marginal but cuts straight to the core meaning of the story: Jews are not bad but good for Persia.[5]

4. Craig, *Reading Esther*, 73.
5. Edward L. Greenstein, "The Scroll of Esther," *Fiction* 9, no. 3 (1990): 55.

After receiving no reward, Mordecai realized that the Jews would have to do more than prevent an assassination to gain Ahasuerus' notice. Perhaps had Mordecai let Esther reveal her birthright from the outset, in the very same chapter where Mordecai stopped Bigthan and Teresh, the king would have acknowledged Jewish loyalty and labeled Haman's decree preposterous from the beginning. Transparency may have spared much of the anguish and the eventual deaths of many, many Persians. Because of his role at the king's gate, Mordecai helped reveal a secret not kept carefully enough and conceal a secret that may have needed to be told.

An Unjust Promotion

In contrast to Mordecai's good deeds, stewardship, and loyalty to the king, we meet Haman in chapter 3 with no prior introduction. The first verse in the chapter uses three strong verbs to communicate Haman's promotion: "Sometime afterward, King Ahasuerus *promoted* Haman son of Hammedatha the Agagite; he *advanced* him and *seated* him higher than any of his fellow officials." In Persian courts, the king sat on a throne above his government ministers. One midrash explains that Haman was elevated when the king literally put him above his colleagues.[6] Sitting higher up and closer to the king's seat indicated the power structure to all in the king's chamber and sent a message to all that the king especially favored one minister. At the gate, Mordecai was not close at all. His position was strategic, allowing him to see and hear the goings-on inside and outside the royal compound, but it was a difficult place to get the king's attention. In one midrash, the rabbis allude to the pernicious nature of Haman's promotion, suggesting that the expression "to elevate him" references the fifty-cubits-high gallows Haman constructed from which he would one day be hanged.[7] His early and visible elevation foreshadows a different kind of public rise.

Oddly, the first two dramatic chapters, filled with ministerial advice, make no mention of Haman. His name did not appear in the list of ministers in chapter 1, and he wasn't involved in the pageant proceedings. The book records no explanation of his promotion. The Sages

6. *Yalkut Shimoni, Esther* 1053.
7. *Midrash Shoḥer Tov* 13:3.

stepped into this lacuna with a suggestion that has become commonly assumed: Memucan is Haman.[8] This association is not far-fetched because Memucan is mentioned first on the king's list of advisors (Est. 1:1), is mentioned once more (albeit last) in a list of his closest advisors (Est. 1:14), gave direct advice to Ahasuerus about Vashti's punishment (Est. 1:18), and clearly had the king's ear when recommending that all men in the kingdom enjoy exclusive rule in their homes (Est. 1:21). Finally, he pushed Ahasuerus to act in ways that would eventually be counter to the king's best interests. The association of the two is character based and not literal. If Memucan was not Haman, then Haman was a character *like* Memucan, the same in spirit if not in person.

The absence of reason for Haman's promotion may have signaled the absence of reason associated with Haman's irrational desire to destroy the Jews. Or perhaps the missing explanation implies that he did not contribute in any meaningful way to the king's political well-being, a detail that can be established retrospectively if not prospectively. It is most likely that shrewd political alliances fueled Haman's meteoric rise. This, too, is suggested in an aggadic quip that could easily be dismissed for its brevity: "Where is there an allusion to Haman in the Torah? *Hamin ha'etz,* 'Have you eaten from the tree of knowledge?' (Gen. 3:11)."[9] A symbolic alliance between the snake in the Garden of Eden and Haman is a delicious association and a telling one. The snake presented itself as wise and innocent, masking a voice of cunning and deceit. The snake was highly persuasive and ultimately destructive. Haman, like the snake in Genesis, was not a nuanced character; he had no redeeming features or positive contributions. The Talmud regarded him as more arrogant than Ahasuerus, whose desire to be popular and loved communicated an oafish generosity but a generosity nonetheless.[10]

If Haman was consistently evil, then Mordecai, another static character, was consistently good and loyal, observant and steady amid courtiers who were self-serving, impulsive, arbitrary, and thoughtless. Mordecai was patient, some might claim overly so, and strategic. These

8. Megilla 12b.
9. Ḥullin 139b.
10. Megilla 15a.

characteristics are embodied in a detail throughout the scroll. Mordecai is almost always seated at the king's gate, just as he was when he overheard two courtiers plot to kill Ahasuerus. "At that time, when Mordecai was sitting in the palace gate, Bigthan and Teresh, two of the king's eunuchs who guarded the threshold, became angry, and plotted to do away with King Ahasuerus" (Est. 2:21). "At that time" suggests that Mordecai happened to be in the right place at the right time to protect the king against these assassins. Yet Mordecai is almost always at the king's gate (2:19, 5:13, 6:10). Craig invites us to compare this with Haman's behavior: "In contrast to Mordecai, Haman is described as sitting only on one occasion – the scene where he and the king sit down for a celebratory drink just after the pogrom edict is dispatched to the provinces (3:15)."[11] Craig sees significance in this contrast: "Haman is a plotter, a contriver, and a man of action who is frequently on his feet."[12] The disparity between sitting and moving is highlighted in another biblical parallel of archetypes Esau and Jacob: "When the boys grew up, Esau became a skillful hunter, a man of the outdoors, but Jacob was a mild man who sat in tents" (Gen. 25:27). The hunter is always on the move. The pious man is content to sit in place. The Hebrew infinitive *lashevet*, "to sit," is related to the Hebrew expression for achieving peace and equilibrium: *yishuv hadaat*. Mordecai sat while Haman stood.

Danger Averted

Chapter 2 ends with an assassination attempt that Mordecai thwarted, providing ample proof that Mordecai is the just choice for promotion. He is, however, overlooked in favor of a courtier who demonstrates no reason for his governmental upgrade. The Talmud credits Mordecai's knowledge of the conspiracy to a facility with seventy languages as a member of the Sanhedrin and elsewhere accorded him prophetic status.[13] As a judge, Mordecai was expected to know multiple languages, rather than rely on translation, in order to be a better judge and advocate.[14]

11. Craig, *Reading Esther*, 71.
12. Ibid.
13. See Megilla 10b, 13a, 15a; Menaḥot 64b–65a; Ḥullin 139b.
14. Sanhedrin 17a.

The Sages who characterized Mordecai thus must have believed that the only reason he was able to eavesdrop on Bigthan and Teresh was that the stewards assumed Mordecai did not speak Persian, or whatever language in which they devised their scheme.

We are told of the plot to kill the king to explain Mordecai's eventual promotion, but there may be two other cogent reasons for its early inclusion in the book. First, it helps readers understand that despite Ahasuerus' focus on pleasing his subjects, many of them were not pleased with him: "Two of the king's eunuchs who guarded the threshold became angry," angry enough to commit murder. We do not know what induced this anger, but its placement right after the contest suggests that it could have been stirred by the yearlong pageant. The king, so busy with his narcissistic pleasures, was not ruling responsibly. Bigthan and Teresh may have had daughters trapped in the king's second harem whom they would never see again. They may have liked Vashti, disliked Esther, or understood that a false move in the royal palace might result in death and so planned to eliminate the threat. Unlike Haman's obvious desire to replace the king, these courtiers did not seek his position. They simply did not want Ahasuerus to rule over them. A second reason to include this mutiny is that it sheds light on the political intrigues lurking at every turn of the book. Haman's attempt to rid the empire of the Jewish people is less outlandish given that murder was a reasonable response to anger. There is no greater control than to have power to determine someone else's future existence. If the book is about power gone awry, little illustrates this like murder. Conspiracy to murder is a way to recalibrate or gain control.

This chapter affords a glimpse into palace life that primarily illustrates the trustworthiness of Mordecai, a characteristic which will be highly prized later in the book. As a palace servant, this act alone should have ensured Mordecai's future in the court. The fact that he went initially unrewarded without complaint becomes yet another endearing affirmation of his loyalty, the insignia of every worthy courtier. It also highlights the injustice baked into political life.

Mordecai's Dangerous Decision

> All the king's courtiers in the palace gate knelt and bowed low to Haman, for such was the king's order concerning him; but Mordecai would not kneel or bow low.
>
> Then the king's courtiers who were in the palace gate said to Mordecai, "Why do you disobey the king's order?" When they spoke to him day after day and he would not listen to them, they told Haman, in order to see whether Mordecai's resolve would prevail; for he had explained to them that he was a Jew. (Est. 3:2–4)

Many exegetes are understandably confused by Mordecai's refusal to bow. There is apt biblical precedent for bowing to or acknowledging a pagan or gentile authority figure. In Genesis 47, a verse twice mentions that Jacob acknowledged Pharaoh when they met: "Joseph then brought his father Jacob and presented him to Pharaoh; and Jacob greeted Pharaoh" (Gen. 47:7).[1] We are not sure what took place in this encounter,

1. For more on this story and the role of royal formalities, see Erica Brown, "Strange Words Between Strangers," in *Torah of the Mothers: Contemporary Jewish Women Read Classical Jewish Texts*, ed. Ora Wiskind Elper and Susan Handelman (Jerusalem: Urim Publications, 2000), 244–61.

but Rashi on 47:7 writes: "This was a greeting of peace, as is usual in the case of all who are granted an interview with kings on occasion." Rabbi David Kimhi (Radak, 1160–1235) on 47:7 directs readers to II Kings 4:29, another incident of acknowledging kings when in their presence. He can find no reason why such an encounter was included in the Jacob narratives if it was not meant to be more than a verbal or physical nod to authority. He believed it signified standard royal protocol.

Elias Bickerman suggests that Mordecai refused to bow to Haman because Haman received a promotion for doing nothing, while Mordecai was overlooked after saving the king's very life. Mordecai, in this reading, was "fighting for his honor." Honor was so consequential to Mordecai, according to Bickerman, that the courtier put his life at risk in protest: "A man from whom the due reward is withheld by the king protests even if it would cost him his life."[2] Gestures, Bickerman writes, were an important part of court protocol and indicated Persian power structures.

This reading, however, does not accord with Mordecai's repeated appearance at the king's gate even after the ludicrous episode of Haman dragging a horse through the city, parading Mordecai in a very visible and unwanted tribute. Mordecai returned to the gate, seemingly nonplussed by the fanfare. He did not leverage this opportunity to seek political power or any form of self-aggrandizement. He was unaffected and, it seems, unimpressed. This is not the behavior of a man who covets honor and would sacrifice his life to demand it. If he failed to give Haman honor because he believed a promotion was rightly his and wrongly assigned, Mordecai need only make this gesture in the king's presence to signal that an injustice had occurred. Mordecai could have explained as much to the courtiers who told him he was transgressing the king's orders (Est. 3:3–4). Instead Mordecai told them he was a Jew, suggesting that it was the revulsion of Haman's hatred that generated Mordecai's response. He was able to spot a threat to both his people and his king. Who better to know a threat to the king's power and position than one who had already revealed a murderous conspiracy? By not bowing to Haman, Mordecai was not drawing attention to himself but putting Haman in the glare of a spotlight so bright than even a dim-witted king

2. Bickerman, *Four Strange Books of the Bible*, 179–80.

would one day take notice and redeem the situation. That Ahasuerus failed to see Haman's character for what it was continued to be true to the very end of Haman's life. Ironically, Ahasuerus did not have Haman killed for something he did do but for something he had no pretension of doing, namely sleeping with Esther on her couch.

There was rabbinic discomfort at the thought that Mordecai, a loyal courtier, would be dismissive of someone appointed and favored by the king. In an almost absurd attempt to understand Mordecai's mindset, Ashkenazi suggests that as a Jew, Mordecai was not counted among the king's official servants and that he was trying to publicize this widely to all: "Although the rule of the king was to bow and prostrate oneself to him, it extended only to those who fulfilled two conditions: they were servants of the king, and they stood at the king's gate.... According to this, Mordecai honored Haman as other officials did by rising and praising but not with bowing and prostration."[3] But far from resolving the tensions inherent in Mordecai's decision, Ashkenazi aggravates them. If this was simply a matter of technicalities, Mordecai could have just bowed through gritted teeth and been done with it.

The Sages of the Talmud understood Mordecai's response differently. It was inconceivable to them that Mordecai would not obey royal orders unless a value far greater than being a good citizen was at issue. Josephus suggests that Haman demanded that Mordecai pay homage to a person, something that, according to him, was prohibited by Jewish law.[4] Honor can be given only to God. Yet, this does not accord with Genesis, chapter 47, when Jacob greeted Pharaoh, or the later rabbinic law to confer blessings upon gentile rulers and recite a prayer weekly in synagogue following the prescription of Jeremiah.[5]

A popular midrashic reading suggests something darker: Mordecai refused to bow because Haman had an idol on his person.[6] The

---

3. Ashkenazi, *Yosef Lekaḥ* 3:2.
4. Josephus, *Antiquities* 11:6. See also Louis H. Feldman, "Hellenizations in Josephus' Version of Esther," *Transactions and Proceedings of the American Philological Association* 101 (1970): 143–70.
5. "And seek the welfare of the city to which I have exiled you and pray to the Lord in its behalf; for in its prosperity you shall prosper" (Jer. 29:7). See also *Pirkei Avot* 3:2.
6. See Rashi on Est. 3:4: "Mordecai would never prostrate himself because he is a Jew

text of this midrash had an outsized influence on readers of Esther and has come to shape the way the story is understood, even down to the minutiae of the historical record:

> When his servants told him [Haman] that Mordecai refused to kneel, Haman remarked that Mordecai's ancestors, Jacob, Rachel, and their children, had prostrated themselves before Esau, Haman's ancestor. Upon hearing Haman's remark, Mordecai replied that he was a descendant of Benjamin, who was born after Jacob's meeting with Esau, and who had thus never prostrated himself before Esau.[7]

In this strange passage, Haman studied Mordecai's ancestry, searching for a precedent to permit Mordecai to honor him without transgressing Jewish law, as if Haman actually cared. Mordecai, however, claimed that his tribal line had never bowed to Esau. This reading also places Esau in a similar category as Haman, even though Esau was the son of Isaac and Rebecca. Ibn Ezra concurs with the rabbinic view that Haman carried an idol and suggests that since Abraham bowed to the Hittites,[8] bowing itself was not the issue.[9]

The Talmud, as mentioned earlier, tries to justify Mordecai's dangerous decision not to bow and concedes that for a courtier who tried not to attract any attention to himself, there can be only one worthy explanation: idol worship. R. Huna gathers the interpretation of four Sages on the verses "Therefore, because of all the words of this letter, and of that which they saw concerning this matter, and that which had befallen them, the Jews ordained...that they would keep these two days" (Est. 9:26–27). R. Huna wanted to know who the subject of these verses was and what was it he or she saw that inspired the recording of this whole remarkable story.[10] One opinion posits that Ahasuerus said that the

and was admonished against idolatry."

7. Esther Rabba 7:8.
8. "Thereupon Abraham bowed low to the people of the land, the Hittites" (Gen. 23:7).
9. Ibn Ezra on Est. 3:4 (second version).
10. See Megilla 19a.

Jews had not been released from exile after the predicted seventy years. Consequently, the king believed they would never be delivered and were fair game as victims. According to another reading, Haman was incensed that Mordecai refused to bow, since the fate of the empire's Jews was in his control. Haman was not merely holding an idol. He was an idol.[11]

If idolatry motivated Mordecai's refusal to bow, as the Sages and many later interpreters believed, then it could have only been born out of deep intention and conviction.[12] Mordecai's fellow courtiers asked him again and again to explain himself, and he gave the same reason again and again: "For he had explained to them that he was a Jew" (3:4). The Rabbis took this to mean that Mordecai would not compromise his Judaism by bowing down to an idol. In this portrait, Haman was either holding an idol or established himself as an object of worship. As mentioned earlier, Haman may have been named after a local god of Susa, making his very name associated with pagan worship.

This situation is not dissimilar to a rabbinic reading of Numbers 25:1–2: "While Israel was staying at Shittim, the people defiled themselves with Moabite women, who invited the people to the sacrifices for their god. The people partook of them and worshipped that god." Here cohabitation is conflated with idol worship in a bacchanalian-like loss of control. This led to the midrashic interpretation favored by Rashi on Numbers 25:1: "When anyone's passions overpowered him [an Israelite man] and he said to her [a Moabite woman], 'Submit to me,' she took out for him an image of Peor from her bosom, saying to him, 'First prostrate yourself before this.'"[13] The seduction worked in two ways. Men could receive sexual favors only in return for idol worship, an unusual but seemingly effective recruitment strategy.

The Greek Esther expands on the notion that Mordecai rejected idol worship. By stating he was Jewish, Mordecai meant God-fearing; the totality of this commitment would not be compromised by mere human demands:

11. Ibid.
12. In addition to Megilla 19a, see Sanhedrin 61b.
13. *Tanḥuma, Balak* 18.

> You know, O Lord, that it was not in insolence or pride or for any love of glory that I did this and refused to bow down to this proud Haman; for I would have been willing to kiss the soles of his feet to save Israel! But I did this so that I might not set human glory above the glory of God, and I will not bow down to anyone but you, who are my Lord; and I will not do these things in pride. (Greek Esther, Addition C; 13:12–14, NRSV).

These texts on idol worship view this incident through a purely legal lens instead of an ethnic or historic one. When Mordecai referred only to his Jewish background to his colleagues as a sufficient explanation, he obviously felt no more need be said. Jewish practice was, according to this reading, well known enough to merit no further explanation. Gersonides on Esther 3:6 suggests that the king's servants let Haman know that Mordecai refused to bow only because he was a Jew.

Perhaps an aggravation far deeper was surfacing at this point in our story.

Haman was an Agagite, a descendant of the Amalekites, and therefore represented evil incarnate to the Jews. If Mordecai was conscious of a fraught history with the Amalekites, then perhaps he could not help himself from treating Haman derisively. Mordecai, in this reading, revisited the history of his own family and the absolutism of the command to be rid of Amalek permanently. Mordecai may not have taken out a sword and finished Haman off, but neither could he bring himself to honor a member of the nation that had done so much harm to his vulnerable extended family long ago, as described in I Samuel 15:2–3:

> Thus said the Lord of Hosts: I am exacting the penalty for what Amalek did to Israel, for the assault he made upon them on the road, on their way up from Egypt. Now go, attack Amalek, and proscribe all that belongs to him. Spare no one, but kill alike men and women, infants and sucklings, oxen and sheep, camels and donkeys!

This command to Saul is consonant with an uncompromising legal mandate dating from Moses and Joshua in Exodus:

> Then the Lord said to Moses, "Inscribe this in a document as a reminder, and read it aloud to Joshua: I will utterly blot out the memory of Amalek from under heaven!" And Moses built an altar and named it Adonai-Nissi. He said, "It means, 'Hand upon the throne of the Lord!' The Lord will be at war with Amalek throughout the ages." (Ex. 17:14–16)

The command is later reiterated in Deuteronomy, in a passage read in synagogue on the Sabbath before Purim, *Shabbat Zakhor*. All members of the community are commanded to be present for the reading, in order to keep the sting of the past alive and ever-present:

> Remember what Amalek did to you on your journey, after you left Egypt, how, undeterred by fear of God, he surprised you on the march, when you were famished and weary, and cut down all the stragglers in your rear. Therefore, when the Lord your God grants you safety from all your enemies around you, in the land that the Lord your God is giving you as a hereditary portion, you shall blot out the memory of Amalek from under heaven. Do not forget! (Deut. 25:17–19)

One midrash posits that every year when we read this Torah passage we are erasing the Amalekites from the world.[14] Erasing or blotting out the memory of the Amalekites is the obverse of remembering them to preserve the sanctity of what it means to be human. In this sense, Maimonides writes that it is a commandment to remember this cruelty not merely once a year but constantly.[15] The Sages understood the harshness and severity of this demand but couched it as a personal and national statement of dignity and integrity: "Whoever is compassionate to those who deserve cruelty ends up being cruel to those who deserve compassion."[16] With all this history in mind, Mordecai would not bow.

---

14. *Pesikta Rabbati* 12.
15. Maimonides, *Mishneh Torah, Hilkhot Melakhim* 5:5.
16. *Tanḥuma, Metzora* 1.

A Shared Past

The deep antagonism between Mordecai and Haman, regardless of any idol Haman may have carried, is echoed in yet another midrash:

> When Mordecai saw Haman, he did not stand up for him. Haman passed by him and he [Mordecai] neither stirred nor greeted him. Haman came to Mordecai's right, and pretending that Mordecai greeted him, replied to him, "Peace be to you." Mordecai responded, "There is no peace, said my God, for the wicked" (Is. 57:21).[17]

This communicates the depth of Haman's anger. He tried hard to befriend Mordecai but could not squeeze a kind word out of him. Mordecai did not give the slightest indication that he was interested in Haman's overtures.

The personal tensions between Haman and Mordecai as archetypes and opposites predate the events recorded in the Book of Esther, as showcased in one lengthy talmudic passage that discusses their differences while hinting at Jacob's relationship to Esau:

> There was a quarrel between them [Mordecai and Haman]. In the days of Ezra, when the Jews were building Jerusalem's walls, enemies came and obstructed them: "You are building without permission of the king," they said. They [the Jews] replied, "But it is with his permission." The enemies said, "Select one of your men, and we will select one of ours, and let them present this before the king." They selected Haman, and Israel selected Mordecai. Both prepared provisions. Mordecai ate his bread in small morsels, while Haman ate carelessly and ran out of food. He approached Mordecai and asked to borrow bread from him but he hesitated to lend him a loaf. Mordecai then said, "If I give you a loaf, will you sell yourself to me?" "Yes," Haman said, "but we have no parchment on which to write the deed." Mordecai responded: "Here is my shoe. Write on it." Thereupon Haman

17. *Aggadat Esther* 3:7.

> wrote on Mordecai's shoe: "I, Haman the Agagite, am slave to Mordecai, the Jew, to whom I sold myself for a loaf of bread."[18]

That Haman was an enemy to the Jews long before his appearance in Esther explains his long-standing and pervasive hatred for them. Haman was an obstructionist, bent on stopping the Jews from protecting their holy city. But rather than highlight the drama of nations, the midrash takes us into a prosaic moment that explains the characters of both men. Mordecai was a strategist and a planner when it came to his meals. He also had the self-discipline to restrain his appetites for the sake of survival. Haman, on the other hand, was willing to give it all up for a loaf of bread, not unlike Esau's sale of the birthright to purchase a bowl of soup.[19] Men who give in easily to their physical needs and prioritize the momentary over the eternal may get in the way of the Israelites temporarily, but just as the truth endures, the ultimate victory always belongs to Israel.

Another linguistic detail aligns the stories of Mordecai and Haman with Jacob and Esau: "But he disdained (*vayivez*) to lay hands on Mordecai alone" (Est. 3:6). It was beneath Haman to issue a punishment to Mordecai alone, says the verse, using a verb also found in the story of Esau and the birthright.[20] Famished, Esau returned from his hunt and sold his birthright for the meal Jacob had cooked. After eating and drinking and leaving, the verse ends this incident with telling words: "Thus did Esau spurn (*vayivez*) the birthright" (Gen. 25:34). It was not enough to sell his blessing of inheritance for something as temporal as lentil soup; he justified his actions by spurning that which he had but would have no longer. Rashi on the verse extends this verb to suggest Esau's wickedness; in the very thought to sell the birthright, Esau "despised the service of God." Rabbi Ovadia Sforno on this verse adds an aftermath to the story, suggesting that his diminishment of the birthright's worth did not precipitate the sale but followed it. The transaction was of little value to him. He just ate his food and left without the regret that naturally follows a foolish act of impulse. What is evident in

18. Ibid. 5:9.
19. Gen. 25:29–34.
20. Esther Rabba 2:5.

this linguistic comparison is that scorn has an aftereffect. The feeling of disgust or revulsion gets projected beyond the act or person and seeps into a shift of perspective on what took place. Like Esau, if Haman had any regrets, the biblical text did not communicate them.

And like Jacob and Esau's fraught relationship and ongoing saga was the friction between Mordecai and Haman; *Targum Esther* weaves a picture of these two men with Haman indebted to Mordecai, rather than the other way around:

> When Haman perceived Mordekhai and the children who were occupied in (the study of) the words of the Law, among the Sanhedrin which Esther established for them at the king's gate, and Mordekhai neither standing up in respect for his [Haman's] image nor trembling in his presence except to stretch out his right foot and to point to the sales contract that he [Haman] sold himself to him [Mordekhai] for a loaf of bread in the letter that was written in his [Mordekhai's] legging opposite his ankle, immediately his [Haman's] anger kindled.[21]

Mordecai in this aggadic passage was not passively skirting his responsibility to honor the one whom the king honored but actively churning his disrespect for Haman. Mordecai let Haman know through a gesture alone that he owned Haman. The sales contract was visible each time the two met. Haman was troubled every time he saw Mordecai. Each interaction presented an opportunity to show Mordecai and Haman who had the real power over whom.

---

21. *Targum Esther* 5:9, as translated by Bernard Grossfeld, *The Two Targums of Esther*, 66.

Haman's Rage and Revenge

> When Haman saw that Mordecai would not kneel or bow low to him, Haman was filled with rage. But he disdained to lay hands on Mordecai alone; having been told who Mordecai's people were, Haman plotted to do away with all the Jews, Mordecai's people, throughout the kingdom of Ahasuerus. In the first month, that is, the month of Nisan, in the twelfth year of King Ahasuerus, *pur* – which means "the lot" – was cast before Haman concerning every day and every month, [until it fell on] the twelfth month, that is, the month of Adar. Haman then said to King Ahasuerus, "There is a certain people, scattered and dispersed among the other peoples in all the provinces of your realm, whose laws are different from those of any other people and who do not obey the king's laws; and it is not in Your Majesty's interest to tolerate them. If it please Your Majesty, let an edict be drawn for their destruction, and I will pay ten thousand talents of silver to the stewards for deposit in the royal treasury." Thereupon the king removed his signet ring from his hand and gave it to Haman son of Hammedatha the Agagite, the foe of the Jews. (Est. 3:4–10)

Mordecai broke a long and respected honor code by not bowing down to Haman. There was a price to pay for this outrageous and public insult. If the Book of Esther is a humorous critique of court protocols and procedures, it is this act of disobedience that most highlights the farce and danger of power. A slight to a higher-ranking courtier is enough to set off explosive rage with disastrous consequences. The French theorist Pierre Bourdieu writes that "the ethos of honor is fundamentally opposed to a universal and formal morality which affirms the equality and dignity of all men and consequently the equality of their rights and duties."[1] An honor code can undermine a moral code when all men and women are not regarded equals. Kwame Anthony Appiah in *The Honor Code: How Moral Revolutions Happen* argues that honor in a moral system must be earned rather than demanded: "It's important to understand that while honor is an entitlement to respect – and shame comes when you lose that title – a person of honor cares first of all not about being respected but about being worthy of respect."[2] Haman was not worthy of respect; thus he had to demand it as an outgrowth of power. And demand it he did.

Mordecai, the target of Haman's ire, was only one person, insufficient to satisfy Haman's bottomless need to punish those who punished him by not showing appropriate obsequiousness. "But he disdained to lay hands on Mordecai alone; having been told who Mordecai's people were, Haman plotted to do away with all the Jews, Mordecai's people, throughout the kingdom of Ahasuerus" (Est. 3:6). This verse may be the only place in the Hebrew Bible to describe true discrimination. Hate for one becomes hate for all, projecting outward until it becomes all-consuming. Esther 3:6 also indicates that Haman did not bear this prejudice toward the Jews before assuming his position. He was told who Mordecai's people were, on the assumption that this knowledge alone would explain Mordecai's disrespect. Haman felt diminished; thus he diminished. He let a trivial bruise to his sense of superiority grow and translate into the sudden mistreatment of an entire nation. True

1. Pierre Bourdieu, "The Sentiment of Honor in Kabyle Society," in *Honor and Shame: The Values of Mediterranean Society*, ed. J. G. Peristiany (Chicago: University of Chicago Press, 1966), 288.
2. Kwame Anthony Appiah, *The Honor Code: How Moral Revolutions Happen* (New York: W. W. Norton & Company, 2011), 16. For more philosophical and historical ruminations on the place of honor, see Tamler Sommers, *Why Honor Matters* (New York: Basic, 2018); James Bowman, *Honor: A History* (San Francisco: Encounter Books, 2007); and Frank Henderson Stewart, *Honor* (Chicago: University of Chicago Press, 1994).

to human nature, Haman took his own bruises so seriously that it was not hard for him to turn anger into indignation and justify the brutal killing of many for the slight of one. But when he later made his case to the king, he could not express it in this crass, base way. Not wishing to appear petty, Haman never mentioned to Ahasuerus Mordecai's perceived disrespect even though this was the underlying reason for the entire plot against the Jews.

Ibn Ezra, in defining the Hebrew term for "anger," *ḥema*, used in Esther 3:5, suggests its root *ḥ-m-h* means "heat," because "anger heats up the body." It is an intensely visceral emotion. This may explain why one opinion in the Talmud compared anger to idol worship[3] in the way it dominates the mind, causing one to forget the very presence of God.[4] R. Shmuel b. Naḥmani added to this ancient debate on the deleterious effects of anger that "one who loses his temper is exposed to all the torments of purgatory."[5] The debate raged on:

> R. Yirmeya said, "He [an angry person] forgets his learning and becomes more and more foolish, as it is written, 'Anger rests in the bosoms of fools' (Eccl. 7:9), and it is written, 'The fool is laid open to folly' (Prov. 13:26)." R. Naḥman b. Yitzḥak said, "It is certain that his sins outnumber his merits, as it is written, 'A furious man abounds in transgressions' (Prov. 29:22)."

Another Sage elsewhere claimed that anger can cause an intelligent person to lose his wisdom and forfeit his greatness.[6] To avoid this, Adda bar Ahava, in his management of anger, claimed that anger never went to bed with him. By the time the day ended, he had made peace with the world.[7] These rabbis of old described the fierceness of an unstoppable anger, the very kind of fury that overtakes an individual's conscious-

3. Shabbat 105b.
4. Nedarim 22b.
5. Ibid.
6. Pesaḥim 66b.
7. Taanit 20b.

ness, creating the loss of control. It is the kind of rage that characterized Haman's limited emotional range.

Rabbi Moshe Chaim Luzzatto in *The Path of the Just* describes several types of anger: The first type is a fury born out of one's inflated sense of self. When an arrogant person is insulted, Rabbi Luzzatto writes, "his heart is no longer with him, and his judgment vanishes."[8] The problem for the Jews of Persia was that Haman, the person who lost his judgment, also had power and sufficient influence to manipulate history. "A man such as he would destroy the entire world," Rabbi Luzzatto writes of this kind of pervasive anger, "if it were within his power to do so, for he is not in any way directed by reason and is as devoid of sensibility as any predatory beast."[9]

We cannot help but make associations with Haman, the predator. The power he enjoyed was not sufficient. Haman needed control and respect in an absolute way, and he needed the praise and adoration of all in Shushan, of every courtier in the king's palace. Mordecai would not legitimize Haman's fury by bending to its will. While many may judge Mordecai's behavior as risky, as it certainly was, perhaps Mordecai understood that a person like Haman fed off his anger. Rather than feeding Haman's monstrous and cavernous appetite for irrational hatred, Mordecai starved it instead.

Haman's Revenge and His Lottery

Mordecai's disrespect came with an immediate consequence: "When Haman saw that Mordecai would not kneel or bow low to him, Haman was filled with rage. But he disdained to lay hands on Mordecai alone; having been told who Mordecai's people were, Haman plotted to do away with all the Jews, Mordecai's people, throughout the kingdom of Ahasuerus" (Est. 3:5–6).

The events of chapter 3 take place in the twelfth year of Ahasuerus' reign: "In the first month, that is the month of Nisan, in the twelfth year of King Ahasuerus" (Est. 3:7). This detail is not insignifi-

8. Rabbi Moshe Chaim Luzzatto, *The Path of the Just* (Jerusalem: Feldheim Publishers, 1980), 161.
9. Ibid.

cant. Nine years after the book's opening and five years after Esther was chosen – "Esther was taken to the king… in the seventh year of his reign" (Est. 2:16) – Haman made his audacious proposal. By this time, the king was fully settled on the throne, the queen was comfortable (or at least not new) in her role, her identity remained securely hidden, and Haman had long before been promoted. Each character had a well-established place in the royal hierarchy, a place that was soon to be toppled. This change came about as the result of an insult and a lottery, a petty sentiment and an arbitrary game, as indiscriminate, haphazard, capricious, and undisciplined as Haman's hatred. In the novel *Four Meals*, Meir Shalev has the central character Jacob explaining something to a child beyond his comprehension at the time: "Two brothers Fate has. The good brother is Luck and the bad brother is Chance. And when those three brothers laugh, the whole world quakes."[10]

In the Hebrew Bible, we signify the casting of lots as a *goral*, usually implying the casting of dice.[11] We do not use the term *pur*, a Persian word that reflects a purely Persian worldview not shared by the Israelites. W. W. Hallo identified a dice cube, "the die of Iahali," that is inscribed twice with the word *pur*, dating from the ninth century BCE,[12] and explained the significance of the *pur* in Persian society:

> The dice serves a wider purpose, in that it illustrates how widespread was belief in a predetermined fate, with which it was considered important for men to co-operate if they were to succeed in their enterprises…. Given that the Jews lived in a fate-ridden culture while they inhabited Persia and the other lands of exile, we can readily comprehend a belief in the power of their God to overrule the way the dice fell (Proverbs 16:33). The book of Esther took the matter further; even when the dice had fallen, the Lord was powerful to reverse its good omen into bad, in order to deliver his people.[13]

10. Meir Shalev, *Four Meals* (Edinburgh: Cannongate Books, 2002), 285.
11. See, for example, Lev. 16:8, Num. 26:55, and Ps. 22:18.
12. W. W. Hallo, "The First Purim," *The Biblical Archeologist* 46 (1983): 22.
13. Baldwin, *Esther*, 23.

Even one barely acquainted with the text of Esther knows that the holiday is named after the lots drawn by Haman to predict the optimal day for a collective massacre. Yet the way the lottery was constructed must have been complex, as communicated by the text itself: "*Pur* – which means 'the lot' – was cast before Haman concerning every day and every month, [until it fell on] the twelfth month, that is, the month of Adar" (Est. 3:7). Rashi points out on 3:7 that the tense is passive, implying that the lot may have been drawn for Haman. It was cast day by day, in this view, because Haman was dissatisfied with the arbitrary results; he tried again and again until he selected a day that was auspicious to coincide with the lottery's selection. If this were the case, it is unclear why a lottery was necessary at all unless it was royal protocol to have a lottery determine important court events.

Rashi on 3:7 comments that the lots were selected more than once, first to determine the month and then to determine the day. Each decision was significant for a day marked in infamy. Ibn Ezra on 3:7 cites a midrash to explain Haman's process: "When the lot fell in the month of Adar, he [Haman] rejoiced, saying, 'The lot has fallen on the month of Moses' death.' Haman did not know that Moses died on the seventh of Adar but that Moses was also born on the seventh of Adar."[14] The Sages noted the timing of the fallen lot in the auspicious month of Adar. Rabbinic time often frontloads and groups important occasions together, as if to suggest that certain times portend tragedy, freedom, or joy.[15] In this reading of the lots, they saw no coincidence and attributed to Haman intimate knowledge of significant Jewish events: Haman plotted not only to kill the Jews but to do so on the anniversary of their greatest leader's death, connecting the tragic loss of one with the loss of many. His strategy backfired, however, because for all his Jewish knowledge Haman failed to realize that the same day also marked the birth of Judaism's greatest hero, who was saved through what appeared to be a series of coincidences. This choice of day intimated that a hero would rise to confront Haman's decree and that a nation on the cusp of death could

14. Megilla 13b.
15. The best example of this may be the association of five tragedies on one day, Tisha BeAv. See Mishna Taanit 4:6 and Tractate Taanit 29a.

be wondrously saved. R. Yosei in the Talmud appreciated the importance of timing when he stated, "A fortunate matter is brought about on an auspicious day, and a damaging matter on an inauspicious day."[16]

Lots and Astrological Forecasting

Ibn Ezra sees a role for astrological forces in the story. He suggests an alignment of the stars, in keeping with his controversial view that astrological forces were predictive. Ibn Ezra on Esther 1:13 described the "wise men, who knew the times" as the "astrological scholars or forecasters who were employed by ancient kings." Commenting on 1:7, Ibn Ezra understood the lottery as Haman's way of determining a fortuitous time to act on his destructive plan:

> "To cast lots": This is a Persian word whose meaning is lottery... there are those who say that he chose the month of Adar to destroy Israel because that is the month that Moses died. He did not know, however, that that was the month that Moses was born. Others say that it was on account of the constellations uniting at Capricorn, which is the twelfth month in astrology, and not a month of good tidings for Israel. And the correct reading is that it was according to the lottery, for God judged and extended the time until Israel would repent and would escape [this fate].

Ibn Ezra believes that the lottery was a function of an astrological forecast and also a means of providing the Jews with sufficient time to examine their ways, repent, and thereby avert the evil decree.

Rabbi Isaac Arama writes that the king used astrologers in the first chapter because he wanted to find Vashti blameless and punish her privately. He therefore consulted the "knowers of times" to find out if the moment was auspicious for such a punishment. The severity of a crime, according to Arama, is always judged relative to societal norms: "Even if it were a sin or small transgression, he could have offered a heavy punishment dependent on the time." Punishment is not only related to

16. Arakhin 11b.

the crime but to the time period in which it was given.[17] If the climate necessitates it, a minor crime can be found to be a major offense. Arama states that if Vashti had not refused in front of the king's officials on a public occasion, she would have been exculpated.[18] This leveraging of astrology to support what one wants to do applied equally to the king and to Haman.

The connection of fate and providence with astrology was important for many Jewish scholars; they would have seen in the *pur* an expression of astral forces colliding with divine providence in ways that most modern readers would dismiss as irrelevant.[19] Many medieval scholars believed astrology to be a credible system; some thought it was repugnant and an insult to God. Others ignored it. Maimonides believed that astrology was irrational, not efficacious, and limited one's free will.[20] In the *Mishneh Torah,* he wrote:

> Whoever believes in these and similar things and in his heart holds them to be true and scientific and only forbidden by the Torah is nothing but a fool, deficient in understanding. Sensible people, however, who possess sound mental faculties, know by clear proofs that all these practices that the Torah prohibited have no scientific basis but are chimerical and inane.[21]

Maimonides' dismissive approach lived side by side with astrological explanations for exegetical difficulties in the study of the Hebrew Bible. The Book of Esther was no exception:

---

17. Carey Moore observes on Est. 1:12 that "although Vashti is no more disobedient here than Esther is later on in refusing to stay away at the king's command (4:11), they provoke a very different response: Vashti raises the king's anger while Esther stirs his mercy" (*Anchor Bible,* 9). Like Arama, Moore concedes that the context, and not only the crime, was considered in the decisive judgment.
18. Arama, 233 fn 28.
19. For a general outline of the issues and scholars involved, see the entry "Astrology," in *Encyclopedia Judaica,* vol. 3 (Jerusalem, 1971), 790–95.
20. Maimonides, *Mishneh Torah, Hilkhot Teshuva* 5.
21. Maimonides, *Mishneh Torah,* "Laws of Idol Worship" 11:15, trans. Moses Hyamson (New York: 1962).

> In the Jewish world, Maimonides was one of the few uncompromising opponents and critics of astrology, calling it foolishness and not at all worthy of being called a science.... In such a climate of general acceptance, it is therefore not surprising to find many references to astrology and its influence in Esther commentaries.[22]

Even earlier than Maimonides, Bahya ibn Pakuda condemned astrology and connected its use to the courtier class, an important perspective for those who study Esther.[23] Court astrologers appear in many biblical texts in addition to the Book of Esther: Genesis 41:33, 39; Daniel 2:27; Isaiah 44:25, 47:10–15; Jeremiah 50:35, 51:57; and I Chronicles 12:32. Rabbenu Bahya's opposition was based more on psychological and theological grounds than on scientific reasoning. He compared astrology to pagan worship and believed it could cause a loss of faith in God and possibly denial of God's very existence.[24] Astrology was commonly studied and used in royal courts, but Bahya believed it to be a superficial and misleading art. It was used merely to enhance one's title. He was concerned that Jewish statesmen, when encountering ideas in astrology counter to their own belief system, found ways of living with the contradiction. "Courtiers apparently found it possible to live on two existential levels. They maintained an intellectual commitment to the religious doctrines of providence, free will, reward and punishment; but simultaneously gave poetic expression to their experience of a capricious fate and an apathetic nature."[25]

Astrology makes an appearance in a commentary on the story of Balaam, particularly on the verse "For there is no enchantment in Jacob, neither is there any divination in Israel" (Num. 23:23). This may have been the inflection point for the later rabbinic expression: *Ein mazal*

---

22. Walfish, *Esther in Medieval Garb*, 55.
23. Bezalel Safran, "Bahya ibn Pakuda's Attitude toward the Courtier Class," in *Studies in Medieval Jewish History and Literature*, vol. 1, ed. Isadore Twersky (Cambridge, MA), 161–65, particularly 162.
24. Ibid., 163. Citation from Ibn Pakuda from Joseph Kapah's edition of *Torat Ḥovot HaLevavot* (Jerusalem, 1973), 255.
25. Safran, "Bahya ibn Pakuda's Attitude," 164.

beYisrael, "There is no astrological luck (*mazal*) in Israel."[26] Haman may have believed that an arbitrary process would reveal an auspicious date, but it did just the opposite; the date chosen ended up being the date for the death of tens of thousands of Persians, not Jews. Some exegetes read that Haman used the lots to determine two matters: when the Persians would be at their greatest point of strength and when the Jews would be at their greatest weakness.[27] But, because Jews are not affected by astrological forces, the very reverse happened. Ibn Ezra, however, uses the very same phrase, "There is no *mazal* in Israel," to demonstrate that Haman's lots were effective:

> Whatever the configuration of stars existing at birth has decreed for an individual will surely befall him, unless he be protected by a power superior to the stars. If he attaches himself to it, he will be saved from the decrees.... This is what the Sages have said, "Israel has no planets (mazal)," [that is] as long as they observe the Torah. But if they do not observe it, the stars will rule over them.[28]

The Jews can avoid the predictions of astrology only by protecting themselves with divine law as shield and cover. The moment they stop observing, they become subject to these irrational forces.[29]

---

26. See Nedarim 32a, Shabbat 156a–b.
27. See, among others, Ashkenazi, *Yosef Lekaḥ*, on 3:7.
28. Ibn Ezra, *Sefer HaYashar*, Ex. 33:23. Translation is that of Y. Tzvi Langermann in "Some Astrological Themes in the Thought of Abraham ibn Ezra," in *Rabbi Abraham Ibn Ezra: Studies in the Writings of a Twelfth-Century Polymath*, ed. Isadore Twersky and Jay Harris (Cambridge: Harvard University Center for Jewish Studies, 1993), 50.
29. Ibn Ezra's belief in astrology is described this way: "He was committed to astrology, using astrological ideas to represent an invocation of cosmic metaphors of a general sort, or perhaps a schematic representation of cosmic processes, rather than a belief that the events and rituals in the Bible – which involve some of the most basic features of Jewish life – are susceptible to detailed astrological analysis, down to the finest technical details" (Langermann, "Some Astrological Themes in the Thought of Abraham ibn Ezra," 30).

The Game of Exile

The *pur* of Purim and the Book of Esther also highlights the difference between luck and risk. These words are often used coterminously, but they do not mean the same thing. Haman relied upon a combination of control and luck. Mordecai and Esther, by contrast, relied upon a combination of strategy and calculated risk. The journalist Morgan Housel discusses this critical difference in his essay "Ironies of Luck":

> Luck is the flip side of risk. You cannot understand one without appreciating the other. If risk is what happens when you make good decisions but end up with a bad outcome, luck is what happens when you make bad or mediocre decisions but end up with a great outcome. They both happen because the world is too complex to allow 100% of your actions to dictate 100% of your outcomes. They are mirrored cousins, driven by the same thing.[30]

And yet here is where the two come apart, according to Housel:

> Experiencing risk makes you recognize that some stuff is out of your control, which is accurate feedback that helps you adjust your strategy. Experiencing luck doesn't. It generates the opposite feedback: A false feeling that you are in control, because you did something and then got the outcome you wanted. Which is terrible feedback if you're trying to make good, repeatable long-term decisions.

While both luck and risk involve knowns and unknowns, a risk taker adjusts his strategy in line with his experience to sharpen his chance of a better outcome, allowing for a modicum of control and intelligence to mitigate the randomness of chance. Unlike risk, luck lulls one into taking credit for a random win, thereby not learning from experience to make a positive outcome sustainable and repeatable. Haman's promotion, decisions, and strategies counted on luck – none more than the

30. Morgan Housel, "Ironies of Luck" (March 14, 2018), http://www.collaborativefund.com/blog/ironies-of-luck/.

goral itself – that he attributed to his own fine skill without analyzing why and taking proper precautions lest the winds of favor turn on him. When they did, he was unable to save himself.

Contrast this to Mordecai's behavior throughout the scroll. Sitting at the king's gate, walking past the king's courtyard, Mordecai was constantly taking in information to calculate his risks and making wiser decisions in a climate that favored the unwise.

The introduction of lots to the story is confusing, but the very root *pur* unlocks what this book is really about: politics. Politics is a game of chance and control as much as it is about governance, and an exile must learn to play it. Lots and lotteries suggest the game-like intricacies of politics: the winners are not those who rule most wisely but those who play the game most shrewdly. Those who want to rule are often, by virtue of desire, the least competent to do so. And yet, even if some players are better primed, prepared, or experienced, a pinch of bad luck could change everything in an instant, like a game of Chutes and Ladders. It is no surprise God's name appears nowhere in the book. God transcends the purely human enterprise of politics, while humans are hopelessly trapped in it.

It is the very paradox of control and luck that attracts players to the game: plotted choreography and strategy are countermanded by unforeseen tensions, making the game a mirror of life itself. This fragility that hypnotizes players is wonderfully depicted in Francis Spufford's novel *Golden Hill*. In a telling scene in eighteenth-century New York, a wealthy politician challenges a group of associates to a game of cards and waxes on about the similarity of cards to the English monarchy, an apt description of Haman's lots and their application to a royal court: "Because in miniature, with a pasteboard monarch and a pasteboard court, it [the card game] offers the situation that most closely resembles the situation of political life. At least, political life as it appears if one is in the midst of it, paying close attention, with a clear mind."[31] With each drop of his cards, he explains his meaning. A strategic player at some point in the game can almost surmise who holds what cards,

31. Francis Spufford, *Golden Hill* (New York: Scribner, 2016), 124.

> being nearly but never quite completely, informed. We see *almost* the whole of the picture, but never absolutely the whole of it.... Between your cards and my cards, and what we have seen when we exchanged, we can deduce virtually the disposition of the entire pack. Yet not quite; never to a complete certainty. And in that little space of imperfection, chance reigns, playing havoc with our plans.[32]

In the Book of Esther, that little space of imperfection wreaked havoc with the plans of a minority group. An unassuming cluster of exiles, scattered throughout the great expanse of Ahasuerus' empire with no desire for attention, suddenly came under intense and irrational scrutiny by a man bloated with a sense of supremacy and a taste for revenge.

Later in Spufford's novel, the card player, with more cards dropped in the spill of light, finishes his lesson on politics and chance by demonstrating that even gifted players can lose. "So chance is a power... which every wise man must acknowledge. The largest conditions may be the consequence of the smallest of circumstances; may be chosen by none, but determine in the end, the fate of all."[33] One upturned card determines the fate of the entire game. The expected winner who loses becomes despondent; the expected loser, within that little space of imperfection where chance resides, can just as unexpectedly shine.

The King's Approval

Once Haman had a date, he needed a plan and he needed to persuade the king to buy into his grand scheme. Haman first had to identify the people, then demonstrate their negative distinctiveness, convince the king that they were subversive, and create a reasonable pretext to condemn them all to death. In only two verses, this is neatly accomplished.

> Haman then said to King Ahasuerus, "There is a certain people, scattered and dispersed among the other peoples in all the provinces of your realm, whose laws are different from those of any

32. Ibid.
33. Ibid., 125.

> other people and who do not obey the king's laws; and it is not in Your Majesty's interest to tolerate them. If it please Your Majesty, let an edict be drawn for their destruction, and I will pay ten thousand talents of silver to the stewards for deposit in the royal treasury." (Est. 3:8–9)

The king hardly blinked. There are times we anticipate a reaction from Ahasuerus, and he offers none. He was prepared to put an entire people in harm's way without even asking why. Haman's outrageous plot gets no real reaction, not even a question. It seems that Ahasuerus was barely paying attention.

The talmudic discussion of these verses describes Haman as a minister with a cunning tongue who devised clever reasons to destroy a nation based on his own personal vendetta against Mordecai.[34] Haman contemplated the king's response and readied himself for any scenario. Should the king say that his kingdom would become depopulated, Haman would contend that they were not one nation living contiguously; rather they were "scattered and dispersed" among all of his provinces. Should the king contend that he gained benefit from the Jews, Haman could claim they were *meforad* (using a play on words for *pered*, "mule"); like a mule, they do not bear fruit, implying they are unproductive. In terms of their laws being different from those of the king's empire, Haman staked his claim that Jews were lawbreakers. The Jews were dangerous and worthless interlopers, ethnically, culturally, and ritually different from other Persians.

According to these talmudic passages Jews were criticized not for directly subverting the law but for socializing differently. Jewish law is described as a way to separate people from others and make them lazy:

> "Their laws are different from all the other nations": For they do not eat from our food and they do not marry our women and they do not marry their women to us… and they waste the whole

34. Megilla 13b. Rava claims that Haman first wanted to kill only Mordecai but then decided to kill "his people."

> year, avoiding the king's work with the excuse: Today is the Sabbath or today is Passover.
>
> "And it is no benefit to the king to tolerate them": For they eat, drink, and mock the throne, for even if a fly falls in a glass of wine of one of them, he casts it away and drinks. But if my master, the king, touches a glass of wine of one of them, that person throws it to the ground and does not drink it.[35]

These peculiar behaviors were offensive to the king. Rashi in his remarks on this talmudic discussion mentions, not one, but several types of taxation that the king did not receive from the Jews.[36] The fact that Jews neither integrated socially with the rest of the kingdom nor contributed enough taxes to support the king's lifestyle were compelling reasons to do away with them.

Rashi has few comments on Esther 3:8 but understood the "laws of the king" to refer specifically to taxation. By telling Ahasuerus that the Jews did not pay taxes, Haman implied there was little reason to keep them. When Haman told the king not to tolerate them, Rashi interpreted this to mean "do not pay them regard," essentially giving license for the king to persecute them. Ibn Ezra on 3:8 interpreted *dateihem shonot*, "their laws are different," as Haman's false claim that the Jews did not keep the king's laws. Ibn Ezra is dismissive of the talmudic discussion that highlighted the distinctiveness of the Jews as a source of irritation for Haman.

Rabbi Isaac Arama on 3:8 contends that there *was* truth to Haman's claim. In order to convince the king, Haman had to mix some truth with his exaggeration and disgust for the Jews. When saying that the Jews were scattered and dispersed, Arama believed this an accurate assessment of the separation between Jews due to their dislike for one another, a condition he attributes to "the sins of our days." This *sinat ḥinam*, baseless hatred, had reached the point of excess so that it was no longer an internal problem alone but noticeable to outsiders. Arama

35. Megilla 13a.
36. Rashi on Megilla 13a.

also acknowledged that the Jews do have laws which are unlike those of other nations, such as the prohibition of mixing different fabrics, animals, and plants, and the ashes of the red heifer. This did not imply, however, that it was worthwhile for the king to annihilate them, since the Jews generated important tax revenues. For this reason, Haman had to add a monetary incentive to compensate for the king's loss of taxes.

Arama understood the expression "one nation" as an intentional reference to a people who have one God and one Torah or set of laws. In other words, the use of the word "one" is a positive description of Jewish uniqueness and a nod to monotheism. He uses various biblical prooftexts to describe Jewish unity as it is signified by the term "one." In contrast to the argument of separation is the opinion of *Siftei Ḥakhamim*, Shabbethai ben Joseph Bass (1641–1718), who blames Jewish participation at the king's party for Haman's decree.[37] Ironically, by behaving like all of the other member nations of the king's provinces, the Jews were singled out by Haman for their lack of total integration. Being too similar to the nations surrounding them compromised Jewish distinctiveness but also paradoxically brought greater attention to them.[38]

The *Rishon LeTziyon*, Hayyim Abenatar, who lived in the seventeenth to eighteenth century, observed that Haman did not refer to the Jews directly in his petition, calling them only "one nation" among the king's many provinces. Abenatar cites a passage of Talmud, Avoda Zara 10b, about a king who had a wart on his leg and asked advice about its removal. He was advised to remove the wart but not the leg. But Ahasuerus could not eliminate the Jews as easily as advised metaphorically by this talmudic statement, because they were dispersed. Yet they remained one nation and only the king had sufficient authority to order the genocide.[39]

Adele Berlin, in her commentary on Esther for the series *Mikra LeYisrael*, divides Haman's statement into three parts: the geographic dispersion of the Jews, their different customs, and their transgression of the king's law. Berlin then deals with the historical issue of anti-Sem-

37. This comment reflects one rabbinic view found in Megilla 12a.

38. *Siftei Ḥakhamim, Mikraot Gedolot HaMaor* (Jerusalem: 2000).

39. *Rishon LeTziyon, Mikraot Gedolot HaMaor.*

itism and if such irrational hatred of the Jews was a historical reality in Esther's Persia. She finds it unlikely. She also questions why geographic dispersion would trouble a Persian ruler since many peoples were similarly spread out in host countries. Rather than understand *dat* as "belief," Berlin translates it as "custom" or "accepted behavior" and explores the possibility that in the ancient world, the dietary restrictions of the Jews or their unique holidays may have been relatively unknown, prompting Haman's observations to the king. In other words, Berlin, like Arama, understands Haman's statements as essentially true and reflective of an outsider's perspective on Jewish life. Berlin, too, emphasizes the fiscal aspect of Jewish existence in Persia, claiming that Haman's anger was that Jews were not contributing their share to the king's treasury; therefore, the king should exempt them from payment altogether by having them killed for avoiding their civic responsibilities.[40]

As You See Fit

One of the most difficult verses to understand in the *Megilla* is a simple statement made by Ahasuerus to Haman: "The money and the people are yours to do with as you see fit" (3:11). That there are evildoers in the king's empire who desire the destruction of others within that kingdom is no surprise. What is more astonishing is that Ahasuerus, the very king who had taken every opportunity to accommodate his citizens, be it the party, the letters in each and every language of his empire, or the tax remission upon Esther's coronation, agreed to Haman's plan. Even were he not seeking approbation at every turn, a king willing to rid his kingdom of a nation would create a security tremor in every other religion and nationality in the empire. It could lead to rebellion and insurrection. Some might regard it as political suicide, but Ahasuerus agreed to Haman's dangerous suggestion without need of much convincing. Haman was deliberately vague about the fate of this nation, expressing it in ambiguous terms so that the king would not disagree with him. When the king replied in 3:11, "Do with them what is right in your eyes," the king assumed, according to the sixteenth-century Ottoman scholar who

40. *Mikra LeYisrael* (Tel Aviv: Am Oved, 2001).

moved to Safed, Moses Alsheikh, that Haman would treat them justly. Ashkenazi on 3:8 has a similar reading:

> No king desires the destruction of a nation without a reason that would justify it because of the harm that would result from it, as it says (Prov. 29:4): "The king by justice established the land." If he destroyed a nation unjustly, his kingdom would not stand nor could he supplement the loss that he would have incurred from this action.

It is not hard to understand why the Sages condemned Ahasuerus as either stupid or evil.[41] One rabbinic passage even attributes to Ahasuerus more hatred toward the Jews than Haman ever had.[42]

The dialogue between king and chief courtier reveals the transactional way the king viewed those who lived in his empire. Subjects were not humans. They were taxpayers. If they did not pay taxes, there was no reason to let them live. If a courtier had designs on a nation, Ahasuerus was fully prepared to hand over his signet ring, have a drink, and then sleep with another woman. The plight of his people had no tangible impact on the king's lifestyle. In *The Beginning of Politics*, Moshe Halbertal and Stephen Holmes describe this kind of political callousness:

> If the sovereign is powerful enough to protect the people against hostile neighbors, he will also be powerful enough to abuse the people for reasons having nothing to do with collective security. The possibility that rulers will betray the ruled is inherent to the nature of rule itself and may or may not be rooted in the psychology of those who inhabit high office.[43]

---

41. Megilla 12a. The Talmud here, as discussed in an earlier chapter, debates whether Ahasuerus was shrewd or stupid, implying an intelligence that may be used for evil purposes.
42. Esther Rabba 7:20.
43. Moshe Halbertal and Stephen Holmes, *The Beginning of Politics: Power in the Book of Samuel* (Princeton: Princeton University Press, 2017), 166.

Rulers will betray the ruled. Whatever sardonic view we take of the way ancient Persia's governance is communicated in the Book of Esther, its inefficiencies and the ineptitude of its leaders, Haman's decree and Ahasuerus' nonchalance chills us. Incompetence slides into irresponsibility. Poor leadership creates a vacuum that wickedness fills.

In the Aftermath of the Decree

What does one do with oneself after making a declaration to decimate an entire nation? The text tells us explicitly, adding a poignant detail and another shiver to the chill the reader already feels: "The king and Haman sat down to feast" (Est. 3:15). In this intimate meal, two leaders of a vast swath of the ancient world gorged themselves, an apt metaphor for their narcissism. The king's self-absorption throughout the book was a function of wealth without limits, of judgments without consequences. Haman's own selfishness was tinged with deviousness. The meal they shared suggests that it mattered little what fueled their capacity to block out humanity and focus only on their own satiation; the outcome was the same.

The simple breaking of bread becomes an act of cruelty. In talmudic law, a judge was not allowed to eat on the day he condemned a person to capital punishment lest he develop callousness in judgment.[44] But Haman was already callous, Ahasuerus oblivious, and neither was interested in being otherwise. One passage of Aggada stresses Haman's despicable character and heartlessness while highlighting Mordecai's curiosity. It helps the reader prepare for this feast of the dead that Haman and his king were about to eat.

> When the letters were sealed and given to Haman, he and all the members of his group went away happy. They encountered Mordecai running after some schoolchildren and followed him. When Mordecai caught up with the children, he said to one of

44. See Moed Katan 14b. In an explication of Lev. 19:26, R. Akiva arrived at this conclusion: "From where is it derived with regard to the Sanhedrin who put someone to death that they may not taste any food or drink for the entire rest of the day? The verse states: 'You shall not eat with the blood' (Lev. 19:26)."

> them, "Tell me the verse you are learning." "Be not afraid of sudden terror" (Prov. 3:25). Thereupon the wicked Haman angrily declared, "My first victims will be the children!"[45]

The cruelty Haman displayed in *Megillat Esther* led to this even icier dialogue in the Midrash, unquestionably making Haman the true heir to the Amalekites who targeted the most vulnerable of the Israelites.

Haman's victory meal is not dissimilar to what the brothers did after they threw Joseph into a pit: "When Joseph came up to his brothers, they stripped Joseph of his tunic, the ornamented tunic that he was wearing, and took him and cast him into the pit. The pit was empty; there was no water in it. Then they sat down to a meal" (Gen. 37:23–25). In both narratives, the lack of empathy allows an innocent person's potential demise to become a source of celebration. Commentators on Genesis are virtually silent about this meal, focusing their exegetical energies instead on the selling of Joseph. Ibn Ezra does make a comment on 37:25, noting that only nine brothers sat down to eat, and R. Joseph Bekhor Shor on the same verse observes that shepherds never eat in a full group; some eat while others watch the flocks. Reuben, thus, was not with them when this happened.[46] *Ḥizkuni* suggests that the brothers sat at a distance from the pit, hinting at a scrap of compassion but then enhances their inhumanity by adding that they moved away "so they did not have to listen to his [Joseph's] pitiful pleas."[47]

The Malbim, the nineteenth-century exegete Rabbi Meir Leibush ben Yehiel Michel Wisser, on our verse in Esther is perplexed that the king would ever eat at such a grim occasion and believes that Ahasuerus was not fully apprised of the situation because of the speed at which the decree was posted. He assumes this because of the first part of the verse: "The couriers went out posthaste on the royal mission, and the decree was proclaimed in the fortress Shushan" (4:15). The cunning Haman arranged the meal to distract the king, causing confusion that spread

---

45. Esther Rabba 7:17.
46. Rabbi Joseph Bekhor Shor on Gen. 37:26.
47. *Ḥizkuni* on Gen. 37:26.

beyond the table to the entire city of Shushan. The Malbim offers the same overtones of false protection of the king that appear elsewhere.

A City Confused

We also learn that while this meal of two was laced with hard-heartedness, Shushan itself was profoundly confused: "The king and Haman sat down to feast, but the city of Shushan was dumbfounded" (3:15). Rashi and Ibn Ezra on 3:15 interpret this as the Jews of Shushan rather than the general population. Outside the walls of the city, Jews were an almost invisible and forgettable people. The city was dumbfounded because Jews throughout the empire posed no threat or danger. This reading assumes that the Jewish presence was so minimal that the news would not have had a deep reach in society. It touched only those who were to be most affected by it.

Rashi based his interpretation on a midrash that states there was little confusion for the non-Jews of Shushan, who stood poised to benefit from the massacre: "The gentiles of Shushan began to harass and taunt the Jews by telling them that they would be killed and their money would be confiscated."[48] In other words, the Jewish residents were shocked and confused at this sudden human loss and monetary gain. The unity that Ahasuerus strove to create with his lengthy opening celebrations collapsed into dissension at this sudden divide between the hunter and the hunted in this new political landscape. This reaction to Jewish death is sadly all too familiar to students of Jewish history. Rashi died in 1105. The First Crusade was in 1095.

Ibn Ezra also connects this verse about Jewish confusion to the first verse of the next chapter. The Jewish masses had no idea how to react to the news, in contrast to Mordecai, who immediately tore his clothes and dressed in sackcloth. Without saying so directly, this observation demonstrates that Mordecai, as opposed to his coreligionists, understood and was perhaps waiting for the grim lining that accompanied Jewish assimilation in exile. He was prepared; as an exile, he anticipated that at any time news could worsen and his people would come under danger, much as they had before. He was introduced as an exile because he had

48. Esther Rabba 7:25.

the mentality and apprehension of an exile. His very presence in Shushan was for the purpose of keeping track of current events. While the Jewish people went unnoticed, Mordecai saw no reason to do other than sit at the king's gate. But when the Jews suddenly became the focus of laser attention, Mordecai stopped sitting and opted, instead, to stand at that very gate in the clothes that shaped his identity. Confusion for others inspired leadership in Mordecai, who moved out of the shadows and into a place of prominence and influence, unafraid to demonstrate his Jewish commitments publicly. Where others held back, he held forth.

Why the Holiday Is Called Purim

As we reflect on the terrible turn of events, it is natural to question why the name "Purim" was chosen for posterity. In the second book of Maccabees, the holiday is referred to as the Day of Mordecai, a name that makes far more sense.[49] C. A. Moore writes that "many scholars believe ... that the word *purim* represents a later folk etymology for a Judaized pagan festival, that is purim was a name supplied by Babylonian Jews to a Jewish festival which had been initially pagan in both origin and character."[50]

The term *pur* appears eight times in the Book of Esther and hearkens back to Haman's decree rather than Jewish victory, memorializing a sinister game of chance to determine randomly the best day for extermination:

> For Haman son of Hammedatha the Agagite, the foe of all the Jews, had plotted to destroy the Jews, and had cast *pur* – that is, the lot – with intent to crush and exterminate them. But when [Esther] came before the king, he commanded: "With the promulgation of this decree, let the evil plot, which he devised against the Jews, recoil on his own head!" So they hanged him and his sons on the gallows. For that reason these days were named Purim, after *pur*. In view, then, of all the instructions in the said letter and of what they had experienced in that matter and what had befallen them. For Haman son of Hammedatha the Agagite,

49. II Maccabees 15:36.

50. Moore, "Archeology and the Book of Esther," 76.

> the foe of all the Jews, had plotted to destroy the Jews, and had cast *pur* – that is, the lot – with intent to crush and exterminate them. (Est. 9:24–26)

Ibn Ezra explains in the second version of his commentary on 9:26 that because two days of Purim are celebrated, the term *pur* became a plural, without dwelling on the reason for the name. It would appear that most classical commentators read these verses literally and were not puzzled that the holiday was named after Persian lots. The Malbim on 9:26 writes that the name captures this season of marvels: "Haman's lot turned into our lot since fortune did not initially side with Israel but turned into divine providence." But this obvious reversal of fortune could be captured in other words, in Hebrew words. Twice in these three verses we are informed about the lot and that it was cast "with intent to crush and to exterminate." It is as if the word *pur* itself is a lightning rod, instantly explaining the blessed irony of the situation. Three letters capture both Haman's intent and its opposite, since he was to die a death of chance.

There are many other more appropriate themes than fate and chance that emerge from the story. The holiday could have been called "triumph" or "victory" or "miracle." Purim as a name is neither celebratory nor religious, eliding the fact that God, not fate, brought the Jews of Persia to a magnificent denouement. If one believes Esther is essentially a comedy, then "lots" might make sense only if placed in proverbial quotation marks, suggesting that while Haman thought he could destroy the Jews with random "lots," the King of kings had other plans. The holiday's name reminds us that one's fate is as tenuous as politics, as a game of chance, as an overturned lot. If you do not want to lose, do not play the game. Some are forced to, and, in the event that one must play, it is best to know the game's rules and take calculated risks.

Chapter Four

Clothing Makes the Leader

Hatakh and the Role of Minor Characters in Esther

The Destiny Moment

Clothing Makes the Leader

> When Mordecai learned all that had happened, Mordecai tore his clothes and put on sackcloth and ashes. He went through the city, crying out loudly and bitterly, until he came in front of the palace gate; for one could not enter the palace gate wearing sackcloth. Also, in every province that the king's command and decree reached, there was great mourning among the Jews, with fasting, weeping, and wailing, and everybody lay in sackcloth and ashes. When Esther's maidens and eunuchs came and informed her, the queen was greatly agitated. She sent clothing for Mordecai to wear, so that he might take off his sackcloth; but he refused. (Est. 4:1–4)

Mordecai's response was unequivocal. While Haman and Ahasuerus ate, Mordecai tore his clothes to publicize the decree loudly and personally. Some commentators wonder how Mordecai knew this news,[1] and others wonder why only he knew it, since it was soon to apply to the entire kingdom. The confusion about Mordecai's knowledge is odd in light of the fact that we know Mordecai made it his business to learn hidden information and to act on the knowledge he received. As a courtier, his advancement in position was dependent on it. As a Jewish leader, his

1. Midrash Rabba 7:18, as cited by the *Torah Temima* on Est. 4:1, contends that Mordecai knew because Elijah the prophet, holder of secrets and hidden information, revealed it to him.

very survival depended on information and his ability to forecast, prepare, and act strategically.

It is Mordecai's response rather than his knowledge of the situation that is worth exploration. He did not turn to God in this time of distress. Our chapter opens with the traditional response to tragedy: wailing and the donning of sackcloth and ashes.[2] The closest biblical parallel points us to another courtier who struggled to represent the position of the Jews: Daniel. He, too, dons sackcloth and ashes, not to appear at a king's gate but to appear before the King of kings:

> I turned my face to the Lord God, devoting myself to prayer and supplication, in fasting, in sackcloth and ashes. I prayed to the Lord my God, making confession thus: "O Lord, great and awesome God, who stays faithful to His covenant with those who love Him and keep His commandments! We have sinned; we have gone astray; we have acted wickedly; we have been rebellious and have deviated from Your commandments and Your rules, and have not obeyed Your servants the prophets who spoke in Your name to our kings, our officers, our fathers, and all the people of the land." (Dan. 9:6)

The significant difference between the texts is their context. Mordecai's outcry was in response to an external enemy, where Daniel's supplication was in response to Israelite sin. And yet we expect that all situations of crisis generate both responses: looking outward and looking inward. The Book of Esther is filled with instances where the Jews are observed by outsiders, from the way the king stared at Esther, to the way Esther looked at Mordecai when he showed up at the king's gate in inappropriate attire, to the way Haman glared at Mordecai, to the way the Jews gazed upon Mordecai after he donned the garments of the court. Clothing in the Book of Esther draws us into this larger motif of social optics, suggesting the almost allergic reaction across Persia to internal reflection or the capacity to see beyond the immediate.

2. See Gen. 37:34, Is. 15:3, Jer. 49:3, Job 16:15, 42:6, Lam. 2:10, Joel 1:8, I Chr. 21:16, Neh. 9:1, Jonah 3:5–9.

The Torn Garment

Norman Cohen, in *Masking and Unmasking Ourselves: Interpreting Biblical Texts on Clothing and Identity*, connects Mordecai's rending of his garments to his tribal affiliation. Mordecai was a descendant of Benjamin. Jacob rent his clothes when he thought Joseph was dead and prepared to mourn when Benjamin was taken from him (Gen. 43:14). "It is not surprising…that years later, Mordecai, who was a descendant of the tribe of Benjamin, would rend his garments and don sackcloth when the lives of his brothers and sisters, the progeny of the twelve tribes, were threatened. Mordecai, a Benjaminite, reciprocated the response to his ancestor's peril."[3] Mordecai was also a descendant of Saul, who ripped Samuel's garment in a last attempt to hold on to the prophet: "As Samuel turned to leave, Saul caught hold of the hem of his robe and tore it" (I Sam. 15:27).

Mordecai's tearing of his own clothing had to speak to Esther in the language of absences. The non-verbal gesture of tearing sought to convey to her that something had been irreparably ripped. Esther was torn from her family, and Mordecai was now torn from his people. The tear is a primal gesture, connecting Mordecai to his grief, to his niece, to his people beside him, and to those long before him who also tore into garments to capture the pain that transcended words, like the sound of a heart breaking.

Jewish law demands that mourners never stitch the tear they made upon hearing of a death. The tear is a tangible testimony to loss, a wordless signal to others that the world is not the same, cannot be the same. Tearing clothing has a rich biblical history, signaling death, tragedy, or compromised leadership. Our first torn garment appears in the Joseph story when Reubern tears his garments, believing Joseph was dead: "Now Reuben returned to the pit, and behold, Joseph was not in the pit; so he tore his garments" (Gen. 37:29). Jacob next rips his clothes also believing his son Joseph was dead (Gen. 37:31–33). All the brothers then ripped their garments when a silver goblet was found in poor Benjamin's sack: "Then they tore their clothes, and when each

3. Norman J. Cohen, *Masking and Unmasking Ourselves: Interpreting Biblical Texts on Clothing and Identity* (Woodstock, VT: Jewish Lights, 2012), 146.

man loaded his donkey, they returned to the city" (Gen. 44:13). This tear was over the anticipated death of Benjamin or perhaps of all of the brothers because Joseph's generosity had been repaid with "theft." The first tear presages the second.

Tears appear throughout the Joseph narrative. When Potiphar's nameless wife, known only by the relationship she did not honor, tried to seduce Joseph and he refused, she fought truth with power: "She caught hold of him by his garment and said, 'Lie with me!' But he left his garment in her hand and got away and fled outside" (Gen. 29:12). The torn garment here supports a false accusation, a piece of evidence for a lie that opened the door to Joseph's second incarceration. First, the pit. Then the cell.

In completely different circumstances and many moons later, Samuel's clothing became a significant marker of his changing status: "Samuel was engaged in the service of the Lord as an attendant, girded with a linen ephod. His mother would also make a little robe for him and bring it up to him every year, when she made the pilgrimage with her husband to offer the annual sacrifice" (I Sam. 2:18–19). Young Samuel, in training under the high priest Eli, wore the clothes of a priest without ever being able to occupy the title, even though he deserved the position more than Eli's sons. Additionally, Samuel received a robe each year that his mother made, the gift of a woman who prayed for the gift of a child. Much love was woven into these robes that tracked Samuel's development far from home.

Years later, when Samuel had already become a prophet of note, Saul seized Samuel's robe, as mentioned above. It may have been one of the very robes that his mother Hannah made for him, but Saul tore it: "As Samuel turned to go, Saul seized the edge of his robe, and it tore" (I Sam. 15:27). Here Saul, a desperate man and a failed king, grabbed onto the only shred of redemption he thought he still possessed: Samuel. But Saul could not hold on to Samuel; the prophet left him physically and emotionally; the kingdom Saul never wanted was violently taken from him by the same prophet who anointed him. All of this was signified by the symbolic piece of cloth that remained in Saul's shaking hand.

Saul would be at the center of yet another torn garment. When he maliciously pursued David to the death, David secretly infiltrated Saul's camp. He could have killed Saul but instead took away a piece of his garment while the king slept, recognizable enough that Saul could identify it as his own: "The men of David said to him, 'Behold, this is the day of which the Lord said to you, "Behold; I am about to give your enemy into your hand, and you shall do to him as it seems good to you."' Then David arose and cut off the edge of Saul's robe secretly" (I Sam. 24:4–5). This tiny piece of fabric expressed a compassion so deep it inspired Saul to broker an uneasy peace with David, one he ultimately could not sustain.

Mordecai's tear may have captured all of these other narrative rippings and is reminiscent of a scene in Milan Kundera's novel *Immortality*. Brigette, relating her pain and anger to her father, kept making the same gesture repeatedly. Kundera writes: "We have encountered this gesture before: it expresses indignant astonishment at the fact that someone wants to deny us our most self-evident rights. Let us therefore call this *the gesture of protest against a violation of human rights*."[4] The body must express itself when it feels powerless against the world or when it faces the existential threat of non-existence. Mordecai's gesture was even more than that. It was made in public, made to tell the world that the powerless must grieve and then the powerless must fight.

Clothing Tells the Story

Throughout the Book of Esther, clothing is a prop that supports the story and, in certain ways, actually tells it. Clothing traces the trajectory of Mordecai's leadership, from the exile who tore his garments in anguish to the courtier who celebrated his leadership with garments reminiscent of the high priest. In between, we have the anxieties and events that led from sackcloth to "royal robes in blue and white" (Est. 8:15). The sackcloth was as religiously and culturally meaningful as the priestly robes were. Mordecai, unable to access Esther with words, spoke to her with clothing. He armored himself in the traditional garments of mourning,[5] using an encoded Jewish signal that may not have been evident to onlookers but would have been startling to Esther.

4. Milan Kundera, *Immortality* (New York: Harper, 1999), 135. Italics in original.
5. Sackcloth first appears in Gen. 37:34, when Jacob mourns his son Joseph. It also appears in II Sam. 3:31, I Kings 21:27, Is. 15:3, Joel 1:8, Jonah 3:5–9, Job 16:15, 42:6,

In sending him a new set of clothes to supplant those he selected for the moment, Esther told Mordecai much about her own shift. She was no longer sensitive to the Jewish language of ritual and loss. She now spoke the Persian king's language of rules and royalty. "She sent clothing for Mordecai to wear, so that he might take off his sackcloth, but he refused" (Est. 4:4). Gersonides, in his explication of this verse, assumes positive intent: Esther, like the rest of Shushan, was confused. Mordecai had instructed her to hide her identity, not to display it openly and brazenly as he was currently doing. She had no idea what prompted Mordecai to blatantly break with royal protocol. Perhaps his clothing had been forcibly taken, which would explain why he showed up in sackcloth. When she sent him a new set of replacement clothing and he refused it, Esther understood that something else was taking place, something of great urgency for their people.

When speaking through an intermediary, decoding is critical and elusive. Cohen captures this difficult means of communication when observing that "without speaking a word, Mordecai attracted Esther's attention through the garments he wore. The garments of mourning were an intimation of the violence and chaos that simmered beneath the veneer of the beauty and wealth of the palace in which she lived."[6] The Malbim and Eliezer Ashkenazi centuries before him, in their explications of Esther 4:4, both assumed that Mordecai wore sackcloth under his appropriate clothing or he would simply not have been allowed to come to the king's gate at all. This creative approach demonstrates more than Mordecai's respect for the law; it captures the abundant tensions of a courtier life that constantly demanded dual allegiances.

Mordecai put on sackcloth by choice, not due to accidental circumstance or external pressure, to show that when his allegiances were put into conflict, his primary allegiance was to his people. This is communicated baldly in two Hebrew words: *velo kibel*, he outright refused. Here Mordecai was teaching Esther a critical leadership lesson about obedience and disobedience, conformity versus conviction. The Malbim here interprets the expression "he refused" as a statement about

---

and Lam. 2:10, among many, many examples.

6. Cohen, *Masking and Unmasking Ourselves*, 147.

Mordecai's state of utter despair. He did not want to lose a moment of supplication and completely ignored the king's rules and Esther's compliance to demonstrate that only God's intervention could change his situation. No human action, let alone a change of clothing, would matter unless God willed it.

It was at this point that Esther understood something was profoundly wrong; an injustice brewing inside the very walls that trapped her gave rise to an unimaginable crisis. Her next step was to send Hatakh to Mordecai to interrogate him and gain the clarity she lacked.

Biblical Clothing Tells a Story

Clothing is not incidental, neither in Esther's story nor in the Hebrew Bible generally. In stories of change and transformation, clothing is often the first sign of the reversal of fate. When the clothing changes, the plot follows. After Adam and Eve realized they were naked in the Garden of Eden and covered themselves with fig leaves, God punished them, and then, to close the narrative outlining their banishment from the garden and the individual consequences they would suffer, reattired them. God offered them an added layer of protection with clothing made of animal skins rather than plants: "The Lord God made garments of skin for Adam and his wife and clothed them" (Gen. 3:21). Clothing in this story of primordial man and woman signifies, as in Mordecai's refusal, disobedience. God changed and improved the clothing, offering a covering of compassion in the midst of punishment.[7] Esther did much the same when seeing Mordecai, believing that a change of clothing could ameliorate the situation but was, in this instance, insensitive to its meaning.

Clothing as compassion is communicated in several other verses from the Pentateuch. Twice in Deuteronomy, we are told that the clothing of the Israelites remained intact during their time in in the wilderness: "Your clothing did not wear out on you, nor did your foot swell these forty years" (Deut. 8:4). This is repeated many chapters later for emphasis: "I have led you forty years in the wilderness; your clothes have not worn out on you, and your sandal has not worn out on your foot" (Deut. 29:5). Much later in Scriptures, this image resurfaces: "Indeed,

7. I am grateful to Rabbanit Chana Henkin for this insight.

forty years You provided for them in the wilderness and they were not in want; their clothes did not wear out, nor did their feet swell" (Neh. 9:21). In Ezekiel, the clothing God placed on the people was not basic but an elaborate testimony to divine care and attention: "I also clothed you with embroidered cloth and put sandals of porpoise skin on your feet; and I wrapped you with fine linen and covered you with silk" (Ezek. 16:10).

Clothing in the Genesis stories of Joseph represents favoritism, danger, and deception. Jacob, and later Pharaoh, gave Joseph a new set of clothes: "Now Israel loved Joseph more than all his sons, because he was the son of his old age; and he made him a varicolored tunic" (Gen. 37:3). When Joseph's brothers wanted to kill him, they smeared that coat with blood and brought it back to their father: "Then they took Joseph's tunic, slaughtered a kid, and dipped the tunic in the blood. They had the ornamented tunic taken to their father, and they said, 'We found this. Please examine it; is it your son's tunic or not?'" (Gen. 37:31–32). Deception and clothing feature prominently in the Tamar and Judah debacle: "So she removed her widow's garments and covered herself with a veil, and wrapped herself, and sat in the gateway of Enaim, which is on the road to Timnah; for she saw that Shelah had grown up, and she had not been given to him as a wife" (Gen. 38:14). The garments that told a lie in Joseph's story told the truth one chapter later when Tamar took out Judah's personal items as an accusation.

Clothing signifies a change of status not only for individuals; it can have that effect collectively as well. The Jews of Egypt were admonished three times to take the clothing of Egyptians before leaving for the mass exodus.[8] The silver and gold they took would serve as recompense and help them prepare for their future. The clothing may have had another function: to make them look like the free men and women they were charged to become; this external shift helped them see how little truly stood between them and their masters.[9] Changing clothing

8. In Gen. 15:13–15, God told Abraham about the future exodus and the wealth to be amassed upon leaving. Later, in Ex. 3:21–22, 11:1, and 12:34–36, this wealth is mentioned with specific reference to Egyptian garments.

9. For more on the significance of clothing and redemption in the Passover story, see Erica Brown, "Slave Wealth," *Seder Talk: The Conversational Haggada* (Jerusalem: Maggid/OU Press, 2015), 95–112.

did not change their destiny, but looking the part may have helped them act like free men and women.

Clothing was also a means to transform the sanctity of community, as evidenced by the detailed description of priestly vestments during the appointment of Aaron as the first high priest. An entire chapter of Exodus is devoted to outlining what Aaron was to wear. The chapter that follows communicates what was to be done with the clothing: "You shall take the garments and put on Aaron the tunic and the robe of the ephod and the ephod and the breast piece and gird him with the skillfully woven band of the ephod" (Ex. 29:5–6). When Aaron finished his service to the people and his time on earth was drawing to a close, his change in status was again told through his clothing. Moses was commanded to "take Aaron and his son Eleazar and bring them up on Mount Hor. Strip Aaron of his vestments and put them on his son Eleazar. There Aaron shall be gathered unto the dead" (Num. 20:25–26). Moses did as he was commanded, disrobing his brother to dress his nephew. Here clothing tells the story of leadership succession; Aaron left his people and Eleazar stepped in to replace him. The smooth transition from one generation to another took place in view of all of the Israelites, suggesting that not a moment was unconsidered in the spiritual leadership of the nation. We can imagine Moses taking off Aaron's tunic and placing it on Eleazar. Neither were stripped bare to accomplish this. Little by little, the shift happened incrementally. Sforno explains that the four standard garments worn by every priest remained upon Aaron. Thus, he may have been stripped of position but not of his holiness or his essentially priestly role. According to a midrash, the perfect death follows the ceremony on Mount Hor. It was the kind of passing that Moses himself longed for but would be denied:

> He [God] told him [Aaron], "Enter the cave," and he entered. "Get up on the bier," and he got up. "Stretch out your hands," and he stretched them out. "Close your mouth," and he closed it. "Shut your eyes," and he shut them. At that very moment, Moses said, "Happy is one who dies this kind of death!" Thus it says, "As your brother Aaron died," the death he longed for.[10]

10. *Sifrei, Haazinu*, #339. See Erica Brown, "In Death as in Life," *Bible Review* 15, no. 3 (June 1999): 40–47.

Sforno concludes that what remained with Aaron upon his death were the kind of garments that angels wear when they appear to humans. In leaving this world, Aaron indeed became angelic, a sacred figure shrouded in leadership memories, an ending told in clothes.

Appearance and the Jewish Courtier

In contrast to the Aaron narrative, the Hebrew Bible records the cynical view that clothing alone makes the leader, embodied in a verse in Isaiah: "You have clothing, be our ruler" (Is. 3:6); followers are drawn to leaders who look the part but may not exhibit the characteristics of leadership. The verse pokes holes at governance, suggesting that leadership is a shallow activity, relegated to surface appearances.

This reading of the externalities of leadership is supported by a verse introducing Esther's distant ancestor, Saul. The hapless young Saul lost his donkeys, had no knowledge of the prophet Samuel, and hid behind baggage at his own inauguration. And yet, the text suggests he was the perfect choice because he looked like a king. Saul was "an excellent young man; no one among the Israelites was handsomer than he; he was a head taller than any of the people" (I Sam. 9:2). Good looks in the Bible can be either a portal to leadership or a clever distraction from the business of competent management. Like Saul, Esther's looks are described as vital for the obtainment of royal position.

The same could be said of Joseph, whose looks were, not incidentally, described only after he achieved a degree of success in Potiphar's house: "The Lord blessed his house for Joseph's sake, so that the blessing of the Lord was upon everything that he owned, in the house and outside. He left all he had in Joseph's hands and, with him there, he paid attention to nothing save the food that he ate. Now Joseph was well built and handsome" (Gen. 39:5–6). Rashi, ad loc., observing the odd placement of this verse about his appearance, cites a well-known midrash that makes the causal relationship between success and appearance explicit: "As soon as he saw that he was ruler, he began to eat and drink and curl his hair."[11] In this midrash, power had gone to Joseph's head, quite literally. The text mentioned his beauty only because it was instrumental in

11. *Tanḥuma, Vayeshev* 8.

getting attention at court where his wisdom would eventually be noticed. Sforno on Genesis 39:6 adds another intriguing detail to the mix. He says that once Joseph had been promoted in Potiphar's house, he had time to devote to personal grooming and preening: "Joseph found time to make himself look handsome, having no longer to perform demeaning physical labor assigned to most slaves." Rabbi Joseph Bekhor Shor's reading of the same verse is less favorable: "Once he became important in the household, he forgot his suffering and his ancestral home and perseverated on his appearance." Ibn Ezra uses only one Hebrew word here in his commentary: "like his mother." Rachel's beauty is described in much the same way, and was, no doubt, instrumental in intensifying Jacob's love for her. Joseph's good looks, however, made him the object of the wrong kind of love, ironic after having once been the object of the wrong kind of hate.[12]

Mordecai, perhaps aware of the cost of good looks, challenged Esther to use her looks to achieve position but then to ignore them in order to focus on the higher goal of good leadership. Esther's prominence was achieved by beauty and *ḥen*, or grace. Grace is difficult to define but may be described as the elusive combination of charm, compassion, and thoughtfulness that is the humane side of beauty, suggesting an interior that parallels and complements the exterior. Grace is not only beauty but receptivity to beauty and the capacity to see beauty in that which does not appear beautiful to the eye. It was this charm that Hegai noticed and that the king observed. This deeper sense of attractiveness is in contrast to someone whose exquisite good looks contribute to a sharp, remote, superior, and distant demeanor.

By contrast, Saul's looks only drew attention to ways in which he was not wise. His failure as a shepherd, the emblematic occupation of Jewish leaders from Abraham to David, highlighted Saul's incompetence. Having lost his donkeys, he sought out a prophet to learn their where-

12. It is worth noting that while Abraham sent Eliezer on a search for the perfect mate for Isaac, a woman who fell off a camel when seeing him (Gen. 24:64), and Jacob wept when he saw Rachel at a well and kissed her (Gen. 29:10–12), Joseph, the only one of this line distinguished for good looks, was paired with an Egyptian woman by Pharaoh with no reason stated or narrative detail offered (Gen. 41:45).

abouts. Prophetic visits, one usually assumes, were reserved for those with questions of spiritual urgency. Asking for the location of one's donkeys hardly seems worthy of a prophet's limited attentions. Saul had the looks of a leader without the requisite talent, and, as his story revealed, not the requisite wisdom, courage, or fortitude either.

Clothing as Status

Clothing for courtiers in the Hebrew Bible often signals a change of position, as it did for Joseph. When Pharaoh appointed Joseph as his economic advisor, he needed to communicate Joseph's new status: "Then Pharaoh took off his signet ring from his hand and put it on Joseph's hand and clothed him in garments of fine linen and put the gold necklace around his neck" (Gen. 41:42). In the Book of Daniel new clothing and jewelry convey Daniel's elevated status after he interprets a confusing dream:

> The king called aloud to bring in the conjurers, the Chaldeans and the diviners. The king spoke and said to the wise men of Babylon, "Any man who can read this inscription and explain its interpretation to me shall be clothed with purple and have a necklace of gold around his neck and have authority as third ruler in the kingdom." (Dan. 5:7)

The dream was opaque, and no one could interpret it: "Then all the king's wise men came, but they could not read the writing or make known its meaning to the king" (Dan. 5:8). Only one man in the kingdom understood: Daniel. The new clothing as reward made Daniel stand out visibly when he already stood out spiritually and intellectually from the rest of the king's many ministers.

The same happened to Mordecai. His torn sackcloth was replaced by majestic garb: "Mordecai left the king's presence in royal robes of blue and white, with a magnificent crown of gold and a mantle of fine linen and purple wool. And the city of Shushan rang with joyous cries. The Jews enjoyed light and gladness, happiness and honor" (Est. 8:15–16). Immediately after describing Mordecai's clothing the text describes the emotional state of Mordecai's people. They were full of pride, as if they themselves were clothed in royal robes of blue and white. Mordecai here is not just a member of the court; he was likened to a king himself, at least in the eyes of his onlookers, who saw in his crown their own elevation. The colors Mordecai wore drew immediate attention to the visuality of triumph. This moment was foreshadowed in chapter 6, when Haman dressed Mordecai in royal robes, but that moment was not yet ripe for Mordecai. Two chapters later, the clothes were given to him out of merit, not because of someone else's maniacal dreams of grandeur. Mordecai dressed himself, suggesting that this clothing was an expression of his authentic leadership rather than a decorative garment placed upon him with no transformative powers, inside or out. They also had to be clothes distinctive from the king's garments, to demonstrate Mordecai's position, as announced in the very last chapter. Mordecai became second to the king, and the clothing demonstrated his wisdom, loyalty to, and lower status than Ahasuerus.

Mordecai's crown is the last crown to be mentioned in the Book of Esther, and aside from the king, Mordecai and Esther, the real heroes of the story, are the only ones to wear crowns. The first mention of a crown is the request that Vashti appear in hers at the king's party (1:11). She, however, refused; thus no crown was worn. The second mention of a crown appears during Esther's coronation (2:17). The third mention was Haman's request for the crown (6:8) – a request that went unfulfilled. Mordecai was given the royal garb, but the verses in which this took place, 8:10–11, did not specify that the crown was included. Clines observed that when Mordecai was crowned in 8:15, the standard word for "crown," *keter*, was exchanged for *ateret zahav gedola*, "a great golden diadem."[13] It may not have been the king's crown, but "it is the next best thing to it."[14]

Female courtiers also wore special dress in the Hebrew Bible, as suggested in Psalms: "The king's daughter is all glorious within; her

13. See II Sam. 12:30: "The crown (*ateret melakhim*) was taken from the head of their king and was placed on David's head – it weighed a talent of gold and had on it precious stones."
14. David J. A. Clines, *The Esther Scroll: The Story of the Story* (Sheffield: JSOT Press, 1984), 66.

clothing is interwoven with gold" (Ps. 45:14). This is confirmed in a narrative context during the grim story of the other Tamar: "Now she had on a long-sleeved garment; for in this manner the virgin daughters of the king dressed themselves in robes. Then his attendant took her out and locked the door behind her" (II Sam. 13:18). The clothing worn to cover her was to be shorn in an act of rape and humiliation at the hands of Amnon. Her clothing signals a painful transition, from a desirable and desired virgin to a woman used and scorned, who, like Mordecai, tore her garments in grief, mourning her fate: "Tamar put dust on her head and rent the ornamented tunic she was wearing; she put her hands on her head, and walked away, screaming loudly as she went" (II Sam. 13:19).

Esther had to make the opposite transition; she went from the status of an orphan to that of a queen, but she recognized that all she had meant nothing if she could not defend her people. The story of Esther in the Apocrypha relies on the message of changed clothing more than the MT text. In the former, parallel to Mordecai, Esther engaged in mourning behaviors when she learned of the decree against her people. Note that here she not only dressed like a mourner, but even injured herself physically in her distraught state:

> Queen Esther, also, being in fear of death, resorted to the Lord: And laid away her glorious apparel, and put on the garments of anguish and mourning: and instead of precious ornaments, she covered her head with ashes and dung and humbled her body greatly, and all the places of her joy, she filled with torn hair.[15]

In contrast to the canonized MT version, this Esther matched and exceeded her uncle in piety. She put away her finery, but went further, covering herself in dung, ashes, and torn hair. She looked and smelled undignified, caring little about appearances when life itself was at stake. Esther put the clothing back only before appearing in front of the king: "And upon the third day, when she had ended her prayer, she laid away her mourning garments, and put on her glorious apparel."[16] Before the

15. Book of Esther, Apocrypha 14:1–2.
16. Ibid. 15:1

crisis, the royal garb was an external expression of Esther's internal, unconcerned state. Haman's decree transformed the clothing into a mask for Esther's deepest emotions of fear and loss.

Among the Bible's Jewish courtiers generally, clothing represents a necessary outer layer of leadership that is to be confirmed by the behaviors of the one who dons the garments. Clothing cannot be dismissed as a superficial concern or materialistic flourish. For the psalmist, God appeared robed in elegant transcendence: "The Lord reigns, He is clothed with majesty; the Lord has clothed and girded Himself with strength; indeed, the world is firmly established, it will not be moved" (Ps. 93:1). Majesty and strength are the coverings of a God who has no physical appearance. These intangible properties demonstrate power tempered by beauty, a regal and noble outreach to a material world where clothing can serve as an end rather than a means. Clothing for biblical courtiers signifies achievements earned through wisdom, an imitation of a God clothed with majesty.

Hatakh and the Role of Minor Characters in the Book of Esther

> Thereupon Esther summoned Hatakh, one of the eunuchs whom the king had appointed to serve her, and sent him to Mordecai to learn the why and wherefore of it all. Hatakh went out to Mordecai in the city square in front of the palace gate; and Mordecai told him all that had happened to him, and all about the money that Haman had offered to pay into the royal treasury for the destruction of the Jews. He also gave him the written text of the law that had been proclaimed in Shushan for their destruction. [He bade him] show it to Esther and inform her and charge her to go to the king and to appeal to him and to plead with him for her people. When Hatakh came and delivered Mordecai's message to Esther, Esther told Hatakh to take back to Mordecai the following reply. (Est. 4:5–10)

Trapped behind thick palace walls and an even thicker invisible wall of distance between her current life and her past, Esther had no way to maintain ties to her uncle and her people except to trust in those who served her. Like Hegai before him, Hatakh became a critical go-between whose very existence symbolized the difficulty of straddling two unrelated worlds. Mordecai may have falsely assumed that as an insider, Esther would have naturally heard about Haman's decree. But not only did she have no knowledge of it, she also had no idea of her people's travails. Ill-informed of both palace life and public life, Esther lived suspended in detachment.

Hatakh, a eunuch who suffered castration, perhaps understood Esther's plight in an embodied way, and felt compassion for this young woman, who, like himself, was entombed in a golden prison. His name is a play on the word "severing," and he is arguably the most important minor character in the Book of Esther. More than relay information, Hatakh had to communicate the emotion behind the words. He was entrusted with subversive information that could have put his position and very life in jeopardy. The peril of his role is captured in a rabbinic observation about a witness to the interplay: "When Haman saw Hatakh coming and going [he witnessed this servant going between Mordecai and Esther], he kicked and killed him."[1] While we have no indication of any of this in the text, we can imagine that a man as paranoid and angry as Haman could easily have seen or been informed of nefarious behavior that suggested betrayal and rushed to stop it. This would explain Hatakh's name as one cut off; Haman cut him off.

Hatakh had to help Mordecai understand how insulated Esther was from the fate of her people and help Esther understand that Haman's decree had important consequences for her life as well. Not only did Esther have a life-changing decision to make; she had to make this transformation through the agency of another person. Hatakh was regarded as a person of such importance to this transformation that he is identified as Daniel in one view in the Talmud: "Hatakh is the same as Daniel. Why was he called Hatakh? Because he was degraded (*ḥatakhuhu*) from his position. Shmuel said: 'Because all affairs of state were decided (*neḥtakhin*) by his voice.'"[2] Rashi suggests Daniel was demoted from the leadership role he held during the reigns of Belshazzar, Darius, and Cyrus to service Esther. This association, while far from the literal reading, makes sense in terms of the way the rabbis regarded the significance

1. *Yalkut Shimoni, Esther* 1056.
2. Megilla 15a.

of Hatakh's contribution and also Daniel's background, ignoring, of course, the problem of chronology. Who better to guide those in Persia's royal court than one who was so deft at maintaining a strong spiritual identity while ably executing his courtier responsibilities?

Other Minor Characters

The range of minor characters in Esther varies from the singular mention of a name, as in Meres or Carshena (1:14), the king's legal advisors, or Parshandatha and Dalphon, two of Haman's ten sons (9:7), to Memucan, Hegai, and Hatakh, who have central roles in moving the plot along. Those who are mentioned only once, undistinguished by any specific activities, may serve as unnamed crowds who populate the palace and create the impression that the king was never alone. Surrounding the king with a beehive of bureaucrats with no distinct roles left him in the midst of noisy sycophants. As such he lived under the constant scrutiny of others and was open to their counsel. The continual presence of others diminished any time or inclination for the king's personal reflection.

Virtually every role that a minor character plays is presaged in the first chapter of Esther: large groups, bureaucrats who fulfill the king's orders, sages who are regularly consulted as a matter of protocol, and close advisors who are asked for counsel. Our first group of seven minor characters, named but without any distinguishing features or contributions, were tasked with bringing Vashti to the king's drinking party. We are unsure if Ahasuerus would have done this himself had he not been very drunk – "when the king was merry with wine, he ordered Mehuman, Bizzetha, Harbonah, Bigtha, Abagtha, Zethar, and Carcas" – or if it was typical to have seven eunuchs do one task. He may have assigned them as a group because he was unsure Vashti would come without a show of force and power. Eunuchs play an important role in all of court life and overcompensated for castrations by wielding control as gatekeepers to the king.

The king next consulted a group of unnamed sages or soothsayers to satisfy standard protocol: "Then the king consulted the sages learned in procedure. (For it was the royal practice [to turn] to all who were versed in law and precedent)" (Est. 1:13). Rashi on 1:13 explains this verse in precisely this fashion: "For such was the king's custom in every judgment, to present the matter 'to all who were versed in law and precedent.'" This procedure should have slowed down the king and made his decision making less impetuous, but, at least according to a passage of Aggada, it was not to have this effect. Ahasuerus wanted these legal advisors to judge Vashti, but because they feared it could have potentially dangerous repercussions on them, they told the king they were unfit to judge capital cases.[3] On this same verse, Ibn Ezra identifies this group of minor characters as court astrologers. Gersonides, however, believes that the king brought his case before two groups mentioned in this verse: lawyers and state philosophers, who were able to judge the case, and then astrologers, who would be able to forecast the best time to act upon the judgment.

Ahasuerus then sought out the advice of his "closest advisors": Carshena, Shethar, Admatha, Tarshish, Meres, Marsena, and Memucan, who are described as having "access to the royal presence and occupying the first place in the kingdom." Rashi on 1:14 defines "closest" as those before whom the king could present all his affairs, even ones as intimate as marital disagreements. Ibn Ezra on 1:14 explains that access to the royal presence was significant because "there are places where the king is not seen by all." He also describes four levels of advisors in the royal hierarchy. Gersonides on 1:14 adds that these advisors had constant access to the king because of their wisdom. He also suggests that this list of advisors was strategically grouped by wisdom in ascending order, with the least wise first. This was done intentionally, so that the king would hear counsel from each and minimize the intimidation of the least wise in front of the most sagacious. Yet Memucan advised first, and Ahasuerus went with his advice right away, not giving full measure to an array of opinions. Memucan's advice, as well as other pieces of counsel that come later, cohered with the natural impulses of an intemperate individual making decisions. Given this, one wonders if the counselors merely occupied a formal role without contributing much other than to foment what they regarded as the king's primal inclinations. This echo chamber of opinions travels throughout the scroll, suggesting that those

3. Ibid. 12b.

in power surround themselves by others who will keep them in power and make them even more powerful.

In chapter 1, Memucan stepped forward in a climate of inebriation, lust, and anger and inflated Vashti's refusal into outright disobedience that would have repercussions throughout the kingdom. We can even imagine Ahasuerus being drawn into a vortex of anxiety, realizing that his masculinity, his very leadership, would be in jeopardy if he did not act swiftly and publicly. In chapter 2, the king also took the counsel of minor characters: "the king's servants who attended him." The literal translation is "the king's lads," young, thoughtless colts who abated the king's anger and distracted him with a new plan to gather virgins from throughout the land. The fact that these are unnamed young men who came up with a rather preposterous recommendation quite suited to young men (they are not the eunuchs of the previous chapter) and Ahasuerus granted permission suggests another failure of good judgment. While the contest winner happened to be Esther, thousands of young women were prevented from normal family life as a result. The first proposal diminished women in their own homes. The second proposal took them out of their homes and diminished the losers in a harem filled with women. Yet, "the proposal pleased the king, and he acted upon it" (2:4).

Who Is Hegai?

Hegai, our next minor character, is introduced as "the guardian of the women" (2:8). He functioned not only as a guardian for Esther but also as a gatekeeper. His opinion of her mattered greatly: "The girl pleased him and won his favor, and he hastened to furnish her with her cosmetics and her rations, as well as with the seven maids who were her due from the king's palace; and he treated her and her maids with special kindness in the harem" (2:9). Rashi on 2:9 explains the causal relationship between the first half of the verse and the second. Hegai showed Esther favor by being "more expedient and quicker in bringing her [cosmetics] than all the others." This is a somewhat problematic reading because Esther asked for nothing – "she requested nothing beyond what Hegai advised" (2:15). One midrash posits that although Esther did not seek beauty treatments or ways to enhance her looks or magnetism, Hegai asked her continually why she did not adorn herself the way the other women did, worrying that if the king found out, he would have him executed for failing in his responsibilities.[4] Hegai played a central role as *shomer hanashim*, "guardian of the women" (Est. 2:8). He served as Esther's key protector and took her maidens under his caring supervision as well. A talmudic Sage may have picked up on the religious connotation of *shomer* rather than its denotation – one who observes – when suggesting that Esther asked Hegai for unprepared food so that she could *observe* the rules of *kashrut*. In other words, he was a *shomer* in that he helped Esther with her religious observance, her *shemirat mitzvot*.[5] This is nowhere indicated in the biblical text but perhaps is an outgrowth of a passage in Daniel that shows the lengths one must go in order to protect one's religious observances on foreign soil:

> Daniel resolved not to defile himself with the king's food or the wine he drank, so he sought permission of the chief officer not to defile himself, and God disposed the chief officer to be kind and compassionate toward Daniel. The chief officer said to Daniel, "I fear that my lord the king, who allotted food and drink to you, will notice that you look out of sorts, unlike the other youths of your age – and you will put my life in jeopardy with the king." Daniel replied to the guard whom the chief officer had put in charge of Daniel, Hananiah, Mishael, and Azariah, "Please test your servants for ten days, giving us legumes to eat and water to drink. Then compare our appearance with that of the youths who eat of the king's food and do with your servants as you see fit." He agreed to this plan of theirs and tested them for ten days. When the ten days were over, they looked better and healthier than all the youths who were eating of the king's food. So the guard kept on removing their food, and the wine they were supposed to drink, and gave them legumes. (Dan. 1:8–17)

In the very first chapter of Daniel, this young exile was determined not to compromise his spiritual integrity even at the cost of his life. He refused

4. *Aggadat Esther* 2:15.

5. Megilla 13a.

the king's food, a risky act of insubordination. Like Hegai and Hatakh in Esther, the unnamed chief officer tended to Daniel's needs, paying close attention to what might imperil Daniel. He noticed Daniel's diet before the king noticed it and sought to protect his charge. Rather than insist on obedience, the chief officer and Daniel entered into a pact, really a ruse. Daniel, bolstered and emboldened by his faith, told the chief officer that his simple legume and water diet would suffice so that he not break the laws of *kashrut*. It worked, and Daniel looked even better than the others who dined on the king's wine and food. The chief officer and guards all took part in this deception, because Daniel, like Esther, gained their favor through natural charm and intelligence.

Zeresh the Philosopher

Zeresh, Haman's wife, ironically became a key figure in her husband's demise. Haman would likely not have died without her and the advice of his friends, who goaded him to take a more expeditious role in executing Mordecai. Their suggestion of the gallows brought Haman to the king's chambers in the middle of the night and instantly made him an object of suspicion. In addition, Zeresh played an odd role as observer of societal truths: when fortune changed, her husband would not be able to surmount the powers of Mordecai and his people. One midrash contends that Zeresh was wiser than 360 of Haman's other advisors, informing the reader that Haman, like the king, sought counsel at every turn and from a great number of people – perhaps almost one per day or, in turning, one at every point of rotation – yet his wife surpassed them all.[6]

As with every notable character in the Book of Esther, however minor, the Sages sought an antecedent to connect Zeresh with someone else with similar distinguishing features and found one in her "father." Zeresh, according to the *Targum* on Esther 5:10, was the daughter of Tattenai, who is mentioned in the Book of Ezra: "At once Tattenai, governor of the province of Beyond the River, Shethar-Bozenai, and their colleagues descended upon them and said this to them: 'Who issued orders to you to rebuild this house and complete its furnishing?'" (Ezra 5:3). This identification has Zeresh related to a man with royal power

6. *Midrash Abba Guryon* 5.

who tried to stop the building of the Second Temple, continuing the rabbinic interpretation of the Book of Esther as a referendum on Temple rebuilding. Zeresh, who suggested a means of death for the most notable exile in Persia, could have come from only such stock. Certainly because she mentioned the family roots of Mordecai (Est. 6:11), her own family background could not be ignored. Like Haman, Zeresh had to emerge from a family with long-held biases against the Jews.

Zeresh and Haman's friends serve first as advisors and then as a motley Greek chorus. Haman wanted to boast to his closest supporters about his recent elevation in stature, but instead the group pronounced the impossibility of Haman's success as long as Jews gained the upper hand, as if this supposition were fact. Their critical role in propelling the plot explains the appearance of minor characters but does not mine the larger question of why the narrative employs minor characters in the first place.

The Literary Function of Minor Characters

After cataloguing the primary minor characters and their roles, we can reflect on their function. It is the minor characters in the Book of Esther who advance all of the major events. Minor characters pass on information and create access among those who could not communicate with each other or who could not gain attention or distinction on their own merits. Without them, the king would not have made his disgust at Vashti a national crime, and the contest for her replacement would not have happened. Esther may not have won the contest had it not been for the assistance of Hegai, and without Hatakh, Mordecai and Esther would have had no method of communication to save their people. Without the presence of minor characters, Zeresh may never have had the last word on her husband's predictable demise, and Haman's sons would not be listed and proclaimed in one exhausting breath. Minor characters play an important role supporting major characters and propelling them to make decisions based on counsel. They also serve as critical gatekeepers and informers.

Minor characters also function as crowds: revelers, partygoers, and postal servants in chapter 1; beauty contestants and beneficiaries of tax remissions in chapter 2; soldiers in Haman's plan against the Jews;

and, ultimately, victims when Haman's decree was reversed. One may argue that a crowd is not a "minor character" because faceless and amorphous groupings have no discrete function, but they do in the Book of Esther. Having a host of servants, for example, is a manifestation of the opulence of the royal estate and may also serve the deeper literary purpose of exposing the reader to the king's profound loneliness, a loneliness managed by the nightly parade of women brought to him for the pageant. They may distract the king, but they do not distract the reader of the king's tale. In ancient Shushan, the constant collection of people makes the king's isolation even more acute.

One compelling explanation for the glut of minor characters is theological. People who describe the book's central miracle as its reversal of fortune for the Jews of the Persian Empire build their case on dozens of unlikely scenarios with a lightning-fast sense of cause and effect, propagated by a staple of unlikely figures who make brief appearances and then disappear as quickly as they appeared, simply in order to facilitate the next event. Traveling back in time, one who observed the chain of events might begin with this narrative glue: had this not happened, that would not have happened, tracing it all back to the Prime Mover. God is, in this reading, the catalyst and coagulant who is represented by the string of minor characters. Humans take the foreground. God takes the background, but, of course, it is God who has made all the events happen along the way.

The Sages, without articulating this explicitly, may have had some notion of this role for minor characters in the Hebrew Bible. Take, for example, a character so minor that he is not named. In Genesis, Joseph was told to seek out his brothers in Dotan but he got lost on the way, and an anonymous man came to his aid: "A man came upon him wandering in the fields. The man asked him, 'What are you looking for?'" (Gen. 37:15). Basing himself on an explicit midrash, Rashi identifies the stranger as Gabriel: "This was the angel Gabriel,[7] as it is said,[8] 'And the man Gabriel.'[9] He answered, 'I am looking for my brothers. Can you tell

7. See Genesis Rabba 84:14.

8. Dan. 10:21.

9. *Tanḥuma, Vayera* 22.

me where they are pasturing?'" Without the appearance of this man, it is likely that Joseph would have made his way back home with an apology to his father. Joseph, not eager to confront an overpowering sibling gang of those who hated him, may have genuinely or subconsciously lost his way. The stranger's simple kindness ensured that Joseph followed the right path, a circuitous one that led to his rise to power in Egypt. It was inconceivable to ancient interpreters that a person of such importance in catalyzing the future of the Jewish people from family to tribe to nation would be unnamed. According to the authors of the midrash, the man was an angel, a messenger from God. With such an important role, he had to be given a name.

Readers who are sensitive to detail and understand the role of minor characters in this theological way will follow the intimations given by their appearance as a suggestion of the way that God operates in the biblical universe. Concealing divine providence behind these figures creates the illusion that humans determine their own fate, when, in theological terms, it is always God's doing. Not everyone, however, makes this association. Jonathan Grossman, in *Esther: The Outer Narrative and the Hidden Reading*, suggests that even serious readers of the text of Esther "have fallen into the trap that the author laid for them, failing to notice what was happening beneath the surface of the story"[10] since the book does not contain religious imagery or any reference to God. He believes that this phenomenon "is so startling that it constitutes proof positive of deliberate concealment."[11] He invites readers to pay close attention to all the events of the book that allude to God's active presence. The deliberate concealment of God's presence may have had to do with Persian censorship of the document or a cynical suggestion to the reader that political machinations fool us into believing that humans control outcomes when only God does that work:

> To highlight the element of concealment in a narrative (as a central development) the author may give this element a role in the

10. Jonathan Grossman, *Esther: The Outer Narrative and the Hidden Reading* (Winona Lake, IN: Eisenbraunds, 2011), 11.

11. Ibid.

> development of the plot. In other words, if in a certain story there is someone (or something) that is hiding behind a mask, perhaps a character that withholds the truth and operates in secrecy, then the issue of concealment rises in the reader's consciousness, and he pursues it throughout the narrative. The reader gains a clue as to the existence of concealed elements; not everything is exposed. He seeks the messages that have been hidden from him, with a view to discovering them.[12]

While Grossman does not explicitly mention minor characters as embodiments of this thesis, his general understanding may support this specific reading.

These minor characters may even have a teaching role for the reader, an "intended and calculated pedagogical device designed to embody and convey the Bible's most important ideas to the learner in a non-propositional manner."[13] The major characters do not tell the whole story. The major characters in relation to the minor characters complete the textual picture, offering observations, foils, and opportunities for a major character to be incrementally revealed and known. The minor characters in Esther highlight the text's gaps of information, provide an alternative perspective, or suggest a new pathway or direction for a major character to follow. They protect, conceal, or reveal a major character's secrets and are responsible for the promotion or demotion of those very characters.

Political Pawns and Movers

Another possible explanation for the appearance of minor characters is political. In Esther, many minor characters hold power that the major characters do not, suggesting that perceived power and real power are different. Perceived power is about position. People obey not because they believe a leader is capable or competent but because the authority

---

12. Ibid., 9.
13. Elie Holzer, "Allowing the Biblical Text to Do Its Pedagogical Work: Connecting Interpretive Activity and Moral Education," *Journal of Moral Education* 36, no. 4 (2007): 498.

of position dictates that they must follow. Real leadership and capable decision making, which may or may not be accompanied by title, induce a devoted following and sincere obedience. The text does not explicitly state this distinction between perceived and real power. It shows it. Ahasuerus and Haman had perceived power but followers regarded one as a fool and the other as a bully. Nevertheless, each had to be followed. Mordecai had real power but not perceived power in the first half of the scroll. This may also explain why Mordecai did not bow to Haman and why this angered Haman so much. Both knew who was a genuine leader and who was not. The reader awaits the moment when Haman's perceived power will be toppled and Mordecai's real leadership will be coupled with a real title, when the holders of perceived power will get duped or manipulated by a man and woman with real leadership abilities.

The Upstairs/Downstairs Genre in Literature

It is a common theme in literature to have a story told on two floors: the upstairs, where the monarchy or aristocracy resides, and the downstairs, where the courtiers and servants abide. Shakespeare's *The Taming of the Shrew*, Austen's *Mansfield Park*, or, in more contemporary literature, Ishiguro's *The Remains of the Day* are perfect examples of this genre. On each floor there are quibbles, larger dramas, heroes, and villains. There are hierarchies of power above and hierarchies of power below. Some servants have no role other than to populate estates as a display of wealth and also to suggest, by virtue of their very person, their own lack of importance. But the two floors also interact, and in a flourish of irony, the servants or courtiers on one floor often have more power than those above them because of the secrets they hold. Knowledge is power, and the covert exchange of information or a whisper of recommendation in a private moment between servant or minister to lord and lady often drives a plot. The genius of this structure is that the servant never expects, gets, or needs credit from the head of the house or its members; there are minimal opportunities for promotion and no real possibility of role exchange. The lower floors and the upper floors never fully interact, and it would appear unnatural for either side to have it any other way.

Each work of literature that sustains this structure assumes that hierarchies are the most natural organizational structure, often pitting the shrewd or wise servant as an ironic contrast to the malleable, impulsive, or undisciplined aristocrat. This hierarchy goes, to some degree, unquestioned. Sometimes, however, there are tensions among those on the lower floor who feel the injustice of their position. The inverse is rarely the case. Stevens, Ishiguro's butler in *The Remains of the Day*, expresses an almost regretless serenity at the lack of control in his life, implying that to serve others who are great makes one great vicariously. There is pleasure in the service of those in power. Being able to manipulate them through one's very obsequiousness becomes its own reward:

> What can we ever gain in forever looking back and blaming ourselves if our lives have not turned out quite as we might have wished? The hard reality is, surely, that for the likes of you and I, there is little choice other than to leave our fate, ultimately, in the hands of those great gentlemen at the hub of this world who employ our services. What is the point in worrying oneself too much about what one could or could not have done to control the course one's life took? Surely it is enough that the likes of you and I at least try to make our small contribution count for something true and worthy. And if some of us are prepared to sacrifice much in life in order to pursue such aspirations, surely that is in itself, whatever the outcome, cause for pride and contentment.[14]

The tiny contribution referenced here may actually be very large indeed in the life of the protagonist. Thus, a minor character may or may not be minor in terms of his role or contribution, even if minor in appearance.

Upstairs/Downstairs in Shushan

The maze-like warren of rooms in Persian palaces does not lend itself to quite the same spatial dichotomy of upper and lower floors, but space seems the only real difference in this ancient story. Persian royalty, it appears, sat with their coterie of ministers beneath them in a pyramid-like structure. This created the immediate visual impact of having all understand the levels of power. Thus, as mentioned earlier, when Aha-

14. Kazuo Ishiguro, *The Remains of the Day* (New York: Vintage, 1990), 244.

suerus promoted Haman in chapter 3, he also had him literally elevated above others in this pyramid structure: "He advanced him and seated him higher than any of his fellow officials" (Est. 3:1). There are also places reserved for royalty that brook no access to the commoner in the book, protecting the role of the major character from the very presence of the minor ones. Royal chambers cannot be entered without very special permission by some and without hesitation by others. Where Esther was worried lest her very life be at risk if she approached the king without being summoned, in chapter 6, Haman had full and easy access to the king's most private rooms:

> "Who is in the court?" the king asked. For Haman had just entered the outer court of the royal palace, to speak to the king about having Mordecai hanged on the gallows he had prepared for him. "It is Haman standing in the court," the king's servants answered him. "Let him enter," said the king. (Est. 6:4–5)

The king granted Haman permission to enter, but this seems merely a slight formality. Haman did not wait to be summoned to kill someone. Esther was petrified to speak up in order to save someone. Even without floors to clearly demarcate the status of characters and their points of intersection, the Book of Esther makes the demarcating lines firm. The Book of Esther uses the upstairs/downstairs structure but also upends it. Ministers, courtiers, and eunuchs showcase the impotence of the king and his impressionability, highlighting the dissonance between themselves and those without power who have the intelligence and capacity to manipulate those with power but no self-discipline. Those who have much power cannot control themselves. Those with little manage to control themselves and others.

The Minor Character as Foil

Uriel Simon posits that there are not many minor characters in the Hebrew Bible generally, and specifically points to the Book of Esther; no more than two or three are active in any one scene.[15] The crowd is

15. Uriel Simon, "Minor Characters in Biblical Narrative," in *Reading Prophetic Narra-*

thinner than one expects when scrutinized. Simon argues that the focus for the minor characters is always to put a spotlight on the activity or dialogue of the main characters. Critical knowledge about minor characters like where they are from, what they do, and information about their family or tribe is routinely absent; there is no character development, and they often appear for only one cameo appearance:

> The actions and feelings of secondary characters are described only when they are required to advance the plot or to shed light on another actor, and not out of a genuine interest in these characters themselves. Protagonists are subject to a different rule. Their personality is an organized part of the themes of the story; hence the narrator paints them in greater detail – not only what is essential to an understanding of the plot, but also what is necessary for a fuller knowledge of their distinctive nature.[16]

There is something troubling about this thesis, however. In the Hebrew Bible, we get virtually no glimpses into the interiority of any character, making everyone, both minor and major, somewhat flat and virtually monochromatic. We know all characters largely through their actions rather than their personalities. Additionally, in the Book of Esther, the minor characters do genuinely interest us. We want to know what prompts Memucan to suggest that the king make a public declaration of male dominance. Did he project onto the king the burden of his domestic woes with his comic recommendation? We are intrigued by Hegai, who takes a liking to Esther and sees something in her beyond surface beauty, and by Hatakh, who holds a secret about the queen that could put her in danger were he to be less of a confidant. We ponder if Haman's sons were killed because they, too, were morally stained.

---

tives, trans. Lenn J. Schramm (Bloomington, IN: Indiana University Press, 1997), 263 and *JSOT* 46 (1990): 11–19. This appeared in Hebrew in *Proceedings of the World Jewish Congress* (1969), Jerusalem: 31–36.

16. Simon, "Minor Characters," in *Reading Prophetic Narratives*, 265.

Once the minor character has acted, there is no longer a need for him. Jonathan Grossman focuses on the timing of the characters' appearance in the Book of Esther. He posits:

> The manner in which a character enters a story naturally attracts the attention of the reader, and is considered to be of great importance. The timing of a character's introduction into the narrative sequence, as well as the way a character is introduced, can contribute to the design and purpose of the story.... In contrast, a character exiting the stage attracts less attention, particularly when the character is a minor one. From a literary standpoint, the moment a minor character's role is completed, the character becomes dispensable, and the reader no longer expects the character to be part of the narrative.[17]

When the minor character has completed his or her role, the character vanishes with no expectation of remaining. The author may choose to accentuate the character before the character disappears to shed light on the protagonist, the setting, or an event.[18]

In very rare instances a minor character comes out of the shadows and becomes a major one. Mordecai left the safety of the king's gate, and Esther left the safety of her throne. The two could have stayed on the margins, but then there would have been no story.

17. Jonathan Grossman, "The Vanishing Character in Biblical Narrative: The Role of *Hathach* in Esther 4," *Vetus Testamentum* 62 (2012): 562.
18. Ibid., 564.

The Destiny Moment

> Esther told Hatakh to take back to Mordecai the following reply: "All the king's courtiers and the people of the king's provinces know that if any person, man or woman, enters the king's presence in the inner court without having been summoned, there is but one law for him – that he be put to death. Only if the king extends the golden scepter to him may he live. Now I have not been summoned to visit the king for the last thirty days." When Mordecai was told what Esther had said, Mordecai had this message delivered to Esther: "Do not imagine that you, of all the Jews, will escape with your life by being in the king's palace. On the contrary, if you keep silent in this crisis, relief and deliverance will come to the Jews from another quarter, while you and your father's house will perish. And who knows, perhaps you have attained to royal position for just such a crisis." Then Esther sent back this answer to Mordecai: "Go, assemble all the Jews who live in Shushan, and fast in my behalf; do not eat or drink for three days, night or day. I and my maidens will observe the same fast. Then I shall go to the king, though it is contrary to the law; and if I am to perish, I shall perish!" (Est. 4:10–16)

Esther challenged Mordecai to remove his sackcloth. He refused. Mordecai challenged Esther to approach the king. She refused. Both invitations and rejections were transmitted through a foreign source, a minor character presumably reliable enough that neither feared exposure. The book's author, by using Hatakh to deliver very difficult and intimate news and the subsequent reactions and requests related to it, demonstrates that the protagonists trusted in his services. Furthermore, the use of a messenger for matters of such serious consequence displays the great emotional disparity between the experiences and surroundings of the one in exile versus the one in the palace. Perhaps the greatest indicator of this distance is that Queen Esther shows misplaced distress when hearing of the decree:

> Also, in every province that the king's command and decree reached, there was great mourning among the Jews, with fasting, weeping, and wailing, and everybody lay in sackcloth and ashes. When Esther's maidens and eunuchs came and informed her, *the queen was greatly agitated*. She sent clothing for Mordecai to wear, so that he might take off his sackcloth; but he refused. (Est. 4:3–4)

We find ourselves relieved by Esther's agitation; it demonstrates that even in the palace, she retained a strong feeling of community and could be appropriately empathic and alarmed. But as we continue reading the verse, our feelings as readers abruptly shift. Esther was not anxious about the fate of her people but about Mordecai's wardrobe choices. As explored above, Esther sent him clothing that he refused to wear. There is only one set of clothing that Mordecai will wear from the palace; the robes he earns by the story's end. On a practical level, it seems odd that Esther had a change of clothing for her uncle on the ready. On a spiritual level, we are chagrined that Mordecai's emotional state did not itself elicit a reaction. As public as it was in the middle of the streets of Shushan, Haman's decree was totally ignored inside the palace. This striking interaction between uncle and niece is cluttered with people – maidens and eunuchs – a possible indication that Esther had one face for the public and another for the expression of her most private emotions. This is the interpretation that Gersonides favors when explaining that Esther next sent Hatakh to find out "*al zeh ve'al ma zeh*" (Esther 4:5), the why and wherefore of it all: "When she sensed that he would not accept [the clothing], then she knew that it was on account of great mourning and immense suffering. Thus, she sent Hatakh to Mordecai to investigate what this was all about."

One opinion in the Talmud reads Esther's distress differently, seeing it as an emotional and physical sensation so intense that the anxiety hijacked her body:

> The verse states: "Then the queen was exceedingly distressed (*vatitḥalḥal*)" (Est. 4:4). The Gemara asks: What is the meaning of *vatitḥalḥal*? Rav said: This means that she began to menstruate out of fear, as the cavities, *ḥalalim*, of her body opened. And R. Yirmeya said: Her bowels were loosened, also understanding the verse as referring to her bodily cavities.[1]

On every level, Esther's distress was understandable. She feared for her uncle. She feared for her people. She feared for herself. The Sages who commented on this unusual verb, *vatitḥalḥal*, tried a lexicographical jump – *ḥalalim* – to indicate that her very body cavities had a visceral reaction to the news. This reaction could have amounted to a number of physical complications, and Rav and R. Yirmeya entertain two: menstruation or defecation. The latter might seem a more natural response, but bleeding would have other implications. Bleeding foreshadows death; menstrual bleeding is a sign that new life has not been created. From a Jewish legal standpoint, it would have engendered a sexual separation between the king and queen. Yet in this reading, more than any physical impurity on the queen's part might have been the disgust Esther had for this monster who lent his approval to her very destruction. The response of defecation suggests this level of revulsion.

A Dual Identity Further Divided

In addition to possible emotional distance between uncle and niece, a host of other issues crop up in this interaction that are interpretation

1. Megilla 15a. For whether or not it would be possible for menstruation to be brought on by stress, see Jeremy Brown, "Queen Esther, Mood, and Menstruation," http://www.talmudology.com/jeremybrownmdgmailcom/2015/11/10/sotah-20b-queen-esther-mood-and-menstruation?rq=menstruation.

worthy and create the groundwork for the impending transformation. Laniak suggests that diaspora life is defined by having a peripheral identity and that Esther experiences this marginal status twice over: "Esther, like other figures in diaspora stories, lives at the edge of two worlds: her Jewish world with its center in Palestine and the Persian world in whose center she now lives. She is marginalized in both contexts, in one by physical distance, in the other by emotional distance."[2] To highlight the internal conflict and drama of Esther's charged turnaround, the text presents several obstructions: the inability for Mordecai and Esther to communicate directly, the supposed palace bias of the intermediary that makes Hatakh potentially suspect, the rules of court life around appearance, in terms of both clothing appropriate to the palace and the presentation of court members to the king unannounced. This maze seems, to the young and naive Esther, absolutely impenetrable. Levenson adds to this mix:

> How Mordecai knows of the plot when Esther, much closer to the seat of power, does not is one mystery. Another involves the knowledge that Esther's staff obviously have of her relationship to Mordecai when her Jewishness itself is a secret. In any event, given her ignorance of the cause of his public mourning, her extreme agitation would seem to be the result not of the genocidal decree against her people, but of her embarrassment at his grossly inappropriate appearance amid the opulence of the fortified compound of Susa. Perhaps she is also discomfited by the thought that Mordecai's public demonstration of his Jewishness will eventually undermine her own persona as a Gentile queen. The effect of vv. 4–11 is thus to highlight the distance between Mordecai the Jew and Esther the Persian. A critique of Jews who fail to identify with their people may be implied here.[3]

The contrast that Levenson points to of Mordecai's knowledge versus Esther's ignorance begins the chapter and will only truly resolve when

---

2. Laniak, "Esther's 'Volkcentrism,'" 79.
3. Levenson, *Esther*, 78–79.

they are both fully knowledgeable. This knowledge relates not only to a detailed report on the nature and force of the decree, the cognitive understanding that Esther lacked as the chapter began, but to the metacognition of all that this means for Esther and her people. Mordecai inducted her into this knowledge incrementally, balancing fact and consequence, statements and questions. In this sense, Mordecai fulfilled his role as *omen*, a guardian to his niece, not only as caregiver but also as mentor.

That Mordecai knew of the plot and Esther did not may not be the mystery that Levenson depicts. We do not know how Mordecai knew of the conspiracy to topple the king, only that he was in the right place at the right time. As mentioned previously, Mordecai was a leader who wanted to know and so placed himself in situations and locations where knowledge was the currency. Esther, by contrast, strikes the reader as a person who embraced willful and volitional ignorance. Life may be safer and easier as the passive individual who is acted upon, a lesson she surely understood and perhaps internalized from the beauty contest. Had she wanted to know the fate of her people, she could have easily obtained the information. Levenson's observation that this scene may be a critique of those who fail to identify with their people is well taken. Fortunately for the story and its outcome, Esther would soon enough identify with the fate of the Jews. Mordecai had to tease out this identification carefully, questioning her about her own sense of self, family, community, and purpose until she was able to formulate a personal and compelling answer herself. In this process, Mordecai became not only her teacher but an instructor to all future readers.

Once the distance between the two was well established in chapter 4, Mordecai's challenge to Esther could serve as either a bridge or a more final separation. Commentators, ancient and modern, failed to ask what would have happened had Esther not accepted Mordecai's challenge. Imagining possible alternatives highlights the importance of what Esther signed on to, with a realization of all of its consequences. In this sense, she was very unlike her husband. Where his knee-jerk reaction was to say yes too quickly, often irrationally, to be loved and then get trapped by the implications of his yes, Esther's initial reaction was to say no, reflecting a more cautious and judicious approach to major decisions. Ahasuerus could not change his mind, even when it was critical that he do so. Esther was able to be persuaded through a rational process, as evidenced by the dialogue between Queen Esther and Mordecai that must be analyzed step by incremental step. The first phase in the conversation was Esther's initial refusal:

> Hatakh went out to Mordecai in the city square in front of the palace gate; and Mordecai told him all that had happened to him, and all about the money that Haman had offered to pay into the royal treasury for the destruction of the Jews. He also gave him the written text of the law that had been proclaimed in Shushan for their destruction. [He bade him] show it to Esther and inform her and charge her to go to the king and to appeal to him and to plead with him for her people. (Est. 4:6–8)

In Mordecai's mind, laying out the edict in documentation would have been enough to spark Esther's willingness to lead. He perhaps naively mistook information for persuasion. Esther said no. Her refusal may have shocked Mordecai. It may also have surprised Esther that a woman of her docility – she seemed to go along with all the instructions given her – would stop at this one life-threatening demand. Some may believe that Esther, enjoying the privileges of the royal class, was not eager to let them go to benefit her people. The gate separating her from her uncle in sackcloth and ash signaled two wholly distinctive universes. She had crossed to safety. Mordecai and his people were left in the hands of a cold-blooded enemy. The wall between them, embodied by the human form of an agent delivering messages, could not have been higher. Such a reading may not be fair to this young and inexperienced woman, who was only just learning the policies and politics of Shushan's sprawling palace and her infinitesimally humble place in it. The feast and tax remission days celebrating her coronation as the new queen were long past, and we wonder what was running through the young queen's mind. Was her refusal an instinctive reaction of fear? Having not been summoned for a month, Esther feared she was already out of favor and that a bold request by Mordecai might have her facing the same fate as her predecessor. At least Mordecai was with his people. Isolated and unsure, Esther may have felt how little her cherished uncle understood her position.

To add to the anxiety, Josephus includes a threatening detail to the narrative as he imagined it. Ahasuerus, Artaxerxes in his telling, had men with axes to surround his throne. The message of intimidation and danger was unmistakable.[4] Bearing in mind that Esther was no longer a new bride but an "old" wife of five years who had not been summoned in thirty days, the idea of approaching the throne with this absurd request must have felt completely out of reach, literally and metaphorically. As we read the text of her rejection, we become mindful of the fast and slow pacing of the text. Mordecai is swift to come to the king's gate and urgent in his need to reach Esther. Esther is halting and long-winded in her refusal:

> When Hatakh came and delivered Mordecai's message to Esther, Esther told Hatakh to take back to Mordecai the following reply: "All the king's courtiers and the people of the king's provinces know that if any person, man or woman, enters the king's presence in the inner court without having been summoned, there is but one law for him – that he be put to death. Only if the king extends the golden scepter to him may he live. Now I have not been summoned to visit the king for the last thirty days." (Est. 4:9–11)

The refusal is filled with courtier jargon and is among the longest verses in the *Megilla*.[5] It suggests a long-held truth about the acceptance or

4. Josephus, *Antiquities* 11:6, 469.
5. The longest verse in the scroll, at forty-three Hebrew words, is 8:9, which also happens to be the longest verse in the Hebrew Bible as well. It also contains one of the longest words in Tanakh, *haashdarpanim*, "satraps": "So the king's scribes were summoned at that time, on the twenty-third day of the third month, that is, the month of Sivan; and letters were written, at Mordecai's dictation, to the Jews and to the satraps, the governors and the officials of the one hundred and twenty-seven provinces from India to Ethiopia: to every province in its own script and to every people in its own language, and to the Jews in their own script and language." This is not surprising, since, as demonstrated above, the verse's length alone communicates the slow, winding ways of Persian government. When it comes to bureaucratic structures, where one word suffices, seven are used.

rejection of leadership roles. A strong yes often stands alone as an affirmation. A no is often followed by lengthy excuses.

There is an underlying question that Mordecai assumed was answered, namely, would a woman at this time in Persia have been able to exert this kind of force and pressure on a king to do her bidding? We have already noted the role that women have played in his empire thus far. Thamar Gindin insists that a woman of this period could have had such power, and that "according to Greek historians, Iranian women (of noble birth, of course) enjoyed a much higher status than their sisters in other lands, and that royal women had far-reaching influence in the king's court. This holds true in matters of life and death as well."[6] She brings as examples Atosa, daughter of Cyrus, who controlled the royal court, and Amestris, wife of Xerxes, who made her son execute the leader of a rebellion who killed one of her other sons. She was also able to stay an execution. Artemesia, queen of Caria, Greece, was an ally of Xerxes who gave him valuable advice he disregarded to his peril. Some have tried to link Esther directly with Amestris or Amestris with Vashti but either identification is improbable. Perhaps there is precedent for a woman of power in Persia to make her views known, but this seems like an imaginative stretch since Esther was young and not long in the household. One cannot assume she had any of the swagger and confidence to sway her new and intemperate husband.

Mordecai's Strategy

Rather than acknowledge Esther's fears, validate them, and calm her, Mordecai exacerbated her heightened stress. He shifted in strategy from a declarative statement to a posture of humble inquiry, punctuated by nuanced warnings:

> Do not imagine that you, of all the Jews, will escape with your life by being in the king's palace. On the contrary, if you keep silent in this crisis, relief and deliverance will come to the Jews from another quarter, while you and your father's house will perish.

6. Gindin, *Book of Esther Unmasked*, 170.

> And who knows, perhaps you have attained to royal position for just such a crisis. (Est. 4:13–14)

Out of context, Esther's refusal had to be met with a multipronged approach. Unable to see her and the wrinkle in her brow or the consternation at the edges of her mouth or to observe anything other than her reaction to his wardrobe choice, he had to devise a brief and clever way to move her. He utilized multiple approaches without overtly suggesting that Esther would be guaranteed success. The first was modeling disobedience by coming to the king's gate in sackcloth. This seditious behavior did not work. He then proceeded to use the following four approaches to convince her, not relying merely on one but on the strength of them in combination:

- the argument of unity
- the argument of posterity
- the argument of history
- the argument of uncertainty

Being inaccessible at an urgent time, Mordecai needed to employ whatever rhetorical tools were at his disposal to communicate the severity of the moment and the unique opportunity that his niece had to rise to the call of leadership.

In the argument of unity, Mordecai suggested that Esther's allegiances must not be divided. She may have been in the king's house, but she was not of the king's house. Therefore, she was subject to whatever the king decreed against her own people, a people in desperate need of a heroine. Initially, this response unfairly assumed that Esther no longer saw herself as part of her nation, an odd and unsettling assumption given that she was raised by Mordecai. Yet it made sense given Mordecai's earlier instruction that she not reveal her ancestry. If her Jewish identity was so tightly concealed, Mordecai may have thus been suggesting that despite hiding her faith, she was still at risk. Mordecai's thoughtful provocation might have seemed illogical to her, confusing Esther as it still confuses readers today. If she had thus far been successful at concealing her identity, she would likely be able to continue hiding it and get around the decree. Having told her unequivocally to be silent, Mordecai now challenged Esther to speak out suddenly and unexpectedly.

We cannot imagine Mordecai ever revealing her secret, nor should we read this as an implied threat to Esther that he might expose her. This would have forced her to come forward to the king because her life would be at risk in either instance. More likely, Mordecai understood that Esther could conceal her identity for only so long. In the new wave of anti-Jewish sentiment, she, too, would be outed eventually, and this revelation would cost her dearly. In this, Mordecai was once again giving her wise counsel, echoing a sentiment in Ecclesiastes with a royal undercurrent: "Do not revile the king even in your thought, or curse the rich man, for a bird of the heavens will carry the sound and the winged creature shall tell the matter" (10:20). Words travel. Esther was not safe. She could no longer trust the forces in power inside the palace. She should, thus, openly embrace the plight of her people.

In the argument of posterity, Mordecai stated outright that the Jews would be rescued come what may: "Relief and deliverance will come to the Jews from another quarter" (Est. 4:14). To that end, Mordecai asked Esther if she wanted to be a lead actor in this majestic story or not. If she remained silent, the story would go on without her, and the credit and congratulations would go to someone else. Should she decide, however, to take a leadership role, she would be remembered for posterity. Posterity may be thought of as a legacy limned with vanity; the desire to achieve immortality always assumes that one is worthy of being remembered. Vanity may seem out of place as an incentive for action until we recall what happened two chapters earlier. Esther was part of another public event: a pageant. Her outside was on display in a contest she won. Now her inside was being tested. Her uncle encouraged her to pass the test.

Mordecai also implied another test and benefit in rising to this challenge that again, initially sounded harsh: the redemption of her father's house; relief would come, "while you and your father's house will perish" (Est. 4:14). Yet Esther as an orphan did not have a father's house, making Mordecai sound unnecessarily cruel and punishing. This is where the argument of history enters. Perhaps Mordecai was not referring to her father literally but to her ancestral or paternal home, a home that connected her to King Saul. Her uncle, who lived with the family stain that Saul had failed the Israelites for not ridding them of the Amalekite violence that birthed the likes of Haman, saw in Esther a chance to make good on the royal association generations later. Esther, by confronting Haman and securing his execution, would offer an alternate end to the family story, a much-needed corrective. The family reputation of failure would be upended by a narrative of redemption. Esther was a family ambassador; she, and only she, could reconfigure the legacy that burdened her family, her tribe, and her people. Without this, relief and deliverance would come to the Israelites, but the opportunity to redeem the tribe of Benjamin would end. Her Jewish genealogical line would be over and further marked by an inexcusable number of Jewish deaths in Persia. Yitzhak Berger makes this even more explicit and argues for a strong thematic link between the Book of Esther and the tribe of Benjamin, as described in the Book of Samuel, supporting his claim that "the author of Esther is fundamentally concerned with the reputation of Benjaminite leadership."[7]

There is, in this reading, a compelling political agenda hidden in the book's pages. "The initiatives taken by Esther and the Jews, to an even greater extent than has been appreciated, stand as reactions to unfavorable depictions of Saul; and, in the process, they counteract a running theme of Davidic moral superiority in the realm of justice and retribution."[8] The linguistic ties between the books cannot be ignored, particularly in this argument of personal history, since the expression "you and your ancestral home" appears in both Saul's and Esther's narratives. Samuel first used it elliptically when Saul lost his donkeys and sought out Samuel the seer for guidance. Samuel seemed to ignore the matter of the lost animals in favor of a much larger role for Saul as the next king, but, in a display of prophetic talent mixed with a dose of cynicism, he told Saul that the lad's work had already been accomplished: "As for your donkeys that strayed three days ago, do not concern yourself about them, for they have been found. And for whom is all Israel yearning, if

---

7. Yitzhak Berger, "Esther and Benjaminite Royalty: A Study in Inner-Biblical Allusion," *Journal of Biblical Literature* 129, no. 4 (Winter 2010): 626.
8. Ibid., 627.

not for you and *all your ancestral house*?" (I Sam. 9:20). Samuel, dubious of the kingship enterprise from the start, was not yearning for a king. He regarded himself as the leader but suggested to Saul that the people awaited him to take charge, linking him directly to a long line of leaders before him from the tribe of Benjamin. There is irony in this because leadership was supposed to come from the tribe of Judah.

The expression "you and your ancestral house" connects both texts even though their contexts are dramatically different. Saul found himself tossed by fate into a leadership role he neither wanted nor arguably deserved, for an undeserving people who merely wanted to be "like all the other nations" (I Sam. 8:5). The two narratives are also connected by virtue of other expressions, as Berger outlines. When Esther was agitated or confused by Mordecai's sackcloth, the text uses the unusual word *vatitḥalḥal* to describe her condition (Est. 4:4). She then announced a fast of three days. While there are many three-day periods in the Hebrew Bible, this is only one of two instances where the three days were devoted to abstention from food.[9] The only other is in I Samuel in reference to a battle of David's against the Amalekites. A servant who led David and his warriors to the enemy was sick and left without food for three days and nights by his Amalekite owner until David and his band restored him to health. The term used to describe his sickness shares the same root as the one in Esther 4.

Esther was told that salvation could be hers but that it would come regardless of her, but Saul was told by Samuel that when the kingship was taken from him, the Lord would "bestow it on another more worthy..." (I Sam. 15:28). Berger notes: "As is widely assumed, this parallel signals that while Saul lost his kingship to a 'more worthy' David, Esther will regain for the family its position of royalty, if only in the Persian exile."

Mordecai closed his plea to Esther with the argument of uncertainty: "And who knows, perhaps you have attained to royal position for just such a crisis" (Est. 4:14). Arguably, it is the question he posed rather than the declarative statements he made that pushed Esther to

9. For more on examples and the significance of this three-day period, see Erica Brown, "The Liminality of Three Days and Three Nights," in *Jonah: The Reluctant Prophet* (Jerusalem: Maggid/OU Press, 2017), 77–90.

reconsider. The argument of uncertainty assumes that an outcome is inherently unknowable but that conditions can be created and actions taken that may lead to a desired outcome, another example of a calculated risk. The situation in Persia for Jews was not ambiguous. Nothing could have been clearer than Haman's request and Ahasuerus' accommodation of him. If Mordecai truly communicated the details of Haman's perfidious arrangement to Esther, he was placing risk against risk. In reality, Esther had nothing to lose – as a Jew herself, she could not escape the fate of all Jews. But she needed to get to the point where the arguments Mordecai made moved her from head to heart and back to head again.

From an emotional perspective, the orphaned Esther had a chance of achieving posterity and bringing respect back to her family name. If she lacked a past, she could shape a future. Mordecai closed by asking a question that Esther could not possibly answer: What are you here in this world to do? None of us knows the answer to this question. In the biblical era, this gift of knowledge and purpose was given to a few prophets explicitly. Mordecai was not a prophet. He could not petition Esther in the name of God, only in the name of her people.

Fox believes that Mordecai was just as uncertain as Esther. He was not using the argument of uncertainty as a false motivation but believed that solutions were not crystallized and forthcoming:

> "Who knows" both expresses a possibility and grants that it is only that. Mordecai believes that it *might be* precisely for a time like the present that Esther has come to the throne. He raises the possibility that even before events began sliding toward disaster, some force was preparing the way for deliverance. This notion is teleological and thus assumes the working of some hidden guidance of history beyond human powers. This is not stated as a confident religious affirmation but as a possibility proffered with a hesitancy uncharacteristic of Mordecai. He is confident that the Jewish people will survive but uncertain how this will come to pass.[10]

---

10. Fox, *Character and Ideology*, 245.

Mordecai's uncharacteristic hesitancy may not be that uncharacteristic for a man of faith. Exile was long regarded in biblical literature as a punishment, a hiding of God's face, as recorded in this exhortation in Deuteronomy: "Then My anger will flare up against them, and I will abandon them and hide My countenance from them. They shall be ready prey; and many evils and troubles shall befall them. And they shall say on that day, 'Surely it is because our God is not in our midst that these evils have befallen us'" (Deut. 31:17). Mordecai may have felt genuinely despondent and uncertain that God would offer help at this vulnerable time because His people may not have deserved it. Nevertheless, Mordecai proceeded.

The argument of uncertainty is compelling because it speaks to the elemental drive that humans have to control their surroundings and their futures, without necessarily disciplining or controlling their own most frightening impulses. We desire, almost demand, to know that which we can never know, to remove ourselves from doubt and to rid ourselves of the burden of that which is vague or not fully formed. Simone de Beauvoir in *The Ethics of Ambiguity* believes that although humans try hard to escape from the human condition, they can never free themselves from it. Thus, a human being

> experiences himself as a thing crushed by the dark weight of other things. At every moment he can grasp the non-temporal truth of his existence. But between the past which no longer is and the future which is not yet, this moment when he exists is nothing.... As long as there have been men and women and they have lived, they have all felt this tragic ambiguity of their condition.[11]

Even failure can be more rewarding that uncertainty. Because ambiguity is such a treacherous condition, de Beauvoir observes two reactions to unburdening the self in doubt: either "by yielding to eternity or enclosing oneself in the pure moment."[12] These are the two impulses that Mordecai

11. Simone de Beauvoir, *The Ethics of Ambiguity*, trans. Bernard Frechtman (New York: Philosophical Library/Open Road, 2015), 7.
12. Ibid., 8.

strives to uncover in his niece. What he saw in Esther's response was her enclosure in the moment. Literally enclosed in a palace, trapped and protected by its many rules, her life became momentary, focused on the fleeting importance of beauty. Mordecai appealed to the competing impulse without demanding submission. Esther could, instead of staying in the moment, yield to eternity. And she did.

Sometimes only a few words can encourage transformation. One brief conversation through an intermediary totally reshaped the lives of Esther and Mordecai and the Persian Jewish community. Fox observes the significance of this destiny moment for Esther and her people:

> At this moment, she undergoes a profound, almost inexplicable change, as if Mordecai had stirred up in her a latent sense of destiny. She now takes the initiative. In a foreshadowing of the role she is about to assume, she immediately commands Mordecai to assemble the Jews to fast for her. She has begun initiating plans of her own, and she is becoming a leader of her people. Then she declares with quiet determination, "I will go to the king unlawfully, and if I perish, I perish" (4:16).[13]

Esther fought ambiguity with submission to a mission far greater than her life: the life of her people. Hegel reminds us that it is only through such life-and-death decisions that we know who we truly are: "It is solely by risking life that freedom is obtained ... the individual who has not staked his or her life may, no doubt, be recognized as a Person; but he or she has not attained the truth of this recognition as an independent self-consciousness."[14]

Mission Impossible

The reader is ill-prepared for the end of the scene where Esther makes a sudden and surprising shift toward duty and service, understanding the full ramifications such a decision has for her very life. Braced with

13. Fox, "Three Esthers," 53.
14. George Hegel, *The Phenomenology of Mind* (New York: Harper Torch Books, 1967), 233.

the knowledge she lacked at the chapter's beginning, she was ready to take charge of both herself and others: her maidens, her uncle, and her people. Fox argues:

> In convening such an assembly and issuing directives to the community, Esther is assuming the role of a religious and national leader and doing so prior to Mordecai's own assumption of that role. She has taken control, giving Mordecai instructions, enjoining a fast on the Jews, and deciding to act contrary to law. Her resolute behavior marks a woman determined to work her way through a crisis, not one cowed into obedience.[15]

Esther as an orphan went to the home of her uncle and then to the home of the king, each time losing herself. Nevertheless, as the Talmud described this destiny moment, Esther gained self-confidence. She clothed herself in royalty; not literal clothing but a royal bearing, a bearing that reflected divine inspiration; the garments of holiness were draped across an otherworldly queen. Esther was girded with majesty:

> The verse states: "And it came to pass on the third day, that Esther clothed herself in royalty" (Est. 5:1). It should have said: Esther clothed herself in royal garments. R. Elazar said that R. Ḥanina said: This teaches that she clothed herself with a divine spirit of inspiration, as it is written here: "And she clothed herself," and it is written elsewhere: "And the spirit clothed Amasai" (I Chr. 12:19).[16]

Esther's sudden declaration of a fast marked the intensity of her newfound commitment. Where the chapter opens with the people weeping and fasting in verse 3, Esther demanded more: a three-day fast. She asked this not only of herself but of all the Jews in the royal city. Interestingly, she also demanded this of her non-Jewish maidens, whose fate

15. Fox, *Character and Ideology*, 200.
16. Megilla 15a.

was bound with hers not through faith but through service. Anyone associated with Esther must feel her plight viscerally, as she did: "Go, assemble all the Jews in Shushan, and fast on my behalf; do not eat or drink for three days, night or day; I and my maidens will observe the same fast" (4:16). One talmudic reading of this declaration is puzzling:

> Esther sent a message to Mordecai: "Go, assemble all the Jews in Shushan, and fast on my behalf; do not eat or drink for three days, night or day; I and my maidens will observe the same fast, and so will I go in to the king, not according to the custom" (Est. 4:16). R. Abba said: It will not be according to my usual custom, for every day until now when I submitted myself to Ahasuerus it was under compulsion, but now I will be submitting myself to him of my own free will. And Esther further said: "And if I perish, I perish" (Est. 4:16). What she meant was: Just as I was lost to my father's house ever since I was brought here, so too, shall I be lost to you, for after voluntarily having relations with Ahasuerus, I shall be forever forbidden to you.[17]

In addition to fasting, the "new and improved" Esther would appear before the king, "not according to the custom." At face value, this means that she would breach the rules and appear without a summons. The Talmud here twists this reading and interprets Esther's change of custom with satisfying the king's lusts without her usual resistance. What could have inspired such a preposterous reading? The loss of Esther's life – "if I perish, I perish" – according to this interpretation, represented the death of her purity, a grace and modesty she maintained by not submitting to the king's advances willingly. Esther, to persuade the king to save her people, was prepared to invest more in her relationship with Ahasuerus. Bringing him closer meant that he would have more to lose if the edict came to fruition, but also meant a deep part of her would die. This reading takes the word *avadeti* from the same infinitive as "to lose." With this new understanding of her role, she was lost to herself

17. Ibid.

and would be lost to Mordecai (her supposed husband according to one talmudic opinion). The deliberate use of the word "to lose" demonstrates how Esther shed one identity for another, losing herself in a genuine attempt to finally find herself.

Chapter Five

Between Fasting and Feasting

Half of the Kingdom

Haman's Happiness

Between Fasting and Feasting

When Mordecai learned all that had happened, Mordecai tore his clothes and put on sackcloth and ashes. He went through the city, crying out loudly and bitterly, until he came in front of the palace gate; for one could not enter the palace gate wearing sackcloth. Also, in every province that the king's command and decree reached, there was great mourning among the Jews, with fasting, weeping, and wailing, and everybody lay in sackcloth and ashes. (Est. 4:1–3)

Then Esther sent back this answer to Mordecai: "Go, assemble all the Jews who live in Shushan, and fast in my behalf; do not eat or drink for three days, night or day. I and my maidens will observe the same fast. Then I shall go to the king, though it is contrary to the law; and if I am to perish, I shall perish!" (Est. 4:15–16)

"If it please Your Majesty," Esther replied, "let Your Majesty and Haman come today to the feast that I have prepared for him." The king commanded, "Tell Haman to hurry and do Esther's bidding." So the king and Haman came to the feast that Esther had prepared. At the wine feast, the king asked Esther, "What is your wish? It shall be granted you. And what is your request? Even to

> half the kingdom, it shall be fulfilled." "My wish," replied Esther, "my request – if Your Majesty will do me the favor, if it please Your Majesty to grant my wish and accede to my request – let Your Majesty and Haman come to the feast which I will prepare for them; and tomorrow I will do Your Majesty's bidding." (Est. 5:4–8)
>
> So the king and Haman came to feast with Queen Esther. On the second day, the king again asked Esther at the wine feast, "What is your wish, Queen Esther? It shall be granted you. And what is your request? Even to half the kingdom, it shall be fulfilled." (Est. 7:1–2)

Food and drink – though more so drink – plays an outsized role in the *Megilla* and calls for analysis. The Book of Esther is told through feasting and fasting, beginning with one feast, ending with another, and placing a fast in the center. Alter observes, "The story of Esther is a vehicle *for instituting* a feast, and Mordecai's grand gesture at the end as a newly appointed viceroy is to enjoin an annual obligation of feasting on his fellow Jews."[1] The feasting can be understood as a lighthearted expression of happiness, included for its comedic value – the slapdash, silly way that too much food and drink weaken judgment:

> There is abundant comedy here of a sort that would scarcely be allowed by the usual preconceptions about biblical gravity, and if it seems an exception to the rule, it may well exemplify the rabbinic interpretive principle of "the exception that comes to teach us about the rule." Feasting in Esther is intimately associated with sexual comedy, and the inventive deployment of sexual comedy in the story is not readily reconciled with the sober purposes of covenantal faith.[2]

The association of food with other carnal needs makes sense at the book's opening but does not explain the use of a drinking party as a strategic

1. Robert Alter, *The World of Biblical Literature* (New York: Basic Books, 1992), 30–31. Italics are his.
2. Ibid., 31.

instrument of revelation, the use of a feast as an expression of existential relief, or the sharing of food parcels as a way of creating unity and transactions of kindness in a community that was "scattered and dispersed."

Food tells its own ethnic story. Sharing it can remove invisible separations; both ones that need to be broken and ones that need to be maintained. Abnegation, by contrast, tells a different kind of story, sends a different kind of message.

Fasting Before Feasting

We have no indication in the scroll's beginning that Jews ate or even participated in Ahasuerus' lavish affair, despite the midrash that suggested this as the sin that precipitated Haman's decree. This uncertainty is unsurprising, since eating does not feature highly anywhere in the Bible as an activity of its characters unless it supports a narrative theme. We do know that there is concern about courtiers and food from the beginning of Daniel (Dan. 1:5–16), as discussed in a previous chapter, but that concern makes no similar appearance in the Book of Esther.

For the Jews in the Book of Esther, fasting came before feasting. Some scholars believe that the fasting theme in Esther creates an envelope structure for the entire plot development of the book, an opening with two royal feasts and a closing with two Jewish ones.[3] Fasting punctuates the ribbon of banquets as if to call silently for the opposite of excess, a stripping away of the intoxication to acknowledge a dramatic break of the festivities with life-threatening news. Berg notes:

> The communal fast of 4:16 may be similar in its purpose to the fast of 4:3. That is, this fast may be a sign of mourning in anticipation of Esther's expected fate. Esther's resigned words in 4:16, "if I perish, I perish," suggest that she does not anticipate a favorable reception by Ahasuerus. But her words also suggest that she retains the slim hope that her intercession somehow will prove successful. The fast of 4:16 thus represents a communal response to Esther's desperate act. The Jews fast in anticipation of Esther's

3. See Fox, *Character and Ideology*, 156–58.

> fate; but also in the hope that, despite the odds, Esther will succeed in averting the catastrophe that awaits them.[4]

The feasts happen in important couplets, with ten banquets in total. Each special occasion is marked by two feasts or pairs of eating binges. The book opens with the two banquets of Ahasuerus, one for his courtiers and the other for everyone in the empire (or the men); two for women, that of Vashti and later of Esther; Haman and Ahasuerus' feast after the decree to rid the kingdom of Jews; the two drinking parties that Esther ordered; the Jewish feast celebrating Mordecai's promotion; and finally the two feasts of the Jews after they triumph, one throughout the empire and one in Shushan proper. Following the reversal-of-fate theme, the empire-wide feasts begin with the king and end with the Jews. Vashti's last meal is followed by Esther's first royal occasion, and Haman's private celebration with Ahasuerus precedes the public meal made to honor Mordecai's new position. In other words, if you want to know where the story is going, follow the food. Some commentators look for a chiastic structure in the feasts. Baldwin, citing Yehuda Radday, notes that "three banquets take place in the first half of the book and three in the second; the royal chronicles are referred to at the beginning (2:23), middle (6:1) and end (10:2). But, as Radday himself admits, the stylistic elements do not occur in the inverse order which chiastic structure strictly demands."[5]

Jon Levenson offers a different structure for the banquets that maintains the theme of reversals of fortune while incorporating the fasting incidents in relation to the feasting: a bilateral chiastic structure.[6] Right after Ahasuerus and Haman's banquet, we learn of Mordecai's mourning and fasting. Right after Esther fasted and obligated others to fast, she organized two drinking parties, and Haman mourned between

4. Berg, *The Book of Esther*, 39.
5. Baldwin, *Esther*, 31.
6. For another depiction of this structure, see J. P. Fokkelman's well-known treatment of the Tower of Babel story in *Narrative Art in Genesis: Specimens of Stylistic and Structural Analysis*, 2nd ed. (Sheffield: Sheffield Academic Press, 1991), 11–45. For more on this chiastic structure in Esther, see Berg, *The Book of Esther*, 106–13 and Yehuda T. Radday, "Chiasm in Joshua, Judges and Others," *LB* 27/28 (September 1973): 9–10.

the first and the second (although there is no suggestion in the text that he fasts; the contrast is between jubilation and grief symbolized by food or its absence). Levenson draws attention away from a bookend structure to a pyramid structure whose apex lies in chapter 6 and whose major events parallel and unravel each other from beginning to end, even if the symmetry is not exact. Thus, where chapter 1 features Ahasuerus' grandeur, chapter 10 highlights Mordecai's. The two banquets in chapter 1 are paralleled by the two Jewish banquets in chapter 9. Esther identifies as a gentile in chapter 2 (or, more accurately, does not distinguish herself as a Jew) and gentiles identify as Jewish in chapter 8. Chapter 3 is about the promotion of Haman, and chapter 8 focuses on the professional elevation of Mordecai. In those same chapters, the anti-Jewish edict of chapter 3 is matched by the pro-Jewish edict of chapter 8; the fateful exchange between Mordecai and Esther in chapter 4 is paralleled by the fateful exchange between Ahasuerus and Esther in chapter 7; and then, just as the story converges, there is the first banquet of Haman, Esther, and Ahasuerus in chapter 5 to parallel the second in chapter 7. Sandwiched between chapters 5 and 7 is the expectation that Haman will be rewarded when Mordecai is rewarded instead. As Levenson says:

> The reversals in the book of Esther are so frequent, and the suspense so high, that it can be misleading to speak of any given scene as the pivotal moment of its plot. But chap. 6 surely defines the pivotal moment, for the royal procession foreshadows the reversal of Mordecai and Haman, as the former sheds his sackcloth and ashes for royal garb, and the latter hurries home in mourning. Note that this occurs between Esther's two banquets with Haman and the king, a point that 6:14 nicely underscores.[7]

In these discussions of structure, eating is not only the background activity; it is the setting where intense interactions take place: the humiliation of Vashti, the coronation of Esther, the revelation of Haman.

Jorunn Økland makes an important distinction between the royal feasts and the Jewish feast near the book's end: "In the case of the

7. Levenson, *Esther*, 6–7.

Persian feasts, the drinking is emphasized, whereas in the descriptions of Jewish feasts toward the end of the book, the emphasis is on gladness and sharing."[8] Drink, though consumed here in copious amounts and with the revelry of much company, provides individual rather than communal pleasure as an expression of happiness. It is a hedonistic pleasure that, when its full impact is felt, removes one from the group, often compromising personal dignity as an unpleasant consequence. By contrast, the idea of sharing food portions with others, and particularly the needy, signifies a different type of feasting altogether. Okland also notes that alcohol goes unmentioned at the Jewish festivities even though he assumes that drinking must have accompanied the meals.[9] We pick up the strain of transitioning from the Jews' intense anticipated anxiety to the release and merriment they suddenly enjoyed. Yet this joy had to be shared to be fully experienced: "And the same days on which the Jews enjoyed relief from their foes and the same month which had been transformed for them from one of grief and mourning to one of festive joy. They were to observe them as days of feasting and merrymaking, and as an occasion for sending gifts to one another and presents to the poor" (Est. 9:22). The text distinguishes between sending gifts to one's friends and to the poor; both are meritorious expressions of happiness. The scarcity induced by fear is met and surpassed by abundant generosity all around. By contrast, the joy that comes from royal libations will never result in generosity. Ahasuerus may have prided himself in offering staggering amounts of alcohol, but the beneficiaries of this gift likely resided within the confines of Shushan and his courtier set; they probably had more alcohol than they could safely handle.

The contrast between the Persian court's notion of joy and the Jewish sense of deliverance is amplified by examining the use of the Hebrew term *manot*, or portions. At the end of Esther, the word is used twice – in 9:19 and 9:22 – to refer to parcels of food distributed to friends and the poor. The same term, however, is also used earlier in 2:9 at the

8. Jorunn Okland, "Ancient Drinking in Modern Bible Translation," in *Stones, Bones, and the Sacred: Essays on Material Culture and Ancient Religion in Honor of Dennis E. Smith*, ed. Alan H. Cadwallader (Society of Biblical Literature, 2016), 92.
9. Ibid., 97.

beauty pageant, where each contestant is allowed to take parcels or items to accessorize herself and achieve the king's favor. Esther, before shining in this competition, was given special portions by Hegai to signal preference: "The girl pleased him and won his favor, and he hastened to furnish her with her cosmetics and her rations (*manotehah*), as well as with the seven maids who were her due from the king's palace; and he treated her and her maids with special kindness in the harem" (Est. 2:9). It would seem patently unnecessary to furnish her with cosmetics in addition to a twelve-month immersion in oils and cosmetics. Esther may have rejected these parcels and cosmetics specifically because she did not want to gain the king's favor by enhancing her chances: "When the turn came for Esther daughter of Abihail – the uncle of Mordecai, who had adopted her as his own daughter – to go to the king, she did not ask for anything but what Hegai, the king's eunuch, guardian of the women, advised. Yet Esther won the admiration of all who saw her" (Est. 2:15). In winning, Esther demonstrated that beauty was not about enhancements. Her essence was sufficient. Later, when *manot* are given among Jews and to the poor, readers hearken to this earlier usage in the story and are reminded that the book concludes only when meaningful rather than superficial gifts are distributed.

There is an additional critical consequence of banqueting. The feasting in the penultimate chapter is followed by a three-verse addendum opening with new taxes. Large parties cost large amounts of money. Taxes bring in money to pay for them. This is implicitly a warning of sorts: the book may begin with a party and end with one, but too much celebration and the everyday work of the government gets ignored, and the people are taxed. By assuring that taxation was put in place and knowing that the Jews in exile had a trusted courtier in high places, Mordecai was able to stabilize the Jewish community in the empire. There was less risk that at the next soiree Ahasuerus would lose self-control and put Jews in jeopardy again.

Fasting and Feasting Together

Up to this point, we have treated fasting and feasting as two separate, opposing acts. Instead, we may view them as interrelated. Baldwin notes that fasting and feasting are powerfully connected in the Book of Esther:

> The contrast between fasting and feasting, and perhaps the importance of what happens during the fasting as a key to the events of the feasting, are maintained in the institution of Purim. Though rejoicing is the main emphasis, fasting is also to be recapitulated in the commemorative annual event (9:31). Though the feasts are more prominent than the fasts, as they would have been in court life, it is in connection with the fasts that the turning-point comes in the story (4:14).... A hopeful outcome to the fast is therefore anticipated.[10]

Each act of fasting presages feasting, despite the fact that those who fast do not know their abstention from food will eventuate in an abundance of it. Fasting represents readiness for transformation, a willingness to sacrifice creature comforts and join communal suffering. When Mordecai, a loyal courtier, rushed out to the streets of Shushan, the public square of a capital city, and to the king's palace wailing, he created an awareness for all those around him of an injustice that could not be tolerated. This awareness, created by an act of communal fasting and mourning, eventually overcomes Esther, who shifts her sense of community awareness and belonging and then adds to the demands of the fast with a three-day commitment from all around her. The growing, public nature of this protest did not go unnoticed and precipitated the consciousness of a grave injustice that could no longer be ignored.

Rabbi Joseph Soloveitchik captures this human movement from suffering to the consciousness of needs to redemption that begins with human frailty and vulnerability, the state induced by fasting:

> Judaism, in contradistinction to mystical quietism, which recommends toleration of pain, wants man to cry out aloud against any kind of pain, to react indignantly to all kinds of injustice or unfairness. For Judaism held that the individual who displays indifference to pain and suffering, who meekly reconciles himself to the ugly, disproportionate and unjust in life, is not capable of appreciating beauty and goodness.... For Judaism, need-

10. Baldwin, *Esther*, 29.

> awareness constitutes part of the definition of human existence. Need-awareness turns into passional experience, into a suffering awareness.[11]

Esther's destiny moment was tied into this new awareness of suffering, a capacity to internalize and feel the burden of her people experientially for the first time. It makes sense that her first charge to herself, her uncle, and the others was to fast. In that act she was essentially catching up to the rest of the community, who had been fasting from the chapter's beginning. But the fast within the palace instead of outside on the streets was more official; it concretized the raw emotions of the moment into action. These same raw emotions surfaced later when the Jews were victorious and the fasting turned to feasting. And just as fasting was a communal activity, food needed to be shared, a joy given out in little parcels to friends and those in need.

11. Joseph B. Soloveitchik, "Redemption, Prayer and Talmud Torah," *Tradition* 17, no. 2 (1978): 65.

Half of the Kingdom

> "What troubles you, Queen Esther?" the king asked her. "And what is your request? Even to half the kingdom, it shall be granted you." (Est. 5:3)

> At the wine feast, the king asked Esther, "What is your wish? It shall be granted you. And what is your request? Even to half the kingdom, it shall be fulfilled." (Est. 5:6)

> On the second day, the king again asked Esther at the wine feast, "What is your wish, Queen Esther? It shall be granted you. And what is your request? Even to half the kingdom, it shall be fulfilled." (Est. 7:2)

> Queen Esther replied: "If Your Majesty will do me the favor, and if it pleases Your Majesty, let my life be granted me as my wish, and my people as my request. For we have been sold, my people and I, to be destroyed, massacred, and exterminated. Had we only been sold as bondmen and bondwomen, I would have kept silent; for the adversary is not worthy of the king's trouble." (Est. 7:3–4)

Esther's three-day fast ended with an anxiety-ridden visit to the king's chamber. As with other three-day periods of anticipation and worry in the Hebrew Bible, such as Abraham's difficult journey to Mount Moriah to bind his son, the three-day wait for revelation at Sinai, or Jonah's three days in the belly of a large fish, we the readers are trapped with Esther in the thick of her three-day wait.[1] She waited once before, in chapter 2, to meet the king for the first time, but perhaps with no desire to triumph. It may have been a wait of many months, even after the six months of pampering in oil and another six in myrrh. But there is no comment on the anxiety of that wait. Esther's second visit portended much more, and the waiting was not about her fate alone.

"There is no growth, no development without waiting," Andrea Kohler writes in *Passing Time: An Essay on Waiting*.[2] Waiting is a state of anticipation and anxiety. It can be characterized by tedium or tension, depending on what one is waiting for. "We can never shake the constitutive duality of our existence," writes Kohler, "indelibly marked as it is by the unremitting interplay between sleeping and waking, absence and presence, the not-yet and the no-longer."[3] As Esther awaited her visit, she remained suspended between the antipodes of breathing and the holding in of breath, the temporal and the permanent. This sentiment may have been felt, if not expressed, in the urgency of the moment, when Esther initially refused Mordecai's challenge: "All the king's courtiers and the people of the king's provinces know that if any person, man or woman, enters the king's presence in the inner court without having been summoned, there is but one law for him – that he be put to death. Only if the king extends the golden scepter to him may he live. Now I have not been summoned to visit the king for the last thirty days" (4:11). Esther's loquaciousness at this moment may have hidden her fear; the refusal hid the cowardice or insecurity behind excuses.

From the time Mordecai issued his challenge, Esther understood that her life and that of her people was about to change radically, but she had no idea how. Her only imagined choices were execution, banishment, or toleration. Without stating it explicitly, Esther meditated on

1. For reflections on the three-day period in the Hebrew Bible, see Erica Brown, "The Liminality of Three Days and Three Nights," in *Jonah: The Reluctant Prophet* (Jerusalem: Maggid/OU Press 2017), 77–90.
2. *Passing Time* (New York: Upper West Side Philosophers, Inc., 2017), 18.
3. Ibid., 20.

Vashti's fate. Queens were disposable in Ahasuerus' universe. A minority people was absolutely fungible.

We can almost imagine Esther tiptoeing into the antechamber, trying to go unnoticed to all but the king, as we visualize the intimidation she must have experienced in the verse: "On the third day, Esther put on royal apparel and stood in the inner court of the king's palace, facing the king's palace, while the king was sitting on his royal throne room facing the entrance of the palace" (5:1). Esther must have felt weak indeed as her maids put on the appropriate clothing and jewelry. "Putting on royalty," the literal translation of *vatilbash Esther malkhut,* makes little sense. Gersonides is quick to point out a missing word; she wore the *garments* of royalty. What would it mean to wear royalty itself? Rashi, citing the Talmud, states that when Esther was garbed in majesty this was no reference to her clothing but to *ruaḥ hakodesh,* divine inspiration. As mentioned earlier, she wore majesty itself. One could interpret this as a woman stepping into clothing that transformed her entire appearance, giving her grace and bearing. We might call this leadership presence; the gravitas of authority combined with an air of beauty that originally made Esther an instant pageant winner. She was royalty itself; clothing was simply a propaedeutic to meet the king. There was no need to share this detail had the text not told us what she truly needed: divine guidance, an inner voice of wisdom and transcendence that was to inform her every word if she could hear its resonances. Ibn Yahya contends that the text tells us that "Esther put on royal apparel" (Est. 5:1) to mark the transition from the sackcloth and ash she wore until this point.

There was much at stake as Esther stood in this vast and cavernous space, humbled and daunted by what lay ahead. The verse offers us stage directions, explaining how Esther positioned herself to be noticed. Ahasuerus' throne faced the palace. She stood in the part of the palace permitted to her, facing his throne. With a likely constant flow of human traffic entering and exiting, Esther may have had to stand for hours until the king took note of her. Ibn Ezra on 5:1, perhaps in a spate of wishful thinking, writes that because the text stresses that the king's throne faced the entrance of the palace, "he noticed her immediately." Such was Esther. She stood out, and the king noticed her immediately. Ibn Ezra may have picked up on Esther's self-consciousness; each piece of clothing she put on, each step of her foot in the palace heightened her awareness of the consequences of her untoward approach. She both wanted to be noticed and feared being seen.

The King Notices

Disobedience worked in Esther's favor. The king did not chastise her for impropriety, nor did he comment on her clothing, nor tell her to wait. The moment he saw her, Ahasuerus bellowed a greeting that showed he noticed something desperate and pained about her, the pathos of the fasting woman riddled with distress. The very king who was trapped by laws that entangled him and his court suddenly dropped all protocol: "What troubles you, Queen Esther?" the king asked her. "And what is your request? Even to half the kingdom, it shall be granted you" (Est. 5:3). Here, Gersonides, a careful reader of Esther, wonders why Ahasuerus immediately assumed something was wrong with Esther and not that she merely sought his company. Perhaps he knew that breaking the rules must have been precipitated by the most grievous of difficulties. The Malbim is quick to add on 5:2 that because of his love for Esther, Ahasuerus would never have prevented her from entering. The prohibition to enter the inner chamber was only for those who did not have the king's favor. "Even when she came to the king's palace it was beloved and treasured to him, and he had no thought to cause her anguish by having her wait until he extended his scepter."

A scepter does not appear often in the Bible. It is used in the penultimate chapter of Genesis: "The scepter shall not depart from Judah nor the ruler's staff from between his feet" (Gen. 49:10). It is Judah's instrument of power: "What I see for them is not yet. What I behold will not be soon: a star rises from Jacob, a scepter comes forth from Israel; it smashes the brow of Moab, the foundation of all children of Seth" (Num. 24:17). God is also referred to as having a scepter as a symbol of might: "Your divine throne is everlasting; Your royal scepter is a scepter of equity" (Ps. 45:6). The scepter, or *sharvit,* as opposed to the *shevet,* the rod of leadership, appears only four times in the Hebrew Bible, all in the Book of Esther, and twice in one verse.[4] All uses are

4. Esther 4:11, 5:2, 8:4.

combined with the verb "to extend," and it appears to be an Akkadian loan word.[5]

The extension of the scepter, according to Ibn Ezra, was the way that the law of the king was promulgated. It was the visual symbol that welcomed or dismissed the king's supplicants. "The king extended to Esther the golden scepter that he had in his hand, and Esther approached and touched the tip of the scepter" (5:2).[6] Later, at the second of Esther's parties, when she beseeched the king again, the king extended his scepter before she pleaded with him:

> Esther spoke to the king again, falling at his feet and weeping, and beseeching him to avert the evil plotted by Haman the Agagite against the Jews. The king extended the golden scepter to Esther, and Esther arose and stood before the king. "If it please Your Majesty," she said, "and if I have won your favor and the proposal seems right to Your Majesty, and if I am pleasing to you." (8:4–5).

Here, the Malbim adds an important detail. The extension of the scepter gave permission for her to speak with the king in private. We can imagine Ahasuerus pointing with his scepter for Esther to stand and then using it to point to his attendants to leave. Esther was told to rise from her prostrate position and state her case. She began to do so dispassionately by recounting Haman's decree but then made her petition personal: "For how can I bear to see the disaster which will befall my people! And how can I bear to see the destruction of my kindred!" (8:6). She was not simply stating and restating her relationship to the issue;

---

5. See Dalley, *Esther's Revenge*, 171.
6. According to several modern Bible scholars, touching the scepter carries a sexual connotation that is difficult to ignore. Alter writes: "This is obviously a gesture symbolizing the conferral of royal favor. But in light of the sexualized atmosphere of the tale, and the oblique hint of a question about royal sexual performance in the nightly testing of the beautiful virgins, it seems legitimate to suggest that a sexual double meaning is lurking here." Such a reading coheres with the king's depraved sexual needs; even in a maudlin state of distress, the king saw Esther first as object and then as person. But this reading, however tempting, does not accord with the king's general demeanor in the text. He expressed genuine concern about her, not about himself. See Alter, *Strong as Death Is Love*, 105.

she was adding something new, appealing not to the king's concern for her people but his concern for her.

In this scene in chapter 8, "disaster" was not as final as "destruction." Esther began with the Hebrew *ra'a*; the evil she might have to see could have been any number of terrible incidents, but *ovdan* speaks to a total decimation. First, she pointed out that her people were in danger but then moved to her very family: *moladeti,* those of her birthplace. She asked the king several times if she found favor in his eyes. With his affirmation, she was ready to put the ultimate question to him: If I find favor in your eyes, how can those who were responsible for my birth not find mercy in your eyes? It was a gambit, and one that worked.

The King's Reaction

One of the striking aspects of Esther's approach to the king is that he seemed to notice her distress when he asserted, *Ma lakh Esther*? – "What distresses you, Esther?" (5:3). Ibn Yahya on 5:3 understands this question as utilitarian in nature. Esther would not have come to the king's chamber had it not been a serious matter because there were consequences for coming unbidden. She must have wanted something, and the king was as direct as possible in getting it out of her. Gersonides follows a similar reasoning and adds, as another interpretation, that Esther looked anguished. Fasting and weeping obviously changed her appearance. The king, who picked Esther after a twelve-month required process of excessive pampering had, no doubt, an expertly trained eye for beauty and its absence. He could not help but notice that the grace he saw at first had morphed into something else. But none of the classical commentators make an obvious connection to this very same question asked in a different context. The expression the king used appears in Genesis 21 when an angel appeared to Hagar after she became lost and ran out of water. He saw a woman in distress over her dying son and inquired: "God heard the cry of the boy, and an angel of God called to Hagar from heaven and said to her, 'What troubles you, Hagar? (*Ma lakh, Hagar?*) Fear not, for God has heeded the cry of the boy where he is" (Gen. 21:17). Virtually every medieval commentator comments on other aspects of the verse. The fact that God had compassion on Ishmael and responded to his situation rather than Hagar's desperation led to a reading of this question as a criticism, more "What's the matter with you?" than "What is wrong?" There seems implicit in the question a sense that Hagar did not do all she could have done to save her son. When the angel opened her eyes and she saw a well right in front of her, her flagrant inability to tap into the resources around her became obvious. Ahasuerus may have meant similarly: "What is wrong with you, Esther, that you came to my chamber unsummoned?" But what may have been initially harsh or perceived that way softened into the desire to fulfill any request, up to half of the kingdom.

A Generous Offer?

"Up to half of the kingdom" is a heady offer for a young queen. Repeated like a drumbeat, it seems to signal the very kind of opening Esther required to plead her case. Half of the kingdom seems an unwarranted promise, even for the overly generous Ahasuerus. If it was a sincere offer, we wonder, was the kingdom truly Ahasuerus' personal property to dispose of at will? Could Caesar have promised half of the Roman Empire to a royal consort? It seems unlikely. If it were a mere slip of the tongue, however, it would not have been repeated an additional three times. Some scholars regard it as an idiomatic expression not to be taken literally. It is "a figure of speech born out of exaggerated good manners which is not to be taken seriously."[7]

Levenson alerts us to the subtle changes among the three times the king offered Esther up to half the kingdom. Rather than a repeated offer, it may be one that built up in intensity and urgency with each request:

> There are some interesting variations in the phrasing among the three occurrences. In the first (5:3), which comes during the highly charged scene of Esther's approaching the king unbidden, we find the shortest version. "What is bothering you?" there takes the place of the half of the parallelistic utterance, this underscoring the irregular nature of Esther's approach and perhaps the king's favorable disposition as well. The title "Queen Esther,"

7. Brenner, *A Feminist Companion*, 31.

> which appears there and here (but not in 5:6), may also serve to underscore the king's favor in these two enormously suspenseful scenes. More intriguing is the gender of the verb "it shall be granted," which is masculine in the first two occurrences, but feminine in the climactic third position. This change helps signal that this time Queen Esther will ask for something vastly more important, it turns out, than just another banquet.... This time Esther asks not for a banquet but for her very survival.[8]

No less likely is the midrashic response Rashi cites on 5:3. A Sage of the Talmud takes the measurement of the kingdom quite literally. What marks the halfway point in Ahasuerus' empire? The Temple in Jerusalem, of course. What motivated this fanciful talmudic reading if not connecting Esther to the only property in the kingdom she could possibly desire: the Temple? In this equation, the Temple itself is worth half the kingdom or at least it would have been valued that way to Esther. Ahasuerus did not know that Esther was Jewish at this point, so the Temple, in this reading, was a place generally acknowledged as prime spiritual real estate. Rashi on 5:3 concludes with a more literal, less fanciful interpretation: even had Esther requested half the kingdom it would have been granted. Ibn Ezra, ad loc., takes a more sparing view: Ahasuerus, sensing Esther's despondency, was trying to appease her with some kind of material support. Those who sought the king normally wanted something from him, and were he to confer a gift to anyone, it would have been the woman who captured his heart, who saved him from his despair and renewed his masculinity and virility throughout his entire kingdom. It was only fair, then, to offer her half of it.

The setting in which the king's offer was originally uttered also seems unusual and disconcerting. Esther appeared before the king after three days of fasting; in her bedraggled state the gift of half the kingdom seems unlikely. If she desired to appear confident, fasting would have weakened her to the point of near death. And that is the point; seeing Esther near death instantly piqued the king's attention. Having lost one wife, he might have been wary of losing another.

8. Levenson, *Esther*, 100–101.

This state of desperation and pathos may serve another critical role. If Esther personified her people, her fragile appearance and vulnerability before a king who could punish or spare her would have served as the microcosm for the exilic condition of her people. She stood in place of them near the brink of death as they awaited the implementation of Haman's decree. In some way, this encounter parallels the very way that the Jews in the ancient world lived. Dependent on the king, pleading with those of influence for their very existence, the Jews in exile were forced to beseech those in charge. An aleatory, unwritten contract between them and a monarch made for an imbalance of power, especially when, like Esther, the people had either been neglected for a long period of time or spurned.

Esther's Wait

Esther made not one party but two. Yet she was not able to get more out of the king than half the kingdom. If she was hoping for more, it was foolish. Why the delay and the additional party if she would not get more than the very generous offer presently on the table? Gordis believes Esther made a shrewd psychological calculation. She knew well of the king's temper and wanted to make sure he was in a good mood when she made her request. The king always enjoyed an ongoing wine feast.[9] Berg challenges this reading, since the king already promised that her request would be granted before the drinking. She did not need this second party, as she already achieved what she sought at the first.[10] Instead, Berg contends that the delay presents another example of Esther's subtle disobedience. "By refusing to tell Ahasuerus her real request, Esther continues to disobey the king (5:8). She disobeys Ahasuerus twice: by her unsummoned appearance, and by her continued refusal to state the reason for her first crime."[11]

Whatever this second wait represented, it was also part of a deliberate strategy on Esther's part. Perhaps precisely because Esther understood the difficulty and anxiety of waiting did she understand that

9. Gordis, *Megillat Esther*, 42.
10. Berg, *The Book of Esther*, 78.
11. Ibid.

she needed to create some anxiety for Ahasuerus, where the immediate gratification of knowing was suspended in an air of tense mystery. She knew the king's reliance on Haman, and she knew the king's insecurities about his own male dominance. The only way she could effectively undermine Haman was by stirring doubt about his fidelities without seeming as if she were trying to encourage Haman's affections. Loyalty trumped incompetence for the king, but fidelity trumped loyalty. Esther understood that Haman's plan could be toppled or manipulated only by Haman's personal fall from grace. Esther did not need half the kingdom. The scattered and dispersed Jewish exiles did not take up that much room. If we understand *malkhut* not only as "kingdom" but as the rights of royalty generally, Ahasuerus was offering Esther an expansion of executive power, and she refused. In so doing, she shined a more intense light on the one who likely wanted to make a power grab for the whole kingdom, not just half.

Haman's Happiness

That day Haman went out happy and lighthearted. (Est. 5:9)

As Haman would become consumed with anger and then mourning, we may mistakenly overlook his fleeting happiness. The Malbim on 5:9 observes that no mention of Haman's happiness had been recorded before. The most obvious place to showcase his happiness would have been at his initial promotion in 3:1, when he was elevated to a preeminent position at court. After his plan to exterminate the Jews was approved and he received the royal ring, Haman ate and drank with the king, but there was no notable change of emotion. It is only here, in the privacy of a wine party with the king and queen that Haman experienced a notable state of elation. We can imagine him leaving the party with a bounce in his step, feeling a new sense of superiority and exuberance. Ibn Ezra adds that the additional expression of happiness – *tov lev,* "lighthearted" – is the result of the drinking. The Malbim notes that whatever Haman had achieved thus far was negligible in his eyes. Only when he sat with the king, on the same level as the king, did he have his first real day of joy. Given the court seating mentioned in an earlier chapter, Haman had always been beneath the king physically and professionally. Sitting at the same table – which ironically allowed Esther to look Haman in the eye and condemn him – filled him with pride.

Most exegetes ignore Haman's happiness, perhaps because it quickly devolved into fury. Fury is so vehement that it distracts us from seeing any range in Haman's emotions, but it is precisely this capacity to experience joy that alerts us to Haman's singular focus. His happiness was rooted in the same source that drove him to rage: his insecurity. When his ego was stoked, he was blissful. When his ego was threatened, he was angry beyond belief. It is not hard to manipulate so simple a man, and we can only imagine the flattery he received at the hands of his toadies and flatterers. Like all insecurities, his hunger for adulation needed constant feeding and was likely fed by court climbers; any diminishment to his honor became an intolerable blight. We can imagine him gathering everyone around to crow about the party he just attended, until a dark furrow fell across his forehead:

> He sent for his friends and his wife Zeresh, and Haman told them about his great wealth and his many sons, and all about how the king had promoted him and advanced him above the officials and the king's courtiers. "What is more," said Haman, "Queen Esther gave a feast, and besides the king she did not have anyone but me. And tomorrow, too, I am invited by her alone with the king. Yet all this means nothing to me every time I see the Jew Mordecai sitting in the palace gate." (Est. 5:10–13)

Haman sought an audience with whom to boast and to seek validation. The minor characters listened to him talk not to learn new information, but to support his ego. No doubt, not one member of this group was unaware of Haman's wealth and position or how many sons he had. Ibn Ezra is quick to point out that Zeresh would have known exactly how many sons her husband had because she birthed them. Haman was passing on the extent of his good luck, which meant little to him or which he could not fully enjoy as long as the niggling and persistent threat of his nemesis continued to exist. Mordecai, of course, was no real threat, but he was not one to validate Haman, and that was enough of a threat to merit revenge.

Encountering Mordecai at the very moment of his greatest pride shook something deep and primal in this small-minded bureaucrat:

> Scene i is framed by Haman's leaving a feast "merrily" at the beginning of the scene and his going to a feast "merrily" at its end. Haman leaves the palace swelled with pride by his invitation to two private banquets with the king and queen. His smug pride soon clashes with pride of another sort – Mordecai's sense of dignity.[1]

Fox's observation here is profound but possibly insufficient to explain Haman's visceral reaction. What Haman saw in Mordecai was more than a refusal to treat Haman as all the others in court did and were mandated to do: Haman passed Mordecai and saw a man secure in his conviction, secure in his sense of personhood, secure in his ethnicity, secure in his God, and secure in his mission. An insecure man in the face of this degree of security could not help but fall apart.

One of the prominent themes of the Book of Esther is obedience versus disobedience. Insecurity often manifests as obedience, a rigid adherence to rules in the hope that the system provides the structure of security not found within an individual. The king had an undisciplined approach to obedience, creating rules when they suited him and tossing them out when they didn't. As king, he had that luxury. Haman was obedient to the system of governance because as someone close to the top of the power structure, it served him well until it didn't. His happiness was related to his ability to scale the system and have others be obedient to him. Haman failed when he showed his true self as disobedient to the king, desiring the king's personal effects. Mistakenly lying on the queen's couch was the final straw, and, unfortunately for Haman, the king was equally insecure and could not abide the slight to his honor caused by Haman's perceived disobedience.

We are invited to contrast this to the story's protagonists. Esther shifted from obedience to disobedience when she moved from protecting herself as an individual to taking on an ambassadorial role for her people. Mordecai is the only character to engage in principled disobedience, succeeding because he was the only truly secure person in the narrative.

---

1. Fox, *Character and Ideology*, 74.

Eric Fromm puts these polarities into a useful construct for understanding obedience and its relationship to authenticity: "For centuries kings, priests, feudal lords, industrial bosses and parents have insisted that obedience is a virtue and that disobedience is a vice."[2] Obedience always serves the insecure person in power. Disobedience for Mordecai, subsequently, was an act of freedom and ultimately authenticity to self over system:

> Obedience to a person, institution or power (heteronomous obedience) is submission; it implies the abdication of my autonomy and the acceptance of a foreign will or judgment in place of my own. Obedience to my own reason or conviction (autonomous obedience) is not an act of submission but one of affirmation. My conviction and my judgment, if authentically mine, are part of me. If I follow them rather than the judgment of others, I am being myself.[3]

Mordecai tutored Esther in disobedience to help her actualize a truer, more authentic self than a political system could ever provide. When she countered his disobedience with an offer of new clothing and then a refusal to reveal her identity, Mordecai understood what was happening; she had begun the descent into obedience that would soon obscure her from the principles by which she was raised. She was hiding again but could hide no longer, for her strength would only manifest in challenging the system. Mordecai helped her see that disobedience was not simply an act of rebellion against the king but was something larger and transcendent. Disobedience, Fromm, contends, "is not primarily an attitude directed against something, but for something: for man's capacity to see, to say what he sees, and to refuse to say what he does not see."[4]

Levenson points out another thematic strain in the book that is manifest through Haman's happiness and then his rage. Haman's happiness,

2. Eric Fromm, *On Disobedience: Why Freedom Means Saying "No" to Power* (New York: Harper Perennial, 2010), 1.
3. Ibid., 5.
4. Ibid., 24.

fueled by superficial sentiments and drives, was short-lived, quickly eclipsed by pettiness and anger, making this kind of happiness fragile indeed. This must be contrasted to the happiness the Jewish community of Persia experienced at the book's end, which was sourced in salvation, unity, and justice:

> Foolishness lies not only in his [Haman's] joy and merriment at the thought of the banquet that will, in fact, prove to be his downfall, but also in his inability to sustain any happiness and to suppress his anger when just one courtier refuses to pay him homage. The expression "merry" has already occurred once before, in 1:10, where it describes Ahasuerus's mood just as he issues the fateful order to bring Vashti to the banquet. The use of this rare expression in these two contexts reinforces the similarity of Haman's character to Ahasuerus's and leads us to expect that here too the merriment is ill-considered and will be of short duration. One of the themes of Esther is the contrast between wise and foolish joy. Haman's joy is clearly foolish and transient, whereas that of the Jews, when events have at last gone their way, turns out to be wise and enduring.[5]

Haman's happiness, according to Levenson, was another manifestation of foolishness. Yet perhaps it is not foolishness alone but something far more pernicious. Both Ahasuerus' happiness and Haman's led to their enemies' banishment or death. The happiness of many was sacrificed for the happiness of the king and his advisor. Happiness in these instances was rooted in narcissism.

Haman's Rage

Rage is an unpredictable constant in the Book of Esther. The rage of Haman matched and surpassed the rage of his king. Not unlike Ahasuerus, Haman was an intemperate man. The combination of power and impulsivity brought with it much collateral damage, not for Mordecai ultimately, but for Haman and his sons. With Haman's enhanced role

5. Levenson, *Esther*, 91–92.

in chapter 3, he exerts his power in absolute ways over the powerless, a common behavior of the bullying personality. He could not possibly imagine that this exertion of dominance might backfire on him because of another man who was quieter, more strategic, and far more loyal. Haman could not control his antipathy to Mordecai. It first manifested only a few verses after his promotion and became increasingly worse with his tenure in office:

> When Haman saw that Mordecai would not kneel or bow low to him, Haman was filled with rage. But he disdained to lay hands on Mordecai alone; having been told who Mordecai's people were, Haman plotted to do away with all the Jews, Mordecai's people, throughout the kingdom of Ahasuerus. (Est. 3:5–6)

Riddled with insecurity, Haman could do naught else but project Mordecai's perceived mistreatment of him as a problem nestled into the heart of every Jew in the kingdom. Haman, as the verses above illustrate, was an angry man whose need for absolute subservience dominated his actions and reactions. It narrowed his field of vision and made him hyper-focus on the insult of Mordecai's very presence.

Two chapters later, Haman's intense happiness over the elevation of his status in Esther's eyes led him to even greater anger at the sight of his nemesis, Mordecai. "That day Haman went out happy and lighthearted. But when Haman saw Mordecai in the palace gate, and Mordecai did not rise or even stir on his account, Haman was filled with rage at him" (Est. 5:9). Haman's joy quickly dissipated. He saw out of the corner of his eye the only person in the entire empire who paid him no mind. Note the text stresses not only that Mordecai did not bow; he did not even move or offer any slight gesture that could have been interpreted by Haman as a sign of respect, even grudgingly so:

> Not only does Mordecai refuse to bow to Haman, he shows no lesser sign of fear or awe, such as quaking or rising. For the author, Mordecai's refusal to show respect is not stubborn and foolhardy, but a heroic trait, a refusal to accord the wicked man the fear he wants to inspire. Of course, this time Mordecai is

> endangering only himself if he enrages Haman further, and that danger is rendered insignificant by the doom awaiting him along with the other Jews.[6]

At this stage, Mordecai had nothing to lose by showing his true feelings to Haman. Unsure of Esther's success in changing the king's mind, Mordecai would have been killed anyway, so he lived out his conviction until the very end.

Because Haman's happiness was so short-lived, his fury appeared with much force and focus. Great joy transmogrifies to even greater wrath. This anger was illogical. The greater Haman's success, the more likely he should have been to ignore Mordecai entirely. Mordecai's indifference should have meant little, unless, of course, Haman's arrogance enflamed an unbearable sense of entitlement. If the queen herself requested a private audience with Haman, elevating him to new professional and personal heights, then Mordecai's dismissiveness was all the more outrageous. The fact that Mordecai in a brief sliver of time would be exterminated was not enough for Haman.

Haman's Restraint

Haman managed to control himself and left. Astonishingly, for a man both rash and calculating, Haman withheld his feelings until he arrived home to sort out this tangle of vehement emotions: "Nevertheless, Haman controlled himself and went home. He sent for his friends and his wife Zeresh" (Est. 5:10). Rashi on 5:10 explains that the restraint was forced and unnatural: "He restrained himself, controlling his anger since he was afraid to take revenge without [the king's] permission." Haman's boasting, it seems, was a way to combat a matter that confused him. It did not make sense that all of his life's bounty did not amount to anything every time he saw Mordecai. It was bewitching and inexplicable, as many base impulses are. By telling this to his friends he was not stating the obvious but presenting what was not obvious to him, struggling to recalibrate and make himself whole when his nemesis was present,

6. Fox, *Character and Ideology*, 74.

lest these heavy feelings of hatred and dread undermine all that he had proudly achieved.

The Malbim suggests that this restraint was over his impulse to return immediately to the palace, tell the king of his hatred for Mordecai, and act on it with haste. Instead he opted to return home and consider the matter with those closest to him. Rashi explains what this self-restraint was about. Gersonides, like Rashi, also uses the term "restraint"; Haman had to discipline himself to conceal his fury from others. Ibn Ezra on 5:10 sees this verb less as the moderation of impulse than a withholding of Haman's secret longing and the *sevel,* or suffering, that accompanies the duplicity of having to act counter to one's authentic self in a context that does not permit it: "He did not disclose the secret to anyone until he got home." Ibn Ezra offers us another glimpse into the role of minor characters; they showcase the difference between who courtiers must be in the royal household versus the thoughts, behaviors, and feelings that a human being can express in his own home.

The biblical text used the same verb of restraint, *lehitapek,* when Joseph withheld his tears when his brothers brought Benjamin down to Egypt (Gen. 45:1). There, too, a courtier withheld his innermost feelings in the presence of the royal court. Joseph actually asked all the Egyptians to leave so that he could reveal himself to his brothers. The two selves of the courtier Jew could not be fully expressed at the same time. Like Joseph, Haman masked his emotions until he was surrounded only by family and friends. Only the king could be fully at home, emotionally, in the palace. Haman asked for permission to kill the Jews and sought to constrain his impulse behind royal protocol so that he could actualize a "final solution" to this Jewish problem. Ibn Ezra says Haman "did not want to reveal this secret to a soul, not until he arrived home." Some emotions bring shame in public or are so complex they can only be fully discussed among one's closest confidants.

Ashkenazi draws a stunning linguistic parallel between Haman's anger and an incident of Sarah's outrage. When Sarah was at the height of her good fortune, at the party she and Abraham made upon weaning Isaac, she caught sight of Ishmael playing with her son and became indignant:

> She said to Abraham, "Cast out that slave woman and her son, for the son of that slave shall not share in the inheritance with my son Isaac." (Gen. 21:10)

Note the counterpoise of the feast to sight and outrage, as if they are causally connected in both narratives. Sarah was so incensed she did not even call Ishmael by name and referred to Hagar using the Hebrew term for "slave" rather than the kinder term for "servant" used to describe her in Genesis 16.[7] With her harsh dismissal, Sarah reduced the child to Hagar's progeny alone, willfully ignoring Abraham's or her own part in the creation of this inconvenient heir. It is noticeable that at a moment of triumph, Sarah would pay attention to what was happening at the margins of Isaac's feast for the same reason that Haman noticed Mordecai's place at the gate when his own status was at its peak.

On Esther 5:9, Ashkenazi links these two stories and observes that it is precisely when one is at the height of one's personal power that any insult grabs one's attention and becomes painfully magnified to the point that there is an almost total loss of perspective. Ironically, what prompted the loss of perspective was not anger; it was sheer and unadulterated delight, a happiness so beyond comprehension that anything that reduced it had to be instantly and emphatically removed. Imagine, for instance, that one was invited to an elegant ball. Each piece of expensive clothing was carefully selected, and in front of the mirror, what looked back was a portrait of near perfection. The dress, the shoes, the hair, the jewelry... wait, what about the little stain on the bodice or a slight skin abrasion? Suddenly, as if magnified, the mirror screams back "Imperfection!" so loudly that every other aspect of beauty is erased immediately.

---

7. See Jo Ann Hackett, "Rehabilitating Hagar: Fragments of an Epic Pattern," in *Gender and Difference in Ancient* Israel, ed. Peggy Liday (Minneapolis: Fortress Press, 1989), 12–16; Phyllis Trible, "The Other Woman: A Literary and Theological Study of the Hagar Narratives," in *Understanding the Word: Essays in Honor of Bernhard W. Anderson*, ed. J. T. Butler, E. W. Conrad, and B. C. Ollenburger (Sheffield: *JSOT*, 1985), 221–46; and F. Ch. Fensham, "The Son of a Handmaid in Northwest-Semitic," *Vetus Testamentum* 3, no. 19 (July 1969): 313–21.

Perhaps, to use our earlier framing, Sarah, too, suffered from the profound insecurity that infertility can bestow. While Hagar conceived immediately, Sarah remained childless for years. And when God finally gave her Isaac, the thought that Ishmael as firstborn would threaten the future inheritance and leadership of her young son was unbearable. Happiness hard-won feels tenuous and breakable, making the one who finally experiences it constantly aware of the peril of losing it at any time. Haman, too, lost perspective. Sarah, unlike Haman, however, was motivated not only by her own fragile happiness but also by concerns about Abraham's legacy and the future leadership of what the couple had built together.

Of Jewish Stock

When Haman finished complaining about Mordecai, the group had only one solution, hearkening back to the advice of the king's ministers about Vashti. Again, if you eliminate the person, you eliminate the problem:

> Then his wife Zeresh and all his friends said to him, "Let a gallows be put up, fifty cubits high, and in the morning ask the king to have Mordecai hanged on it. Then you can go gaily with the king to the feast." The proposal pleased Haman, and he had the gallows put up. (Est. 5:14)

This suggests another important role of minor characters in the Book of Esther. They offer solutions but typically only violent solutions to violent men who are prone to select such solutions.

Not only did Zeresh and company recommend hanging Mordecai,[8] they felt that the punishment for his offensive behavior needed to be advertised across the empire with gallows about seventy-

8. Ibn Ezra on 5:14 says that Zeresh is mentioned first because it was she who began to speak: "It is the custom of women to act on impulse and not see the consequences [literally, *ro'ot et hanolad*]." Ibn Ezra makes similar comments about the "custom of women" elsewhere. See, for example, his interpretation of Ex. 3:22 and Ex. 38:8, where the custom of women was to care greatly about looks. (He suggests that on Num. 12:2 Zippora may not have been beautiful.) This may have had to do with a tendency to asceticism or a personal understanding of human behavior that he

five feet in height. Ibn Ezra points out that the gallows would be visible beyond Haman's courtyard. The Malbim on 5:14 suggests that making this a punishment for those who disrespected Haman was itself an act of respect to Haman. Hanging Mordecai was a deterrent for all. This also explains the suggestion that this punishment be meted out in the morning; when people woke up and left their homes, Mordecai's limp body would be a sign of personal victory over this difficult Jew. While Malbim does not state this, the impact of this visual for the Jews of Shushan specifically would have been profoundly frightening and a harbinger of terror to come. This terror and Mordecai's demise may have repaired the emotional fracture Haman experienced; nothing of his success mattered without total obedience to him, personified by Mordecai's subversive refusal to bow. Head bowed on the gallows, Mordecai would bow to Haman in death if not in life. Haman's response comes as no surprise: "The proposal pleased Haman" (5:14).

Height is significant here: Haman's accomplishments were personal heights and those who invalidated them would suffer at a height unattainable to normal humans. It is hard to imagine how this hanging would be logistically possible, but it foreshadows the fact that Haman himself, known throughout the kingdom for his high visibility in the court, would be highly visible in his own death. From Haman's height, his eventual fall would be much greater. The great paradox is that Zeresh, his own wife, explained that Haman's fall was inevitable: "If Mordecai, before whom you have begun to fall, is of Jewish stock, you will not overcome him; you will fall before him to your ruin" (Est. 6:13). Haman's first fall was in 6:10–13, then he fell on Esther's couch in 7:8, and then he totally fell from grace with his death of shame.[9] The man who believed in random lots and astrological forces to bring others down was told a truth with great certainty from those who cared for him the most. Haman was going down. It was just a matter of time.

---

shared in his *peshat*-based interpretation. His commentary is not, however, always literal. See H. Norman Strickman, "Abraham Ibn Ezra's Non-Literal Interpretations," *HaKirah* 9 (2010): 281–96.

9. See Craig, *Reading Esther*, 124.

Chapter Six

Sleepless in Shushan

Reversals of Fortune

Mordecai's Gate

Sleepless in Shushan

> That night, sleep deserted the king, and he ordered the book of records, the annals, to be brought; and it was read to the king. There it was found written that Mordecai had denounced Bigthana and Teresh, two of the king's eunuchs who guarded the threshold, who had plotted to do away with King Ahasuerus. "What honor or advancement has been conferred on Mordecai for this?" the king inquired. "Nothing at all has been done for him," replied the king's servants who were in attendance on him. (Est. 6:1–3)

What kept Ahasuerus up at night? It may have been a nagging insecurity about his chief advisor's plans of ascendency, a subliminal awakening that all was not right in Shushan. The king, tossing about on his royal bedding, could find no solace, so he rose to review the annals of his kingdom, searching for respite. No doubt, his victories, major and minor, were spelled out on every page, but something was amiss that even reading these accounts could not solve. The king did not sleep that night.

Ahasuerus had good reason to be awake. A few chapters earlier, an assassination plot was revealed, and now his wife was asking him to a private party that could have been romantic had she not also invited Haman. Perhaps Ahasuerus watched the way Haman fawned over Esther, how the odd triangle of their grouping portended something insidious or masked a budding relationship in the king's full view. All of this heightened Ahasuerus' sense of physical and emotional insecurity.

In chapters 4, 5, and 6, each central character in the scroll experiences a deep and unsettling anxiety followed by an epiphany. These defining moments help the plot unfold. In chapter 4, Esther had anxiety about approaching the king that manifested itself in initial hesitation and then in fasting. When she arrived at her defining moment, she was able to see her life in all of its humility and power. She became a vessel for a higher purpose and, as that conduit to salvation, she used her position to influence the story's outcome. In the next chapter, Haman's anxiety followed the only state of happiness recorded in his life, his boost in status as a result of the queen's party. He then experienced intense fury at Mordecai, the only one to disrespect him in the land. As chapter 6 unfolds, Haman's anxiety will become his undoing when he seeks to punish Mordecai at the exact moment Ahasuerus wanted to reward him. Ahasuerus' angst and sleeplessness was to culminate in the ridiculous charade of mimicking the king that revealed with great clarity and wisdom who protected the king and who threatened him. Mordecai may have had anxiety at the hollowness of being paraded around with no chance at a real reward, his own life in exchange for saving the king's life. But this, too, came with an observation that held a glimmer of hope. Justice may take its time, but it is destined to arrive. If the king finally remembered him, then justice, insignificant as it felt then to the course of history, may possibly win the day.

All of these epiphanies converge in chapter 6.

Royal Insomnia

Ahasuerus was unable to sleep, disturbed as he was by the nocturnal churnings that haunt us all as we review our days: the petty insults, the punctures of pleasure, the slight bruising. Nighttime sings of all these ghosts that hide in the day. One opinion in the Talmud suggests that no one slept that night, not even God.

> The verse states: "On that night the sleep of the king was disturbed" (Est. 6:1). R. Tanḥum said: The verse alludes to another king who could not sleep; the sleep of the King of the Universe, the Holy One, blessed be He, was disturbed. And the Sages say:

> The sleep of the higher ones, the angels, was disturbed, and the sleep of the lower ones, the Jewish people, was disturbed.[1]

In this figment of the rabbinic imagination, the tumultuous revelations about to surface precipitated unease across the created world. The ripples of uncertainty troubled and offset basic functions of the body, like sleep. Good news or bad news, it did not matter; the universe trembled on the precipice of change. God trembled. Angels trembled. Jews trembled. This was not divine insomnia, but the expected reaction when a truth fierce and intense is finally revealed, and the world stands alert to receive it.

Rava, in the continuation of this talmudic passage, was more pedestrian in his understanding of Esther 6:1. The king literally could not sleep. He had too much on his mind, an inner emotional landscape clouded with consternation:

> Rava said: This should be understood literally: The sleep of King Ahasuerus was disturbed. And this was the reason Ahasuerus could not sleep: A thought occurred to him and he said to himself: What is this before us that Esther has invited Haman? Perhaps they are conspiring against that man, i.e., against me, to kill him. He then said again to himself: If this is so, is there no man who loves me and would inform me of this conspiracy? He then said again to himself: Perhaps there is some man who has done a favor for me, and I have not properly rewarded him, and due to that reason people refrain from revealing to me information regarding such plots, as they see no benefit for themselves. Immediately afterward, the verse states: "And he commanded the book of remembrances of the chronicles to be brought" (Est. 6:1).[2]

In this jumble of nocturnal stream-of-consciousness thoughts, Ahasuerus considered not only the oddity of Esther twice inviting Haman to a party but also what he himself may have done to precipitate any wrongdoing.

---

1. Megilla 15b.
2. Ibid.

This rabbinic perception of the king's self-scrutiny is itself radical. In his self-doubt, Ahasuerus checked his chronicles.

> The verse states: "And they were read before the king" (Est. 6:1). "And they were read" teaches that they were read miraculously by themselves. It further says: "And it was found written (*katuv*)" (Est. 6:2). The Gemara asks: Why does the *Megilla* use the word *katuv* [written], which indicates that it was newly written? It should have said: A writing (*ketav*) was found, which would indicate that it had been written in the past. This teaches that Shimshai, the king's scribe who hated the Jews (see Ezra 4:17), was erasing the description of Mordecai's saving the king, and the angel Gabriel was writing it again. Therefore, it was indeed being written in the present. R. Asi said: R. Sheila, a man of the village of Timarta, taught: If something written down below in this world that is for the benefit of the Jewish people cannot be erased, is it not all the more so the case that something written up above in heaven cannot be erased? "The king ordered that the book of records be brought": Haman's son Shamsai was reading. When he came to the place listing Mordecai, he rolled [the record] to a different place but the pages rolled back on their own."[3]

Much is disturbing about this midrash.[4] Among the many battles of the story, there was another waging: the battle of the word. Jewish goodness could be erased, or preserved and wait to be discovered. Justice was so

---

3. *Midrash Abba Guryon* 6.
4. Shamsai, for example, was not a son listed in ch. 8:7–10. This may reflect the midrashic reading that Haman had 40 sons, 10 of whom were royal scribes and 30 who were scattered throughout the provinces (*Pirkei DeRabbi Eliezer* 50). This reading suggests that only the 10 in the king's service were killed and those who remained would, no doubt, seed more hatred toward the Jews in successive generations. Based on *gematria,* another midrash states that Haman had 208 sons (Megilla 15b). This, too, while offering a larger family portrait, hints that Haman was far from a lone and isolated figure. His hatred was likely a legacy that filled his many sons with latent biases and prejudices, prejudices that would far outlive one influential cabinet minister.

obvious, it had to be articulated. As the talmudic passage begins, the chronicles themselves spoke, as if to suggest that Mordecai's contribution spoke for itself. The truth that needs to be revealed will find a way to speak, but hatred against the Jews was not in the preserve of Haman alone. A royal scribe shared Haman's irrational hatred and tried to erase them from history. The angel Gabriel would not allow it. This aggada injects another dose of hatred where none had existed. Nothing suggests that the record books were tampered with, only that they were ignored by the king. This midrash has a son of Haman trying to manipulate the historical record by passing it over to include, instead, something more pleasant to put the king to sleep. His efforts, like those of his father, were doomed to fail. The midrash may also offer a reason that Haman's sons were killed with him. They, too, were complicit in their father's plan.

The Chronicles

Many assume that Ahasuerus asked for the chronicles as a sleeping pill. Their dry, soporific nature would have settled the king. The talmudic passage above assumes that the chronicles were read not for this reason but to make sure that whatever bothered the king was not a matter of personal or state importance, the neglect of something critical or inexcusable. Unlike Haman, the king did not rely on lots when making a decision. He turned to documentation. Ashkenazi on 6:1 dismissed the notion that reading the chronicles would put the king to sleep, since the "book of chronicles and stories would engage man's ears and heart to pay attention and, thereby, actually prevent sleep and fatigue." Note the different approach to history subtly presented in this interpretation. Ashkenazi believed history to be so exciting that it would discourage sleep; as long as the king was unable to sleep, he would make himself most fully awake by reading historical annals.

Radday regards verse 6:1 as the pivot of the entire book. He proposes that the book is structured in three distinct phases: mortal danger, crisis, and salvation. The verses of salvation remedy the buildup of the mortal danger, with the crisis as a midpoint captured in one verse that represents the apex of the augmenting tension and becomes the turning point: 6:1.

Mortal Danger:
Introduction and background – chapter 1
The king's first decree – chapters 2 and 3
The contention between Mordecai and Haman – chapters 4 and 5

Crisis:
"On that night, the king could not sleep" (6:1)

Salvation:
Mordecai humiliates Haman and bests him – chapters 6 and 7
The king makes another decree to challenge the first – chapters 8 and 9
Epilogue – chapter 10

The night the king could not sleep represents the nexus, the tectonic shift, that changed everything.[5]

In many biblical stories, as in the stories of Jacob, Joseph, and Daniel, dreams or dream interpretations propel the plot. In the Book of Esther, the absence of dreams, the waking terror, stimulates the reversal of fortune that is about to take place.

A Delayed Reward

"What honor (*yakar*) and advancement has been conferred on Mordecai for this?" (Est. 6:3) is a strange question asked on a strange evening. That a king would be unable to sleep and suddenly take under review the reward issued to an unimportant person in his empire was astonishing enough. It is not in keeping with the king's position to involve himself with specific rewards. Status and material boon came together routinely in courtier life; the king naturally assumed that the person who revealed a conspiracy against him had already been rewarded. The *yakar* mentioned here is closest in the king's understanding to its use in the first chapter as munificence: "For no fewer than a hundred and eighty days he displayed the vast riches (*yakar*) of his kingdom and the splendid glory of his majesty" (1:4). *Yakar* will be used later in reference to Jewish relief and triumph to suggest happiness and material

5. See Radday, "Chiasm," 9.

security in apposition to material excess. The king believed he could buy his way out of any situation. Little did he realize that he failed to reward the very person who sought no material reward, only the survival of his people.

Reversals of Fortune

"What honor or advancement has been conferred on Mordecai for this?" the king inquired. "Nothing at all has been done for him," replied the king's servants who were in attendance on him. "Who is in the court?" the king asked. For Haman had just entered the outer court of the royal palace, to speak to the king about having Mordecai hanged on the gallows he had prepared for him. "It is Haman standing in the court," the king's servants answered him. "Let him enter," said the king. Haman entered, and the king asked him, "What should be done for a man whom the king desires to honor?" Haman said to himself, "Whom would the king desire to honor more than me?" So Haman said to the king, "For the man whom the king desires to honor, let royal garb which the king has worn be brought, and a horse on which the king has ridden and on whose head a royal diadem has been set; and let the attire and the horse be put in the charge of one of the king's noble courtiers. And let the man whom the king desires to honor be attired and paraded on the horse through the city square, while they proclaim before him: This is what is done for the man whom the king desires to honor!" "Quick, then!" said the king to Haman. "Get the garb and the horse, as you have said, and do this to Mordecai the Jew, who sits in the king's gate. Omit nothing of all you have proposed." So Haman took the garb and the horse and arrayed Mordecai and paraded him through the city square; and he proclaimed before

> him: This is what is done for the man whom the king desires to honor! (Est. 6:3–11)

The constant reversals of fortune in Esther keep readers attentive, no matter how familiar the text. Reversal of fortune as a central theme of the book was apparent not only to modern scholars. "Ahasuerus," one midrash states, "who put his wife to death on account of his friend, is the same Ahasuerus who put his friend to death on account of his wife."[1] The rabbis clearly had a sense of sardonic wit and understood the many inversions, both the significant and relatively insignificant, that are woven throughout the Book of Esther as both a kind of spiritual and comedic glue that would eventuate in joy and justice. Some scholars believe that the entire book has a chiastic structure, with later verses upending earlier verses in content and theme, thus making the entire literary structure one of reversal, as mentioned in Radday's reading cited a chapter before.

The reversal of fortune is a well-studied device. Aristotle's *Poetics* describes tragedy as "*peripeteia*," a dramatic reversal of fortune. In literature this moment signals "a change by which the action veers round to its opposite, subject always to our rule of probability or necessity."[2] Hubris is usually at the heart of a noble character's downfall as the cause of the pivot in fortune. Comedy is rooted in a similar reversal but in the opposite direction. Often the seriousness of theme and intent is upended in comedy by the absurdity of the ambition or an ill-fated miscalculation. This is certainly true for the Book of Esther.

> Greek comedy reverses the norms of Greek tragedy; heroes are replaced by anti-heroes and "unhappy" endings are rendered worthy of laughter. One can thus perceive an oblique relationship between that tradition and the book of Esther: the reversal of fortune is a happy, not unhappy, turn of events for the hero and heroine; the demise of Haman and his sons is, for the audience, laughable; and everyone celebrates by allowing the fun of

1. Esther Rabba 1:1.
2. Aristotle, *The Poetics of Aristotle*, trans. S. H. Butcher (London: Macmillan and Co., 1904), 27.

> the story's finale to spill off the stage (and off the narrative page) into a raucous festival.[3]

Nowhere is this reversal of fortune more evident than in chapter 6. Scholars debate the significance of this extraordinary chapter with its supposedly meaningless parade, because it is this chapter, more than any other, that catalyzes every other reversal of fortune to be disclosed. It is here where the concealed world of intentions meets the revealed world of envy, greed, and humiliation.[4] Once the inner whispers of character were brought to the fore, the rest of the plot quickly unraveled, even if on the surface the ridiculous street parade changed nothing. Mordecai put on the king's clothing and rode on the king's horse in public, but remained in the shadow of the gallows erected by Haman. It was both meaningless and insulting to reward Mordecai if his life would ultimately be taken. It was equally meaningless to Haman because, regardless of this temporary humiliation and public setback, Haman was still in power, was still going to Esther's second party, and was still able to settle the score with his archrival. Thick with a spirit of reprisal, Haman could still look forward to his rival's defeat. A date had already been set, the method of Mordecai's execution was already determined, and the fifty-cubit gallows would be a much more public and gruesome event than a quick and embarrassing turn in the public square.

Ultimately, despite the apparently comedic tone of this chapter, the absurdity of the king's charade hints that much more elation is on the way. How it is to be achieved, however, was not yet clear.

To Whom Shall Honor Go?

When Haman entered the king's chambers unbidden and at an hour usually closed to courtier traffic, the unsettled Ahasuerus suspected Haman of some kind of foul play without knowing exactly what it was. Ahasuerus, on high alert, first sought to determine the identity of the person who entered his private domain. He may have sounded shrill: "Who is

3. Soltes, "Images and the Book of Esther," 140.
4. For a comprehensive treatment of the humiliation presented in this chapter and the reversal of honor, see Laniak, *Shame and Honor in the Book of Esther*.

in the court?" (Est. 6:4). The king's second question invited Haman to relax his judgment and let his imagination travel, disarming this high-ranking court officer: "What should be done for a man whom the king desires to honor?" (Est. 6:6). For Haman, the answer was patently obvious: all honor should be directed to him, as Hazony notes:

> Haman's conception of the ordering of the Persian state allows for only one interpretation of the king's question: Truly an idolater to the core, he continues to identify the good of the realm with his own perfect control. For him there is in fact only one appropriate address for all honor. To honor someone else is to create rivalry and danger, allowing another to vie for the favor of the king, to him an impossibility.[5]

The reader of this scene is amused by Haman's lack of self-awareness and also equally surprised by Ahasuerus' sudden shrewdness. An accusation would have been inappropriate at this point and led to mere defensiveness; a question well placed and open-ended, however, was entirely reasonable and effective and gave the king a portal to understanding Haman's inner workings.

In answer to the question, Haman lacked only ultimate power. Of all the rewards one could want, from money to change of title to special access, Haman wanted only one delusional, impossible gift: the chance to look like someone he could never be, the king. Rashi believes that Haman never asked directly for the crown, "because he saw that the king became jealous when he said that they should place the crown on [another] person's head." Sasson observes that "when Haman advises that he whom the king wishes to honor be dressed to look and act like royalty, he is in effect proposing treatment reserved for substitute kings."[6] This must have been immediately obvious to Ahasuerus, an instant alert that something was out of order.

Some scholars suggest that when Haman proposed a ride on a horse with a crown on its head – "A horse on which the king has ridden

5. Hazony, *The Dawn*, 163.
6. Sasson, *Esther*, 341.

and on whose head a royal diadem has been set" (6:8) – it was a literal suggestion. A horse with a crown appears as an image on Assyrian palace reliefs in Nineveh and Chorsabad.[7] Others suggest because of the relative particle in the sentence *asher* that Haman was asking for a robe like the king's and a horse like the one the king rode at his inauguration. In other words, Haman requested items that were actually used by the king rather than mere simulacrums.[8]

This robing effect may have been for more than show. Berg mentions historical examples where the king's robes were actually associated with the king's powers: "The belief that a king's garment possessed special significance, if not magical power, was widespread in the ancient world. The manner by which Mordecai is honored in Esther 6 thus suggests more than a simple reward of his deed."[9] Berg wonders how it would be plausible, given the robe's significance, that Ahasuerus was willing to let another wear his garments. She concludes that it is another manifestation of the king's foolishness and no less plausible than any other narrated event in the book. Alternatively, it may point to the king's naive magnanimity. Berg also offers the possibility that dressing Mordecai in royal robes was significant to the scroll's audience: "A Jewish audience, living under foreign rule, undoubtedly delighted in any allusion to royal power secured by the Jews at the expense of the ruling administration."[10] While Berg does not state this, perhaps the robes were like the king's in their finery, and this was enough for a Jewish audience who wanted, indeed needed, to see Mordecai as their own royalty but not a replacement for the actual king.

Pirkei DeRabbi Eliezer presents the crown issue as an exegetical problem needing to be solved. A crown was mentioned in Haman's first recommendation to the king in 6:8 but then not mentioned in verse 6:9, when the king ordered Haman to do just as Haman desired...but for

7. Berg cites this reading from Hans Bardtke, *Das Buch Esther*, KAT 17/5 (Gutersloh: Gutersloher Verlagshaus Gerd Mohn, 1963), 348. See Berg, *The Book of Esther*, 61.
8. Oswald T. Allis, "The Reward of the King's Favorite (Esth. 6, 8)," *Princeton Theological Review* 21 (1923): 630–31.
9. Berg, *The Book of Esther*, 63.
10. Ibid.

Mordecai. The crown detail is also missing from 6:11, when Haman actually humiliated himself at the parade. According to *Pirkei DeRabbi Eliezer*:

> Haman said in his heart: he does not desire to exalt any other man except for me. I will speak words so that I shall be the king just as he is. He said to him, "Let them bring the apparel which the king wore on the day of the coronation and the horse that the king rode at the coronation and the crown put on the king on the day of his coronation." The king was very angry because of the crown. The king said, "It is not enough for this wicked man. He even wants the crown upon my head." Haman saw that the king was angry because of the crown and said, "Let the robes and the horse be delivered to the hand of one of the king's most noble princes."[11]

If Ahasuerus could not sleep because he worried about another attack on his life, having his chief courtier request his crown paradoxically settled the matter. He finally understood the real threat to his power. As Hazony astutely points out, with each word Haman uttered, the king increasingly saw Haman as a rival and needed a way to demote him publicly.[12] These suspicions reached their ultimate and inaccurate crescendo when the king suspected Haman of foul play with his wife. In a note of irony, Vashti refused to come in her crown while Haman wanted to be seen publicly wearing Ahasuerus' crown. "Uneasy lies the head," Shakespeare wrote in *Henry the Fourth,* "that wears the crown."[13]

Haman initiated his plan to get rid of the Jews before letting the king know and did the same in his plot to eliminate Mordecai. The king may have become suddenly aware of the lack of transparency. Berg notes that "Haman's presumptuous actions suggest that he, not the Jews, usurps royal prerogatives and hence poses a threat to the king."[14]

---

11. Gerald Friedlander, *Pirkei de Rabbi Eliezer* (New York: Hermon, 1965), 404.
12. Hazony, *The Dawn,* 161.
13. William Shakespeare, *Henry IV, Part 2* (New York, Simon and Schuster, 2006), 111.
14. Berg, *The Book of Esther,* 74.

The staged dress up showed the public that change was possible in Shushan; the imagined became real, and the real suddenly became unimaginable. Haman was shown to be worthy of defeat, Mordecai worthy of promotion. But in the real world, a number of critical factors needed to change to realize the impossible and the just.

The Fantasy of Revenge

The Sages of the Talmud revel in their exegesis of chapter 6 and spend pages interpreting it, almost line by line. One can almost sense the fun they had as they embellished the already ludicrous charade. The events on their own are a premonition of the Jewish future in Persia, but in the hands of the rabbis, the fantasy of revenge was too sweet not to mine at each and every turn. We will cite large swaths of Tractate Megilla 16a–b broken into excerpts, while visualizing ourselves in a study hall with an intimate group of sages, their faces pocked with gloating.

The verse states that Ahasuerus was told with regard to Mordecai: "Nothing has been done for him" (Est. 6:3). Rava said: It is not because they love Mordecai that the king's servants said this, but rather because they hate Haman.

When Ahasuerus' young servants told him that nothing had been done for Mordecai, they said this in unison, with a surety that indicates the injustice was a piece of well-traveled palace gossip. Saying it together also prevented the king from blaming any one member of his court for making the error. No one had rewarded the only person in the scroll who had the king's best interests in mind, and everyone seemed to know this except for the king. Instead, Haman was promoted at the exact time that Mordecai should have been rewarded. The king's servants understood that this failure to recognize loyalty would eventually have psychic costs for this insecure king, who would now likely go out of his way to recompense Mordecai. The rabbis were quick to add that rectifying this mistake had nothing to do with the courtiers' high regard for Mordecai but was fueled by their growing hatred of Haman. The Talmud continues:

> The verse states: "Now Haman had come into the outer court of the king's house, to speak to the king about hanging Mordecai

> on the gallows that he had prepared for him" (Est. 6:4). A Sage taught in a *baraita*: This should be understood to mean: On the gallows that he had prepared for himself (*lo hekhin*).[15]

With a play on words that switches the order of the verb and direct object in the verse (*hekhin lo*), the rabbis saw, in essence, that Haman built his own gallows, a visual metaphor to suggest he literally dug his own grave. The reversal of word order forecasts the reversal of outcomes.

In fact, in the previous chapter, Zeresh had suggested that the gallows be built in the morning. It is clear from 6:4 that in his zeal to rid his world of Mordecai, Haman immediately set about his task that night, entering the king's chamber at odd hours, defying protocol to let the king know his intentions.[16] Mordecai was going to die anyway, but Haman wanted to expedite the death, relishing his personal arrangement of the execution and ensuring it took place as soon as possible. The Sages elaborate on Ahasuerus' order, to delve into what they regarded as Haman's utter disbelief:

> The verse relates that Ahasuerus ordered Haman to fulfill his idea of the proper way to honor one whom the king desires to glorify by parading him around on the king's horse while wearing the royal garments: "And do so to Mordecai the Jew who sits at the king's gate; let nothing fail of all that you have spoken" (Est. 6:10). When Ahasuerus said to Haman, "And do so to Mordecai," Haman said to him in an attempt to evade the order: Who is Mordecai? Ahasuerus said to him: "The Jew." Haman then said to him: There are several men named Mordecai among the

15. Megilla 16a.
16. We do not know if Haman built the gallows himself, which would indicate another act of overenthusiasm, not dissimilar to the rabbinic understanding of Abraham and Balaam each saddling their own donkeys for their respective missions, as discussed in Genesis Rabba 55:8: "Love upsets the natural order. Hate upsets the natural order." These high-profile figures would ordinarily never do this kind of menial labor themselves. The strong emotions of love or hate spurred each to act immediately rather than wait for assistance.

> Jews. Ahasuerus then said to him: I refer to the one "who sits at the king's gate."[17]

It could not be that the very person he plotted to kill would now be receiving a reward! Who is Mordecai? To rub salt in the vast wound of Haman's ego, the rabbis state the king's pronouncement to enhance Haman's suffering – "Mordecai the Jew," the king declared to a man who hated the Jews. Mordecai was mentioned as the one who sits in the gate to Haman, who was infuriated each time he saw Mordecai there.[18] This reading likely surfaced because the Sages noticed a detail that was carefully dropped into Ahasuerus' order; the king knew Mordecai was Jewish. This information was told to Haman, but we have no prior record that the king knew Mordecai was Jewish. Haman, at this juncture, may have been seized with panic – Ahasuerus would soon realize that the very loyal Mordecai was a member of the very people Haman sought to annihilate. The larger, devious plans Haman had made for Mordecai and his people, the plans he minimized to the king, would come to haunt him. Haman did not speak back in the biblical text but does in this stretch of aggadic literature:

> Haman said to him: Why award him such a great honor? It would certainly be enough for him to receive one village (*disekarta*) as an estate, or one river for the levy of taxes. Ahasuerus said to him: This, too, you must give him. "Let nothing fail of all that you have spoken," i.e., provide him with all that you proposed and spoke about in addition to what I said.[19]

---

17. Megilla 16a.
18. This reading, too, had a midrashic parallel in one rabbinic reading of Gen. 22:2. Rashi cites that when God told Abraham to take his son, his only son, the one that he loved, Abraham replied he had two sons and loved them both. In each instance, the nouns and adjectives are interrogated and drawn out to slow down the identification intentionally. In these midrashim, slowing down the identification was a form of resistance. Abraham resisted God's call to bind his son, and Haman resisted Ahasuerus' demand that he parade Mordecai.
19. Megilla 16a.

With each utterance, Haman made his situation worse, tossing out possible gifts that the king subsequently added to the original award, making Haman's humiliation all the greater.

As the midrashic passage continues, we enter the study hall with Mordecai as he debated the minutiae of Temple sacrifices. The depiction of Mordecai as an expert in Jewish legal matters is perhaps a projection of what the Sages believed represented true Jewish leadership: scholarship. As a member of the Sanhedrin, Mordecai was expected to have legal expertise:

> "Then Haman took the apparel and the horse" (Est. 6:11): When he went, he found Mordecai as the sages were sitting before him, and he was demonstrating to them the laws of the handful, i.e., the scooping out of a handful of flour from the meal-offering in order to burn it on the altar.[20]

Not only was Mordecai teaching in this scenario, he happened to be teaching what was commonly viewed as an intricate and difficult Temple ritual. This would not only have demonstrated Mordecai's legal expertise; it would also subtly connect him to the Temple, a connection noticeably absent throughout the biblical text. The Sages sought to rectify the absence with their additions and emendations. By interrupting the group study, Haman followed a long line of despots throughout history who prevented Jewish study, adding yet another reason to mark him an enemy of the Jews. He not only hated the nation; he prevented them from engaging in their most sacred duty of communal continuity.

Next, Mordecai is depicted as a spiritual hero who saves the life of those around him through prayer, much as he would save a nation:

> Once Mordecai saw him coming toward him with his horse's reins held in his hands, he [Mordecai] became frightened, and he said to the sages: This evil man has come to kill me. Go away from him so that you should not get burnt from his coals, i.e., that you should not suffer harm as well. At that moment Mor-

20. Ibid.

> decai wrapped himself in his prayer shawl and stood up to pray. Haman came over to where they were and sat down before them and waited until Mordecai finished his prayer.[21]

Mordecai pushed his fellow sages to safety and then took refuge in prayer. Again, as no prayer appears in Esther, it is not hard to understand why the authors of this alternate narrative supplemented the story with rituals that would characterize their own response to danger. The precious image of Haman patiently waiting for Mordecai to finish praying shows respect both for God and for a man in the midst of supplication. The story becomes increasingly fanciful:

> In the interim, as he waited, Haman said to the other sages: With what were you occupied? They said to him: When the Temple is standing, one who pledges a meal-offering would bring a handful of fine flour and achieve atonement with it. He said to them: Your handful of fine flour has come and cast aside my ten thousand pieces of silver, which I had pledged toward the destruction of the Jewish people. When Mordecai finished praying, he said to Haman: Wicked man, when a slave buys property, to whom belongs the slave and to whom belongs the property? As I once bought you as a slave, what silver can be yours?[22]

Haman not only waited for Mordecai to finish, he struck up a conversation with Mordecai's scholarly colleagues, who had not vacated the scene. Haman was hardly interested in the details of the ritual, yet he used it to further his malicious purposes, perhaps suggesting that no amount of fine flour would help the Jews seek atonement with the Temple gone and the Jewish people about to disappear. Mordecai may not have had the best prayer session because he responded to the conversation with a quip. The conversation will again take a turn from the merely absurd to the ridiculous:

---

21. Ibid.
22. Ibid.

> Haman said to him: Stand up, put on these garments, and ride on this horse, for the king wants you to do so. Mordecai said to him: I cannot do so until I enter the bathhouse and trim my hair, for it is not proper conduct to use the king's garments in this state that I am in now. In the meantime, Esther sent messengers and closed all the bathhouses and all the shops of the craftsmen, including the bloodletters and barbers. When Haman saw that there was nobody else to do the work, he himself took Mordecai into the bathhouse and washed him, and then he went and brought scissors from his house and trimmed his hair. While he was trimming his hair he injured himself and sighed. Mordecai said to him: Why do you sigh? Haman said to him: The man whom the king had once regarded above all his other ministers is now made a bathhouse attendant and a barber. Mordecai said to him: Wicked man, were you not once the barber of the village of Kartzum? If so, why do you sigh? You have merely returned to the occupation of your youth. It was taught in a *baraita*: Haman was the barber of the village of Kartzum for twenty-two years.[23]

Mordecai sought to delay the absurd parade, and insisted that a haircut was warranted before a royal visit, revealing Haman's low past as a barber in the process. Esther worked behind the scenes to ensure that Haman used his own skills to get Mordecai ready. Haman had no choice; this was, after all, the king's request, and he had to satisfy it. Mordecai here even questioned Haman's obvious involuntary sighing, a sigh of denigration that needed no explanation. By bringing attention to it, Mordecai further exposed Haman's vulnerability. Haman could not believe he had been reduced to this by a king who once favored him, an observation he shared with his least likely sympathizer. But Mordecai had not exhausted his capacity for irony:

> After Haman trimmed his hair, Haman dressed Mordecai in the royal garments. Haman then said to him: Mount the horse and ride. Mordecai said to him: I am unable, as my strength has

23. Ibid.

> waned from the days of fasting that I observed. Haman then stooped down before him, and Mordecai ascended on him. As he was ascending the horse, Mordecai gave Haman a kick. Haman said to him: Is it not written for you: "Do not rejoice when your enemy falls" (Prov. 24:17)? Mordecai said to him: This statement applies only to Jews, but with regard to you it is written: "And you shall tread upon their high places" (Deut. 33:29). The verse states: "And he proclaimed before him: Thus shall it be done to the man whom the king delights to honor" (Est. 6:11).[24]

Haman tried to order Mordecai, and again, the Jew protested. Weak from fasting and supplication, Mordecai used his once-powerful adversary as a lowly footstool. Here we find a commentary on Jewish-gentile relations through the odd mechanism of the pagan rival citing biblical wisdom to the Jewish hero. As it happens, the verse from Proverbs was cited as a biblical prooftext against gloating over one's enemies because all are creatures of one God, an application used after the Egyptians drowned in the Reed Sea.[25]

The long midrashic reading moves quickly back to the farcical. It deepens Haman's humiliation by including not only those in the public square as witnesses to the parade but also those in his very household. In the biblical text, Haman disclosed his hate for Mordecai openly, and, no doubt, those around him understood what this parade signaled. According to the midrash, however, Haman tried to quickly conceal his identity during the parade but was, nevertheless, completely humiliated in front of all the onlookers:

> As Haman was taking Mordecai along the street of Haman's house, Haman's daughter was standing on the roof and saw the spectacle. She thought to herself that the one who is riding on the horse must be her father, and the one walking before him must be Mordecai. She then took a chamber pot full of feces and cast its contents onto the head of her father, whom she mistakenly took

24. Ibid.
25. See Megilla 20b and Sanhedrin 39b.

> as Mordecai. When Haman raised his eyes in disgust afterward, and looked up at his daughter, she saw that he was her father. In her distress, she fell from the roof to the ground and died. And this is as it is written: "And Mordecai returned to the king's gate" (Est. 6:12). R. Sheshet said: This means that he returned to his sackcloth and his fasting over the troubles of the Jewish people. Simultaneously, "but Haman hastened to his house, mourning, and having his head covered" (Est. 6:12). "Mourning" over the death of his daughter. "And having his head covered" due to what had happened to him, as his head was full of filth.[26]

The authors of this midrash constructed a scene in crowded Shushan, where distance blurred the identities of horse, rider, and steward, enabling a complete reversal – *nahafokh hu* – to occur. Haman's daughter threw feces upon her father because in no scenario could she contemplate that her father would *not* be the one on the horse dressed in royal robes. Yet when the eyes of daughter and father locked, the terrible truth surfaced. Out of shame, Haman's daughter leapt to her death. The real suffering in the midrash is not Haman's abasement but at the suicide of his daughter when she realized her active role in her father's denigration.

The covering Haman wore that hid his face was not a garment of mourning but the excrement his own daughter threw upon him. He was covered in dung and stricken with grief over the loss of his daughter. While there is humor in this reading, there is poignancy and even a little tenderness, too. The pathos lies in the fact that the daughter's action signaled a truth about her father; she unintentionally punished him for his crime against Mordecai and humanity, unintentionally upholding a truth. Remember that the previous passage of this very midrash alerted us to the prohibition against smirking over our enemy's troubles. For one sympathetic moment, we are absorbed in this embellished reading, left to feel the pain and loss of both daughter and father.

We understand why, exegetically, the Sages opted for such an odd reading of Esther 6:12: "Then Mordecai returned to the king's gate, while Haman hurried home, his head covered in mourning." The two

---

26. Megilla 16a.

responses read almost like stage directions, inviting analysis. The reader assumes Haman's mourning was due to personal mortification at parading his enemy; the Sages read it as literal mourning, perhaps skeptical that Haman would be in mourning over his reputation. The reader shares no such skepticism, especially with Haman's self-important behavior on full display in chapter 6. Regardless of what caused Haman's mourning, Esther 6:12 shows two men in mourning, rather than one. Haman returned to his home sad and troubled, while Mordecai returned to his court position at the king's gate, garbed once again in sackcloth and ashes.

Haman's Return Home

Ibn Yahya comments on the pace of Haman's walk. As soon as the slow ceremonial trot ended, "Haman hurried home" to minimize his shame and grief. The Talmud's midrashic reading associates grief with only one event: death. Haman's devastation was overpowering, and the verse's use of a term that indicates loss – *avel* – foreshadows Haman's approaching execution. Ibn Ezra also reads the verse literally. Haman covered his own head when the march of Mordecai was over; recoiling in embarrassment, Haman hid his identity. Covered, he was able to escape public recognition but still had to confront the internal torment. In the second version of his commentary, Ibn Ezra further details the shame of 6:12: "He covered his head so that he would not lift his eyes or be seen from a distance because of the humiliation and degradation." Ibn Ezra says Haman did not want to see those who could see him. This may also have been picked up in the midrash as an explanation for why Haman's very daughter could not distinguish her father from her father's enemy.

This inability to recognize Haman, the king's top advisor, is reminiscent of another courtier story: that of Joseph. "Although Joseph recognized his brothers, they did not recognize him" (Gen. 42:8). While medieval commentators offer various explanations (perhaps Joseph was bearded or was newly clean-shaven, as if this could throw off his brothers), the issue of recognition goes beyond physical appearance. The brothers could not believe Joseph was alive, let alone a member of the royal court; it never would have occurred to them to recognize Joseph as the Egyptian official. Of course, even if they had not thought Joseph dead, they never before recognized his greatness. This reading suggests not only their trouble identifying Joseph, but the difficulty in seeing him for who he really was all along. Similarly, Haman's daughter in the midrash could not believe her father would be low in anyone's esteem. Consequently, she did not think for a moment that he was the man leading the horse.

Haman, in his state of grief, did not receive comfort and support when he needed it most. Instead, he was told by those closest to him that what happened to him had to happen. It was inevitable, literally written in the stars: "If Mordecai, before whom you have begun to fall, is of Jewish descent, you will never overcome him. You shall collapse altogether before him" (Est. 6:13). If this were a self-evident truth in the manner in which Zeresh expressed it, it is unclear why she did not make this known earlier, in chapter 5, instead of advising Haman to do away with Mordecai with very visible gallows: "Then his wife Zeresh and all his friends said to him, 'Let a gallows be put up, fifty cubits high, and in the morning ask the king to have Mordecai hanged on it. Then you can go gaily with the king to the feast.' The proposal pleased Haman, and he had the gallows put up" (Est. 5:13–14). Keeping this information from Haman earlier makes her appear cold, detached, and politically cunning, siding with whoever was triumphant. She should not have suggested gallows unless she believed at the time of the suggestion that Haman was moving up, which meant that Mordecai was descending. When the scales turned, she saw only one direction for her hapless husband. Zeresh becomes the ultimate predictor of events in a way that suggests a comic relief for the audience. When even one's own wife sides with her husband's enemy, we can imagine readers laughing at how profoundly the political landscape had changed. Paradoxically, Haman was chastened by his wife despite Ahasuerus' earlier proclamation of male superiority and domination in the home.

Zeresh, one midrash contends, had her own courtier connections and understood the universe of politics. Another midrash suggests that Haman actually had 360 wives, but none were as wise as Zeresh.[27] Her wisdom came through powers of observation. When she observed that Mordecai was of Jewish descent, she understood he was in favor. One

27. *Midrash Abba Guryon* 5.

midrash pieces together the two conversations in which she participated; in the first conversation, she suggested gallows because she knew about the Book of Daniel where Hananiah and his other colleagues were delivered from a fiery furnace and Daniel survived a lion's pit. This prompted Zeresh to suggest gallows:

> His wife said to him, "If this man about whom you are asking [Mordecai] is of Jewish stock, you will not be able to overcome him unless you cleverly contrive something that no member of his people has ever experienced. Hananiah and his colleagues were delivered from a fiery furnace. Daniel emerged from a lion's pit. Thus hang him on a gallows, for we have not found that any of his people were saved from that.[28]

Jews evidently had enough magical power to escape fire and ferocious animals, but gallows had not yet been tested.[29] Rashi, basing himself on the Talmud, suggests that Zeresh was not referring to acts in the Book of Daniel but to earlier promises made to Abraham: "'But you shall fall (*nafol tippol*) before him' (Est. 6:13). Why is there a doubling of verbs here? The Jewish nation is compared to the dust and it is compared to the stars. When they descend, they descend to the dust, and when they rise, they rise to the stars."[30] This talmudic observation suggests a falling down countered by a falling "up." Craig draws attention to the way in which this truth about Mordecai's people and Haman was written into the fabric of existence:

> It appears that Haman's destiny, according to his wife and friends, is guided by something – and they do not call it God – beyond themselves or this world.... It is Mordecai's Jewishness that somehow foreshadows victory over Haman. According to those who speak now, it is not because Mordecai has power over him-

28. Esther Rabba 9:2.
29. Ibid.
30. Megilla 16a.

> self to overcome Haman, but because he is part of an inevitable movement.[31]

When Haman told his story of woe in chapter 5, Mordecai was in a state of abject despair. By chapter 6, circumstances had changed so radically that when Haman returned home dejected and shared what had happened in the middle of the night, Zeresh understood a truth not evident before. Mordecai was on the rise, and there was nothing Haman could do to stop him.

To Rise and to Fall

We recognize the kind of dichotomy Zeresh created from the Jacob and Esau narratives. One's success signals another's tragedy in a zero-sum game. This dichotomy is also redolent in the Book of Ovadiah, where Jacob and Esau become the personifications of Israel and Edom, or Rome. Edom gloats over its triumph while God mandates that its height of power is only an illusion soon to be shattered: "Your arrogant heart has seduced you, you who dwell in clefts of the rock. In your lofty abode, you think in your heart, 'Who can pull me down to earth?' Should you nest as high as the eagle, should your aerie be lodged among the stars, even from there I will pull you down – declares the Lord."[32] Edom will be laid low, and Israel will ascend. Pitting Haman against Mordecai or even a wife against a husband plays to either the dramatic or the comic irony of opposites that repel. It seems, according to another midrashic treatment, that the diametric opposition of good and evil – Mordecai versus Haman – was evident to Ahasuerus as well:

> When the wicked Haman said to Ahasuerus, "Let us destroy Israel," Ahasuerus replied, "You will not win because their God will never forsake them. See what He did to the kings of old who attacked Israel. These kings were stronger and mightier than I, but in the end they became a laughingstock throughout the world. Therefore, stop pressing me on this matter." Nevertheless, the

31. Craig, *Reading Esther*, 123–24.
32. Ob. 1:3–4.

> wicked Haman continued to press Ahasuerus constantly and to give him evil advice about Israel. "If so," said Ahasuerus, "let us consult the sages and sorcerers." He gathered all the sages of the nations of the world. They all came up before him and said in unison, "If you destroy Israel, the world will cease to exist."[33]

This midrash paints an unlikely portrait of a humble Ahasuerus, ready to admit that others were more powerful than he and that Israel enjoyed insurmountable divine protection. It was a cosmic truth, obvious to Zeresh, plain to Ahasuerus, completely unknown to Haman. By depicting Ahasuerus gathering many sages for consultation, this midrash presents its characteristic and consistent view that all were aware of the special status the Jews occupied in the world. Against this, Haman's plans did not stand a chance.

Where's the Change?

There are those who might question the value of this chapter since it apparently did not change anything. No matter what status Mordecai achieved with his ride on the horse, it altered neither his fate nor the fate of his people. And yet, perhaps something did radically shift. This parade was a chance for both Haman and Mordecai and their many onlookers to glimpse the future. The king saw, for the very first time, the true greatness of Mordecai, who did not need or value the finery and thus was no threat. Mordecai may have received a reward he never wanted, but he also got the unimaginable chance to be seen and to see himself as the true leader he knew himself to be in private: loyal, protective, strategic, wise. Visualizing oneself as a leader can leave a powerful and indelible impression. Even as Mordecai returned to sackcloth, he did not have to imagine what a powerful advocate for his people he might look like given the chance. This visual enabled him, and Esther watching him, to be bolder and more courageous. Esther and Mordecai were able to take risks because they were finally witness to Haman downtrodden and Mordecai uplifted. This foretaste of the truth could not be "un-seen." The fact that this picture was fully displayed allowed

33. Esther Rabba 7:13.

the public, including the Jews, to imagine another world, one where evil was degraded and goodness promoted. It was only a short step from this to Mordecai's real promotion.

Mordecai's Gate

"Quick, then!" said the king to Haman. "Get the garb and the horse, as you have said, and do this to Mordecai the Jew, who sits in the king's gate. Omit nothing of all you have proposed." So Haman took the garb and the horse and arrayed Mordecai and paraded him through the city square; and he proclaimed before him: This is what is done for the man whom the king desires to honor! Then Mordecai returned to the king's gate, while Haman hurried home, his head covered in mourning. (Est. 6:10–12)

At that time, when Mordecai was sitting in the palace gate, Bigthan and Teresh, two of the king's eunuchs who guarded the threshold, became angry, and plotted to do away with King Ahasuerus. Mordecai learned of it and told it to Queen Esther, and Esther reported it to the king in Mordecai's name. (Est. 2:21–22)

When Mordecai learned all that had happened, Mordecai tore his clothes and put on sackcloth and ashes. He went through the city, crying out loudly and bitterly, until he came in front of the palace gate; for one could not enter the palace gate wearing sackcloth. (Est. 4:1–2)

That day Haman went out happy and lighthearted. But when Haman saw Mordecai in the palace gate, and Mordecai did not

> rise or even stir on his account, Haman was filled with rage at him. (Est. 5:9)
>
> "Yet all this means nothing to me every time I see that Jew Mordecai sitting in the palace gate." (Est. 5:13)
>
> For Mordecai was now powerful in the royal palace, and his fame was spreading through all the provinces; the man Mordecai was growing ever more powerful. (Est. 9:4)

After the parade around downtown Shushan, Mordecai did not go home. He returned to where he could once again make himself useful to the king and to Esther: the king's gate. Rashi on 6:12, with perhaps a touch of irony, says that Mordecai returned "to his sackcloth and to his fasting."[1] There was no reason to celebrate. Mordecai's fame was a trifle, a vanity. If he was to die, then royal robes did nothing for him. Only sackcloth could capture the tone and tenor of the moment. Ibn Yahya on 6:12 adds that despite the hoopla, Mordecai "was not filled with pride over all this honor."

For all the time he spent there, the king's gate might be more aptly named Mordecai's gate. Mordecai's character is exemplified by this location; an in-between space, neither in nor out. It was a place where someone with an insider/outsider status, someone like an exile, might find himself. Not entirely welcome but also not entirely foreign to court, Mordecai's position at the king's gate symbolized his evolution from outsider to insider. Mordecai, the exile, placed himself in this liminal space because real leadership is most necessary in ambiguous places. The gate was also an apt metaphor for the Jewish people in Persia, who were neither in nor out. Life in the diaspora was not an entrance and not an exit. The gate held promise and fear; approaching it had the potential to change lives. After all, it was this very location where Mordecai overturned a plot to kill the king, and it was to where Mordecai turned with the terrible news of the decree. If he protected the king in this space, perhaps the king would, in turn, protect him and his people.

1. Rashi bases himself on Megilla 16a.

Fox believes that the term *shaar hamelekh,* "the king's gate," is not a reference to a specific opening in the walls of the royal court but a designation for "the entire palace administrative complex."[2] Sitting at the king's gate thus implied holding a government position. As discussed earlier, the gate was not a modest entranceway into the palace but likely an enormous thoroughfare separating the palace from the rest of Shushan. It was a place buzzing with activity and commotion, a place where the comings and goings of notables could be marked and observed.

Mordecai's position parallels what we know of another biblical courtier's location: "At Daniel's request, the king appointed Shadrach, Meshach, and Abednego to administer the province of Babylon; while Daniel himself was at the king's gate" (Dan. 2:49). Ibn Ezra, ad loc., makes the connection between the two gates explicit and describes Daniel's placement at the king's gate as a promotion: "And Daniel was at the king's gate because it represented a significant ascension since this is where the magistrates and judges sat." This suggestion is not arbitrary but contextual. Daniel had just identified and interpreted Nebuchadnezzar's dream, gaining himself accolades, gifts, and a position of political privilege: "The king then elevated Daniel and gave him very many gifts, and made him governor of the whole province of Babylon and chief prefect of all the wise men of Babylon" (Dan. 2:48). The Malbim on this verse adds that when the king saw that Daniel did not enjoy the proper honor in the court (literally, *kevod elohut*), he promoted him politically and "gave him many and substantial gifts and made him ruler over all of the provinces of Babylonia and more powerful than any other official of Babylonia." That the king took proper notice of Daniel and his contribution highlights the fact that Ahasuerus forgot to honor Mordecai, his only loyal servant. While one could counter that Daniel solved a problem with a stated reward (so he was explicitly owed one), the stakes were much more consequential in Ahasuerus' case.[3] Mordecai did not just interpret a king's dream; he saved his very life.

---

2. Fox, *Character and Ideology*, 39.
3. Nebuchadnezzar promised gifts and honor to the one who could properly interpret his dreams: "If you tell the dream and its meaning, you shall receive from me gifts,

From Accidental to Intentional

The royal household expected Mordecai to be at the king's gate. It is where Mordecai turned to with the terrible news of the decree: "He went through the city, crying out loudly and bitterly, until he came in front of the palace gate; for one could not enter the palace gate wearing sackcloth" (Est. 4:1–2). We know Haman strongly associated Mordecai with this location: "But when Haman saw Mordecai in the palace gate, and Mordecai did not rise or even stir on his account, Haman was filled with rage at him" (Est. 5:9). This association became so strong that Haman must have had a difficult time in any situation that demanded he pass through or nearby the gate: "Yet all this means nothing to me every time I see that Jew Mordecai sitting in the palace gate" (Est. 5:13).

One wonders if Mordecai's irritation of Haman was intentional, or if it was a convenient by-product of his being at the gate for other reasons. Mordecai leveraged the negative associations Haman had with the area to cripple him. If so, Mordecai was successful. In order to attend to his royal business, Haman had to pass this place, possibly multiple times in the course of a day. If the entrance and exit to the royal household became haunting and threatening, the site became associated with a paralyzing sense of failure. Mordecai's return to the gate after the horse parade signaled that he would always be a strangling, inescapable presence for Haman, an eddy of insecurity.

Mordecai may also have had something personal to gain from returning to the gate again and again: he was patiently awaiting a reward that took a long time coming. His constant presence may have alerted other courtiers to Mordecai's first act of loyalty there, and maybe someone would eventually point out to King Ahasuerus that Mordecai's service was never acknowledged. Stay in one place long enough, and people begin to notice.

---

presents, and great honor; therefore, tell me the dream and its meaning" (Dan. 2:6). He also threatened that if the interpreter was wrong, he would be ripped limb from limb.

Moving from the Outside In

Mordecai may have spent a long time on the sidelines, but he did not stay there forever: "For Mordecai was now powerful in the royal palace, and his fame was spreading through all the provinces; the man Mordecai was growing ever more powerful." (Est. 9:4). By patiently staying in the same spot, and growing his influence, Mordecai eventually became a figure of much influence in the royal household itself, moving from the outside to the inside. The Malbim on 9:4 shares a fascinating observation about political life in the palace. He believes that there are essentially three types of courtiers: those who run the king's household, those who run state affairs, and those who wage war for the king against external threats and expand his empire. Success in each venture expands the muscle and authority of a courtier. Mordecai succeeded in each of these roles: he eventually ran the king's household, as second to the king he ran affairs of state, and through taxation he helped expand the king's empire. This, according to the Malbim, explains the expression used in 9:4: "Mordecai was growing ever more powerful (*holekh vegadol*)." He became greater and more instrumental to governance than before. While we do not witness this shift in status directly, we imagine that to become second to the king, as indicated in 10:3, Mordecai had to climb incrementally up a ladder. When Haman's seat was vacated, Mordecai may have been moved from his seat at the king's gate to right beside the king himself. We know that there is some record of this even if its details are not offered in the scroll because the closing chapter indicates as much: "All his mighty and powerful acts, and a full account of the greatness to which the king advanced Mordecai, are recorded in the Annals of the Kings of Media and Persia" (Est. 10:2). Mordecai's advance was significant enough to merit a full reckoning in official records. His initial decision to stay at the king's gate and remain an outsider with access to inside information paid important dividends.

Dangers of the King's Gate

This dream of proximity to the king, who desperately needed Mordecai's advice, achieves its most memorable depictions not in the Hebrew Bible but in the Talmud. There another unusual relationship between an important Jew and an important gentile unfolds, but the Jew is a sage rather than a courtier.

A talmudic passage in Tractate Avoda Zara begins with a complex legal discussion about hereditary kingship among the nations and then quickly devolves into a discussion of the relationship between R. Yehuda HaNasi, redactor of the Mishna, and the Roman emperor Antoninus, sometimes identified as Marcus Aurelius Antoninus, who ruled Rome from 211 to 217 CE. Without prior talmudic context (the setting is unclear, and we don't know if the rabbi was summoned for this or already present), Antoninus poses a question to R. Yehuda: "I wish for Asveirus, my son, to rule instead of me and that Tiberias be released [from taxation]. If I ask for one [from the Roman Senate], they will do it, but two they will not."[4] Here, even the most powerful man in the Roman Empire cannot get all that he wants from his Senate, so he takes guidance from an unlikely counselor, a scholar from an embattled minority over whom Antoninus reigned. R. Yehuda immediately responds with a role play that masks a solution: "He brought a man, placed him [on the shoulders] of another man, and put a dove in the hands of the one on top and said to the one on the bottom: 'Tell the one on top that he should let the dove fly from his hands.'" Antoninus understood R. Yehuda's elusive advice. He should ask the Senate for his son to succeed him and then tell his son to release Tiberias from taxes, thus achieving both his wishes. Commentators on this encounter explain that Antoninus wanted to exempt Tiberias from taxes because it was home to Jewish scholars. The Roman emperor wanted to honor his relationship with R. Yehuda by releasing an entire city from taxation, hearkening to the reprieve from taxes that Ahasuerus granted his empire upon his marriage to Esther. Later, in Esther, it was Mordecai the Jew, whose presence is associated with a firm reinstatement of taxes, who was able to bring the king's empire back to fiscal health. Royalty, taxation, and the Jewish people are linked, revealing the Jewish community's historical dependency on the whim and material support of the monarch and the king's need for Jewish financial support in the form of taxes.

4. Avoda Zara 10a.

The dialogue between king and sage continued. Antoninus confided in R. Yehuda about Roman politics: "Important Romans are upsetting me." Again, R. Yehuda responded elliptically, bringing Antoninus to his vegetable garden for a series of days and uprooting a radish each day. Antoninus also read into this theatrical move. He should kill these Romans one by one and not threaten them as a group. If the first story sounds unlikely, the second enters into the theater of the absurd. It sounds almost treasonous for a Jew to advise a king to kill members of his own empire, but it was the advice Antoninus wanted. We begin to understand the potency of this dialogue, as if a Jew could will the next government into existence and had the power to kill at will by bending the ear of the most powerful man of the land. The brilliance of the narrative is that R. Yehuda said nothing. His innocent gestures gave nothing away. The king interpreted his every word to have political import.

But our story does not end there. Antoninus needed advice not only on his successor and the management of his court but also about his family. His daughter behaved promiscuously, and the king of the Roman Empire needed parenting advice.[5] The passage continues, and in gratitude for his friendship and counsel, every day Antoninus sent R. Yehuda crushed gold in large sacks covered with wheat. The wheat hid the gold, much like R. Yehuda's gestures hid his dramatic advice. The fantasy deepens even further. R. Yehuda rejected the gold, replying simply and humbly with another lesson: "I do not need it. I have enough."[6] In these few words, he may have also been creating a distinction between Jew and emperor. Authority does not come from things. It comes from wisdom. This may have also been a lesson for Jews who were drawn to the trappings of foreign rule: live humbly in exile. Do not be seduced by the trinkets of other lands. Antoninus, however, insisted that R. Yehuda keep the gold for later generations; a future regime might one day reinstitute taxes in Tiberias.

If these tales ended here, they would be wonderful daydreams of Jewish influence. The magic, however, continues:

5. Avoda Zara 10b.
6. Ibid.

> Every day, he [Antoninus] would minister to R. Yehuda; he would feed him and give him to drink. When the Rabbi wanted to alight on his bed, he [Antoninus] would bend down in front of him and say: "Ascend upon me to your bed." The Rabbi protested: "It is not proper conduct to treat the king with such disrespect." He [Antoninus] responded, "O that I were a mattress under you in the World-to-Come!"[7]

Power yields to wisdom in this unimaginable conversation, reminding us of an earlier aggada about Mordecai stepping on Haman's back to alight his horse.[8] Antoninus was R. Yehuda's valet, attending to his every need, even serving as the lowly stepping stool for R. Yehuda, subjugating himself and thereby hoping to gain entrance to the next world by mere association. If this were not enough, after several related debates about foreign power, the Talmud adds an addendum to these passages. Not only had Antoninus served R. Yehuda, but King Arkdan of Persia (Artabanos, who defeated the Romans in 216 CE) did the same for Rav, a first-century *Amora*. While there are no detailed discussions of how Arkdan served Rav, the point is to cap the discussion of revered sages by noting that obsequious treatment of a sage was not unique to R. Yehuda and the Roman emperor. The dream spread across time and geography.

In the aggregate, these tales are as amusing as they are telling. By the time we get to the last of them, we know they could not possibly be true. R. Yehuda may very well have had some connection to Antoninus, but the likelihood that the head of the Roman Empire prostrated himself so that a Jewish sage could step on his back to get to bed is a stretch. The exaggerated reports suggest not what the relationship was in reality, but the dream Jews had of what it could have been. Earlier in the same tractate, the Talmud states that the Jews had twenty-six years of a good relationship with Rome, highlighting almost three decades of peace and tolerance that later sank into intolerance and brutality: "For twenty-six years, the Romans stood faithfully with the Jewish people and did not

---

7. Ibid.
8. Megilla 16a.

subjugate them."[9] Twenty-six years is a wink in historical time. The nostalgic longing for the twenty-six years of yore, during which R. Yehuda enjoyed status and prestige among the Romans, seems paradoxically both an affirmation and a denial of diaspora reality. "Look at what Jews can achieve" is undercut immediately by the reality that even when it is good, it cannot – will not – last. To that point, the Talmud also puts to rest the awe of gentile kings: "When Antoninus died, the bundle was separated. When Arkdan died, Rav said, 'The bundle was separated.'"[10] The tight cord that joined each scholar with a ruler was severed with their deaths; whatever protection or tax exemption the Jews of each period enjoyed as an outgrowth of these intense friendships was over. *Vayakom melekh ḥadash.*[11] A new king came to power.

Jewish friends at court do exist, but when relationships are personal, they may or may not last. Sitting at the gate with close proximity to the king, Mordecai may have given Ahasuerus much-needed advice and the counsel he lacked to handle affairs of state, much in the way R. Yehuda counseled Antoninus. Maintaining proximity to the gate is critical because it becomes easier to know the way out when fortunes eventually change.

And they always do.

9. Avoda Zara 9a.
10. Ibid. 10b.
11. Ex. 1:8.

Chapter Seven

Revelation at Court

Keeping Silent

Death by False Accusation

Revelation at Court

> So the king and Haman came to feast with Queen Esther. On the second day, the king again asked Esther at the wine feast, "What is your wish, Queen Esther? It shall be granted you. And what is your request? Even to half the kingdom, it shall be fulfilled." Queen Esther replied: "If Your Majesty will do me the favor, and if it pleases Your Majesty, let my life be granted me as my wish, and my people as my request. For we have been sold, my people and I, to be destroyed, massacred, and exterminated. Had we only been sold as bondmen and bondwomen, I would have kept silent; for the adversary is not worthy of the king's trouble." Thereupon King Ahasuerus demanded of Queen Esther, "Who is he and where is he who dared to do this?" "The adversary and enemy," replied Esther, "is this evil Haman!" And Haman cringed in terror before the king and the queen. (Est. 7:1–6)

Jan Lievens' portrait of the second wine party, *The Feast of Esther*, completed in 1625, is rich in saturated color and drama. Scholars once assumed it was painted by Rembrandt, and it was sold as such in 1952. The large canvas, stretching four-and-a-half by five feet, invites the onlooker to the table where Haman will be outed for the evil, scheming courtier he was. In the painting, Ahasuerus is covered in a heavy, brocade mantle cinched by a large gemstone. His large, white turban with its crowned peak and jaunty feather sits atop a royal head that dominates the right side of the painting. The king's authority over the others is evident; his eyes have no tolerance for Haman. For days and nights, the king's suspicion about Haman's intentions had intensified, interrupting his sleep and his waking hours. At this scene of revelation, Haman feigns surprise, not that Esther was Jewish, but that he, the constant favorite, was suddenly the subject of disgust. The great manipulator had been manipulated.

Mordecai, who was not invited to this party, appears in this painting between the faces of Esther and Ahasuerus, his eyes also drilling into Haman. Mordecai dominated Haman's thoughts as an obsession he could not shake. Although Mordecai was essentially powerless at this time, he was able to trigger in Haman such intense hatred that whenever Mordecai was present none of Haman's long list of accomplishments meant anything. Mordecai's placement in the painting also suggests that he had finally found his place, quite literally, between the royal couple.

Haman's right hand is lifted in shock and terror as he looks at the king. Ahasuerus lays his right arm on the table with his hand extended in Haman's direction. His left hand is beneath the table, clenched with an anger that shows in his hooded eyes, taking in the shadowy figure of Haman. All eyes are on Ahasuerus, but all the light in the painting is reserved for Esther. She, too, is covered in the intricate finery that would showcase the artist's attention to detail, her gemstone pendant matching the shape and size of the king's. The two were now joined aesthetically, as if to suggest that they were now aligned in their revulsion for the man who joined them at the party.

Esther's Strategy

The banquet of chapter 7 started off much like the previous banquet, with the last of three utterances that displayed the king's magnanimity: "What is your wish, Queen Esther? It shall be granted you. And what is your request? Even to half the kingdom, it shall be fulfilled" (7:1). The king immediately asked Esther the same question he had asked before, offering to satisfy her wishes before she had even articulated them. Willingness to accommodate without fully understanding the details had led Ahasuerus to many poor decisions which did or could come with a high price: the loss of his former wife, the potential loss of the Jews in his empire, the loss of his new queen, the loss of life for his other Persian subjects. One might think that at this late juncture, the king would have been more circumspect in rushing to accommodate. The repetition may then suggest that Ahasuerus did not have the capacity to learn from his mistakes. It also could suggest that this was actually just royal protocol, a standard phraseology not meant to be taken literally. Esther certainly did not take it literally, because Jews did not take up half the kingdom or even a fraction of it.

Esther planned her plea carefully; the unlikely scene of a banquet, a time reserved for pleasure and social niceties, perhaps disarmed the king. Then there was the strategy of asking the king for a favor that might be good for the king himself. Sparing her life benefited her *and* him: "If Your Majesty will do me the favor, and if it pleases Your Majesty, let my life be granted me as my wish, and my people as my request" (Est. 7:3). Esther could have separated the value of her life from that of her nation, pleading for herself without addressing the general decree. Instead, she tried a riskier tactic, effectively prioritizing her people above her husband. Her life would not be worthwhile without her people. This risky plan revealed a deep sense of collective belonging, both primal and inspiring, that Ahasuerus may not have felt, being above all and therefore attached to no one in particular.

Esther also baldly referenced the transactional nature of the decree, slowly drawing the king into how terrible it would be to be sold into slavery but how much worse still to be sold for extermination. "For we have been sold, my people and I, to be destroyed, massacred, and exterminated. Had we only been sold as bondmen and bondwomen, I would have kept silent; for the adversary is not worthy of the king's trouble" (Est. 7:4). Surely being sold into slavery would warrant the king's attention, yet in phrasing it the way she did, Esther suggested her own powerlessness. Moore believes that the word "sold" here should be translated as "delivered over to," citing Deuteronomy 32:30, Judges 2:14, 4:2, and 4:9.[1] It seems that only death merited the king's attention, but Esther also highlighted the fact that the decree was an act of financial exploitation. People in Ahasuerus' kingdom were to be bought and sold

1. Moore, *Esther*, 70.

as chattel. This could not serve the king's best interests, not least of all when one of those sold was his queen:

> Her plea is masterfully constructed. Note that she addresses the king first not in the expected third-person form ("If I have won the King's favor ..."; cf. 5:4, 8) but in the bolder and more personal form of address ("If I have won your favor, O King...", v. 3). She is pleading for her own life but also implying, without being so tactless as to say it directly, that the king is about to lose the person dearest to him and most intimate with him.[2]

The queen did not mention her people by name. Instead, her strategy was to highlight suffering first such that the persecuted could have been any tribe or grouping. She appealed to the king's humanity rather than try to fight the bias against the Jews that the king either felt himself or harbored as a result of the faceless animosity Haman had carefully cultivated. Ahasuerus should have inquired about her nationality, but because of the way Esther strategized and laid out her request, she led the king to identifying the villain before the victim, pegging the one who committed an injustice and shining a light on him. An association with injustice could harm the king and do his reputation damage, hearkening to an earlier Genesis verse: "Shall not the Judge of all the earth deal justly?" (Gen. 18:25). Should not the judge over a vast Persian Empire deal justly?

Esther also had the tricky and delicate task of vilifying and demonizing Haman while studiously avoiding laying any of the blame on the king who permitted the decree to go forward. She had to make the case subtly that the king had been manipulated, indeed, duped; Esther worked with the assumption that Ahasuerus would never have knowingly granted permission for a dishonorable human transaction. Craig observes that the author of the book had Esther use the same language that Haman used in trying to eliminate the Jews:

> The narrator has her use the same key word *shavah* (a word used infrequently in the Hebrew Bible), that Haman had spoken in 3:8.

2. Levenson, *Esther*, 101.

> So the narrator hints that Esther can play the same game – even using some of the same words – that Haman did. Her strategy for convincing the king is not unlike Haman's. Both appeal to what they hope will be interpreted in the king's best interest. You've promised *me* half the kingdom, but my only request is for you to do what's best for *your* kingdom, Esther would have the king believe.[3]

Alerting us to the similarity of language, Craig suggests Esther was manipulating the king as if it were a game that two could play. To call it a game, however, belittles what Esther was doing, reducing it to mere political scheming. Esther was doing something of great urgency and virtue because so much was at stake in this moment. Haman, on the other hand, acted purely for selfish and immoral reasons.

The similarity of language may offer a linguistic way of Esther upending Haman's plan by suggesting that what she is doing is *really* in the king's interest, in counterpoise to Haman's plan. It was not good for the king to jeopardize even one small nation among his empire of 127 provinces, for it would put every other people at potential risk. It was not good for the king to corrupt himself and his empire in order to feed the monstrous vengeance of one courtier. It was not good for the king to forgo the tax money the Jews put in the royal coffers. Haman's actions were in Haman's own interest, sold unconvincingly to a king more eager to please than to act wisely on the throne. Esther was protecting the king's best interests, to rule wisely and well, while trying to protect her people from harm.

Her mounting accusation explains Haman's reaction to the revelation: "And Haman cringed in terror before the king and the queen" (Est. 7:6). The second version of Ibn Ezra's commentary explains Haman's terror: "A fear that came suddenly" and unexpectedly. Initially, the cringe is puzzling. Haman was transparent with the king about his plan, presenting his problem with the Jews, why he believed they should not be tolerated, what was to be done about them, and the amount of revenue that would have made the arrangement worthwhile. By contrast, the

3. Craig, *Reading Esther*, 117.

queen was not transparent in naming her people. But she was very transparent in identifying the enemy, and in the same verse, 7:6, she called Haman an enemy using two nouns, a man who is an enemy and a villain: *ish tzar ve'oyev*. The second version of Ibn Ezra on this verse hints at Haman's duplicity: he was an enemy both in public and in private. One recalls the visual cues present that Lievens used so fittingly in his painting – there was no mistaking the enemy now.[4]

In answer to the king's question about the enemy: "Who is he and where is he who dared to do this?" Esther believed it was just as important to describe him as to name him: "'The *adversary* and *enemy*,' replied Esther, 'is this *evil* Haman!'" She may have added this layer in response to the double nature of the king's question. He wanted to know who was really at the root of the evil plot, and Esther provided not only a name but an explanation: Haman. It was he who acted nefariously not because his proposal was an isolated strategy but because he was, at heart, a person driven by intense hate. Since evil can be hard to name until much damage has already been done, we often soften it, contextualize it, minimize it, even justify it. Esther offered none of that. The soft-spoken, graceful queen suddenly became sharp, definitive, and unmoved by any false pity for her nemesis or fear of reprisal. The truth, when it was ready to surface, had to be told with crystalline surety. Like Nathan condemning David over the Bathsheba incident: "That man is you" (II Sam. 12:7), or Joseph revealing himself to his brothers: "I am Joseph" (Gen. 45:3), there are situations where wrongdoing must be named directly. A moment of revelation, with its horror and flood of emotion, must land with ferocity for full impact.

This is not the first time the king asked the question "Who is this man?" In chapter 6 Ahasuerus asked the same question about a man who entered his chambers in the dead of night. The answer was the same in both chapters, hinting that all bad roads led to Haman. When the truth

---

4. Rashbam on Gen. 37:19 references our verse to explain the word *hazeh* as something or someone close at hand. The fear and intensity of the moment was amplified by the physical proximity to the enemy. While Haman held a more powerful position than Esther, by naming him she was able to undercut his power and show it for what it was: a smokescreen and conduit for unbridled evil.

became clear, the facts leading up to the moment retrospectively took on new color, meaning, and import.

Haman Could Not Hide

Haman's animosities were no secret. That they were to affect Esther so profoundly was the great secret that is no secret to the readers of this book. The secret that Esther was a Jew and related to Mordecai, the queen kept close to her chest, worrying about its consequences perhaps needlessly. We are unsure, however, if it was a real secret in the royal palace. It is difficult to believe the king did not know firsthand Haman's feelings toward Mordecai, or that Mordecai was Jewish, or that the identity of the nation Haman hated was that of his queen. If anyone should have worried or hidden a secret, it was Haman, who may have been wiser to conceal his disgust at Mordecai and who, knowing how much the king loved his queen, had much to lose. Ahasuerus gave Esther every indication that he was committed to helping her and offered assurances that even her rule breaking was to be ignored. Rather than receiving any punishment or negative attention for what Esther did, she was roundly and immediately rewarded with the gift of Haman's house, a promotion for her uncle, and an opportunity for national self-defense. Once revealed, a secret often becomes both momentous and inconsequential at the same time. The same cannot be said of Esther's party and its monstrous revelation, where those who had deep investments in shared confidences suddenly had to function on the narrow edge of the truth.

The unmasking of Haman was an incremental process in the Book of Esther. Haman, in fact, did more to reveal his true nature than the queen ever could. Esther's direct identification of her sworn enemy was merely the final and direct confirmation that Haman was a conspirator, unable to keep his personal hate agenda under control. If there is an emperor with no clothes in this story, it is not the actual emperor but his impostor second.

Did Esther Create This Plan?

We have no indication that Mordecai planned Esther's revelation at court. Esther's previous explicit and indirect contact with Mordecai was in chapter 4. This young woman independently contrived a brilliant plan to disarm her enemy without his suspecting foul play, while catalyzing in Ahasuerus the very suspicion she avoided receiving from Haman. By fomenting Ahasuerus' jealousy and confusion, Esther primed Ahasuerus to harbor bitter feelings toward Haman, associations helped by the previous chapter when the king finally had insight into those loyal and disloyal to him, those who would support him and those who would undermine him. These angry feelings predisposed and prepared Ahasuerus to hear negative information about Haman – an advisor Ahasuerus personally promoted – without allowing Haman to mount a defense. Esther had to bring the unsuspecting and the highly suspicious to the same table in order for her strategy to work.

Some talmudic Sages credited Esther with creating this plan, while others saw it as above her, another act of God performed by one of His trusted conduits. One talmudic passage analyzes Esther's mindset: "What did Esther have in mind when she invited Haman? She was laying a trap for him, thinking, 'I will smile at him [Haman] and then he [Ahasuerus] will slay him and me.'"[5] Making the king envious of a blossoming relationship between his new wife and his chief minister was logical given that the very same man wanted the royal clothing, horse, and honor. Claiming the king's wife represented, for Ahasuerus, the final takeover and makeover in Haman's scheme. The first party, coming directly after Mordecai's parade, which was Haman's idea, may have alerted the king that something was not right. The second party with the same guest list cemented his anxiety. Note that in the rabbinic reading, Esther smiled knowingly at her enemy at the risk of his life and hers. She understood that she would likely have to pay the ultimate price to stop this slaying machine. The king would kill both Haman and Esther out of a sense of betrayal and anger. Having been ready to give up her life earlier – "If I die, I die" (4:16) – Esther was ready to do so again.

Other rabbinic readings of this scene were less certain who the enemy was and less confident in Esther's leadership: "'An adversary and an enemy' (7:6): This teaches that she [Esther] began to point toward Ahasuerus, but an angel came and turned her hand toward Haman."[6]

5. Megilla 15b.
6. Ibid. 16a.

Esther was not promoting jealousy, a compelling but perhaps misguided tactic. She was, instead, going to tell the king the truth, implicating both her husband and his minister in her people's plight. But as she raised her hand to indicate one enemy, an angel pointed her hand at the real foe, upending her plan with a more effective strategy.

In a rabbinic reading a few verses later, another angel appears. This time it was the angel Michael, who cleared the king's line of vision so that even from a distance, he could make out the image of Haman falling on Esther's couch. Adding insult to injury, the angel violently pushed Haman on top of Esther, leaving no doubt about Haman's intentions:

> "The king rose in rage from the wine feast and went into the palace" (7:7): What did the angel Michael do? He began to cut down young trees thereby increasing the king's fury. "Haman fell upon the couch" (7:8): Michael had pushed him on top of Esther, who then cried out, "Your Majesty, he is forcing me in your very presence."[7]

Cutting down trees is an apt symbol for a king whose view of reality was so long obstructed. Ahasuerus had failed to see both the evil and the good in front of him, a failure that prompted him to reward Haman and ignore Mordecai. Now he finally experienced clarity.

The rabbis who devised this reading may have been influenced by another biblical encounter with an angel. When the prophet Balaam traveled to curse the Jews, his path became blocked by a hidden angel only visible to Balaam's donkey. Eventually Balaam was granted sight, too: "Then the Lord uncovered Balaam's eyes, and he saw the angel of the Lord standing in his way..." (Num. 22:31). Balaam's former blindness transformed into clear sight and became a theme in the poetic visions he later shared in rhapsodic form: "Word of the man whose eye is true.... Who beholds visions from the Almighty, prostrate, but with eyes unveiled" (Num. 24:3–4).

Ahasuerus, however, never really saw reality for what it was. Although he was able to recognize evil, what he saw was the wrong evil.

7. Esther Rabba 10:9.

He thought he saw a crime committed against him, when in fact, this was not true. Fox contends that Haman was executed "for attempting to rape Esther (he could not very well have been executed for a deed the king was implicated in)."[8] This is not an insignificant detail to be hemmed in by parentheses. It is a critical and important development. The king wanted to rid himself of the threat of Haman but could not find a legal way to do so within his own governance restrictions. Thus, he needed a fabricated charge and used one without due process. Of course, this begs the question of why he could not do the same for Esther's people: find some way to circumvent the law. What he did for himself, he was not willing to do for her, despite the fact that many lives were at stake.

The king revealed his inability to control the state of affairs. All he could do was leave the room, a sure sign of impotence: "The king, in his fury, left the wine feast for the palace garden" (Est. 7:7). Prepared to give Esther almost anything, he could not actually give her the one thing she truly desired. Offering her the opportunity for self-defense was not a real gift, because in a universe of justice, that should be a right, not a privilege. Furthermore, self-defense in this instance involved the risk of losing everything with no guarantee of winning anything. While Esther's request would have involved no loss of life, only its preservation, Ahasuerus' "solution" – one he arrived at it, oddly, without any ministerial consultations – had a devastating impact on his people. Haman's plan worked in the end, but on an unintended audience. While many modern commentators blame the Jews for this massacre, the blame actually belongs to the king. If there is any blame directed at Esther, it may be her failure to petition the king for the lives of the Persians. Had she been morally outraged rather than relieved when the king granted this dispensation, perhaps the outcome might have been different. Yet given the inexplicable universe of exile, it was unlikely.

"I must reveal a secret that my heart cannot conceal," remarked the French dramatist Jean Racine in *Phaedra*.[9] Not coincidentally, he wrote a three-act tragedy called *Esther* in 1689, based on the biblical heroine,

8. Fox, "Three Esthers," 53.
9. Jean Racine, *Iphigenia, Phaedra and Athaliah* (New York: Penguin Classics, 1964), 117.

produced during the reign of Louis XIV at a seminary for young noblewomen. As a playwright, Racine knew how important dramatic irony was. When an audience knows a secret that a character does not, it holds viewers' attention, building the tension until it bursts with the relief of revelation. A revealed secret then unites the plot, offering direction and resolution. Around the table, when Esther's accusation was made, the direction and resolution for the Jews was not apparent. Esther still had no idea if she or her people would live beyond the date set for their deaths. But she did know that she made something magical happen around the table and that her courage and leadership did not go unnoticed.

Keeping Silent

Esther did not reveal her people or her kindred, for Mordecai had told her not to reveal it. (Est. 2:10)

When the turn came for Esther daughter of Abihail – the uncle of Mordecai, who had adopted her as his own daughter – to go to the king, she did not ask for anything but what Hegai, the king's eunuch, guardian of the women, advised. Yet Esther won the admiration of all who saw her. (Est. 2:15)

When the virgins were assembled a second time, Mordecai sat in the palace gate. But Esther still did not reveal her kindred or her people, as Mordecai had instructed her; for Esther obeyed Mordecai's bidding, as she had done when she was under his tutelage. At that time, when Mordecai was sitting in the palace gate, Bigthan and Teresh, two of the king's eunuchs who guarded the threshold, became angry, and plotted to do away with King Ahasuerus. Mordecai learned of it and told it to Queen Esther, and Esther reported it to the king in Mordecai's name. (Est. 2:19–22)

For we have been sold, my people and I, to be destroyed, massacred, and exterminated. Had we only been sold as bondmen and bondwomen, I would have kept silent; for the adversary is not worthy of the king's trouble. (Est. 7:4)

The wise words of Ecclesiastes frame Esther's leadership experience. There is a time for all things: "A time to keep silent, and a time to speak" (3:7). A Sage in the Talmud elaborates on the meaning of this verse, emphasizing the subject rather than the infinitive: "There are times when one is silent and receives reward for the silence, and there are times one speaks and receives reward for the speech."[1] The absence or presence of language is not significant in and of itself. Silence must have meaning. Speech must have meaning.

We are told several times in the Book of Esther that Esther held her tongue. When told to remain silent, she obeyed. Even though she spoke when necessary, speaking seemed to be a struggle for her. The notion of holding one's tongue assumes a natural impulse to speak that must be controlled. It assumes that Esther was inclined to talk had she not been told otherwise. Yet Esther is generally laconic. She shared a few recorded sentences with Hegai, the eunuch in charge of the pageant, and had a conversation with the king about the conspiracy against him, crediting Mordecai without explaining her relationship to him. Ibn Ezra on 2:22 explains that Mordecai and Esther spoke through a messenger because the protocols of palace life demanded indirect communication, ensuring there were few secrets and many potential layers of bureaucracy with every word (this caution might explain some of the silence). Esther had a brief but potent exchange with Mordecai when she initially refused to plead on behalf of her people and then had limited interactions with the king at her two wine parties. Esther strikes readers as a person who spoke only when she had something to say. Given this, we are unsure why Mordecai needed to warn her to remain silent.

Remaining silent is often a more noble posture than speaking out, as Mahatma Gandhi advised a friend in a letter: "What shall I write to you? Everybody complains that you talk too much. You should sit alone somewhere… I have taken to prolonging my silence. It gives me joy and happiness. It is the only remedy for you."[2] Politics, in particular, offers

1. Zevaḥim 115b.
2. Mahatma Gandhi, *Collected Works of Mahatma Gandhi*, letter no. 285 (January 22, 1940) (CreateSpace, 2015), 242.

many opportunities for foolish, ill-spoken words that often come back to haunt the speaker in the form of broken promises and unmet expectations. Did Mordecai fear that Esther was too young to speak intelligently in the royal court or that she lacked the kind of political or diplomatic know-how to handle a conversation on her background with delicacy and aplomb? If this were the case, she would have been an unlikely candidate to then be told to navigate the rough waters of revealing her background.

Sidnie Ann White makes the case that Esther is herself a model for Jewish life in exile; she must serve and can only rise in influence if she uses her authority and feminine wiles to gain power. Otherwise, she is hopelessly vulnerable.[3]

That silence is rectitude may explain the general preference in the Bible and rabbinic literature for silence over speech. The sound of silence rings loudly at the parting of the Reed Sea (Ex. 14:14), and it whispers in I Kings 19:12 as the still small voice. Silence beckons loudly in Aaron's response to the loss of his two sons: *Vayidom Aharon*. Aaron was silent, or possibly he was silenced by the trauma of loss. Shame can also manifest itself as silence; Aaron's sons offered inappropriate fire on altars for which he himself was the chief steward. We wonder if Aaron's response inspired a talmudic response to suffering in silence; we are told to be both modest and silent in the face of difficulty, since silence is a means to end suffering.[4]

Silence may not end suffering in the technical sense as much as it ends the perseverative nature of suffering, the constant review of our troubles and their implications. Such does a verse in Psalms suggest: "I was mute with silence; I was silent from good, and my pain was strong" (39:3). The Talmud interprets "For You silence is praise" (Ps. 65:2) as a prescription for healing: "The best remedy of all is silence."[5] Ancient folk wisdom suggests that if one word is worth one *sela*, silence is worth two – an expression brought to Babylonia by R. Dimi from the Land

3. White, "Esther: A Feminine Model," 167.
4. Berakhot 62a.
5. Megilla 18a.

of Israel.[6] We find a similar resounding silence in Ezekiel's quiet sigh of *he'anek dom* (Ezek. 24:17). Proverbs and Ecclesiastes repeatedly recommend silence as a way to protect against harmful, hurtful, or trivial speech. R. Akiva touts silence as a fence to wisdom (*Pirkei Avot* 3:13). R. Shimon suggests that there is no balm for problems as effective as silence: "All my days I grew up among the Sages, and I did not find anything good for the body except silence" (Ibid. 1:17).

Silence is a worthy practice, yet we are still unsure why Mordecai asked Esther to remain silent. Rashi on 2:1 explains why Esther was originally not supposed to reveal her background: "So that they should not say she was from an ignoble family and dismiss her, for if they knew she was of the family of King Saul, they would keep her." Speaking would have made Esther either a more attractive or a less attractive candidate. Since both outcomes were possible, keeping quiet was a way to avoid either supposition. Ibn Ezra comments, at unusual length, about the information she was likely withholding: her nation, Israel, her kindred, her tribe or family, which would have associated her with Mordecai. Perhaps had she revealed herself and her association with Mordecai, a known exile, Ahasuerus would not have been interested in her as an orphan of exile. Gersonides takes a similar view: Mordecai believed that Esther would help the Jews achieve salvation but might imperil her chances of winning if the king knew she was from a lowly people in exile. Mordecai's insistence on Esther's silence can be read either as his trying to minimize her chances of winning or as his trying to optimize them. Ibn Ezra adds that he did not believe the king was interested in her lineage. He was solely interested in her physical beauty. Consequently, he was awed by Esther's charm and anxious lest she be taken into the arms of another, so he took her as a wife. As a woman, Ibn Ezra notes, she could hide her Jewish identity easily.

The rabbis in one talmudic reading tied Esther's silence to Rachel's silence:

> "He withdraws not His eyes from the righteous; but with kings upon the throne He establishes them forever, and they are

6. Ibid.

> exalted" (Job 36:7). This teaches that in reward for the silence shown by Rachel she merited that Saul, who was also silent, should descend from her, and in reward for the silence shown by Saul, he merited that Esther should descend from him.[7]

The verse from Job creates a hereditary line of leadership qualities; chief among them is silence. Rachel did not protest her father's cruel switching of brides. This was not regarded as a lack of courage but as a judicious and thoughtful approach to assessing when to speak out and when to observe and act. The silence here that gets passed down to Saul and then to Esther is a manifestation of good judgment, of patience, of bravery, and of an uncanny ability to know when words work and when they do not.

Silence and Beauty

This discussion also raises the ancillary but interesting relationship between silence and beauty. Beauty can almost become marred by words, distracting form through content. Perhaps by keeping her nationality private, Esther was further eroticizing her encounter with the king. Not knowing who she was or where she was from increased her mystique and heightened the distance that sexuality tries to overcome, the desire to know in confrontation with the impossibility of knowing. Esther was, in this way, cryptic. She did not approach Ahasuerus as a representative of a nation or people, much the way that other candidates might have. She transcended those markers. Without knowing her background, the king could make no assumptions; neither could he engage in stereotypes. Additionally, as an orphan, Esther lacked some of the basic anchoring mechanisms that a family identity offers. She could take risks and present herself without the kind of ties that may have made her more familiar and less exotic.

In silencing Esther, Mordecai may have enhanced both her independence and her selection. Revealing her Judaism would immediately align her with Mordecai, not necessarily as a relative but as a coreligionist. Mordecai's Jewishness was to become a source of consternation and potential subversion; it was the only possible explanation given for his

7. Ibid. 13b.

disobedience to Haman. Mordecai needed Esther's compliance so that he could take a principled stand without in any way compromising Esther's safety or effectiveness in bringing about redemption. Mordecai had an exquisite understanding of politics and knew that shifting a deeply entrenched culture required a multipronged approach. He would be the front man for his faith, Esther would handle the back-channeling, and the two would work as a team, atomizing the virtues of speech and silence by dividing them between two different individuals. These virtues were necessary complements to each other when living in a time of risk.

Putting Words to Esther's Silence

Where the Apocrypha's Book of Esther has Esther praying, the version in the Hebrew Bible contains no act of overt prayer. In this book, in this royal court, it is not pleading with God that would achieve the necessary political ends but rather using every political means within one's human arsenal: speech balanced by silence, loyalty to the sovereign balanced by allegiance to one's religion, conviction balanced by accommodation. It is almost predictable that many Christian scholars criticized Esther as a book spiritually deficient. They regarded politics as antithetical to the life of the faithful. Their perception is that the behaviors required to be successful within the complex web of government reduce the intensity of spiritual commitment. But in exile, political acumen is inextricably woven into the lifeblood of the faithful. Without the autonomy to practice one's faith freely, religion atrophies. It becomes less full-throated, influential, and potent as an animating force for both beliefs and behaviors.

Sold into Slavery?

Esther, when she finally told all, said something very odd to the king, that she would have said nothing had her people only been sold into slavery, despite the fact that we know from Egypt that the experience of slavery was exceptionally damaging to the Israelites. Esther's comment seems an exaggeration. Rashi enlightens us with his understanding of "it is not worthy of the king's trouble" (Est. 7:4). Esther conjectured that Haman was unconcerned with the financial loss to the king incurred by ridding the empire of the Jews. Had Haman cared about the king, he would have sold the people as slaves to drive revenue to the king's coffers. This financial reasoning was not explicitly mentioned in Exodus when Pharaoh enslaved the Jews. Slavery was justified as a security measure to prevent a powerful fifth column in Egypt. Ibn Ezra on Esther 7:4 comments that enslavement would not have been worth mentioning, because as slaves, despite their low class in society, the Jews would not have been at risk of death, nor would the king risk loss. This language, of course, parallels Haman's earlier claim that it was not worth it for the king to keep the Jews (Est. 3:8). Esther fought back when given a voice. What she told Ahasuerus with that voice was clear and unequivocal: it is not worth it for the king to tolerate an enemy that would destabilize Ahasuerus' empire.

Silence as a Literary Theme

The fact that Esther was asked to conceal a critical aspect of her background may give us pause as readers, indicating that we are party to a secret, possibly even to many secrets, in the Book of Esther. When readers pause to consider the deliberate masking of identity, we become willing partners in a ruse, suddenly more invested than innocent bystanders. We are, with our complicity, asked to contemplate the nature of secrets, the difference between secrets and lies, and what it is that spouses and families withhold from each other and why.[8]

Grossman suggests that the Book of Esther engages the reader precisely through its secrets:

> When a narrative conceals messages, it allows the reader to become a partner in the process of decoding the narrative and exposing its meaning. The reader's sense of having discovered the narrative's secrets considerably enhances his identification with the narrative. Its message impresses itself on him or her more firmly than it would if the educational message were spelled out explicitly, since overt moralizing often causes the reader to

8. See Moshe Halbertal, "The Hidden and the Sublime," in *Concealment and Revelation: Esotericism in Jewish Thought and Its Philosophical Implications* (Princeton: Princeton University Press, 2007), 13–17.

> become defensive. The inclusion of the reader in the process of decoding the narrative makes him or her an "active reader" or even a reader who "creates the text."[9]

Grossman contends that "even serious readers have fallen into the trap that the author laid for them, failing to notice what was happening beneath the surface of the story."[10]

In watching Esther conceal an elemental aspect of her identity, we begin to contemplate how and under what circumstances we readers might do the same. Esther's dichotomy between internally knowing herself and being publicly known becomes a metaphor for life in exile, a place where one cannot fully be oneself without consequence. And while an optimistic reading of the book might suggest that Esther's revelation prompted a redemptive ending and catapulted Mordecai to a place of greater influence, this was only after the full price in human life had been tallied. The price of revelation was either one people or another. Esther, in the act of hiding, must have become an odd observer of her own situation, measuring what her faith and ethnicity meant to her and what she was willing to sacrifice in both the hiding and in the telling, as George Orwell wrote, "If you want to keep a secret, you must also hide it from yourself."[11] When Mordecai told Esther to keep silent, he muted her identity in an act that ultimately assisted her in articulating a newfound sense of self, one full of conviction and authenticity.

Esther's concealment also becomes a metaphor for God's concealment in exile, an observation highlighted in a talmudic passage:

> Where else in the Torah is Haman found? From "this – *hamin* - tree" (Gen. 3:11). Where else in the Torah is Esther found? "And I will surely hide – *astir*" (Deut. 32:20). Where else in the Torah is Mordecai found? It is written, "Solidified myrrh – *mar dror*" (Ex. 30:23).[12]

---

9. Grossman, *The Outer Narrative*, 1–2.
10. Ibid., 11.
11. George Orwell, *1984* (New York: Signet Classic, 1981), 281.
12. Ḥullin 139b.

We picture the Sages around a table, seeking playful prooftexts or prefigurations in the Pentateuch for later characters based on the vocalization of the names. As mentioned in a previous chapter, Haman, in this scheme, is associated with a text about a snake and its evil machinations from the early days of Genesis. Mordecai is a fragrant spice prepared for an altar in the Tabernacle in its most concentrated form. Esther, on the other hand, is more enigmatic. Her name connects her to the very act of concealment suggested in Deuteronomy, in a verse that deserves full attention and context. God were angry at the Israelites for "waxing fat" and forgetting about God when they lived in a state of abundance:

> You neglected the Rock that begot you. Forgot the God who brought you forth. The Lord saw and was vexed and spurned His sons and His daughters. He said, "I will hide My countenance from them, and see how they fare in the end. For they are a treacherous breed, children with no loyalty in them. They incensed Me with no-gods, vexed Me with their futilities; I'll incense them with a nation of fools." (Deut. 32:18–21)

The literary resonances are redolent here, both linguistically and thematically. Ibn Ezra on Deuteronomy 32:20 interprets this frightening world of an absent God not as an inevitable result of sin but as part of God's intentional concealment to see what will happen when the good in human lives shrivels: "I will hide My face until I see what they do when their troubles overtake them." God's anger and subsequent withdrawal are causally related. After sensing that the Israelites absconded spiritually, God too withdrew and then tested the relationship. The Book of Esther is almost the case study for these verses in Deuteronomy. How would Israel fare if God were no longer overtly present as they confronted the difficulties of living among those with no gods or a nation of fools? It is hard not to see fools at virtually every turn in the Book of Esther.

The hiding of the face is not the only evident similarity between Esther and these verses in Deuteronomy. Rashi on 32:20 notes that the term *omen* in "children with no loyalty," *lo omen bam*, has the same meaning as the word has in Esther 2:7 describing Mordecai as Esther's caretaker, "one who nurtures." But in Deuteronomy, the Israelites act as if they have no God, no caretaker: "My training is not evident in them, for I showed them the good way and they deviated from it."

Hiddenness becomes a deliberate act of concealment in order to reveal the real relationship between God and the Israelites when they are not dependent upon God for every need. Mordecai, by asking Esther to conceal her identity, for whatever pragmatic reasons, was also asking her to embody, as a leader, the condition of her people in exile. It is hard to stay silent, to mask one's identity for long; to carry the spiritual weight of a nation is exhausting and discourages wholeness. But sometimes it is only through the act of concealment that a confrontation with the inner self is possible. Who am I hiding when I hide? By the time Esther revealed herself and her nation in chapter 7, she had found her voice… and her calling.

Death by False Accusation

> The king, in his fury, left the wine feast for the palace garden, while Haman remained to plead with Queen Esther for his life; for he saw that the king had resolved to destroy him. When the king returned from the palace garden to the banquet room, Haman was lying prostrate on the couch on which Esther reclined. "Does he mean," cried the king, "to ravish the queen in my own palace?" No sooner did these words leave the king's lips than Haman's face was covered. Then Harbonah, one of the eunuchs in attendance on the king, said, "What is more, a gallows is standing at Haman's house, fifty cubits high, which Haman made for Mordecai – the man whose words saved the king." "Hang him on it!" the king ordered. So they hanged Haman on the gallows which he had put up for Mordecai, and the king's fury abated. (Est. 7:7–10)

The emotional tensions in chapter 7 are mesmerizing and complex. The queen was scared and indignant. Haman was humiliated. Ahasuerus was furious. Rashi on 7:7 adds to the meld that the closing clause, "the king had resolved to destroy him," signaled that all of Ahasuerus' emotions had finally surfaced: "The evil, the hatred, and the vengeance were decided." The emotions culminated in a decision: the king was ready to destroy Haman. Only one verse later, Ahasuerus experienced another wave of destructive emotion when he saw Haman on Esther's couch. It was Harbonah who literally pointed the way to Ahasuerus' next decision as a way to resolve all of this pent-up emotion. Rashi, in explicating the unusual expression *khalta elav* (literally, "closed upon him"), suggests the finishing up of a matter. It is as if the flitter of bad feelings, of uncertainties and tensions, were finally coming together in an emotional panopticon. Ahasuerus finally realized with full clarity that Haman deserved punishment, though he had yet to think of one. Harbonah's interruption in the scene expedited the process by offering a practical resolution to the buildup of negative sentiments. To this the Malbim questions why Haman did not plead in the presence of both king and queen, since it was the king who needed to be assuaged. No doubt, Haman would have begged before the king had he stayed in the room, but Ahasuerus left. This forced Haman to degrade himself before Esther in yet another reversal. Once upon a time, Haman was outraged that Mordecai had not bowed, but in chapter 6 he had lowered himself before Mordecai the Jew and now, one chapter later, he prostrated himself before Mordecai's niece.

All of the characters in this surreal triangle were unsure of their respective futures, some with a fear that was immediate and others with fears prolonged. Would Esther die? Would Haman be killed? Would Ahasuerus be responsible for both deaths and then have to once again search for a replacement wife? The close proximity of a shared table amplified all of these questions to the point of explosiveness. As these stresses mounted, the king had to remove himself physically from the space.

The anger that carried the king out of the room ironically left a vacuum where his suspicions of the two he left behind could fully percolate. Upon what was his initial anger based? The king was guilty of permitting Haman to pursue his treacherous plan in the first place. With the flurry of speed, there was no time to process sufficiently what had occurred in the sleepless night before as Haman was whisked to this inexplicable second wine party. The mix of negative emotions the king felt toward Haman and the compassion he felt toward his new wife simultaneously, no doubt, confounded Ahasuerus, who may have realized he was at the center of this scheme. He promoted an undeserving courtier. He ignored a loyal courtier who saved his life. He accepted the money that made the death of a nation a petty transaction. He handed over his signet ring. The self-loathing for a powerful and insecure man was no doubt a cause for emotional combustion. He may have been angry at himself, angry at his minister who manipulated him, and angry at a Persian system of law that was overly rigid. He projected it all onto Haman.

The king may have left not because he could not stand or literally share space with Haman, but because he could not stand himself. Fury laced with shame, the kind that overcomes those who realize their culpability in terrible events, entraps the one who experiences it. The king's own failure to be vigilant and give a matter his fullest attention led to problems deep and irrevocable. Adding to this misery, the king realized for the first time that two individuals he trusted, with whom he shared very intimate moments, deeply hated each other, a hatred that Ahasuerus fomented through his own negligence. Haman was prepared to kill the object of Ahasuerus' latest affection because of petty insecurities. As the full depth of this realization overcame Ahasuerus, he had to vacate the space where he was physically because he had to vacate the space he occupied mentally. He needed a new framework for thinking about his situation, a different space in which to consider his options.

"When the king returned from the palace garden to the banquet room, Haman was lying prostrate on the couch on which Esther reclined" (Est. 7:8). Esther ate while reclining on a couch, as was the custom in the Persian Empire, and true to the kind of reclining legally obligated on the Passover Seder as a symbol of royalty and freedom.[1] Rashi on Esther 8:8 points out that the queen at this time was likely lying back on one of the opulent couches mentioned in the first chapter, the "couches of gold and silver" (Est. 1:6). This made her physical position vulnerable and submissive, a literal rendering of her existential state at this point in our narrative. Yet it is this very posture that became her enemy's undoing rather than her own: "'Does he mean,' cried the king, 'to ravish the queen in my own palace?' No sooner did these words leave the king's lips than Haman's face was covered." Esther looked like she was being taken advantage of by Haman. And she was. She was very nearly Haman's victim, but not for the reason Ahasuerus falsely assumed.

As readers, we may not be suspicious enough of Haman. Maybe he did have designs on the queen. It would not be unusual for a man who

1. See Pesaḥim 99b, 108a; *Shulḥan Arukh, Oraḥ Ḥayim* 472.

wanted to wear the king's clothes and ride the king's horse to want the queen as well. A parallel exists in Genesis. Reuben, who thought himself second in line to his father, Jacob, slept with Jacob's concubine: "While Israel stayed in that land, Reuben went and lay with Bilhah, his father's concubine, and Israel found out" (Gen. 35: 22). This act to demonstrate Reuben's position backfired. Jacob spoke directly to Reuben before he died with words initially sweet and then condemning: "Reuben, you are my firstborn. My might and the first fruit of my vigor, exceeding in rank and exceeding in honor. Unstable as water, you shall excel no longer. For when you mounted my bed, you brought disgrace: my couch he mounted!" (Gen. 49:3–4). Jacob recalls this subversive act of his eldest with incredulity. How dare he mount my bed!

When King David was away from Jerusalem, his son Absalom, with eyes on David's throne, had a tent pitched on the palace roof, "and he slept with his father's concubines in the sight of all Israel" (II Sam. 16:22). Absalom's friend Ahithophel believed this act would secure Absalom's prominence and encouraged him to do it to gain supporters (II Sam. 16:21). What could be more brazen than to engage in such an act, not with one woman but with many with literal high visibility? The rooftop had its own unfortunate resonances for David, as a place where he spotted the lovely Bathsheba bathing and committed his venal sin (II Sam. 11:1–4). It was hardly a place where David could assert his moral superiority over his son.

Adoniah, another of David's sons, tried to do the same. These were sexual acts not directed at the woman as much as at the authority figure at the center of the story. The women were cruelly used to make a point. The pretenders to the throne slept with these women because they could or thought they could. In the Book of Esther, Haman felt comfortable enough traipsing into the king's chambers unannounced; he was likely not afraid to be in close physical contact with the queen. We can only imagine Esther shuddering at his brutish approach, wondering if he was going to strangle her for being of the same faith and people as Mordecai. Alone in the banquet room, she may have seen herself in peril.

And yet, a sexual framing for the scene seems inappropriate, even tone-deaf to the moment. Ahasuerus terrified Haman, who was neither proud nor flaunting his power; this moment in time was not for sexual conquest but for survival. He crouched near the queen because, paradoxically, she was the only one who could save him.

But when the king re-entered the room, supposedly composed and with a strategy, he saw none of Haman's terror, only his presumption. Ahasuerus unexpectedly experienced a second wave of revulsion at his minster that confirmed his lingering suspicions. If indeed, Ahasuerus' anger was in part directed at him, Haman's appearance on his wife's couch gave him the prerogative of the powerful: the ability to project all of that anger onto Haman. Rashi, citing a passage of aggada on 7:8, adds to the humiliation, mentioning a midrash we encountered earlier. Every time Haman tried to stand up, an angel pushed him back on the couch, further infuriating the king. The midrash paints an almost comical, Kafkaesque image of one who could not resist his own failures and was prone to repeat them and repeat them despite their negative consequences. Haman, now finally exposed for the hateful, spiteful courtier he was, could no longer plead his innocence even though in this instance he was not guilty.

Harbonah's appearance here is also puzzling. At this crucial juncture in the story's plotline, a new character is introduced: "Then Harbonah, one of the eunuchs in attendance on the king, said, 'What is more, a gallows is standing at Haman's house, fifty cubits high, which Haman made for Mordecai – the man whose words saved the king'" (Est. 7:9). It is an odd time to toss someone new into this emotional mix unless the newness of the character is itself a significant detail. Haman's designs were not particularly hidden; only the king was in relative darkness. Harbonah, a eunuch, had information the king lacked, and made not so much a recommendation as an observation with his gesture, helping the king out of his confusion. We can imagine Harbonah theatrically pointing a finger to the gallows, only visible because of Haman's absurd need to advertise his power and hatred far and wide. Harbonah also succeeded in moving the king's gaze from the low couch before him to the gallows high in the distance, refocusing Ahasuerus, transitioning his anger into problem-solving.

One talmudic opinion has a more jaded view of Harbonah, reading him as a classic political opportunist:

> "And Harbonah, one of the chamberlains, said before the king, 'Behold also, the gallows fifty cubits high, which Haman has made for Mordecai, who spoke good for the king, stands in the house of Haman'" (Est. 7:9). R. Elazar said: Harbonah was also wicked and involved in that plot, as he too wanted Mordecai executed. Once he saw that his plot had not succeeded, he immediately fled and joined Mordecai's side. And this is the meaning of that which is written: "It hurls itself at him and does not spare; he would fain flee out of its hand" (Job 27:22), indicating that when God sends calamity upon a wicked person, his friends immediately flee from him.[2]

When Haman was in favor, Harbonah supported him. When Harbonah saw that the royal tide had turned against Haman, he was quick to point to the gallows, signaling Haman's ignoble end. Citing a verse from Job is appropriate to the circumstances, given the way Job's friends were quick to find fault with him to explain Job's suffering. Harbonah may have actually helped put up the gallows, which would explain his role in the chapter. To gain the king's favor, he offered unsolicited advice with a mere gesture.

Thinking Fast and Slow

In an earlier chapter, we discussed the erratic pacing in the book. While the pageant and the posting of official notices were long and protracted affairs, the later actions happen fast and furiously. One party, one parade, another party, and then a hanging took place in a matter of days. The collapse of time prevented the king from changing his mind, a tactic the eunuchs were well aware of in managing Ahasuerus. True to form, the solution once again involved eliminating the problem quite literally.

Chapter 7 is the second-shortest chapter in the scroll and serves as an important follow-up to chapter 6: it provides the resolution to many of the tensions generated the night the king could not sleep. The chapter ends with the deed done: "So they hanged Haman on the gallows which he had put up for Mordecai, and the king's fury abated" (Est. 7:10).

---

2. Megilla 16a.

Since Haman's death did not bring about a revocation or modification of his decree, hanging him may have been a clever and opportune way for Ahasuerus to distance himself from Haman; the king's total disgust may have implied that the king never gave approval to Haman's plan. Hanging Haman, however, accomplished only one desired outcome: "the king's fury abated." Just like the floodwaters that subsided in Genesis 8:1, the king's anger dissipated with the death of his suspicious courtier. Ahasuerus was calm.

It is not lost to readers of the Book of Esther that Haman died for reasons unconnected to his actual crime. The king never heard Haman's explanation, nor did it interest him. Due process was not popular in ancient Persia. The king's decree was forceful and determined: "Hang him on it!" (Est. 7:9). This was how one treated a scoundrel, not a trustworthy advisor. Esther had not asked that Haman's life be taken. She pointed to Haman as an enemy but made no suggestion as to his treatment.

If we regard Haman's death as an ironic injustice, we must consider what the book is trying to communicate in not finding Haman guilty of his *actual* crime against humanity. This could be yet another way the scroll presents the shadowy undercurrents that sustain life without political autonomy and integrity in the diaspora. If true criminals with immense control cannot get a fair hearing, there is little chance that those with less influence and status will receive equitable treatment. Dispensing undeserved punishment haphazardly is yet another demonstration of Ahasuerus' intemperate and impulsive nature that highlights the randomness of life in exile for the Jews.

Chapter Eight

The Signet Ring Changes Hands

The Spoils of War

Joy, Finally

The Signet Ring Changes Hands

That very day King Ahasuerus gave the property of Haman, the enemy of the Jews, to Queen Esther. Mordecai presented himself to the king, for Esther had revealed how he was related to her. The king slipped off his ring, which he had taken back from Haman, and gave it to Mordecai; and Esther put Mordecai in charge of Haman's property. Esther spoke to the king again, falling at his feet and weeping, and beseeching him to avert the evil plotted by Haman the Agagite against the Jews. The king extended the golden scepter to Esther, and Esther arose and stood before the king. "If it please Your Majesty," she said, "and if I have won your favor and the proposal seems right to Your Majesty, and if I am pleasing to you – let dispatches be written countermanding those which were written by Haman son of Hammedatha the Agagite, embodying his plot to annihilate the Jews throughout the king's provinces. For how can I bear to see the disaster which will befall my people! And how can I bear to see the destruction of my kindred!" Then King Ahasuerus said to Queen Esther and Mordecai the Jew, "Look, I have given Haman's property to Esther, and he has been hanged on the gallows for scheming against the Jews." (Est. 8:1–7)

This chapter begins with Ahasuerus requisitioning Haman's property and transferring Haman's powers to Esther and Mordecai. With his death and the death of his sons, Haman's worldly goods could be given to his enemy as an act of goodwill. Why, though, would Esther need Haman's property? Zeresh was still alive and likely living in the house. If she was not, this fact was not disclosed in the scroll. Ahasuerus believed that by removing any trace of Haman's family from the royal compound and giving away Haman's property, he was solving Esther's problem. The king's poor decision-making skills were complemented by his inadequate problem solving. Giving Esther an unwanted gift was a smoke screen for withholding the gift that was most necessary. The token exchange of doorplates, however, would have served as a visible indicator to other courtiers and outsiders that a transfer of power had taken place within the king's cabinet. This gesture sent a strong and unequivocal message to courtiers who had up to this point taken orders from Haman and were intimately familiar with Haman's hatred of Mordecai. They may even have fomented that hatred, contributed to it. Even if they only tolerated Haman's wicked designs on Mordecai, those under Haman's leadership must have been shocked at this public turn of events and frightened for their own positions and lives now that Haman's treachery had been discovered and punished for all in Shushan to see.

The Persistent Threat

Ahasuerus' response to Esther's supplications was atonal. He was neither merciful nor distressed but simply reiterated his earlier offer with the verbal equivalent of a shrug. The king stressed his gift of property and Haman's death, but neither factor eliminated the threat to Jews throughout the empire. Haman's actual death had nothing to do with protecting the Jews, as established in the previous chapter. Rashi on 8:7 notes this problem with the inclusion of the word *hinei* – "Look, I have given" – an indication to regard what he had done for Esther instead of what he had not done: "From now on everyone will see that I favor you and whatever you say, everyone will believe that it comes from me; therefore, you do not have to rescind them but write other letters 'as you see fit.' (Est. 8:8)." Rashi merges verses 8:7 and 8:8 as Ahasuerus' solution. The king would not come up with a solution – governance was beyond his skill set – but instead would empower Esther and Mordecai to create their own solution. Because the two had the king's favor, all would assume their plan met with the king's approval. Their plan would be in their own language and appeal to their people in a cultural idiom that could bring solace and hope. But this generous reading cannot mask Ahasuerus' incompetence or need for validation and praise for half measures. Esther had no need for tokens of affection; she needed a change of outcome, but neither she nor Mordecai could stop what Haman set in motion and neither had the authority to put a better solution in place.

Haman was promoted before Esther, but Esther would outlive him and outstrip his authority. She would not, however, be able to outwit the clever way in which Haman had put his ordinance into law, rendering the transactional and symbolic transition of title and status essentially meaningless. The Malbim on 8:1 bluntly suggests that it was no great accomplishment for Mordecai to be introduced to Ahasuerus; any constituent in the king's empire could have requested an audience with the king (a presumption worthy of debate). He concludes that Mordecai was granted an all-access pass to the king in chapter 8. He could appear before the king "at any time and did not need to wait until he [Ahasuerus] called him [Mordecai] and extended his scepter to him." Nevertheless, revenge, houses, rings, and access still did not amount to the only matter of urgency to preoccupy Esther. Ahasuerus promised half the kingdom, but he could not promise the safety of the Jews within that kingdom. Rather than offer her gratitude, Esther pleaded with Ahasuerus yet again. Prestige and material gain would do little; a dead courtier has no need for signet rings and houses.

The king's signet ring is mentioned on six occasions in the Book of Esther.[1] Like the crown, it conferred dignity and royal validation to the person who wore it. Unlike the crown, it conferred actual decision-making power. That the king took it from Haman's slippery fingers and gave it to Mordecai immediately upon learning of his relationship to Esther, signaled to her and to the court that something extraordinary was taking place. That Esther was not given the ring first suggests that the king did not see her as having judicial authority. Ahasuerus regarded her

1. Est. 3:10, 12, twice each in 8:2, 10.

primarily as consort, not as advisor. This was quite unlike the relationship Haman had with Zeresh. It is also a telling follow-up to chapter 6. Mordecai may have been given royal clothing and a horse for a day – the mere appearance of leadership – but the real object of authority was not given to him until chapter 8.

The Signet Ring

The gift of the signet ring, as noted in a midrash and by many contemporary scholars, was reminiscent of Pharaoh's gift to Joseph in Genesis 41:42: "And removing his signet ring from his hand, Pharaoh put it on Joseph's hand." Rashi on 41:42 observes: "When the king gives his ring it is a sign that the person to whom he hands it is to be second to him in rank." Nahmanides cites Rashi's view and agrees. Rabbenu Bahya affirms this reading of 41:42: "He handed Joseph his signet ring with which he appointed ministers or relieved them of their authority." *Ḥizkuni,* however, regards the ring not as a gift but as a test of loyalty: "This is why he [Pharaoh] entrusted him [Joseph] with executive power: to observe whether he would work for the benefit of the state. If Joseph accepted this task, he would be convinced that he was loyal and upright, as he would know that failure would bring disastrous consequences for himself."

We have several other examples of seals in the Hebrew Bible connected with royalty. Jezebel took King Ahab's seal when incriminating Naboth falsely: "So she wrote letters in Ahab's name and sealed them with his seal and sent the letters to the elders and the nobles who lived in the same town with Naboth" (I Kings 21:8). The *Metzudat David* on 21:8 regards this seal or *ḥotem* as Ahab's signet ring, *tabato*. Gersonides understands that this act was Esther's way of manipulating the system, using the king's signature, in effect, to communicate authority with the elders and nobles while bypassing the people, who surely would have protested this injustice.

A signet ring was also regarded in the biblical world as a hallmark of one's personal identity. When Tamar asked for and Judah gave her his seal, cord, and staff, he essentially gave her the means to expose him later when she revealed that she played the harlot to force him into having relations with her. The seal was an unmistakable sign of ownership: "And he said, 'What pledge shall I give you?' She replied, 'Your seal and cord, and the staff which you carry.' So he gave them to her and slept with her, and she conceived by him" (Gen. 38:18). *Ḥizkuni* on this verse contends that Tamar knew Judah could not live without these very personal items for long because the signet ring allowed him to conduct business. In taking these highly personal and functional items, Tamar ensured that her prolonged desperate situation would have to come to a quick and shocking denouement.

There are other examples of signet rings in the Hebrew Bible, most notably in one of the Later Prophets, Haggai, where a signet ring becomes a symbol for an actual person. God will overthrow foreign rule and treat Zerubbabel, the descendant of David and governor of Judah, as His very own signet ring: "On that day – declares the Lord of Hosts – I will take you, O My servant Zerubbabel son of Shealtiel – declares the Lord – and make you as a signet; for I have chosen you – declares the Lord of Hosts" (Hag. 2:23). Not once but twice did the prophet declare Zerubbabel as God's signet ring, a sign of trust and affection. This is a turnaround from an earlier time in the same family. King Jehoiachin, Zerrubabel's grandfather, was dethroned and exiled to Babylon; Jeremiah depicted God's anger at this king with an image of Jehoiachin as a signet ring violently removed from God's finger for betrayal:

> As I live – declares the Lord – if you, O King Coniah [Jehoiachin], son of Jehoiakim, of Judah, were a signet on My right hand, I would tear you off even from there. I will deliver you into the hands of those who seek your life, into the hands of those you dread, into the hands of King Nebuchadrezzar of Babylon and into the hands of the Chaldeans. I will hurl you and the mother who bore you into another land, where you were not born; there you shall both die. They shall not return to the land that they yearn to come back to. (Jer. 22:24–27)

Rashi on 22:24 paints an image of a seal embossed on God's right arm, but unlike the passionate, intense, and romantic symbol of the engraved seal in Song of Songs – "Let me be a seal upon your heart, like the seal upon your hand. For love is fierce as death" (Song. 8:6) – this seal will be removed and discarded. Jehoiachin deserved banishment to a place of isolation. By contrast, in Haggai, God called Zerubbabel the "signet ring," but one that would not be removed, one that may even herald the coming of the Messiah. The days ahead would be blessed (Hag. 2:19), and Zerubbabel would enjoy military success, ensured God: "I am going to shake the heavens and the earth, and I will overturn the thrones of kingdoms and destroy the might of the kingdoms of the nations. I will overturn chariots and their drivers" (Hag. 2:22).

On Song of Songs 8:6, Rashi describes the seal as a marking on the heart made for the sake of love that is in some way visible and serves as a constant reminder of a relationship. The *Metzudat David* on 8:6 sees this transference from hand to heart as an indicator of its inherently non-transferable nature. A seal or signet on a hand can be removed. A seal on a heart cannot. This theme is further taken up in the Talmud:

> And the congregation of Israel further entreated God unreasonably in another context, saying before Him: Master of the Universe: "Set me as a seal upon Your heart, as a seal upon Your arm" (Song. 8:6). The Holy One, blessed be He, said to her [Israel]: My daughter, you ask that I be manifest to you in a matter that is sometimes visible and sometimes not visible, as the heart and arm are not covered. However, I will act so that I manifest Myself for you like a matter that is always visible, as it is stated: "Behold, I have engraved you on the palms of My hands; your walls are continually before Me" (Is. 49:16).[2]

Israel and God are the lovers in the metaphor of the Song of Songs, and Israel is an insecure partner in need of much assurance that God's love is true and constant. The seal is the insurance policy Israel required to feel whole and secure.

In Haggai's prophecy, God regarded Zerubbabel as this sort of seal and had to assure the governor that what happened to his grandfather was not to be his fate. As God's signet ring, Zerubbabel was chosen for a nobility of purpose and as a continuation of the Davidic line. God was reinstating the Davidic line, skipping over the recidivism between kings.

---

2. Taanit 4a.

Haman's House

Returning to the Book of Esther, the king's ring was his sign of collaboration and approval and his to distribute freely. There is some conflation and confusion in the first two verses of chapter 8, however, between the king's ring and Haman's property, which was presumably Haman's. The words in 8:1 read *beit Haman*, "the house of Haman," which likely refers to a home or suite attached to the palace that was part of the royal assemblage of property. The ring may have been a treasured and precious item with great legal import or a larger embossed-like stamp not worn on the hand but used with the hand. Changing the nameplate on Haman's door to signify Esther's ownership, the king was true to his word. While not half the kingdom in scope, Haman's house represented more than half the kingdom in principle. Ibn Yahya understands this exchange as a way to reimburse Esther for her suffering. She could do, "whatever she may wish," with the property, much as Haman had exercised his will and whim on her people. Ahasuerus had his revenge when Haman was hanged. For Esther, the king chose this symbolic act of material empowerment. It is an odd gift, made odder by the fact that the text goes out of its way to state later that the Jews took no bounty when defending themselves. Once again, what she really wanted, Esther could not have. Ancient Persia was a place of temporary material achievement at the cost of real freedom.

Mordecai's Status

Ibn Yahya understands the last part of the verse as yet another reversal of fortune: "Mordecai presented himself to the king, for Esther had revealed how he was related to her" (Est. 8:1). Where, in 7:8, Haman's head was covered and bowed low before the king as he was brought to his end, Mordecai in 8:1 was brought "before the king," *lifnei hamelekh,* with his head held high, presented by Esther as her relative.

Most classical exegetes on 8:1 focus not on the transference of property but on the revelation that Esther and Mordecai were related. It was indeed a dramatic moment in this series of revelations that the king digested as he pieced together all of the difficult and seemingly inexplicable events of the days before. First Esther revealed her people, and only later, once Haman was eliminated from the scene, did Esther choose to reveal to the king her relationship to Mordecai. It would have made more sense for Esther to introduce Mordecai first as the man who had saved the king. Having just rewarded Mordecai for his loyalty and courage, Ahasuerus with this critical piece of information would have felt even closer to his new bride and more trusting of her uncle. This absence highlights the arbitrary nature of life in the palace, and the king's irrationality. His decisions were based more on personal feeling than on logic and caution. Perhaps Esther felt that introducing him as her uncle rather than as Ahasuerus' savior would elicit more positive favor than reminding the king of an earlier threat that no one else in the palace discovered.

Mordecai rose to power in the king's home without an official change in status. He received no official title after saving the king, no title in chapter 6, and no title in chapter 8. Only in chapter 10 was he called second to the king, and this may not have been an official designation but a description of the way he was regarded in the court. Ashkenazi puzzles over the lack of title and explains it by virtue of Mordecai's modesty. In Esther 8:10 Ashkenazi compares Haman and Mordecai; Haman had someone else handle his correspondence "because he loved to drink with the king," but Mordecai wrote his own letters, because "he loved to perform commandments all by himself." On Esther 8:16 Ashkenazi returns to this question and suggests that Mordecai's status did not change because the status of the Jews had not changed:

> Celebrations were held all over, except in Shushan where Mordecai did not celebrate until the entire miracle took place. The righteous are always wary lest a sin take place. Also, they are not joyous over the fall of the enemy.... Or, possibly, since Israel is like one body, Mordecai could not celebrate until he was assured that the whole nation was alive.... Therefore, the Jews of Shushan had light [relief], but they did not have a banquet.

Mordecai's fate was tied inextricably to the fate of his people. At this stage of the story, there was partial happiness, but complete happiness was still out of range. There was no good or evident option for their future. The author might also be communicating that the only title truly descriptive of Mordecai's status is the way he was first introduced: an exile.

And Esther Wept...

With the transfer of ring and property, Esther wept, tears the text did not communicate in other more dramatic and emotional scenes: "The king slipped off his ring, which he had taken back from Haman, and gave it to Mordecai; and Esther put Mordecai in charge of Haman's property. Esther spoke to the king again, *falling at his feet and weeping,* and beseeching him to avert the evil plotted by Haman the Agagite against the Jews" (8:2–3). Rather than regarding Haman's death and the ring as signs of power, Esther saw them as symbols of powerlessness. The weeping we might have expected from Esther at the pageant or when she approached Ahasuerus unsummoned did not occur. She was even able to divulge her background with confidence, but when she finally saw that it led to only the meager gift of the ring, she could contain herself no longer. The most she was able to secure for her people was the ring Haman used to put the final stamp on his decree; the ring offered no revocation. Power in the future meant little without the power to disable the decree of the past. Clines takes us into this moment with the raw feelings it elicited:

> Esther and Mordecai have only to dictate a letter, it seems, and the deed of Haman will be undone, his letters will be revoked, just as Esther had requested (8:5), and the new decree of revocation will carry permanent and irreversible royal authority. But, on the other hand, those very last words of the sentence, "cannot be revoked" (*'en lehashiv*), as they sink into the consciousness, renew the tension all over again. For, with the best will in the world, the king has brought into the open his powerlessness to do what Esther has asked..."[3]

Esther needed immediate action to counteract Haman's decree. When she pled, weeping, before the king, she added a poignant and personal note, a reformulation of the impassioned concern for her people expressed at the second wine party: "For how can I bear to see the disaster which will befall my people! And how can I bear to see the destruction of my kindred!" (8:6). With the word "destruction," *ovdan,* Esther

3. Clines, *Esther,* 18.

hearkened back to her own willingness to submit to harsh consequences when approaching the king: *kaasher avadeti, avadeti,* "if I am destroyed, I am destroyed" (4:16). She herself was willing to die but was not prepared to see her people sacrificed because of something as trivial and personal as Haman's disgust. This she could not bear. Ahasuerus had little acquaintance with her people; thus Esther built her case on the king's emotions. He would not want his young and beautiful queen saddled with worry and despair. Esther's strategy was similar to others in the scroll who sought to manipulate the king by making the political personal. The difference was her virtue and lack of self-interest.

Something both public and subtle did, however, change in the opening to chapter 8. Mordecai may not have had a change of title but Haman did; he was suddenly referred to with a new moniker: "the enemy of the Jews." With this vilification, his true nature was broadcast. Haman would be remembered as a man scorned and demonized with each utterance; listeners shudder at the mere mention of his name. By calling him an enemy of the Jews, the text assumes this was an essential description of his person for posterity, a legacy of evil. He had lost all perspective in the presence of Mordecai; thus he would become known only by the hostility that he promulgated. The man who hated would himself be hated in perpetuity.

In being called the enemy of the Jews, Haman was joined in a continuity of loathing that originated with the tribe of Amalek, traveled through Agag, and then joined with the Haman narratives as an almost seamless expression of a truth and a reality: the Jews will always have enemies. It is best to know them and name them. Only then can their power be diminished. Craig discusses the custom of making effigies of Haman to be burned or hanged; he claims this practice may go back as far as the fifth century but gained in popularity in the ninth to tenth centuries: "A pole is erected in a courtyard, and the Haman effigy is then doused with a flammable liquid and ignited with the celebrants clapping, singing and rejoicing."[4] Craig also claims that this is still practiced today in Iraq and Kurdistan and even in Tel Aviv.[5] This disgust is

4. Craig, *Reading Esther*, 159.
5. Ibid.

signified today by the ritual to blot out Haman's name with noise and shouts when the scroll is read on Purim.[6]

Modern customs notwithstanding, Haman's name was textually demonized; his ring was given to another, and his property appropriated. But the policy he instituted was not abrogated.

6. I myself saw the practice observed in Israel in a synagogue service I attended on the Purim immediately after the First Gulf War officially ended in February 1991. When Haman's name was mentioned the first time, a large effigy of Saddam Hussein as Haman was thrown over the women's gallery as a mock hanging to the cheers of the congregation and the disruption of the *Megilla* reading. Having never before witnessed this custom, I must confess a degree of shock and discomfort not shared by those around me.

The Spoils of War

> The king permitted the Jews of every city to assemble and fight for their lives; if any people or province attacks them, they may destroy, massacre, and exterminate its armed force together with women and children, and plunder their possessions – on a single day in all the provinces of King Ahasuerus, namely, on the thirteenth day of the twelfth month, that is, the month of Adar. The text of the document was to be issued as a law in every single province: it was to be publicly displayed to all the peoples, so that the Jews should be ready for that day to avenge themselves on their enemies. (Est. 8:11–13)

While readers of Esther revel in its exaggerations and comedic, slapstick style – the buffoonery of its gentile characters, the absolutism of their evil, the ridiculous materialism and inefficiencies of palace life – there is a passage where the book's relationship to gentiles becomes stark and chilling. Any gentile considered an enemy of the Jews was fair game for revenge. How this was determined is never discussed, but later, the book notes that many gentiles were awed by the Jews and possibly converted to become members of a nation awash in God's love and protection. The verses in chapter 8 above, however, stop us in our tracks. A day of revenge, not self-defense, is the way the text presents what happened. A day such as that can only leave a deep mark of despair on the survivors as well as the perpetrators. Blood on the hands stains forever.

Claude Montefiore, a nineteenth-century scholar, was clearly unsettled by this outcome, despite the fact that it was a royally sanctioned means of self-protection: "We can hardly dignify or extenuate the operations of the Jews by saying that they were done in self-defence.... Moreover, the slaying apparently included both women and children."[1]

Some read the midsection of Esther 8 with an I-told-you-so grin. Revenge belonged to the Jews, and it would brook no resistance. It is the stuff of hallucination, the dream of unbridled power, to have the capacity to do to others what they would have done to you had they been able. Others read in chapter 8 the sad, morally confounding details and bristle at the celebrations that followed.

Revenge should have destroyed any semblance of respect the Persians had for their Jewish neighbors. For Ashkenazi, another Purim miracle is that the non-Jewish nations did not seek counter-revenge even after 75,000 Persians were killed:

> For the nations considered them [the Jews] friends and did not seek revenge upon them. This is the principal miracle: After all of this passed, how could it be that despite the victory that you [the Jews] experienced, the other nations forgot their dead brethren?... Haman was the only one among the nations who felt anger at the Jews, since one cannot say that all nations have anger at the Jews.[2]

Ashkenazi on 9:22 explains that divine protection prevented revenge; it would have been natural for Jews to become more despised after killing

---

1. Claude Montefiore, *The Bible for Home Reading*, vol. 2 (New York: Macmillan Company, 1899), 403, as noted in Kenneth Craig; see *Reading Esther*, 133. Craig himself notes on pp. 129–30 that while Esther prepares us for the death of women and children in 8:11, the term *ish*, "man," is used in the actual description of casualties in 9:6 and 9:15. This is an interesting but problematic reading. The fact that men are indicated in the Hebrew does not mean that women and children were not put to death by the sword. The text is explicit, for example, in the same verse, 8:11, in informing us that although the Jews were allowed to take the spoils, they refrained from doing so, as stated in 9:10, 9:15, and 9:16. If they were granted permission to kill women and children and did not do so, one could argue that the text would have made this explicit in a similar fashion.
2. Ashkenazi, *Yosef Lekaḥ* 9:22.

Persians. This, for Ashkenazi, is yet another awe-inspiring feature of the book. Divine protection canceled any bad feelings or anger. Any ill will was placed on Haman, who started the whole debacle and who was the only one in the story who explicitly hated the Jews. This reading also seems out of the pages of a fairy tale but may be understandable given a significant detail in the chapter that could easily be overlooked.

What Happened to the Spoils?

The brutality of events is tempered somewhat by a detail the text repeats; Jews took no spoils of war, neither from those who rose against them nor from Haman's sons. Not taking the spoils would seem an obvious and wise strategy to obviate any accusations that the Jews were acting for monetary gain. Ibn Ezra agrees that it was a wise consideration on the part of Persia's Jews. There was no need to make their situation worse among their neighbors; Jewish restraint was a powerful reminder to the rest of Persia that they were not the ones who devised this devious plan, nor were they interested in profiting from it. Ibn Yahya adds that although the Jews were expressly permitted to take the spoils, in refraining, they were following the example of Abraham, who refused to take even a shoelace from his host nation even when encouraged to take spoils. That text in Genesis bears similarity to the Esther story.

Like Esther, Abraham was favored by a foreign leader: King Malchizedek. As a way of honoring the patriarch, Malchizedek blessed Abraham and granted him permission to augment his own wealth. In the preceding chapter, we are told expressly that Abraham (Abram in these texts) already amassed wealth (Gen. 13:2). Abraham wanted only the men who ventured out with him to be returned:

> He blessed him, saying, "Blessed be Abram of God Most High, Creator of heaven and earth. And blessed be God Most High, who has delivered your foes into your hand." And [Abram] gave him a tenth of everything. Then the king of Sodom said to Abram, "Give me the persons, and take the possessions for yourself." But Abram said to the king of Sodom, "I swear to the Lord, God Most High, Creator of heaven and earth: I will not take so much as a thread or a sandal strap of what is yours; you shall not say, 'It is I who

> made Abram rich.' For me, nothing but what my servants have used up; as for the share of the men who went with me – Aner, Eshkol, and Mamre – let them take their share." (Gen. 14:19–24)

Abraham was forthright in explaining his restraint: he wanted credit for his wealth to go to God, not to a pagan leader. The neighbors, subsequently, may have accused Abraham of taking Malchizedek's money undeservedly. Under these circumstances, Abraham protected his integrity by not taking or wanting more than he needed.

Mordecai's Jews were permitted to take spoils, but their own sense of justice prevented them from doing so. Ibn Yahya insists that the Jews refrained of their own accord to show the other nations and the officers that the "children of Abraham were both generous and, like Abraham, would not take a shoe strap that did not belong to them." This answer assumes that the Jews were motivated out of a self-conscious need to defend themselves to those in their host country. But the motivation was more intrinsic, speaking to the profound sense that justice had been impaired, both for them and even for those who would take their lives. Fox drives home this point in his understanding of Jewish restraint at this key juncture in the story: "The permission to take spoils allows the Jews to *refuse* to do so."[3]

Rashi on 8:11 adds his explanation: "So the king should not cast an envious eye on the money." According to Rashi, this collective restraint was not about maintaining a sterling reputation (this would be supremely difficult given the circumstances) in the empire but a strategic step to prevent the king from taking the loot in the end. The loss of lives would be handsomely compensated by financial gain for the king when Ahasuerus either demanded the items from the Jews or taxed them in kind. Esther and Mordecai did not want the king to increase his wealth at their expense.

Lack of Restraint

This reaction is a sharp contrast to I Samuel 15:17–29, where Saul not only did not kill Agag as he was commanded but allowed the people

3. Fox, *Character and Ideology*, 100.

to take the best of the spoils of war, although expressly forbidden. One even senses that because Esther is both connected and contrasted to Saul, this detail has a polemical overtone, a way of deterring royals who abused their position or did not heed the word of God. In the Book of Esther, it is not God who demanded that Esther and her people refrain from taking spoils. In this instance, Ahasuerus actually gave the Jews free rein with the possessions of their captives: "The king has permitted the Jews of every city to assemble and fight for their lives; if any people or province attacks them, they may destroy, massacre, and exterminate its armed force together with women and children, and plunder their possessions" (Est. 8:11). This permission to take adds a raw dimension of gloating, a material smirk, to the perverse permission to kill. Again, material gifts given to Esther, Mordecai, or the Jews are spurned or ignored as a way of suggesting that Jews were indeed different and that money would not solve their problems.

In the narrative of Saul sparing Agag and the livestock, God turned to Samuel with immense displeasure, telling the prophet that the protégé forced upon him did not carry out God's command. Samuel was angry and "cried out to God all night" (I Sam. 15:11). When confronted, Saul lied to Samuel, brazenly reporting, "I have fulfilled the Lord's command" (I Sam. 15:13), as if a prophet could have been fooled. This displayed a certain naive innocence at best and subversion at worst. In one of the great biblical moments of irony, Samuel responded, "Then what is this bleating of sheep in my ear and the lowing of oxen that I hear?" (I Sam. 15:14). The king could hardly have ignored the sound of sheep bleating but responded as if nothing were the matter: "They were brought from the Amalekites, for the troops spared the choicest of the sheep and oxen for sacrificing to the Lord, your God. And we proscribed the rest" (I Sam. 15:16). Samuel stopped him cold: "Why did you disobey the Lord and swoop down on the spoil in defiance of the Lord's will?" (I Sam. 15:19). Saul then launched into a defense of himself and his troops, suggesting in the way all human machinations and calculations are an outworn justification of bad behavior, that his motives were pure. He left the choicest animals to sacrifice to God in honor of the victory, but God did not want these sacrifices. God did not desire gifts. God desired obedience and compliance. This is in contrast to Esther, who was almost too compliant. In Esther, there was also disobedience against an authority, but only for the higher goal of protecting the relationship of the Jews in exile to their host country. There was nobility in being granted permission and then rejecting personal gain. The long-term gain of protection and respect outweighed the short-term gains of more money or more chattel. In the Book of Esther both taking lives and taking spoils are terrible consequences of life in the diaspora; the Jews expressed no desire to do either.

Spoils Outside of Persia

The attitude to spoils of war was different, however, in verses throughout Deuteronomy and Joshua, where the people were incentivized to take objects, cattle, and captives of war as a benefit of waging a successful conquest of the Land of Israel. There was a protocol when approaching a new area:

> When you approach a town to attack it, you shall offer it terms of peace. If it responds peaceably and lets you in, all the people present there shall serve you at forced labor. If it does not surrender to you, but would join battle with you, you shall lay siege to it; and when the Lord your God delivers it into your hand, you shall put all its males to the sword. You may, however, take as your booty the women, the children, the livestock, and everything in the town – all its spoil – and enjoy the use of the spoil of your enemy, which the Lord your God gives you. (Deut. 20:10–14)

If brokering peace did not work, permission was granted by God to fight and to take loot. In instances where God explicitly forbade the taking of spoils, doing so was a capital offense, as the story of Achan in Joshua demonstrated. Overcome by the seduction of taking what seemed there for the taking, Achan went against an express prohibition. The Jews lost the subsequent battle because God was angry: "Israel has sinned! They have broken the covenant by which I bound them. They have taken of the proscribed and put it in their vessels; they have stolen; they have broken faith!" (Josh. 7:11). When Achan was found out, he confessed. The specificity of his confession reveals the temptation to take what was not his: "I saw among the spoil a fine Shinar mantle, two hundred shekels of silver, and a wedge of gold weighing fifty shekels, and I coveted them and took them. They are buried in the ground in my tent, with the silver under it" (Josh. 7:21).

In contrasting spoils of war in the Book of Esther and I Samuel, Esther and Saul, both royalty, were in very different positions. Saul was king and had ultimate decision-making power. The loot of the Amalekites added incentive for his soldiers to wage war and win, and filling Saul's own treasury would strengthen his throne. In the Book of Esther, with death as a hovering reality and the Jews under the aegis of a king who could change his mind at any moment, the booty of war was less appealing and may have made their position in the empire more precarious in the future.

Not taking the spoils of war, while not a complete reversal of Haman's decree, allowed the Jews to demonstrate a modicum of humanity at a time of inhumane conditions. Paulo Freire in his masterwork, *Pedagogy of the Oppressed,* reminds us that there is no true freedom if fighting against oppression leads to a reversal of who becomes oppressed:

> Because it is a distortion of being more fully human, sooner or later being less human leads the oppressed to struggle against those who made them so. In order for this struggle to have meaning, the oppressed must not, in seeking to regain their humanity (which is a way to create it), become in turn oppressors of the oppressors, but rather restorers of the humanity of both.[4]

Behaving differently than those who oppressed them by not taking spoils, the Jews of the Persian Empire accorded a small measure of dignity to those against whom they were obligated to fight. This alone could not restore, in Freire's words, the humanity of both, but it could remind the Jews not to become like those who wanted to kill them.

4. Paulo Freire, *Pedagogy of the Oppressed* (New York: Continuum Publishing Company, 2000), 26.

Joy, Finally

> Mordecai left the king's presence in royal robes of blue and white, with a magnificent crown of gold and a mantle of fine linen and purple wool. And the city of Shushan rang with joyous cries. The Jews had light and gladness, and joy and honor. (Est. 8:15–16)

One short verse enables the reader to experience the relief felt by the Jews of Persia: "The Jews had light and gladness, and joy and honor" (Est. 8:16). One even wonders why the book did not stop here. Given the summative nature of this all-encompassing joy, it would have been a perfect ending. There were still, however, many loose ends that needed to be brought together as whole cloth to complete the story. Still, the emotional end seems to culminate here. Clines went as far as to suggest that this did, in fact, represent the end of the Book of Esther, with chapters 9 and 10 as later add-ons.[1] He also suggests that the four nouns that communicate joy and relief are a tonic to the four verbs used earlier to signal the destruction of the Jews: mourning, fasting, weeping, and wailing (Est. 4:3).[2]

Levenson describes the intensity of the happiness the Jews experienced as an expression of validation: "The joy with which the city of Susa cries out in Est. 8:15 is the joy of salvation. It parallels the response

---

1. Clines, *The Esther Scroll*, 26–30.
2. Ibid., 97.

of the worshipping community upon learning that their sacrifices have been accepted (cf. Lev. 9:24). The last clause of 8:15 reverses the last clause of 3:15 ('the city of Susa cried out in joy' versus 'the city of Susa was thrown into confusion')."[3] Fox suggests that light is another way to reference joy, as in Psalms 97:11 and 112:4 and Job 12:25.[4]

Ibn Ezra on 8:15 believes that this verse stresses that only Jewish happiness was manifest; this was not the reaction of non-Jews living in Shushan. Verse 8:16 qualifies the happiness quite specifically: "The Jews had light and gladness, and joy and honor" – but not the non-Jews. He explains the connection of happiness and light by describing the movement from darkness to a state of clarity: "Like a person who dwells in the dark and then goes out into the light of the world that is the very opposite [of what he experienced in the darkness] without any intermediary state." This is the blinking kind of light that one would take in when leaving a place of total gloom for bright sunlight. It appears blinding until the eyes adjust. The Jews of the ancient Persian Empire may have had to take time to adjust to this new reality, making sure that it was true, breathing into the reprieve and letting the healing slowly begin.

In the second version of his commentary, Ibn Ezra explains that the Jews had happiness within and without, feeling joy at the way they were viewed by their neighbors. Ibn Yahya on 8:16 examines each of the four expressions of happiness for their distinct nuances: *Ora*, "light," is relief. *Simḥa*, "happiness," is the removal of worry. *Sason*, "joy," is spiritual delight, and *yakar*, "honor," is material satisfaction. Readers sensitive to the linguistic parallels and repetitions of the text understand the potency of the word *yakar* here, which appears four other times in the scroll.[5] The most well-known of these verses is familiar since it forms a call-and-response aspect of Havdala, the parting ritual at the close of Shabbat: "The Jews had light and gladness, happiness and honor (*yakar*)." With the ritual parting of Shabbat, Jews open a new week, hoping that the darkness that has brought Shabbat to a close will only be literal and not metaphoric in the week ahead, hearkening back to a dark time in

---

3. Levenson, *Esther*, 116.
4. Fox, *Character and Ideology*, 104.
5. Esther 1:4, 20, 6:3, 6, 8:16.

Jewish history that resolved itself in abundant light. Ibn Yahya observes on Esther 8:16 that the word *yakar,* which closes a string of nouns about jubilation, refers specifically to "the happiness that comes with the abundance of material wealth and honor that replaced their mourning over being sold as ox to the slaughter." The happiness is specific to the circumstances. The nuance of joy here is of a material nature amplified precisely because from a material standpoint, the Jews had been sold. They became objectified, payment for a debt of cruelty. To reverse fortunes required that they suddenly have objects rather than be objects. Their transactional value disappeared and left in its place a new fiscal security.

By contrast, Alsheikh on the same verse extends the joy that Shushan experienced *beyond* the Jewish community. The entire city erupted in happiness because Mordecai's ascension was regarded as a windfall to the gentile population as well. The joy recorded for them may have been less about Mordecai's ascension as much as Haman's elimination. Justice would finally return to the capital city. Gersonides on 8:15 considers both options – that it was the happiness of the Jews or the happiness of all – and concludes that "it is more correct" to read the verse as a statement of universal joy.

This collective happiness recalls a similar passage from the Book of Nehemiah, when the Jews in exile returned to their homeland and were reunited with the Torah, amid tears. The scribe advised them to stop crying and rejoice:

> He further said to them, "Go, eat choice foods and drink sweet drinks and send portions to whoever has nothing prepared, for the day is holy to our Lord. Do not be sad, for your rejoicing in the Lord is the source of your strength." The Levites were quieting the people, saying, "Hush, for the day is holy; do not be sad." Then all the people went to eat and drink and send portions and make great merriment, for they understood the things they were told. (Neh. 8:10–12)

Like the Purim ritual detailed in the scroll, the moment in Nehemiah was to be celebrated with eating, drinking, merriment, and gifts to others. Joy, properly experienced, translates into sharing and giving. But unlike the Nehemiah story, the reader must question if the happiness of the Jews in exile could ever be complete. Ahasuerus was unpredictable. Joy now, suffering later. The happiness they experienced at this moment could not sweep away all of the heartache and terror of the past months. Relief should never be mistaken for happiness. It is significant, neutralizing the difficulties of the past, but it does not, in and of itself, create the sensation of total bliss, safety, love, and serenity.

A Rabbinic Reading

The classical commentators who categorized happiness may have taken their cue from the Sages of the Talmud, who interpreted each expression of joy as an aspect of this complex emotion. Unlike the medievalists, among whom were literalists, the talmudic readings are more playful, understanding the feelings as related to specific commandments: Torah study, observance of the Jewish holiday calendar, circumcision, and phylacteries.

> R. Yehuda said: "Light"; this is referring to the Torah that they once again studied. And similarly it says: "For the mitzva is a lamp and the Torah is light" (Prov. 6:23). "Gladness" (*simḥa*); this is referring to the festivals that they once again observed. And similarly it says: "And you shall be glad (*vesamaḥta*) on your festival" (Deut. 16:14). "Joy" (*sason*); this is referring to circumcision, as they once again circumcised their sons. And similarly it says: "I rejoice (*sas*) at Your word" (Ps. 119:162), which the Sages understood as referring to David's rejoicing over the mitzva of circumcision. "Honor"; this is referring to phylacteries, which they once again donned. And similarly it says: "And all peoples of the earth will see that you are called by the name of the Lord; and they will be afraid of you" (Deut. 28:10). And it was taught in a *baraita*: R. Eliezer the Great said: This is referring to the phylacteries worn on the head. Haman had banned the fulfillment of all the mitzvot mentioned, but upon Haman's demise the Jews returned to their observance.

Nowhere in the scroll are we told that Jews were forbidden to practice their faith. The king was informed that the Jews were different – "their laws are different from those of any other people and they do not obey the king's laws" (Est. 3:8) – but this knowledge did not translate into any prohibitions. Haman was not specific here about what they observed of their own law or how they failed to observe the king's law. Yet this canard was understood by the rabbis to have practical implications, reverberating with their own experience of Greek and Roman prohibitions on outward expressions and professions of faith. It was Haman, not the king, who forbade Jewish observance.

For the rabbis, happiness was less about salvation and more about the return to Jewish law and order. Mitzvot represented spiritual happiness. Any prohibition to their observance would have generated sadness and anxiety. Unable to be fully Jewish in the religious sense of the word, their very identities were compromised. The rabbis of this period in Babylon may have related all too well to the costs of exile as they looked out at their own diaspora communities. The ability to practice one's faith unobstructed was equal to any other happiness. They may have even found a non-legal, emotional understanding of happiness as a betrayal of true joy, pleasure, and delight. For them, Torah study and its observance was all the happiness a person outside the Land of Israel could hope for or desire.[6]

The Biblical Roots of Joy

Once again, in the spirit of Ecclesiastes, the Jews of ancient Persia experienced a wide range of emotion throughout the Book of Esther's ten chapters: "A time for weeping and a time for laughing; a time for wailing and a time for dancing" (Eccl. 3:4). We can almost pinpoint the chapters and verses when each of these emotions surfaced. When the Jews finally experienced happiness, it was multifaceted, as the nouns expressing it convey.

---

6. For a discussion on the relationship of happiness to study within rabbinic tradition, see Hava Tirosh-Samuelson, *Happiness in Premodern Judaism* (Cincinnati: Hebrew Union College Press, 2003), 101–42.

"Jewish" joy in the Bible generally is related to holiday observance, economic stability, and the sharing of one's bounty with family and the needy. These aspects, present in the Book of Esther, also appear in the biblical mandate to observe Sukkot:

> After the ingathering from your threshing floor and your vat, you shall hold the Feast of Booths for seven days. You shall rejoice in your festival, with your son and daughter, your male and female slave, the Levite, the stranger, the fatherless, and the widow in your communities. You shall hold a festival for the Lord your God seven days, in the place that the Lord will choose; for the Lord your God will bless all your crops and all your undertakings, and you shall have nothing but joy. (Deut. 16:13–15)

If each element is in place, one can experience and must experiece "nothing but joy." The failure to experience joy is regarded as its own transgression in the very same biblical book: "Because you did not serve the Lord your God with joy and with a good heart … therefore you shall serve your enemies" (Deut. 28:47–48). In later rabbinic literature, Maimonides describes *simḥa* as a "very high form of prayer" that one must avail oneself of or be punished for not fully embracing an aspect of God's love.[7]

In wisdom literature, there are many proverbs about what constitutes happiness, and a number of psalms – "wisdom psalms" – begin with the expression "Happy is the one who," using the Hebrew word *ashrei*.[8] According to Tirosh-Samuelson, the word appears over forty times in the Hebrew Bible. Twenty-six of those times are in the Book of Psalms.[9] The number of times it appears in the Bible's wisdom literature suggests that the wise understand the true roots of happiness: a strong relationship with God, virtue, loving and productive relationships, children, friendship, study, and thoughtful decision making. If

7. Maimonides, *Mishneh Torah, Hilkhot Teshuva* 9:1.
8. See its use in Is. 3:12, 9:15; Prov. 4:14, 9:6, 23:19.
9. Tirosh-Samuelson, *Happiness in Premodern Judaism*, 62. The entire chapter (pp. 55–100) discusses the biblical notion of joy.

Esther is to be understood as wisdom literature,[10] the book invites us to contrast the kind of hedonistic or egotistic happiness of Ahasuerus and Haman, which is always short-lived, with the more stable, durable aspects of happiness promoted throughout the Bible that the Jews achieve to some degree by the end of the Book of Esther. Happiness could not be achieved without security. After safety, Jewish happiness came through community-wide observance of a holiday, the sharing of food, economic relief, and the fact that they finally had a representative in the palace who could help promote their security and restore normalcy.

10. This was put forward earlier in the Introduction, "Satire, Drama, Fiction, History, or Theology?" note 10, as the supposition of Solomon Talmon.

Chapter Nine

Fear of the Jews

An Unreasonable Death Toll

Letters: Marking Pain and Joy

Fear of the Jews

Mordecai left the king's presence in royal robes of blue and white, with a magnificent crown of gold and a mantle of fine linen and purple wool. And the city of Shushan rang with joyous cries. The Jews enjoyed light and gladness, happiness and honor. And in every province and in every city, when the king's command and decree arrived, there was gladness and joy among the Jews, a feast and a holiday. And many of the people of the land professed to be Jews, for the fear of the Jews had fallen upon them. (Est. 8:15–17)

And so, on the thirteenth day of the twelfth month – that is, the month of Adar – when the king's command and decree were to be executed, the very day on which the enemies of the Jews had expected to get them in their power, the opposite happened, and the Jews got their enemies in their power. Throughout the provinces of King Ahasuerus, the Jews mustered in their cities to attack those who sought their hurt; and no one could withstand them, for the fear of them had fallen upon all the people. Indeed, all the officials of the provinces – the satraps, the governors, and the king's stewards – showed deference to the Jews, because the fear of Mordecai had fallen upon them. For Mordecai was now powerful in the royal palace, and his fame was spreading through all the provinces; the man Mordecai was growing ever more powerful. (Est. 9:1–4)

One of the most enigmatic expressions of the *Megilla* is the rather unusual detail, *nafal paḥad haYehudim aleihem*, "the fear of the Jews had fallen upon them." The inhabitants of Ahasuerus' empire found themselves frightened of the Jews, where the Jews were once frightened of them. What power this minority people wielded! They had won a beauty pageant, changed the power structure of those closest to the king, won the right to defend themselves, killed thousands in the battle without suffering one casualty, and emerged more influential than ever. Surrounding inhabitants were understandably terrified and awed. They had no idea what would happen next. Assuming that the remaining population did not bear resentment and hatred toward the Jews because they were still alive, they were still unlikely to have neutral feelings.

This turn of events is not dissimilar to the fear displayed in Joshua that also inspired new adherents. Rahab told the two spies reconnoitering the land the stories that had reached her about the Israelites:

> I know that the Lord has given the country to you, because dread of you has fallen upon us, and all the inhabitants of the land are quaking before you. For we have heard how the Lord dried up the waters of the Sea of Reeds for you when you left Egypt, and what you did to Sihon and Og, the two Amorite kings across the Jordan, whom you doomed. When we heard about it, we lost heart, and no man had any more spirit left because of you; for the Lord your God is the only God in heaven above and on earth below. (Josh. 2:9–11)

Unlike the Esther story, here the fear is of the God of Israel and how this God led the Israelites to victory. Rashi on 2:11 fancifully describes the impact this fear had when he interprets the expression "no man had any more spirit left because of you." Rahab, a harlot whose business was in ruin, concluded that the anxiety was so great that men had no desire to lie with women.

Later in Joshua, the Gibonites created an elaborate ruse to avoid being conquered and finally confessed that their dishonesty was rooted in terror: "You see, your servants had heard that the Lord your God had promised His servant Moses to give you the whole land and to wipe out all the inhabitants of the country on your account (*mipeneikhem*); so we were in great fear for our lives on your account (*mipeneikhem*). That is why we did this thing" (Josh. 9:24). In the physical presence of the Jews, the native population trembled.

In other instances in the Bible, the fear felt by non-Jews is again directed toward the God of the Jews, rather than the Israelites themselves. In Exodus 15, the Song of the Sea, for example, the fear is represented by a physical, instinctual experience of shaking: "The people hear; they tremble. Agony grips dwellers in Philistia. Now are the clans of Edom dismayed. The tribes of Moab, trembling grips them. All the dwellers in Canaan are aghast" (Ex. 15:14–15). There is no mention here of the Egyptians, despite the fact that they were the immediate enemy. Their fear was assumed. Fear in these verses spread quickly, moving from one tribe to another, instilling in all of Israel's enemies a troubling insecurity. Word of Egypt's loss traveled across time as well. The reaction is later summed up in Psalms: "Egypt rejoiced when they left, for the dread of Israel had fallen upon them" (105:38). This last verse uses the same noun-verb sequence we find in Esther: *ki nafal paḥdam aleihem*. Ibn Ezra makes this graphic point on 105:38: the meaning of "had fallen" is that the Egyptians were fallen dead. *Metzudat David* contends that what fell upon the Egyptians was not death but fear. Like a dark cloak, the Egyptians moved from rejoicing to trembling, much as the Israelites in Persia moved in the opposite direction.

From Fear to Conversion

As a result of the fear, many Persians converted, *mityahadim,* which some translate as a form of profession to Judaism. The King James Version (KJV) states this outright: "And many of the people of the land became Jews; for the fear of the Jews fell upon them." Rashi on 8:17 translates the action here in the same way: the people converted. Conversion represents the ultimate ideological triumph of the Jews against their enemies. Those who harbored intense ill will against them suddenly wanted to be like them and were willing to take upon themselves the demands of commitment. They crossed from the dark side into light. Again, in the universe of exilic fantasies par excellence, little could prove one's worthiness more than imitation by others, especially when those others had previously demeaned and demoralized the Jews. There was no need for the Jews to proselytize. One needed only see the beautiful Esther, the resplendent Mordecai, and the unusual good fortune these Jews had to arrive at the conclusion that their own lot might be similar if only they adopted the lifestyle and devotions of their successful neighbors.

This kind of pragmatism is not unusual in life or in the Hebrew Bible. Aligning oneself with a winner is a critical strategy for personal survival. Military success begets other peripheral boons to reputation and influence, among them the wholesale adoption of the beliefs and behaviors of the conquerors. But in the Book of Esther, the Jews were neither invading warriors nor imperialists. They had little to gain but neighborly support and validation in this sudden public interest since they had no political autonomy and their fight was only in self-defense. But the Jews were winners, and everyone loves a winner. Unadorned, seemingly undesirous of winning, Esther captured the heart of her steward and the king with her simple grace and beat others who tried harder but failed. Mordecai, through dignity and the strength of conviction, surpassed Haman at his own game. Winning is not everything, but in the harsh and duplicitous universe of Shushan's politics, winning was almost everything, as Haman came to understand with his very life. Winning had collateral impact, making the victors shine and be worthy of emulation and admiration. One would think that more verses would describe this unusual and unanticipated turn of events, but the verse that describes the fear, 8:17, often seems to get overlooked. Absorbed readers who focus on Mordecai's opulent entrance into court life almost ignore the significance and weight of the end of this description: the fear of the Jews had fallen upon the least likely suspects. The author, rather than broadcast this development, seems to downplay it.

The infinitive *lehitgayeir* generally associated with conversion is not used here, making the relationship of these residents to Judaism rather than to Jews somewhat astonishing. They feared Jews thus they became Jews. This is not dissimilar to the sailors in Jonah who, upon experiencing the redeeming powers of Jonah's God, may, too, have changed beliefs: "The men feared the Lord greatly; they offered a sacrifice to the Lord, and they made vows" (Jonah 1:16). Although the verbs in Esther and Jonah are not the same, Rashi on Jonah 1:16 is similarly unambiguous about what took place: "They converted." Rabbi David Altschuler is more modest in his interpretation: the sailors, having experienced God's might and capabilities, swore to offer sacrifices in the Holy Temple and, following Radak's reading, gave charity to the poor.

This fear of the Jews in the Book of Jonah emerges again in a midrashic treatment of its third chapter. In a strange outcome in the royal court, the king of Nineveh did a sharp about-face. When news reached him that his capital city was to be destroyed in forty days, he declared a public fast for his citizens and their animals. In an attempt to explain this sudden and dramatic shift of an Assyrian king and enemy of the Jews, one midrash identifies him as Pharaoh.[1] Pharaoh survived and ran away from Egypt only to go to Assyria to become "reincarnated" as the head of another foreign oppressor. When he heard that a Hebrew prophet predicted doom and gloom for his nation, he took it very literally. He had been there before and was not going to make the same mistake twice.

But conversion may not be the only gentile response to a Jewish victory in the Persian Empire. Ibn Ezra is puzzled by the verb *mityahadim* and calls it a *mila zara*, a strange word. He believes that the gentiles of this story changed their relationship to the Jews as a result of their triumph but separates the literal understanding from the rabbinic one that suggests conversion itself. The word *mityahadim* may have meant an acceptance of the Jews, a positive recognition of their ethnic and religious identity or even a simulacrum of behaviors, rituals, and language associated with Jews. In his second commentary to the book, Ibn Ezra, still troubled by the exact meaning of the word, goes as far as to suggest that the book's scribe may have made a mistake, repeating the first clause with a minor modification so that the term *haYehudim* turned into *mityahadim* in the second clause. Gersonides on 8:17 puts the verb within the context of who the people were; the *amei haaretz*, or "people of the land," are the subject of this verse. In rabbinic literature, this term came to mean the ignorant, simple, or those who were not pious enough to be trusted with the intricacies of certain laws of

1. *Yalkut Shimoni, Shemot* 176.

purity. These are the uneducated or the boorish.[2] Such, however, is not the case with its usage in the Hebrew Bible.[3] It would imply those who regarded themselves as Jewish without necessarily understanding what this meant or demanded of them.

The Beginning of Fear

"And many of the people of the land professed to be Jews, for the fear of the Jews had fallen upon them" (Est. 8:17). To understand the verb *mityahadim*, "profess" or "convert," we must understand the noun *paḥad*, "fear." If Persians were terrorized or converted largely depends on the way "fear" is defined. Rabbi Alan Lew, in *Be Still and Get Going*, describes *paḥad* as "the fear of the phantom, the fear whose object is imagined."[4] The term *paḥad* makes its first appearance in Genesis 31:42, when Jacob confronts Laban after years of exploitation: "Had not the God of my father, the God of Abraham and the fear of Isaac (*paḥad Yitzḥak*), been with me, you would have sent me away empty-handed." Where we expect the expression "God of Isaac" to continue the pattern, the text, by switching suddenly to this most unusual expression, alerts the reader to Jacob's primal anxiety, the fear of his father, a fear decades in the making that began with Jacob's lie. Rashi asks why the strange phrase was used but avoids the issue of the relationship altogether by stating simply that the God of Isaac was not referenced because Isaac was still alive; this expression was apparently used only over the dead.[5] Ibn Ezra's reading is more spiritual in nature: Jacob was suggesting to

---

2. See Pesaḥim 49a–b for the rabbinic distrust of the *am haaretz* in contrast to the scholarly class. Berakhot 47b and Sota 22a stress that Torah study alone was insufficient. One was labeled an *am haaretz* for not sitting at the feet of scholars. "Rabbinic sources use the term *am haaretz*, literally, 'people of the land,' to refer to non-rabbinic or uneducated Jews. This term derives from the biblical books of Ezra and Nehemiah, where it designates the Israelites who had remained in Judea when the aristocracy were deported to Babylonia during the first exile" (Jeffrey L. Rubenstein, *The Culture of the Babylonian Talmud* [Baltimore: Johns Hopkins University Press, 2003], 124).
3. See II Kings 11:14 and Ezra 4:4. Rashi on Ezra 4:4 understands "the people of the land" very specifically as the enemies of Judah and Benjamin. Gersonides on the same verse understands them as the Samaritans.
4. Alan Lew, *Be Still and Get Going* (New York: Little and Brown, 2005), 125.
5. *Tanḥuma, Toledot* 7.

his callous father-in-law that Laban's success was due only to the reverence his own father, Isaac, had for God. One might combine the two and suggest that this *paḥad* was a feeling of dread rather than awe. Laban should have had the kind of fear of God, as his own father had, that would have prevented him from wrongdoing. It was a fear that Jacob, who had lied in the past, had perhaps learned the hard way: the dread of facing the truth and one's own lie. *Ḥizkuni* makes this a physical rather than religious contrast: Isaac was wealthy and important, a man Laban should fear, even if Laban was not motivated by ethics and piety. This contrast of father and father-in-law would, no doubt, have confirmed Jacob's evolving integrity. Nahmanides introduces a subtler childhood association for Jacob: his father's fear at the moment Abraham bound him at Mount Moriah.

We find the word *paḥad* used again in Proverbs 3:25: "Have no fear of sudden disaster or of the ruin that overtakes the wicked." One who lives in sin and hate perseverates on the punishment that might come at any time. "*Pachad*," observes Tara Mohr, "is the overreactive, irrational fear that stems from worries about what *could* happen, about the worst-case scenarios we *imagine*."[6] The Hebrew in the verse in Proverbs, *al tira mipaḥad*, suggests that one should not fear fear itself. Fear is a primitive, intuitive response to wrongdoing in this proverb. A righteous person should have no fear of sudden catastrophe or disaster, because piety offers protection.[7] Again, this sense of a flash of terror assumed in the use of the word *paḥad* appears in Job when he describes his plight, a sudden onslaught of tragedy without letup: "For what I feared (*paḥadeti*) has overtaken me; what I dreaded has come upon me. I had no repose,

---

6. Tara Mohr defines fear this way in her discussion of the differences between *paḥad* and *yira* in *Playing Big* (New York: Avery, 2015), 65.
7. W. F. Albright suggests that this expression means "kinsman of Isaac" (*From the Stone Age to Christianity* [Baltimore: John Hopkins Press, 1957], 248). M. Malul, however, contends that this expression may be rooted in the Aramaic for "thigh," suggesting an oath, as in Gen. 24:9, 47:29–31, in "More on *paḥad yisḥāq* and the Oath by the Thigh," *Vetus Testamentum* 35 (1985): 194–96. The context of an oath makes sense given that only two verses later, an oath is suggested and then taken: "Come, then, let us make a pact, you and I, that there may be a witness between you and me" (Gen. 31:44). This oath does not involve the thigh, an act of trust and intimacy not expected in this relationship.

no quiet, no rest, and trouble came" (Job 3:25–26). Fear, in this image, is a black cloud of one's worst imaginings, the trepidation that the most awful outcome could overtake and overwhelm a blessed life, changing it instantly. Rashi on Job 3:25 adds a first-person confession of vulnerability: "All my days I stood in fear of this." The Malbim on the same verse contributes a note on the constancy and stubbornness of this fear: "Job had had a premonition, but despite all he had done to try to prevent the calamities when their pre-appointed time came, his very worst fears were fulfilled. There was no way he could escape his destiny."

Joan Didion opens her meditation on the sudden loss of her husband with a Jobian punishing reflection. Her husband died of a heart attack while the two were preparing their evening meal: "Life changes fast. Life changes in the instant. You sit down to dinner and life as you know it ends."[8] The expectation of routine is suddenly and irrevocably upended. In our darkest hours, we find ourselves asking, "How could this have happened when everything was normal?"[9] The Jews of Persia experienced this in Esther's early chapters. In another reversal of fortune, now the gentiles of the empire would experience many of the same emotions.

There is a talmudic reading of this verse in Job that offers the same sentiment:

> Yehuda bar Natan was coming and going after R. Hamnuna. Yehuda bar Natan sighed; R. Hamnuna said to him: Do you wish to bring suffering upon yourself; as it is stated: "For that which I did fear is come upon me, and that which I was afraid of has overtaken me" (Job 3:25)? He responded: Is it not said: "Happy is the man who fears always"? R. Hamnuna answered: That verse is written with regard to matters of Torah.[10]

R. Hamnuna found that he had an enthusiastic acolyte who wanted to live in the shadow of a sage but gave the sage no rest. Being in R. Hamnuna's presence kept the fear of God upon Yehuda bar Natan. But the elder

8. Joan Didion, *The Year of Magical Thinking* (New York: Vintage, 2007), 3.
9. Ibid., 68.
10. Berakhot 60a.

sage rejected the exhausting role of being a source of dread to help another maintain his piety, directing the younger man to the words of Torah rather than the fear of other human beings. Fear and awe may work as temporary catalysts, but long-term healthy relationships cannot be predicated on them. If this is true for individuals, it is also true for nations. Fear of the Jews may have been provocative for the citizens of Ahasuerus' empire, but over time, fear would not likely have led to sustained good relations.

Shifting Fears

The short clause of 8:17, arguably an afterthought, about fear of the Jews becomes amplified in the opening of chapter 9: "And no one could withstand them, for the fear of them had fallen upon all the people. Indeed, all the officials of the provinces – the satraps, the governors, and the king's stewards – showed deference to the Jews, because the fear of Mordecai had fallen upon them" (Est. 9:2–3). Where a chapter before only the people of the land, commoners or opportunists, were afraid and re-thought their faith commitments, by the time the dread of Jewish self-defense swept the kingdom, the sentiment was shared by "all the people." This "all" included the most powerful people of the empire, the courtiers in Shushan and the satraps and governors outside it. These two verses signal a dramatic political turn as a result of an equally dramatic overturn of power, signaling a recognizable leadership transition. Once a new leader was introduced, the biases and the agenda of the previous leader could be properly interrogated and discarded in favor of the new with little regard for political continuity. Those who need to ingratiate themselves with those in power change quickly with the shifting political winds. Just as Haman's hate toward Mordecai translated into a general hatred of Mordecai's people, the new reverence of Mordecai translated into a fear of them. One senses throughout the Book of Esther that Mordecai is a living symbol of the Jewish people. Hatred of him becomes a hatred of those he treasures. Awe of him becomes awe of those he treasures: they "showed deference to the Jews, because the fear of Mordecai had fallen upon them" (Est. 9:3).

This transformation may represent the best example of peripety in the entire book and even overshadows the reversal of fortune in chapter 6, when Haman paraded Mordecai in the king's garments, thus achieving for Haman the very opposite of what he came to the palace court to do. The consequence of that masquerade, however, had little impact on the plot itself. Mordecai received a reward he did not want or value, and Haman experienced humiliation without significant other consequence. It is here, in chapter 9, that peripety as a theme has its single greatest outcome. The attitude toward the Jews changed radically and unexpectedly in what seems like a very brief window in a very large empire. Levenson observes this theme in 9:2:

> Mordecai acts to save the king's life, and then the king acts to save the lives of Mordecai's people. Herein again lies a hint of the seditiousness of anti-Semitism, another ironic twist since Haman's initial accusation against the Jews centered on their alleged disloyalty to the king and his laws (3:8). The same principle can be heard in the verb "*menassim*" ("gave honor to") in 9:3. This was the verb that described Ahasuerus' elevation of Haman in 3:1. By refusing to recognize that elevation, Mordecai endangered himself and his people, but he also ensured his own elevation in place of Haman – and now the elevation of all the Jews as well, at the hands of the very officials formerly charged with their annihilation (3:12–13).[11]

Levenson suggests that one verb, used judiciously, first communicates the rise of the villain and subsequently the rise of the hero. In Haman's promotion, evil was given a free hand. Mordecai's rule, however, was characterized by "words of peace and truth."

The Malbim on 9:3 records the change from chapter 8 to 9 and notes that the Persians' fear of the Jews upon Mordecai's promotion was different from the fear experienced by those in government service. The people of Ahasuerus' empire, according to the Malbim, were unaware of all of the documents consigning Jews to their deaths. What they experienced was an arbitrary swing from having one enemy to having another, a transition conveyed through contradictory proclamations. When the

11. Levenson, *Esther*, 120–21.

Jews had the upper hand, the people feared them because their own lives were at risk. Initially, the courtier class, unlike the masses, had no fear of the Jews. They were aware of Haman's decree and acted accordingly. Once Mordecai received the king's ring from Haman's very hand, the courtiers feared his rule, lest Mordecai, "bring revenge upon them." From Mordecai's perch at the king's gate, he likely knew who supported Haman. After all, he knew perfidy intimately, having identified those who betrayed the king in chapter 2 and likely others who were disloyal throughout this painful saga. This moment of truth could only have instilled primal panic in the king's courtiers, who would have had much to fear from this exile-turned-vizier. Waiting on the receiving end of revenge was terrifying.

Ibn Yahya notes the unusual and specific listing of courtiers in 9:3: "All the officials of the provinces – the satraps, the governors, and the king's stewards – showed deference to the Jews, because the fear of Mordecai had fallen upon them," and then proceeds to describe the function of each within the hierarchy of governance. This is not essential information for the reader but rather it illustrates that Mordecai found himself at the very top of this courtly pyramid of power. Ibn Ezra adds that the hierarchy would have been well known because of Mordecai's proximity to the king, a likely physical placement as discussed in chapter 3. He goes as far as to say in 9:4 that the word *gadol* to describe Mordecai's prominence was actually an honorific. If courtiers called him the great one, then each time his name was mentioned, his position in the court became another wound for those who dismissed Mordecai when Haman was in power.

The Malbim adds that courtiers had more to fear. The turn of events had a military and civilian impact in their respective provinces. How could they explain what happened to their constituents? It was a wonder, inexplicable and unnerving. The very feature that made Jews a vulnerable object of derision for Haman – "they are scattered and dispersed among the other nations in all the provinces of your realm" (3:8) – made them enough of a presence everywhere to make them a threat under Mordecai. A concentrated strength of numbers in one region would have been easier to manage or eschew, but not if the Jews were located in all of Ahasuerus' 127 provinces. The Persians everywhere were afraid.

An Unreasonable Death Toll

So the Jews struck at their enemies with the sword, slaying and destroying; they wreaked their will upon their enemies. In the fortress Shushan the Jews killed a total of five hundred men. They also killed Parshandatha, Dalphon, Aspatha, Poratha, Adalia, Aridatha, Parmashta, Arisai, Aridai, and Vaizatha, the ten sons of Haman son of Hammedatha, the foe of the Jews. But they did not lay hands on the spoil. When the number of those slain in the fortress Shushan was reported on that same day to the king, the king said to Queen Esther, "In the fortress Shushan alone the Jews have killed a total of five hundred men, as well as the ten sons of Haman. What then must they have done in the provinces of the realm! What is your wish now? It shall be granted you. And what else is your request? It shall be fulfilled." "If it please Your Majesty," Esther replied, "let the Jews in Shushan be permitted to act tomorrow also as they did today; and let Haman's ten sons be hanged on the gallows." The king ordered that this should be done, and the decree was proclaimed in Shushan. Haman's ten sons were hanged: and the Jews in Shushan mustered again on the fourteenth day of Adar and slew three hundred men in Shushan. But they did not lay hands on the spoil. The rest of the Jews, those in the king's provinces, likewise mustered and fought for their lives. They disposed of their

> enemies, killing seventy-five thousand of their foes; but they did not lay hands on the spoil. (Est. 9:5–16)

Immediately after describing the fear that non-Jews experienced across the empire, chapter 9 tallies casualties. The Book of Esther in a span of only ten verses, 9:6–16, records a staggering number of deaths, a number that itself tells a gruesome story. We as readers are meant to see these numbers and be silenced with the reflection caused by any human loss. The numbers tell the story as the death count mounted; nothing is hidden from the reader: 75,000 were killed in the provinces (9:16). To this must be added the 500 in Shushan's palace (9:6, 9:12), 300 in the city of Shushan (9:15), the 10 sons of Haman (9:7 and 9:12) and Haman himself. This brings the total to 75,811. We can only imagine Memorial Day in Shushan years later. The very date marked for festivities for some became a somber, devastating anniversary for others. This is the inheritance of war, its poison, its waste.

The numbers also told another story. As evidenced by the death toll, within Shushan, in the inner court itself, there was a strong concentration of courtiers and royalists who hated the Jews. They were more than prepared to follow Haman's orders. Lest the reader think that this sentiment "lived" only in the capital, near the center of the rancor between Haman and Mordecai, chapter 9 informs readers that hate's tentacles were widespread and pernicious. Everywhere in the empire, Jews lived. Everywhere in the empire, Jews were hated.

Craig highlights a notable absence of Jewish casualties relative to the decimation of their enemies, what he calls quite literally "overkill":

> More than 75,000 non-Jews are killed without any injury whatsoever to any Jewish partisan, and these victims are spread throughout the kingdom. There is absolutely no mention of blood or pain – only reports of unrealistic casualty figures. Is it possible to execute such a large number without suffering a single casualty? The figure represents such an exaggerated casualty that the Esther (B) translator reduces the number to 15,000![1]

1. Craig, *Reading Esther*, 136.

Other versions of Esther downgraded the disaster to a fraction of the MT numbers, yet still the sheer brutality and one-sided nature of the calamity leads the reader to believe that, like the 187-day party and the twelve months of spa treatments for beauty queens, these numbers are a flight of fancy, tall tales in a villain-meets-hero story of exaggerated success. As Craig summarizes: "Overkill *follows* overstatement."[2]

Much as we might want to avoid the reality that Jewish victory came at the expense of Persian lives – even if it was in self-defense – the verses paint a grisly and disconcerting outcome: "So the Jews struck at their enemies with the sword, slaying and destroying; they wreaked their will upon their enemies" (9:5). Slaying, destroying, and wreaking their will are three strong verbs suggesting a total decimation fueled by anger and connects *ve'avdan*, destroying, with women and children, adding another unmentionable dimension of this life-threatening battle. The same verse Esther used to describe her willingness to give up her life in chapter 4 – *avadeti, avadeti* – is used five chapters later to describe those who really did give up their lives. The second version of Ibn Ezra includes more than the sword in this vast devastation. He says that the additional verbs in 9:5 suggest other forms of killing in addition to the sword.

Uncomfortable to read and more upsetting to digest in all of its particulars, verse 9:5 does not hide from the cruelty of revenge, even if every individual killed was one who rose up against the Jews first. The text invites us to view the day of violence with all the graphic morbidity of a sword slash visited upon gentile neighbors. The Malbim is quick to point this out in the distinction he makes on 9:5 between the two different Hebrew nouns used to communicate enemies: *oiveihem* and *soneihem*: "Certainly, the Jews were not given permission to kill anyone they wanted but rather only to seek revenge on their enemies." These enemies could be categorized in one of two ways. *Oiveihem* are those who scorned the Jews publicly and indiscriminately, whose feelings were well advertised in the empire. *Soneihem* were those who hated the Jews without any outward display, a subtler but no less difficult enemy. In certain ways, the quieter nature of this hate could have been more dangerous, both difficult to detect and to fend off on this day of collective misery. One

2. Ibid. Italics in original.

imagines a Jewish resident of Shushan going about his or her business, hiding on the day of terror from sworn enemies, then suddenly found in the presence of a hidden enemy, one formerly considered a friend. It was a day that revealed aversions, loyalties and jealousies, tremors of shame and guilt, and for some, the better angels of their nature.

All of these interpretive possibilities once again point to the survival techniques needed to weather life in exile. Either condition of existence, victim or oppressor, was intolerable. The Jew of Persia was prepared to be invisible, utterly unnoticeable, but exile did not allow for this luxury. One could be hated or one could hate; one could be too powerless or too powerful. One could be killed or kill. These are choiceless choices.[3] No saner, more moderate, more subtle choice was available in exile. One must, at base, survive. The quality of that survival was dependent on the willingness to be judged by the external measures of what society deemed success. Ahasuerus must have been proud of his queen, her uncle, and her people at this time. Esther and Mordecai may have experienced shame. We will never know. What we can imagine is that they experienced relief. Relief is the emotion that accompanies survival. It is not an expression of one's personal or communal integrity, but a primeval sigh of a minimalist existence that signals one is merely alive, though alive nonetheless.

The same could not be said of many of the Jews' Persian neighbors. Thinking there was no price to pay for their venomous hate crimes, their new-found terror was not only fear of the Jews but fear of consequences they thought they had escaped. It was the fear of the naked, abusive powers within oneself. The Jews after this debacle had to live with these frightening realities about self and other, too. According to Ibn Ezra, those who hated the Israelites rushed to report the killings to the king, believing it would raise his ire. Note, however, that the king seemed nonplussed by what could only have been a national disaster and tragedy for the Persians in his empire. His response was not only nonchalant but was heartless and irresponsible:

3. See Lawrence Langer's application of the term to the Holocaust in "The Dilemma of Choice in the Death Camps," *Centerpoint: A Journal of Interdisciplinary Studies: The Holocaust* 4, no. 1 (Fall 1980): 53–59.

> When the number of those slain in the fortress Shushan was reported on that same day to the king, the king said to Queen Esther, "In the fortress Shushan alone the Jews have killed a total of five hundred men, as well as the ten sons of Haman. What then must they have done in the provinces of the realm! What is your wish now? It shall be granted you. And what else is your request? It shall be fulfilled." (9:11–12)

Ahasuerus' question, which could have been asked with a tone of indignation – What then must they have done in the provinces? – was asked instead with a tone of unexpected pleasure, as if he did not know or believe Esther's people capable of such damage. The king sounded proud of "his" Jews. Esther may have regarded her circumstances as tragic either way, either the loss of her people or, without a choice, the loss of another's, yet Ahasuerus saw some kind of bizarre sport in this completely preventable outcome. How else are we to understand that he followed one question with another, asking Esther yet again for any wish of hers to be granted, almost suggesting that more could die at her hand with the king's imprimatur and approval? Fox also notes this and characterizes Ahasuerus' response as "impressed, perhaps bemused, by the death toll more than by the Jews' deliverance."[4] Perhaps Ahasuerus did not regard the Jews as militaristic and was "pleasantly" surprised by their unexpected agility with the sword, a fact that he may have deemed useful for future purposes when he went to war. He may have equally been taken that Esther, who continued to delight him, was associated with this people who responded to this call to battle with such vehemence and skill, another confirmation of his choice of consort.

There may also have been some shock that as many as five hundred people in Shushan, in addition to Haman and his sons, were willing to kill Mordecai and Esther's people. It is possible that until this moment, Ahasuerus did not understand the depth of animosity and baseless hatred targeted at the Jews. As mentioned earlier, the death toll told the story in ways that narrative could not. The Malbim on 9:12 explains Ahasuerus' disbelief and wonderment at what was happening

4. Fox, *Character and Ideology*, 112.

in the provinces: if this is how the Jews behaved in the capital city, killing half a thousand people directly under the king and queen's aegis, how much more so should the king expect a high toll in the rest of the many provinces? This may explain Esther's odd request for another day:

> "If it please Your Majesty," Esther replied, "let the Jews in Shushan be permitted to act tomorrow also as they did today; and let Haman's ten sons be hanged on the gallows." The king ordered that this should be done, and the decree was proclaimed in Shushan. Haman's ten sons were hanged. (Est. 9:13–14)

Unlike at other times in the book when Esther demurred in the face of Ahasuerus' exaggerated generosity, here she requested more from him. Unsure of how her people fared outside of Shushan and with the unfinished business of Haman's sons still alive, allowing Haman's hatred to survive, Esther was not ready to call a halt to the macabre work. Ahasuerus granted her request.

The Death of Haman's Sons

"In the fortress Shushan the Jews killed a total of five hundred men. They also killed Parshandatha, Dalphon, Aspatha, Poratha, Adalia, Aridatha, Parmashta, Arisai, Aridai, and Vaizatha, the ten sons of Haman son of Hammedatha, the foe of the Jews. But they did not lay hands on the spoil." The first verse in this series mentions that five hundred people in Shushan were killed and "also" the sons, each listed by name, almost as if the text takes us on the hunt for each one, in effect eliminating any residual danger. One talmudic reading suggests the ten sons are read in one breath during the scroll's public recitation in the synagogue to show their thought alignment with their father and each other. They were, in essence, like one person. This is followed up with another opinion contending that they were all hanged on the same gallows.

> "Parshandatha … and Vaizatha, the ten sons of Haman" (Est. 9:6–10). R. Adda from Jaffa said: When reading the *Megilla*, the names of the ten sons of Haman and the word "ten" must be said in one breath. What is the reason for this? It is that their souls all

> departed together. R. Yoḥanan said: The letter *vav* in the name "Vaizatha" is a lengthened *vav* and must be elongated as a pole, like a steering oar of a ship. What is the reason for this? To indicate that they were all hanged on one pole.[5]

James Kugel, in his discussion of the evolution of vicarious punishment in the Bible, the notion that children receive the punishment for the sins of the fathers, looks at this ugly chapter of death in Esther as a late example of this theory playing itself out. Although there is a development throughout the Hebrew Bible from punishing children for the wrongdoings of their parents to punishing only the sinners to forgiving the sinners who relinquish their evil ways, the text of Esther seems a throwback to earlier, more primitive views of punishment. Kugel reflects that

> Haman received classical transgenerational punishment; not only was he killed, but his ten sons were executed after him (Est. 9:7–10) – what did they do, apart from having the wrong father? In fact, five hundred other people (Est. 9:6) were subsequently killed, then three hundred more (9:15), and finally an additional seventy-five thousand for good measure (9:16). True, these corpses may be the fantasy of a subject people eager to imagine that revenge had, at least on one occasion, been theirs; but whatever else these numbers prove, they seem to be saying that vicarious punishment was not altogether dead.[6]

While this may reflect a view of biblical punishment that was long in the dying, it may also, and primarily, represent an expression of the reversal of fate. In a theological view of the universe where both the evil get their just deserts by watching their children suffer *and* the righteous suffer but are eventually vindicated, Haman was actually executed before his sons were killed, and Mordecai was rewarded in his lifetime and initially in ways that were not instrumental to his welfare. The killing of Haman's children may have signaled that the DNA of hatred was being cut off at

5. Megilla 16b.
6. Kugel, *The Great Shift*, 266.

the root; the excessive paranoia at the heart of Haman's enterprise would find no harbor in those who came after him to continue the desperate project of annihilation. Reversing the way that King Saul had spared Agag, which allowed the regeneration of Agag's hostility and violence, Haman's sons, known to us only in name and not deed, were not allowed the time or space to breed their father's ways. This may be less an example of vicarious punishment and more a preemptive strike designed to allay the deep-seated fears of the Israelites.[7] While such thinking appears in a midrashic reading of Enoch's death in Genesis 5:24 – "Enoch walked with God and then he was no more" – namely that Enoch was "taken" before his time to forestall inevitable moral lapses, this view is morally problematic and assumes that sinful individuals had no capacity to repent or to change.[8] Without reasons assigned for their deaths, the sons of Haman were also victims, albeit victims who failed to engender much sympathy in future audiences. The troubling nature of their murder is reflected in Rashi's interpretation of 9:10, after the biblical listing of the names of the sons. He writes that he saw in *Seder Olam*, a chronology of Jewish life from Genesis through Alexander the Great traditionally attributed to the second-century scholar R. Yosei b. Ḥalafta, that a group defamed Judah and Jerusalem (Ezra 4:6) to prevent Jews returning from exile in the days of Cyrus and prevented the reconstruction of the Holy Temple. This group was identified as Haman's sons.[9] Never mind that this was not a capital offense in anyone's lawbooks. It was wrong, and it would not be tolerated:

---

7. Soltes points out the visual demarcation of the death of Haman's sons in most scrolls and compares this to the Ten Plagues in Egypt and the way they, too, are often offset in the Haggada for extra attention. They "share a numerological focus on the suffering of others as the price of Israelite-Judean redemption" (p. 138).
8. Rashi on 5:24 assumes this as a reasonable interpretation of events based on Genesis Rabba on 5:24: "He was a righteous man, but his mind was easily induced to turn from his righteous ways and to become wicked. The Holy One, blessed be He, therefore took him away quickly; and made him die before his full time. This is why Scripture uses a different expression when referring to his death by writing 'and he was not,' meaning, he was not in the world to complete the number of his years." Ibn Ezra, perhaps aware of the theological difficulties of such a reading, explains Enoch's death through similar verb uses in the Book of Psalms.
9. *Seder Olam Rabba* 29.

> "The ten sons of Haman": I saw in *Seder Olam*: These are the ten who wrote an accusation against Judah and Jerusalem, as it is written in the book of Ezra: "And during the reign of Ahasuerus, at the beginning of his reign, they wrote an accusation against the dwellers of Judah and Jerusalem" (Ezra 4:6). And what was the accusation? To stop those who were coming up from the exile during the days of Koresh, who had started to build the Temple, and the Cutheans slandered them and stopped them (*Seder Olam Rabba* 29). But when Koresh died, and Ahasuerus reigned, Haman was promoted, and he prevented those in Jerusalem from the construction, so they [Haman's sons] sent word in Ahasuerus' name to the princes of the other side of the river to stop them [from building].[10]

This is far from a literal reading. In addition to the fact that Haman's sons were not mentioned explicitly in the Book of Ezra, defamation is not a crime worthy of execution, nor is any of this referenced in the Book of Esther.

This ancient reading performs an important, alternate function of "justifying" deaths that are unjustifiable, which is exactly the point. This incident is yet another manifestation of justice gone awry at the hands of this royal court, another symptom of life under foreign rule where fury rather than fairness propelled events forward. Whether Jews suffered from it or benefited from it has important practical implications but does not minimize our critique of this existential reality. Justice cannot be expected.

Craig looks at the death of Haman's sons as part of the literary engine of reversal at play throughout the book. In 5:11, Haman boasted about his riches and the number of his sons and the honor given to him by the king. All this had to be lost to show how fortunes had altered: "The subsequent execution of Haman's sons, *as projected in this narrative world*, is a turnabout image. Haman is not proud of his sons, but of

10. Rashi on Est. 9:10. See Manfred R. Lehman for a discussion of this Rashi and the links between the Book of Ezra and the Book of Esther: "A Reconstruction of the Purim Story," *Tradition* 12, nos. 3–4 (1972): 90–98.

the number of his sons, and the death of all ten in chapter 9 is a literary attack on the (dead) man's pride."[11]

That the number ten seems an exaggeration and a fabricated literary detail to support the story's dominant motif points us in the direction of Job, which opens with a display of Job's achievements. As with Haman, Job's success was measured by his ten children, property, and cattle: "Seven sons and three daughters were born to him; his possessions were seven thousand sheep, three thousand camels, five hundred yoke of oxen and five hundred donkeys, and a very large household. That man was wealthier than anyone in the East" (Job 1:2–3). Job, too, is a reversal-of-fortune story. Unlike Haman, whose children died after he died, leaving nothing of him for the future, Job lost all of his children in the very first chapter in a long, sordid set of circumstances (1:13–19) but had ten more children at the story's end, suggesting all was finally right in his world. Wealth and family had to be his again for equilibrium to be restored. Disturbingly, in the last chapter of Job, money is referenced before children, a reversal of order from chapter 1: "Thus the Lord blessed the latter years of Job's life more than the former. He had fourteen thousand sheep, six thousand camels, one thousand yoke of oxen, and one thousand donkeys. He also had seven sons and three daughters" (42:12–13). Children, like wealth, it seems, can be easily replaced.

To add to this comparison, we get another detail about Job's life that highlights all that Haman lost: "Afterward, Job lived one hundred and forty years to see four generations of sons and grandsons. So Job died old and contented" (42:16–17).[12] Job merited not only the gift of abundance regained but also the satisfaction of seeing multiple generations of children follow him, enough to conclude that his life had been worthwhile and not forever pockmarked by the tragedy of earlier years.

---

11. Craig, *Reading Esther*, 136; italics in original.
12. The detail is reminiscent of Abraham at the close of his life. Perhaps because of this, Bar Kappara in Bava Batra 15b suggests that Job actually lived in the days of Abraham. For an excellent treatment of the two narratives in contrast to each other, see Judy Klitsner, *Subversive Sequels: How Biblical Stories Mine and Undermine Each Other* (Philadelphia: Jewish Publication Society, 2009), xviii–xxii.

The base assumption of the story is so problematic that some Sages of the Talmud believed the story of Job never took place. Whether or not Job is regarded as a fiction, the end of the book is a clear and unambiguous reversal of all that came before, giving Job back what he had lost and more. The Book of Esther uses the theme of reversal more subtly but no less effectively. In fact, where Job is told repeatedly that all was in God's hand, including Job's fate and fortune, the message of the *Megilla* is almost the opposite: the fate of humans is dependent on humans. God acted as a silent partner but was often so silent as to lack the presence apparent in Job and other biblical books.

Berg notes God's absence as one of the distinguishing features of the Book of Esther. The absence left room for, indeed demanded, human action. For Berg, the people of Israel share responsibility with God for the shaping of the future:

> The belief that divine activity remains partially concealed perhaps also explains the theme of dual loyalty in Esther, with its specific ordering of priorities. A Jew's loyalty to his/her people implies an active affirmation of its history as one's own.... Yet a Jew who is faithful to his/her socio-religious heritage must cope at the same time with the vicissitudes of everyday life, which include – particularly for a diaspora Jew – interaction with foreign rulers.... The Book of Esther suggests one solution to this potential conflict of loyalties. It suggests that Jews who prove loyal to both people and king overcome any problems which their dual loyalties might engender.... This dual allegiance goes hand in hand with the understanding that each individual Jew helps to determine the fate of the people as a whole.[13]

This notion that fate is determined in part by human beings who take action and feel accountable for their fate is a sharp contrast to the fate of many Persians. Whereas Mordecai and Esther risk their lives to work on behalf of their people, the same could not be said for Ahasuerus and Haman, who seem distant from and indifferent to the fate of the people

13. Berg, *The Book of Esther*, 178–79.

of their empire. The death toll of the Persians was a problem for the Jews and also a sign of the casual irresponsibility and thoughtlessness of their leaders.

Letters: Marking Pain and Joy

Mordecai recorded these events. And he sent dispatches to all the Jews throughout the provinces of King Ahasuerus, near and far, charging them to observe the fourteenth and fifteenth days of Adar, every year – the same days on which the Jews enjoyed relief from their foes and the same month which had been transformed for them from one of grief and mourning to one of festive joy. They were to observe them as days of feasting and merrymaking, and as an occasion for sending gifts to one another and presents to the poor. The Jews accordingly assumed as an obligation that which they had begun to practice and which Mordecai prescribed for them. (Est. 9:20–23)

"And you may further write with regard to the Jews as you see fit. [Write it] in the king's name and seal it with the king's signet, for an edict that has been written in the king's name and sealed with the king's signet may not be revoked." So the king's scribes were summoned at that time, on the twenty-third day of the third month, that is, the month of Sivan; and letters were written, at Mordecai's dictation, to the Jews and to the satraps, the governors, and the officials of the one hundred and twenty-seven provinces from India to Ethiopia: to every province in its own script and to every

> people in its own language, and to the Jews in their own script and language. He had them written in the name of King Ahasuerus and sealed with the king's signet. Letters were dispatched by mounted couriers, riding steeds used in the king's service, bred of the royal stud, to this effect: The king has permitted the Jews of every city to assemble and fight for their lives; if any people or province attacks them, they may destroy, massacre, and exterminate its armed force together with women and children, and plunder their possessions – on a single day in all the provinces of King Ahasuerus, namely, on the thirteenth day of the twelfth month, that is, the month of Adar. The text of the document was to be issued as a law in every single province: it was to be publicly displayed to all the peoples, so that the Jews should be ready for that day to avenge themselves on their enemies. The couriers, mounted on royal steeds, went out in urgent haste at the king's command; and the decree was proclaimed in the fortress Shushan. (Est. 8:8–14)

Writing, reading records, and disseminating proclamations is a regular feature of Ahasuerus' royal court and bookends the scroll. Ahasuerus promulgates a new law in chapter 1 that must be delivered to all the people of Shushan, and all the events of the *Megilla* are recorded in the annals of Persia and Media in chapter 10. Letter writing and sending began in chapter 1, continued in chapter 3, and then was used more than once in chapter 9. In each instance, letters were designated as proclamations with the full backing of the king, but in no instance was a letter initiated or written solely by the king. This is most clearly illustrated in the very first letter: "If it please Your Majesty, let a royal edict be issued by you, and let it be written into the laws of Persia and Media, so that it cannot be abrogated, that Vashti shall never enter the presence of King Ahasuerus" (Est. 1:19). Rashi here observes that this new law, by protocol, shall be "in the books of the statutes and the customs of the kingdom." The letter, suggested by someone else, needed the king's approval and became a matter of gravitas and law through the act of writing: "Then will the judgment executed by Your Majesty resound throughout your realm" (Est. 1:20). An act cannot achieve full potency without this process. No doubt, Mordecai and Esther realized this when they sought to defend their nation against attack, summarized the story, and then promulgated a new holiday. *Dat,* law, must be kept and preserved despite its absurdity or consequence.[1]

Letters changed in function across the scroll and are a puzzling feature throughout. In chapter 1, letters functioned almost comically to affirm male rule in each household. If a decree had to be made to assure male dominance, it is safe to assume that it was under threat, if not in the homes throughout the empire, then at least in the royal palace. That is not the function that the missives had in chapters 8 and 9. In these later chapters, they may be the sole source of information about the edict against the Jews and its eventual reversal through yet another letter. One delay in delivery could have resulted in chaos. New rules, new developments, and new tellings of history were all conveyed through mail. Dispatching messengers was an act of Persian power that in chapter 9 is given to Mordecai as a sign of his arrival in the upper echelons of Persian politics.

The request for the second letter in the *Megilla,* that of Haman to the same set of provinces, suggests the appropriate royal procedure to send out a missive and, at the same time, alludes to the rigidity of such documents such that once they are delivered, they seal the content irrevocably: "If it please Your Majesty, let an edict be drawn for their destruction, and I will pay ten thousand talents of silver to the stewards for deposit in the royal treasury" (3:9). The king thereupon gave Haman his ring and said obliquely, "The money and the people are yours to do with as you see fit" (3:11). Some believe Haman offered the king money, and he refused. Others believe Haman sought money to do this, and the king delivered. Craig suggests that when Haman offered to place ten thousand talents into the king's treasury, "The king will have none of it: 'Keep the money and do with the people as you please,' he tells Haman (3:11)."[2] Not unlike his repeated generous offer to Esther of up to half the kingdom or his tax remission when she was chosen queen, money never seems to be an issue, yet another demonstration of the king's failure to think. The king's coffers may have suffered under the hand of a leader

1. See LaCocque, *Esther Regina,* 9.
2. Craig, *Reading Esther,* 140.

without economic sense. As will be studied later in detail, Mordecai's promotion in chapter 10 coincides, quite intentionally, with the repositioning of taxes, suggesting overtly that the Jews were not only beneficiaries of the king's favor; they made important strategic contributions to the fiscal health of the empire.

Ahasuerus neither asked questions to interrogate Haman's request nor did he mention the people by name, helping us understand the king's surprise at Esther's revelation. His action reminds us of leadership dissonances that fray the worthiness of the political enterprise: there is often a gap of information, time, and position between an immoral act and the authority for that act that allows for tragedy to occur without any single person taking responsibility. In the Book of Esther, the letter was the ultimate symbol of this distance – an almost totemic icon of political power – that demonstrates the remoteness of the leader to those led. It is formal and impersonal. It makes demands that are didactic yet confusing. It arrives long after the wheels of motion have been set in place and long after anything can be done to stop its violence. Letters in the Book of Esther are a representation of power at a distance in its most devastating form. On this, Halbertal and Holmes share the following analysis:

> Hierarchically organized power is defined by the power-wielder's capacity to act from a distance. Delegation involves the capacity to create extended causal chains, embroiling and implicating multiple subordinates whose actions radiate downward from an apex or outward from a center. The longer the chain, the greater the power of the sovereign who acts invisibly through its multiple links. It is as if the arm of the sovereign literally reached its remote objective through a succession of proxies carrying out his commands.... The ruler's numerous messengers, surrogates, and agents serve not only as tools of his power but, more significantly in the present context, as decoys obscuring the initiator's identity and disguising his stage-management of the way the action unfolds.[3]

3. Halbertal and Holmes, *The Beginning of Politics*, 82. Although the authors make this observation about King David's cruel handling of the Uriah and Bathsheba incident,

In the *Megilla*, letters inform, distract, and confound. They separate the one who makes the decision from the ones who had to live with the consequences of the decisions.

A similar use of letters appears in another biblical story, that of Ahab and Naboth, a story mentioned earlier. It is a haunting tale of biblical abuse of power through letters, resulting in tragic consequences. Ahab desired Naboth's vineyard, so his wife Jezebel viciously acquired it on Ahab's behalf in I Kings 21. She maligned Naboth and falsely accused him of blasphemy with the goal of making him guilty of a capital offense. Once stoned, she was able to take his estate and give it to her sulking husband. She accomplished this, in part, by sending letters "signed" by the king, usurping his authority for brutal ends: "She wrote letters in Ahab's name and signed them with his seal and sent letters to the elders and to the nobles who were in his city" (I Kings 21:8).[4] In both narratives, in I Kings and Esther, one royal figure initiated action on behalf of another, distancing the crime from its originator.

Writing in Chapter 8

At the start of chapter 8, Ahasuerus told Esther and Mordecai to inform their people that Haman's property had been transferred and that he had been "hanged on the gallows for scheming against the Jews" (Est. 8:7). The rest of the message Esther and Mordecai were to devise on their own, and Ahasuerus, in keeping with his aloof approach to governance and lack of oversight, would seal it in his name without examining its contents. This offers confirmation that Ahasuerus, chapters earlier, may have signed on to Haman's decree with little information and no personal animus against the Jews.

The king's message, however, was far from accurate. He did not hang Haman for scheming against the Jews, at least not according to the

---

their conclusions easily apply to any number of biblical texts related to royal power.

4. For more on the relationship of these two texts, see Jonathan Grossman, "The Edicts of Haman and the Vineyard of Naboth," *Megadim* 30 (1999): 55–58; Yair Zakovitch, "The Tale of Naboth's Vineyard, I Kings 21," in *The Bible from Within: The Method of Total Interpretation*, ed. Meir Weiss (Jerusalem, 1984), 379–405; and Yossi Feintuch, "Judah and Jacob; Ahab and Ahasuerus – Comments on the Methodology of the Use of Analogy as an Exegetical Device," *Megadim* 44 (2006): 9–23.

text. Shame or the desire to please led him to manipulate the truth to make himself look good. This may have had one positive benefit. The citizens of his empire would know that the king's feelings toward the Jews had radically altered, and it was best to step in line with the king's new direction. This could have functioned as a dog whistle to those who hated the Jews, forcing them to change their tune to adjust to the new reality and avoid death themselves. Knowing that Haman's scheming against the Jews cost him his life would have given pause to those who shared his prejudices but were far less powerful.

One wonders how the Jews of the empire would have responded to this new and bewildering letter. The first letter made them victims. The second letter would make them murderers. Jews of Ahasuerus' empire could not rejoice. At best, they may have felt initial relief followed by profound confusion. Killing in self-defense may have changed the intent, but it did not change the graphic brutality of the killing fields, or possibly even the outcome, which may have been the same no matter the motivation. The letters gave the Jews permission to defend themselves, but if they could defend themselves only on one day and only if someone was attacking them, they risked dying in every altercation. And how did they know, with this fickle and eccentric king, if there was to be a third letter that was to change their fate yet again? To Esther and Mordecai the message was clear. The king did what he could, which amounted to little, and it was up to them to tell the next part of the story and seek the solution as they saw fit: a solution that was no solution. All of this was to be communicated via a complex postal system; it would take time for the news to travel, which increased the possibility that the change of course be lost in a bureaucratic puddle.

Writing in Ancient Persia and Beyond

The correspondences that inform the plot in the Book of Esther govern events from chapter 1 onward and heighten in intensity and frequency toward the book's end. The relationship between law and writing makes it appear as if an action or event became serious and real in the Book of Esther only if it was written down. This sentiment is not only central to Persian governance and culture; it was critical to the formation of nationhood among the early Israelites as evidenced in several key biblical passages:

> Then Moses turned and went down from the mountain with the two tablets of the testimony in his hand, tablets which were *written* on both sides; they were *written* on one side and the other. The tablets were God's work, and the *writing* was God's *writing* engraved on the tablets. (Ex. 32:15–16)

> You shall *write* them on the doorposts of your house and on your gates. (Deut. 6:9)

> So it shall be on the day when you cross the Jordan to the land which the Lord your God gives you, that you shall set up for yourself large stones and coat them with lime and *write* on them all the words of this law, when you cross over, so that you may enter the land which the Lord your God gives you, a land flowing with milk and honey, as the Lord, the God of your fathers, promised you. (Deut. 27:2–3)

> It came about, when Moses finished *writing* the words of this law in a book until they were complete. (Deut. 31:24)

> And Joshua *wrote* these words in the book of the law of God; and he took a large stone and set it up there under the oak that was by the sanctuary of the Lord. (Josh. 24:26)

> Thus says the Lord, the God of Israel, "*Write* all the words which I have spoken to you in a book." (Jer. 30:2)

> "But this is the covenant which I will make with the House of Israel after those days," declares the Lord. "I will put My law within them and on their heart. I will *write* it; and I will be their God, and they shall be My people." (Jer. 31:33)

Moses wrote. Joshua wrote. God "wrote." Writing solidified expectations into law, into permanent engravings in the hearts, minds, and souls of the people at a time when writing was time-consuming and difficult. Bringing written, stone tablets down the mountain in full public view crystallized and hardened the notion of a collective covenant, as did writing down the rest of the law as demanded in Deuteronomy and then again in the days of Joshua. For the Jews, writing created community and covenant, grounding values with unified messaging.

But the writing in the Persian court system as it appears in Esther is not like the writing with which Jews would have been familiar. Rather than lend clarity and credence, the Persian court letters were suspect. One cannot imagine the contents of the Decalogue, for example, being revoked a few months after they were delivered on Sinai. Yet royal Persian letters suggested messaging that was contradictory and highly personal rather than collective, creating an unequal and unfair power imbalance among spouses and neighbors instead of framing and shaping a national awareness of a master narrative. The fact that the letters were sent out in each language rather than only one testified to the singularity of experience over the cohesiveness that these letters could have achieved in an empire already geographically fragmented. The same holds true for the annals. Major events recorded but neglected and quickly forgotten explain one of the dangers of writing: it leaves open the possibility that what is written will have no influence precisely because the act of recording distances the writer from lived experience.

Rabbinic Readings of Writing

A lengthy talmudic discussion explores what methods of communication count toward an individual's fulfillment of the obligation to read the *Megilla* each year. This discussion about the process by which a text gains significant cultural weight begins with a mishna about a scroll read out of order and in another language:

> With regard to one who reads the *Megilla* out of order, reading a later section first, and then going back to the earlier section, he has not fulfilled his obligation. If he read it by heart, or if he read it in Aramaic translation or in any other language that he does

> not understand, he has not fulfilled his obligation. However, for those who speak a foreign language, one may read the *Megilla* in that foreign language. And one who speaks a foreign language who heard the *Megilla* read in *Ashurit,* i.e., in Hebrew characters, has fulfilled his obligation. If one read the *Megilla* at intervals, pausing and resuming, or while he is dozing off, he has fulfilled his obligation. If one was writing a *Megilla,* or expounding upon it, or correcting it, and he read all its words as he was doing so, the following distinction applies: If he had intent to fulfill his obligation with that reading he has fulfilled his obligation, but if not, he has not fulfilled his obligation. If one reads from a Megilla that was written not with ink but with *sam* or with *sikra* or with *komos* or with *kankantom,* or from a *Megilla* that was written not on parchment but on *neyar* or on *diftera,* a kind of unprocessed leather, he has not fulfilled his obligation. He does not fulfill his obligation unless he reads from a *Megilla* that is written in *Ashurit,* i.e., in the Hebrew language and using the Hebrew script, upon parchment and with ink.[5]

One fulfills the legal requirement to hear the contents of the scroll as long as it is read in sequence, in a language the listener understands, and written with permissible ink and parchment. Even the writer of the scroll can satisfy the commandment while writing it as long as he reads it with this intention. As the mishna is explicated, the significance of the writing is made clear, as is the distinction between knowing something in one's heart and having it written down explicitly, specifically in reference to the command to remember Amalek:

> If one read the *Megilla* by heart he has not fulfilled his obligation. The Gemara asks: From where do we derive this? Rava said: This is derived by means of a verbal analogy between one instance of the term 'remembrance' and another instance of the term 'remembrance.' It is written here, with regard to the *Megilla*: "That these days should be remembered" (Est. 9:28), and it is written else-

5. Megilla 17a.

> where: "And the Lord said to Moses: Write this for a memorial in the book and rehearse it in the ears of Joshua: That I will utterly blot out the remembrance of Amalek from under the heavens" (Ex. 17:14). Just as there, with regard to Amalek, remembrance is referring specifically to something written in a book, as it is stated, "in the book," so too here, the *Megilla* remembrance is through being written in a book.[6]

The Talmud then follows up with another question that gets to the heart of how writing is to be processed from a spiritual standpoint. Is it sufficient to write down these stories or must they also be read aloud?

> From where do we know that this remembrance that is stated with regard to Amalek and to the *Megilla* involves reading it out loud from a book? Perhaps it requires merely looking into the book, reading it silently. It should not enter your mind to say this, as it was taught in a *baraita*: The verse states: "Remember what Amalek did to you" (Deut. 25:17). One might have thought that it suffices for one to remember this silently, in his heart. But this cannot be, since when it says subsequently: "You shall not forget" (Deut. 25:19), it is already referring to forgetting from the heart. How, then, do I uphold the meaning of "remember"? What does this command to remember add to the command not to forget? Therefore, it means that the remembrance must be expressed out loud, with the mouth.[7]

For writing to be meaningful in shaping consciousness, in molding and determining a master narrative, it must be written and must be read aloud, again and again. Narratives of hate and narratives of astonishment can be forgotten if they are placed on a shelf. "Remembrance must be expressed out loud, with the mouth."

Writing in the scroll is an act of agency, expressing the need and desire to be in control over one's history. Stories may be told about us;

6. Ibid. 18a.
7. Ibid.

they are not the same as the stories we tell about ourselves. Mordecai needed to tell the story of his own astonishing rise, perhaps first and foremost for himself. Writing allows one to luxuriate in all the extraordinary details of an experience. It is also clear from the text of chapter 9 that Mordecai was sharing not only "objective" events but also his feelings about the events and the emotional dimensions that related to those facts, taking his readers on a journey from neutrality to confusion, from grief to unbridled joy. Facts alone do not communicate the emotional tribulations set off by the events. Alsheikh on 9:20 observes that Mordecai selected the events most worthy of remembrance. This demonstrative dimension would not likely have appeared in the royal annals, which most likely read as lists of events involving key aristocrats.

The Stamp of Approval

> In view, then, of all the instructions in the said letter and of what they had experienced in that matter and what had befallen them, the Jews undertook and irrevocably obligated themselves and their descendants, and all who might join them, to observe these two days in the manner prescribed and at the proper time each year. Consequently, these days are recalled and observed in every generation: by every family, every province, and every city. And these days of Purim shall never cease among the Jews, and the memory of them shall never perish among their descendants. Then Queen Esther daughter of Abihail wrote a second letter of Purim for the purpose of confirming with full authority the aforementioned one of Mordecai the Jew. Dispatches were sent to all the Jews in the hundred and twenty-seven provinces of the realm of Ahasuerus with an ordinance of "equity and honesty": These days of Purim shall be observed at their proper time, as Mordecai the Jew – and now Queen Esther – has obligated them to do, and just as they have assumed for themselves and their descendants the obligation of the fasts with their lamentations. And Esther's ordinance validating these observances of Purim was recorded in a scroll. (Est. 9:26–32)

After the fighting settled, another missive is sent from both Mordecai and Esther. The purpose of this second letter is unclear. It seems that in the first letter, Mordecai explained what happened and the rituals to be observed in commemoration. In the second letter, Esther added her imprimatur as queen as an additional stamp of approval and to let her people know that this holiday would be observed in perpetuity. Ibn Ezra on 9:29 mentions that Mordecai alone did not have the power to establish Purim as a festival day. The words "confirming with full authority" may then explain why Esther wrote a second letter. Perhaps the first was done with good intention and content but lacked the requisite authority to ensure that these days would be observed by the exiles. Mentioning it again may also suggest that these days were being forgotten and needed the extra heft of the queen's approval to ensure they would be remembered.[8]

Unusually, in 9:29 Esther is called the daughter of Abihail, a title not used since her introduction that may serve the literary function of establishing her allegiances. As a Jew, Esther was the daughter of her father more than the wife of her husband. Ibn Ezra also adds that Esther's letter made sure that the people observed not only the celebratory aspects of Purim but also commemorated the three days of fasting that Esther undertook with her maidens and anyone who joined her. These days fill out the total picture of this time period in all of its multifaceted dimensions.

Rashi on the words "with full authority" in 9:29 cites the talmudic statement that Esther was writing "with all the authority of the miracle of Ahasuerus, Mordecai, and Esther."[9] The Revised Standard Version translation (1952) of 9:29 translates this term as "full written authority."[10] Mordecai and Esther had separate recordings because each experienced the wonders of the story differently. There were enough acts of amazement to go around. Rashi also points out that this letter was sent in the

8. Levenson, among others, notes that the expression "with full authority" is "awkward and obscure." He cites Fox in what he calls "the least radical suggestion as to how to understand this clause" (*Esther*, 125): "a trope for words of authority" (Fox, *Character and Ideology*, 286) such that the holiday would come into proper observance.

9. Megilla 19a.

10. See Greenspoon, "From Maidens and Chamberlains," 222.

second year to remind people to celebrate this holiday. It takes time before a community shapes its rituals and observances, especially when adding new ones.

The contents of Mordecai's letter are unclear. According to Rashi, Mordecai actually sent the scroll of Esther "as it was then." This was not a simple proclamation of a holiday and its observances, but a recording of the story that needed to be lovingly read by each and every Jew in the empire. Transporting such a large document to every household, if indeed the story was told in all of its detail in such a mailing, would have been a challenge for the messengers. Rashi also offers a leadership insight with this reading: From Mordecai's unique perch, word from him would have been both credible and affirmative. It would have boosted his reputation in the eyes of his people. His words would have been trusted and would have enlightened the people who were most likely in the dark about the original decree and its sudden repeal. All of this arbitrariness could only be countered by a story – a full narrative of what had actually happened. Sending the entire story as it was up until that point made the only real sense. The specific rituals would have been secondary to why they were to be kept.

Levenson suggests that the redundancies and oddities of these letters hint at a more complex problem:

> Though Jewish tradition has often seen a reference to the book of Esther itself in the statement that "Mordecai recorded these things" (9:20), the more likely interpretation is that Mordecai included a summary of the key events in the letters he sent to the Jews to enjoin them to observe the fourteenth and the fifteenth of Adar as days of festival.[11]

Levenson adds that the expression "near and far" (9:20) likely hearkens to Isaiah 57:19, where God promised well-being to those near and far as an aspect of their healing. "If so, then the implication is that in the events that have led to the institution of Purim, the Jews are to see the fulfill-

11. Levenson, *Esther*, 125–26.

ment of an ancient prophecy of deliverance."[12] The idea of God caring about those who are far may have resonated with the Jews of Persia, who may have felt in the aftermath of this distressing and alarming chapter of their history that God abandoned them in exile. Mordecai was then not only providing a summary of events and their ritual consequences; he was also providing a broader framework that tied his people's experience into the prophetic, apocalyptic history of Israel more generally. At the same time, Mordecai would have offered the psychic comfort that their specific diasporic condition contained the seeds of redemption.

12. Ibid., 125.

Chapter Ten

Taxes: A Happy Ending?

Respected by Most: The Courtier's Dilemma

The End That Wasn't Written

Taxes: A Happy Ending?

> King Ahasuerus imposed tribute on the mainland and the islands. All his mighty and powerful acts, and a full account of the greatness to which the king advanced Mordecai, are recorded in the Annals of the Kings of Media and Persia. For Mordecai the Jew ranked next to King Ahasuerus and was highly regarded by the Jews and popular with most of his brethren; he sought the good of his people and interceded for the welfare of all his kindred. (Est. 10:1–3)

Taxes appear as early as chapter 2 of Esther. Ahasuerus issued a tax remission to celebrate Esther's elevation in status, a thoughtless strategy for a king preoccupied with wealth and position: "He proclaimed a remission of taxes for the provinces and distributed gifts as befits a king" (Est. 2:18). Rashi says that Ahasuerus did this to honor Esther. The Talmud hints that Ahasuerus used taxes as a means of discovering Esther's nationality.[1] Later in chapter 10, when he knew of Esther's ancestry, he restored taxes. This reading suggests that the king actually cared about the details of Esther's life. A literal reading of the scroll indicates he could not have cared less. He asked her no questions about her background, but, to his credit, did ask what ailed her when she appeared before him.

Verse 2:18 also states that the king gave gifts, which Rashi writes was also to entice Esther to reveal her nationality. This correlation does

1. Megilla 13a.

not seem obvious to the reader. A tax remission and gifts would not alone soften Esther to reveal that she was Jewish unless she valued the perks of her position, which she did not. Overall, this reading seems problematic. Ahasuerus does not appear clever or astute enough to come up with such a complex plan; he left the scheming to others in his administration.

The idea of an empire-wide celebration being a time for tax breaks or some kind of relief from a government's hold on its citizens appears in the Book of Ezra in a discussion about the building of the Second Temple. Some of the Jews' enemies took it upon themselves to impede the building of the Temple, and contacted the king, urging him to halt the construction. They wrote: "Now be it known to the king that if this city is rebuilt and the walls completed, they will not pay tribute, poll tax, or land tax and in the end it will harm the kingdom" (Ezra 4:13). Gersonides elaborates there that the king demanded taxes early because he suspected that when the building and walls were completed the empowered citizens in Jerusalem would rebel and not give the king his tribute. Gersonides on Esther 2:18 takes a similar approach; he interprets the *hanaḥa*, "remission," as a break from the king's rule for one day, the equivalent of a tax free-for-all in Esther's honor.

The reinstatement of taxes is curious and hardly makes for an inspiring end to the scroll. In some synagogues, when this verse is read on Purim a low hiss spreads from pew to pew. While Haman's name is obliterated through ecstatic noisemaking, the mention of taxes is a simmering and enduring irritant, reflected by the hushed but audible sound of consternation. Haman is no longer with us, but taxes are here to stay.

Renewed taxation may reflect a summative outcome of the empire being brought under more responsible governance than the mess the king created. In the Talmud, R. Ḥanina even suggests that Ahasuerus' name "alludes to the fact that everyone became poor (*rash*) in his days, as it is stated: 'And the king Ahasuerus laid a tribute upon the land' (Est. 10:1)."[2] Ministers could no longer get away with overly privileged behavior for themselves and their constituents at the king's cost. This would be a noble bookend to the frivolous and costly party of chapter 1. Alternatively, taxation may have been mentioned so close to the end of

2. Megilla 11a.

the book because Mordecai's presence ensured that revenue was generated through taxation rather than bribery, extortion, or other unethical means. Ibn Ezra on Esther 10:1 suggests that "tribute on the mainland and the islands" is mentioned to show just how far the king's authority reached as a result of Mordecai's perspicacity. The islands, he concludes, were not part of Ahasuerus' empire, but out of fear, their inhabitants paid monetary tribute anyway. David Daube argues, contrary to scholars who see no need or reason for this chapter, that the return to taxation is a positive development to which the scroll was always leading:

> I wish to submit that the last chapter of Esther forms a conclusion worthy of the whole; and that, among some final remarks upon the happy state of Jewry under Mordecai's regime, it embodies, in 10:1, one of the great political arguments of the author – namely, that a government has more to gain by orderly taxation than by giving over the Jews to massacre and indiscriminate plunder.[3]

There are two ways to run a kingdom: in the chaotic, impulsive, overly advised fashion that Ahasuerus originally conducted government affairs or in the stable, structured way Mordecai conducted government affairs, logically and without self-interest. The only interest mentioned in these concluding three verses is that Mordecai sought the good of the kingdom and the good of his people in addition to the good of the land.[4] It is the Jew, the exile, the outsider in the court who finally brings good governance to the empire.

Levenson reads the connection between Mordecai's promotion and Ahasuerus' taxation as another reversal in the book:

> The reference to the king's promotion of the Jew (*giddelo*) again recalls the use of the same term in connection with Haman (10:2, 3:1, 5:11). The only other appearance of the word parasha ("story")

3. See David Daube, "The Last Chapter of Esther," *Jewish Quarterly Review* 37 (1946): 140.
4. If conflicted, one need not wonder what Mordecai would choose. He already let the court know that he was loyal, *and* that he would put the fate of his people first.

> in Esther – or in the whole Hebrew Bible – is in 4:7, where Mordecai tells Esther "the story of the money that Haman had offered to deposit in the royal treasury in exchange of the destruction of the Jews." Now things have altogether reversed themselves, and the story of the money that was paid to destroy the Jews for Mordecai's refusal to bow has become the story of the king's successful imposition of taxes and of Mordecai's power and grandeur.[5]

The connection between Mordecai and taxes suggests that Mordecai's place in the palace was assured because he fortified the economic strength of the kingdom, much as Joseph did in Genesis for Pharaoh. And, true to the similarities of both courtiers, they are each respectively shown as caretakers for their own people first and only then for the economic development of the ruler each served:

> Joseph sustained his father, and his brothers, and all his father's household with bread, down to the little ones. Now there was no bread in all the world, for the famine was very severe; both the land of Egypt and the land of Canaan languished because of the famine. Joseph gathered in all the money that was to be found in the land of Egypt and in the land of Canaan, as payment for the rations that were being procured, and Joseph brought the money into Pharaoh's palace. (Gen. 47:12–14)

The ideal courtier takes care of his own and brings money into the royal household. Fox draws the same conclusion:

> One message of 10:1, in light of this connection, is that not only does Jewish success benefit other subjects of the realm (in this case, by a tax relief), it is good for the royal coffers. This is a message of Gen. 47–13–26, in which Joseph delivers the Egyptians from starvation all the while bringing the entire land into the king's ownership and establishing a 20 percent income tax. Esther 10:1 may be a reflex of that passage, though different vocabulary

5. Levenson, *Esther*, 133.

> is used, and Mordecai is not said to have masterminded the taxation. (Perhaps the author is not eager to have a Jew blamed for taxation.)[6]

But before jumping too quickly to a positive conclusion, there are two aspects of the Joseph story in Genesis 47 that Fox did not mention that are relevant to the conclusion of Esther and the future of Persia's Jews. The first is economic manipulation, which is superior to corruption but manipulation nonetheless. Taxation in these narratives aided the ruling class while fomenting the inequities of society and likely imperiling the working class and the poor. As Joseph's economic preparation continued, he was able to devise a shrewd way to become an instrumental arm of government exploitation. People were willing to sell themselves into serfdom in exchange for bread:

> And when the money gave out in the land of Egypt and in the land of Canaan, all the Egyptians came to Joseph and said, "Give us bread, lest we die before your very eyes; for the money is gone!" And Joseph said, "Bring your livestock, and I will sell to you against your livestock, if the money is gone." So they brought their livestock to Joseph, and Joseph gave them bread in exchange for the horses, for the stocks of sheep and cattle, and the asses; thus he provided them with bread that year in exchange for all their livestock. And when that year was ended, they came to him the next year and said to him, "We cannot hide from my lord that, with all the money and animal stocks consigned to my lord, nothing is left at my lord's disposal save our persons and our farmland. Let us not perish before your eyes, both we and our land. Take us and our land in exchange for bread, and we with our land will be serfs to Pharaoh; provide the seed, that we may live and not die, and that the land may not become a waste." (Gen. 47:15–19)

Joseph purchased goods in exchange for food and then purchased land from the very same people in a time of drought and famine. He had the

6. Fox, *Character and Ideology*, 129–30.

farmers work their own land and give Pharaoh 20 percent of their earnings, while creating a strategy for Pharaoh, in time, to own almost all the land of Egypt. The short-term gains for the masses resulted in a terrible long-term economic situation for them. They praised Joseph for saving them, but one wonders what they said years later in the privacy of their chambers. Perhaps they cursed him because they had nothing to pass down but tenant farming to the next generation.

> So Joseph gained possession of all the farmland of Egypt for Pharaoh, every Egyptian having sold his field because the famine was too much for them; thus the land passed over to Pharaoh. And he removed the population town by town, from one end of Egypt's border to the other. Only the land of the priests he did not take over, for the priests had an allotment from Pharaoh, and they lived off the allotment which Pharaoh had made to them; therefore they did not sell their land. Then Joseph said to the people, "Whereas I have this day acquired you and your land for Pharaoh, here is seed for you to sow the land. And when harvest comes, you shall give one-fifth to Pharaoh, and four-fifths shall be yours as seed for the fields and as food for you and those in your households, and as nourishment for your children." And they said, "You have saved our lives! We are grateful to my lord, and we shall be serfs to Pharaoh." And Joseph made it into a land law in Egypt, which is still valid, that a fifth should be Pharaoh's; only the land of the priests did not become Pharaoh's. (Gen. 47:20–26)

This strategy worked for a time, but it was no guarantee of safety or security for Joseph or his brothers. Joseph was in real danger of being blamed in the future for the economic plight of the masses. The very Joseph who was credited with saving Egypt was, with his death and the appearance of a new king, not remembered at all at a time when his own people's numbers were growing and they needed the protection more than ever: "Joseph died, and all his brothers, and all that generation. But the Israelites were fertile and prolific; they multiplied and increased very greatly, so that the land was filled with them. A new king arose over Egypt who did not know Joseph" (Ex. 1:6–8). So too, a new king would one day arise over Persia who did not know Esther or Mordecai. When protection is personal and the personal connections are gone, the protection goes with it.

Money, like policy, is fickle. So are taxes and the ones who levy them. Jews in the Book of Esther must have been diligent taxpayers because Haman needed to compensate for their losses. Rashi, however, suggests that Haman's description of the Jews as not obeying the king's laws in Esther 3:8 is specifically a criticism that Jews did not pay taxes. This would go against the talmudic notion that "the laws of the land are law."[7] To be good citizens in exile, Jews are mandated to keep the laws of their host country. Those who benefit from taxes must share the responsibility of paying them. "Observe that this must be true. For [the government] cuts down trees and builds bridges, and we cross them," demonstrates another rabbinic expression. Thus, paying taxes is an obligatory burden on all. And it was a burden. One Sage concluded that since the scroll ends with taxes, it demonstrates that Ahasuerus was really "wicked from beginning to end."[8]

Gore Vidal connects taxation and societal inequity that can frame taxation in Esther as a less generous contribution of Mordecai's leadership: "The genius of our ruling class is that it has kept a majority of the people from ever questioning the inequity of a system where most people drudge along paying heavy taxes for which they get nothing in return."[9] It is evident that Ahasuerus' reign cost many Persians their money and their lives in support of a government not worth supporting. When the very last verse in Esther suggests that Mordecai was loved by most, but by inference, not by all, this may have been a subtle suggestion that there were other Jewish leaders at the time who may have been anxious lest taxation be associated with Mordecai and catalyze a groundswelling of hate directed at the Jews yet again.

7. For examples, see Nedarim 28a, Gittin 10b, Bava Kamma 113a, Bava Batra 54b–55a.
8. Introduction to Esther Rabba.
9. See Jay Parini, *Empire of Self: The Life of Gore Vidal* (New York: Doubleday, 2015), 9.

Taxes versus Tithing

The idea of taxes, a portion of one's income given away to support a collective system, is built into the Jewish superstructure of communal living, called not taxes but tithing. The tithe amount is a relatively fixed amount so that, unlike taxes, it did not become onerous, but was still significant enough to create a sense of obligation and ownership for all within a community. Tithing appears as early as Abraham. It was money donated to God, so to speak: "And blessed be God, Most High, who has delivered your enemies into your hand. And Abram gave him a tenth of everything" (Gen. 14:20). Much later, as tithing became codified in Jewish law, it was a means of supporting the spiritual framework of the community and helping the poor and vulnerable:

> At the end of every three years you shall bring out the tithes of your produce in the same year and lay it up in your towns. And the Levite, because he has no portion or inheritance with you, and the sojourner, the fatherless, and the widow, who are in your towns shall eat and will be filled, that the Lord may bless you in all the work of your hand that you do. (Deut. 14:28–29)

The Hebrew Bible made explicit the condition that if these laws were carefully and vigilantly observed, poverty would be eliminated: "There shall be no needy among you – since the Lord your God will bless you in the land that the Lord your God is giving you as a hereditary portion" (Deut. 15:4). In order to keep tithing in the foreground and as almost reflexive behavior, all were adjured to make tithing inherent to the act of working:

> When you reap your harvest in your field and forget a sheaf in the field, you shall not go back to get it. It shall be for the sojourner, the fatherless, and the widow, that the Lord your God may bless you in all the work of your hands. When you beat your olive trees, you shall not go over them again. It shall be for the sojourner, the fatherless, and the widow. When you gather the grapes of your vineyards, you shall not strip it afterward. It shall be for the sojourner, the fatherless, and the widow. (Deut. 24:19–22)

The consequences of not contributing to a culture of tithing and, even worse, exploiting the poor would have reverberations for one's own harvest, as the prophet Amos admonishes:

> Therefore because you trample on the poor and you exact taxes of grain from him, you have built houses of hewn stone, but you shall not dwell in them; you have planted pleasant vineyards, but you shall not drink their wine. (Amos 5:11)

Here, in the prophet's exhortation, the difference between taxes and tithing is apparent. Tithing was a mechanism for creating a more just and compassionate society by leveling economic inequities for all. The societal ideal of eradicating poverty is described eloquently in Deuteronomy. The description of a welfare society is one where exploitation is minimized, where covenantal responsibilities are highlighted, and where wealth is seen as a divine blessing designed to be shared to overcome disparities:

> There shall be no needy among you – since the Lord your God will bless you in the land that the Lord your God is giving you as a hereditary portion – if only you heed the Lord your God and take care to keep all this instruction that I enjoin upon you this day. (Deut. 15:4–5)

> If, however, there is a needy person among you, one of your kinsmen in any of your settlements in the land that the Lord your God is giving you, do not harden your heart and shut your hand against your needy kinsman. Rather, you must open your hand and lend him sufficient for whatever he needs. (Deut. 15:7–8)

By contrast, taxes, as they appeared in the Book of Esther, were arbitrary financial burdens placed on the masses to support the lifestyle of a king and his court without making explicit any benefits to the population at large. They were lessened when the king was happy, raised when the king needed more money, and, as Haman's silver exchange made apparent, even interchangeable with human life when circumstances called for it.

The scroll presents no means by which taxes aided society, making readers wonder what life would have been like for the average Persian living under Ahasuerus' rule. That Mordecai climbed up the political ladder speaks well of him, but also raises questions about how this exile's talents were utilized once he became a courtier. The dream of success in the diaspora should not be to support a ruler like Ahasuerus but to return to a biblical foundation of moral economics. The Joseph narratives provide apt warning. Clever courtiers can protect their own while augmenting the wheels of government but risk exploiting the people in the process. This may backfire on the courtier and on those he or she represents. In time, whatever influence is achieved will matter little. The courtier will be resented by the people and then forgotten.

Respected by *Most*: The Courtier's Dilemma

> For Mordecai the Jew ranked next to King Ahasuerus and was highly regarded by the Jews and popular with most of his brethren; he sought the good of his people and interceded for the welfare of all his kindred. (Est. 10:3)

The Book of Esther ends with Mordecai, an appropriate way to balance and support Esther's rise to power. If one courtier with influence is good, two are even better. While Esther was queen, Mordecai was close to the king. So great was he that Mordecai appeared in the journals of a powerful foreign governing body. Gersonides on 10:2 contends that the formation of royal records should be read as a question – "Are they not written in the chronicles of the kings of Media and Persia?" – to suggest that what was specifically recorded was not only the exploits of the story but also the status and stature of Mordecai. For an exile to be ranked next to or second to the king, as the word *mishneh* is commonly translated, was almost too good to be true. One even suspects that the brevity of this three-verse chapter in relation to the nine that preceded it is to create a full stop at the peak of Jewish political ambition and status. The book aims for a happy ending. One more verse, and all could unravel and deteriorate.

The two-letter word that opens the very last verse of the scroll, *ki*, deserves attention. In his second commentary, Ibn Ezra focuses not on the word *mishneh* but on the subordinate conjunction *ki*, which means "for," "because," or "like." Traditional interpreters translated the word as "because," implying that because Mordecai had achieved this eminent position, he was highly regarded by his people and able to intercede on their behalf to the king. This also made him suspect in the eyes of some who questioned the durability of his Jewish commitments because of the royal demands placed on him. Ibn Ezra, however, reads *ki* as "like." "The king," he writes, "is not like anyone else, but his second is the closest approximation." Ibn Ezra's reading is compelling given the context. Mordecai was highly regarded not just because of his relationship to the king. He was also popular among his people before this verse for having kindled their salvation. By suggesting that he was *like* the king, the verse implies that his people saw him that way. His proximity to power made him like the king of the Jews. Where the book opens with the visual fixation on the palace and the party within, on a place and an activity, it closes with a person, a saintly Jew, an émigré who was responsible for his people's deliverance.

It is this last thought that shapes and informs the end of the *Megilla*. As the Book of Esther ends with the flourish of Mordecai's long-anticipated promotion in the royal court, his place among his own community was secure but not entirely. The insecurity in exile is related not only to the likelihood that safety will be short-lived because of a change in politics or regime. There is also internal ambivalence. *Rov eḥav velo khol eḥav* – Mordecai was respected by most but not all – the verse suggests. The intimation that Mordecai may not have been beloved by all irks the reader because he is beloved to us. It suggests that despite a remarkable political coup, beginning with the rescue of Ahasuerus from conspirators, the deliverance of the Jews, the ridding of their mortal enemies from the top down, and the power that both Esther and Mordecai enjoyed in the royal court, Mordecai was still not loved and admired unanimously by his own people. We may conclude from this that no person can be loved by everyone. It is impossible to make all people happy, especially as a leader. This, then, would reflect poorly on the Jews who did not admire Mordecai rather than on the courtier. Rashi, however, demonstrates that this was not quite the issue. He cites the Talmud in his explanation of the last verse: "But not by all his brethren: Some of the Sanhedrin, this teaches us, separated from him because he was too close to royalty and neglected his learning."[1] The midrash is unequivocal. The discomfort with Mordecai was not from the masses but from the Jewish elite. The business of politics was a distraction from the primacy of scholarship. It is learning that makes the Jewish leader. Mordecai's prestige elicited suspicion from his scholarly colleagues; there were distinct and perhaps inevitable lapses in Mordecai's priorities that took him away from his former devotion and commitments.

Ibn Ezra is not troubled by this seeming diminution of Mordecai. He writes in the second version of his commentary that Mordecai was a great scholar, rejecting the midrashic view above. In his first version, he writes on the last verse that it is simply "not possible for someone to please everyone because of the envy humans feel for each other." For those preoccupied with pleasing others, this message can be hard to swallow. Ibn Ezra regards this verse as a negative statement about Mordecai's detractors rather than a criticism of Mordecai. In the second version of his commentary, he moves away from the emotion of jealousy and suggests that the impossibility of pleasing all is inherent in the very nature of public service, since each person has his or her own distinctive needs. Taking care of one constituent will naturally make a leader unable to address the needs of another. Ibn Ezra adds that despite Mordecai's enhanced power, he maintained his modesty and humility, likening him to Moses. In addition to doing good, Mordecai "desired good for his people." This suggests that even when Mordecai lacked the requisite authority to do good for his people, his intent was always to help.

Ibn Ezra also translates *zaro*, "his seed," as a possible reference not to Mordecai's people generally but rather to his specific children, for

1. Megilla 16b. It is not uncommon for the Sages to imagine biblical characters as projections of their own occupations and dispositions. Here, Mordecai is guilty of prioritizing the court over the study hall. We find a similar phenomenon when Isaac was not mentioned as coming off the mount in Gen. 22. A midrash (Genesis Rabba 56:11) suggests he was studying in the yeshiva of Shem and Eber. Later, Jacob is even said to have kicked inside his mother's womb in the direction of a study hall when Rebecca passed one (*Yalkut Shimoni, Toledot* 110).

whom he sought benefits, perhaps even hoping to give them some of the political advantages he enjoyed in the royal household. Ibn Ezra suggests this reading without any concern about nepotism. Even so, the order of the verse, Ibn Ezra notes, places Mordecai's intercession on behalf of his people before any privileges he bequeathed to his own progeny. Rabbi Baruch HaLevi Epstein, author of the *Torah Temima* commentary, ties Mordecai's request for peace for his people – *dover shalom* – to his earlier inquiries about the welfare of Esther in her early days in the palace: "Every single day Mordecai would walk about in front of the court of the harem, to learn how Esther was faring (*ladaat et shelom Esther*) and what was happening to her" (Est. 2:11). The parallel phrase *ladaat et shelom Esther* suggests that Mordecai did not change an enduring disposition that characterized his leadership. He was a seeker of peace.

Alsheikh poses difficult questions about the need for the final verse and the curiosities of its content. On the surface, this ending adds little to our scroll. We already know from an earlier chapter that the events were written down in the chronicles of the Persians and Medes. We also know that Mordecai was well regarded by his people and sought out their good because that's the role Mordecai played in the story from his very first appearance. Alsheikh is also mystified by the three populations segmented in the verse: his brethren, his people, and his seed. To answer, he takes us back to the very beginning of the book to the magnificent banquet where no expense was spared and no yoke of taxes was mentioned. At that time, the need for financial tribute may not have been urgent or necessary or, more likely, Ahasuerus, in his popularity bid, sought to be a highly regarded leader rather than a fiscally sensible one. Financial security is ultimately what Mordecai brought to the court.

The mention of the chronicles in 10:2, suggests Alsheikh, signifies that Mordecai's achievements, with all their *tokef*, or power, were known not only by the Jews and by Ahasuerus but across Persia and Media. His successes were not just the talk of Shushan and the court, since 10:2 states specifically: "All his mighty and powerful acts, and a full account of the greatness to which the king advanced Mordecai." Here the stress is on all his might and heroism, which went far beyond the Purim story. The scroll offers us only a thin slice of Mordecai's greatness. People all over the empire and beyond wanted to know about Mordecai and his achievements. This explains the outgrowth of interest mentioned in the verse. Even so, the verses continue to state the adoration for him by his fellow Jews. Despite Mordecai's high-profile position, he made his role as head of the Sanhedrin primary. It is in this capacity, Alsheikh implies, and not as a courtier, that Mordecai was not beloved by all. Judges are popular with those who win their cases, less so with those who lose. Nevertheless, Mordecai sought good for all, even those who were unkind to him. Too often, Alsheikh posits, those in power become haughty and promote family members and friends. In the description in 10:3, Mordecai's closest relatives came last on the list.

On Esther 10:3, Ashkenazi offers a similar, if briefer, portrayal: "When it says that Mordecai was great in the eyes of the Jews, this refers to Torah. If it referred to his appointment as second to the king, he obviously would have been revered by the Jews." Ashkenazi wants to assure readers that Mordecai's reputation among his own was first as scholar, not as politician. He always kept Jewish identity foremost in his mind and actions. According to Ashkenazi, Mordecai even modified the command to drink as an expression of joy in Esther 9:23: "Mordecai wanted everyone to drink until they forgot about the exile, but not, of course, so that they would forget about Jerusalem."

Mordecai in this closing is depicted both in the text and through classical interpreters as a great and humble Jewish leader, imbued with piety and good judgment, who did his best to bring about the redemption of the Jews while remaining committed to the king's service. Mordecai is able to pilot the dual allegiances of his courtier position deftly and bring dignity to the king and to his people. As a result, Mordecai became the emblem of what all Jews should be: loyal Jews and upright subjects.

Most end the story here, tying up the stresses of a plot thick with intrigue and action into a neat bow of relief. The spotlight lands on our hero, rather than our heroine. Her golden moment came when the king extended his golden scepter, and she began the intricate process of asking for deliverance. But once Ahasuerus handed over Haman's ring to Mordecai, it is his role, rather than hers, that occupies center stage. She will, of course, continue to be important as the king's favored consort, but not critical in the running of the king's political affairs. The book's end invites us to imagine Mordecai as courtier *after* dispensing with the

Jewish story, suggesting that his court activities and adventures made him an increasingly powerful and important figure, far beyond his early assistance in saving the king's life and the lives of his Jewish brothers and sisters. As court life settled, Mordecai's contributions became increasingly valuable.

But one wonders if this end might just be read ironically. What could possibly be a greater contribution than saving the king's life? Could the scroll's conclusion suggest that Mordecai's new greatness lay in mere taxation and that when he was not loved by all, it had to do with the Jews themselves being taxed or assimilating with their Persian neighbors, all while Mordecai stood at the helm of this campaign? Life was surely better for the Jews of Persia in chapter 10 than it was in the book's midsection, but it is unclear if it was qualitatively better than at the book's beginning. A dual message about diaspora life is nestled into this concluding verse as if it ended with a slight addition not mentioned: Mordecai was powerful, sought the good of his people, and had an excellent royal stage from which to do so, *but* being second to a foreign potentate in someone else's empire could never be as free and meaningful as having one's own independence and right to self-determine, even in a land far less grand. Persia may have become more hospitable to its Jews for a time, but it would never be home.

Courtier Tales

Mordecai's role at the end of the Book of Esther suggests an identity that must traverse conflicting and competing narratives of persecution and success. Lawrence M. Wills explores the possibility of a biblical narrative genre which he calls "the Jew in the court of the foreign king" or "wisdom court legend."[2] Although scholars before Wills highlighted aspects of this theme as it appears in Hebrew biblical literature, most noticeably in the succession of Joseph, Daniel 1–6, and the Book of Esther, they did not develop it as an independent genre. Even during the talmudic era, there was a sense that these texts shared important literary parallels even if the parallels were recorded in a rather inchoate fashion.

2. See Lawrence M. Wills, *The Jew in the Court of the Foreign King*, Harvard Dissertations in Religion (Minneapolis: Fortress Press, 1990).

As an example, in the Talmud, as discussed in an earlier chapter, Daniel makes an oblique appearance in Esther as the minor character Hatakh, creating a parallel between the two figures.

Wills explores the courtier genre and also compares it to antecedent and parallel stories in other ancient Near Eastern cultures. Specifically, Wills believes that the Book of Esther may have been influenced by a strong Persian interest in court legends.[3] John J. Collins takes this a step further and suggests that, given the political structure of Jewish life, a court background for a biblical narrative would have evolved only in the diaspora.

> The original composition of a group of tales which are set in a royal court can most plausibly be located in a milieu where such a court existed and was a focus of attention. It is true that the genre of the court tale was widely known and that such tales could conceivably be composed as pure fictions anywhere. However, there is no apparent reason why Palestinian Jews in the post exilic period should choose such a setting for their tales. The problems with which the tales deal were not likely to arise in the theocratic administration in Jerusalem. On the other hand, those problems were of daily and vital interest to Jews in the Diaspora, and especially to Jews who functioned as courtiers or aspired to be 'wise men' after the manner of the Chaldeans and other Gentile wise men.[4]

Collins believes that such royal tales were anomalous in the Land of Israel. Where they would have been matters of urgency and intrigue in Shushan, they were of no importance in Jerusalem. Jews in the diaspora, however, needed them.

Wills utilizes an interesting distinction (developed by himself and W. Lee Humphreys) between "contests," where a wise but undistinguished person achieves a position of rank in the court through

3. Ibid., 194.
4. John J. Collins, "The Court Tales in Daniel and the Development of Apocalyptic," *JBL* 94, no. 2 (June 1975): 220.

good judgment, and "conflicts," where a courtier enjoys power in the court but is persecuted by other courtiers and finally promoted by the king.[5] Courtier tales, because they involve court intrigues and present battlegrounds of political tension, may use both the contest and conflict approaches in the same story. The Book of Esther involves both Esther and Mordecai in the "contest" position and Haman in the "conflict" position, although Haman was never vindicated by the king. The fact that these court legends involve foreign ruling powers is not coincidental.

Arndt Meinhold calls both the Joseph and Esther narratives diasporanovelle as descriptive of the genre.[6] The reader wonders what Jewish destiny will be in a foreign royal court and what authority, if any, the courtier can exercise to save his people or ingratiate them to the king.

> Court legends offer a response to ethnic competition and a rather benign response to inequities and restrictions on social mobility... they promulgate a wisdom teaching to the effect that the person marked by wisdom receives the just reward, even in pagan society...they affirm a theology of weakness and also a "psychology" of weakness, that is, they provide a wish fulfillment of a scribal ideal of wisdom and righteousness.[7]

Such tales create an aspiration of power, paradoxically showcasing the actual weakness of the diaspora Jew. Levenson offers a broader summation but also one which transforms the notion of weakness used by Wills to one of boldness of identity.

> The scene with which the Masoretic Esther closes is one for which Jewish communities in the Diaspora have always longed: Jews living in harmony and mutual goodwill with the Gentile majority, under Jewish leaders who are respected and admired by the rulers,

5. For more, see W. Lee Humphreys, "A Life-Style for Diaspora: A Study of the Tales of Esther and Daniel," *JBL* 92 (1973): 211–23; and Collins, "The Court Tales," 218–34.
6. Arndt Meinhold, "Die Gattung der Josephgeschichte und des Estherbuches: Diasporanovelle, I, II," *ZAW* 87 (1975): 306–24; 88 (1976): 79–93, as cited by Wills, *The Jew in the Court of the Foreign King*, 9–10.
7. Ibid., 203–4.

> yet who are openly identified with the Jewish community and unashamed to advance its interest and speak out in its defense.[8]

Humphreys posits that at the foundations of this genre are "tales of a particular type, which, along with their considerable entertainment value, develop a particular theological emphasis addressed to the emerging Jewish communities of the Persian and Hellenistic Diaspora. They suggest a certain life for the Jew in his foreign environment."[9] What that lifestyle is, Humphreys clarifies: "Esther and Mordecai skillfully seek the royal benefit and in so doing deliver their people. The tale does not permit any tension to develop between their double loyalty to king and coreligionists; the actual benefit of each party coincides."[10] Dual loyalty to one's homeland and one's nation is what such biblical courtier tales promote. It is not coincidental that the book closes with the addition of taxes and the praise of Mordecai. For the Jew to succeed in the diaspora, particularly the courtier Jew, requires that what is good for the Jews is also good for the ruling power in a harmonistic rather than dialectic sense:

> Through the vehicle of this popular form of tale there is expressed a particular stance that affirms for the Jew of the Diaspora the possibility of living a creative and rich life in the foreign environment, as part of the complex social, political and economic dynamics of that world, and also of remaining a devoted and loyal member of his community of fellow Jews. As in the Joseph narrative, there are two foci for the courtier's life: the king and his own people.[11]

Court narratives involve distinct geographic locations and well-defined political and religious tensions. Collins also argues that specific, deliberate structures frame such narratives:

---

8. Levenson, *Esther*, 133–34.
9. Humphreys, "A Life-Style for Diaspora," 211.
10. Ibid., 215.
11. Ibid., 216.

> a. The tale may emphasize the wisdom or ability of the courtier. In this case the crisis which provides the setting and the specific nature of the message or action of the courtier are of secondary importance.
>
> b. The tale may focus on the drama of danger or humiliation followed by salvation. The wise man is for some reason threatened or imprisoned. However, he is eventually released and exalted more greatly than before. This type of story can serve to highlight the wisdom or skill of the courtier but can also focus on the dramatic manner in which his fate is reversed.
>
> c. The tale may be used as a vehicle for the message of the courtier. The message may be cast in the form of proverbial sayings or the interpretation of dreams.[12]

Collins' theory clearly works well in the stories of Joseph, Esther, Mordecai, and Daniel. Characters are described as wise and competent. Esther and Daniel are taken to the court not of their own volition and become trapped in an outsider's palace. Mordecai and the Jews are slated for extermination. Joseph goes from pit to prison. All use ingenuity to find a way out, and all use their courtier position for the benefit of the people. Dreams play a key role for Joseph, Daniel, and Mordecai in the Apocryphal text.

In the Esther and Joseph narratives, both are given two names, Hebrew and pagan (Gen. 41:45 and Est. 2:7) and both are described using the same terms of beauty (Gen. 39:6 and Est. 2:7). Both are married to gentile royalty or aristocracy with the text noticeably withholding judgment. The seemingly coincidental nature of events in both narratives, the portrait of the foreign leader as trusting but perhaps naive and easily influenced, the role of clothing, and the ultimate success of the Jewish leader and the Jewish nation on foreign soil all confirm the likelihood that the structure of Esther had its literary antecedents in the Pentateuch. Few medieval commentators, however, compared the two. Scholars fre-

12. Collins, "The Court Tales," 219.

quently discern close affinities in the language, themes, and motifs of the two narrative accounts. Berg conducts an extensive comparison of the thematic and linguistic similarities in the narratives.[13] One story in particular, that of Joseph, is often compared to Esther and viewed as a literary antecedent.[14] She lists the verses that draw linguistic parallels:[15]

Genesis	**Esther**
41:42–43	6:11
39:10	3:4
44:34	8:6
41:34–37	2:3–4
43:14	4:16
40:20	1:3, 2:18
44:24	8:6
43:31, 45:1	5:10
50:3	2:12

These linguistic parallels are significant in the way in which they draw thematic parallels. In this regard, Berg adds:

> Both tales are set at the court of a foreign monarch and concern Jewish heroes who rise to prominence at those courts. The heroes suffer a decline in their personal fortunes as a direct result of their positions at court. The heroes, however, overcome their misfortunes, and their success provides the means by which their people are saved. In addition, each story refers to two eunuchs who act against the king (cf. Gen. 40:1–3; Est. 2:21–23). These incidents involving the eunuchs both come to the king's attention and contribute to a reversal in the personal fortunes of the Isra-

13. Berg, *The Book of Esther*, 123–65.
14. Ibid., 123.
15. These were taken from a German study Berg quotes on Esther, Joseph, and Daniel done by Ludwig M. Rosenthal in 1895, "Die Josephsgeschichte mit den Buchern Ester und Daniel verglichen," *Zeitschrift fur die alttestamentliche Wissenschaft* 15: 278–84. For more on the linguistic comparisons, see Moshe Gan, "The Book of Esther in Light of the Story of Joseph in Egypt," *Tarbiz* 31 (1961–1962): 144–49.

> elite servants. This turning point directly results from the king's disturbed sleep, when the monarch (or his servant) remembers the Israelites (cf. Gen. 41:9–45; Est. 6:1–11). In both stories, the heroes eventually are rewarded for their service to the king by the transference of royal power to them. Both accounts also depict a banquet scene where invited guests (Joseph's brothers, Haman) do not know the true identity of their host/hostess. The revelation of Joseph's and Esther's true identities results in a change in the personal lives and fates of their guests. Finally, both stories mention punishment by hanging.[16]

These parallels are not coincidental even though, as Berg points out, not every detail in one narrative is given the same degree of attention or primacy in the other. The comparison between the stories demonstrates that the theme of a wise diaspora courtier in a foreign court offered important insights into leadership, the path to influence, and the way one leverages one's position for good. Esther is likened to Joseph and assumes the role of the Jew who "initially passes for a Gentile in the foreign court and eventually uses his or her high status to rescue his or her endangered people."[17] In a critique of Berg's theory, Glendon E. Bryce questions the reliance the Esther story has on the Joseph narrative:

> Is the dependence of Esther upon the Joseph story, given the rich narrative imagination of the Orient, either likely or even necessary? Do a general setting, formulaic motifs, some similar themes and stylistic parallels add up to dependence?.... Is it not more probable that the general similarities between Esther and the Joseph story are due to the social setting in which they have circulated or to folkloristic channels of transmission?[18]

---

16. Berg, *The Book of Esther*, 126.
17. Levenson, *Esther*, 61.
18. Glendon E. Bryce, Review of Sandra Beth Berg, *The Book of Esther: Motifs, Themes and Structure*, *JBL* 100, no. 2 (1981): 276.

Bryce agrees with Wills that it is not necessarily the similarity between the characters but the similarity of setting that provides the narrative parallels. By contrast, Baldwin contends that each similar detail in the stories of Joseph and Esther on its own is not remarkable but cumulatively, the result is impressive. She suggests dependence on the earlier courtier tale in Esther: "If the older story is well known it may suggest to the author a paradigm for the later situation, and he may deliberately 'borrow' the phraseology because its associations recall the kind of message he wants to convey."[19] In exploring the role of Jew as courtier in the Hebrew Bible and in the Book of Esther specifically, we find the pride, authority, and self-importance of gentile courtiers translated into a very different experience for the Jews in the royal court than for their gentile colleagues. Court life for Jews generated anxiety, suspicion, and vigilance. It also conferred wanted and unwanted attention and influence.

19. Baldwin, *Esther*, 26.

The End That Wasn't Written

> All his mighty and powerful acts, and a full account of the greatness to which the king advanced Mordecai, are recorded in the Annals of the Kings of Media and Persia. (Est. 10:2)

In offering us an abbreviated ending of only three verses, the Book of Esther invites us to complete the chapter and the story of the Jews of Shushan ourselves. The Talmud indicates that Ahasuerus died an untimely death not long after the story unraveled, perhaps suggesting that this king had outlived his usefulness, having played a critical role in the potential decimation and subsequent redemption of the Jews in his empire.[1] Mordecai's and Esther's deaths are nowhere recorded in the Hebrew Bible, but legend has it they were both buried in Hamadan, Iran. It was and still is the custom of Jews in the region to visit their graves before Purim to pay their respects.

Because the Book of Esther ends so abruptly, I have devised four alternative endings. Each of the suggested endings cohere with other endings recorded in the Hebrew Bible elsewhere, making each highly plausible.

1. Megilla 11b.

> *After Mordecai increased taxation, the people grumbled against the Jews, and the enmity they had in the days of Haman was renewed. At this time, Hatakh was elevated to chief steward of the royal house. He suggested that the king celebrate his renewed coffers with another royal feast. Thus the king invited all of his officers in all his satrapies to come to Shushan for a seven-day banquet. And a proclamation was written and delivered throughout the empire in the language of each and every nation that all were to drink without limit. After Ahasuerus was full with wine, he asked for his wife Esther to be brought to his chambers before his nobles to display her beauty.*

> *Esther and Ahasuerus had a child, and the child's name was Darius. Esther went in to the king unsummoned. And the king laid forth his scepter and said, "What is your wish, Queen Esther? Up to half the kingdom and it shall be given to you." And Esther said, "My plea and my request, if I have found favor in your eyes, is that Darius inherit the throne in the fullness of days." And the king was filled with rage: "The son of Vashti is the firstborn heir. It is to him that I bequeath the kingdom."*

> *And it was recorded in the annals of Persia and Media that Ahasuerus was old and was gathered unto his ancestors. And his son took the royal throne. This son was not like his father and did evil in God's eyes. Thus a new king had risen over one hundred and twenty-seven provinces who did not know Mordecai and Esther. The Jews of Shushan had grown numerous as the stars in the sky and the dust of the land. The king said to his people, "Look, the Israelite people are too numerous for us. Let us deal wisely with them so that they do not increase lest in a time of war they join forces against us and rise up from the ground."*

In the first scenario, the people of Persia respond to Mordecai's increased taxation by blaming the Jews and renewing the tensions that Haman had fostered when he was in charge. The cycle begins again. The Jewish victory banquet is not the last banquet in the Book of Esther's pages. With the many changes across his empire and his fiscal situation stabilized,

Ahasuerus celebrated his enhanced security on the throne. Hatakh, who was promoted as a result of his assistance to Mordecai, suggested throwing a party and the king quickly acquiesced, as he usually did to the guidance of his ministers. This time, out of respect for Mordecai, the goblets of the Temple were not used, yet, even so, the drinking was without limit, and the king, never one to miss a moment of intoxication, soon found himself doing what he always did, calling for his beautiful wife in the heat of pleasure to display herself to all of his courtiers. Mordecai paced within the palace walls, sending messages to Esther through the vast network of eunuchs to have her say no. All knew the fate of Vashti, but to have Esther appear would be an indignity to her and to his nation. The king heard about Mordecai's disobedience and gathered his other ministers for counsel and to draw lots.

The second ending reminds us that Esther was to have children with Ahasuerus, as did all good and fertile queens. Up to now, the fairy tale of the Jewish orphan who became a princess over the sprawling Persian Empire was still a fantasy. Frozen as is, the story seems magical. Yet when the fairy dust settled, Esther had to perform her duties and produce children to add to the ever-increasing number of the king's progeny. This was a central responsibility of female royals. With children came battles over heirs and spares. Esther, no stranger to making her needs foremost in the king's mind, would want to secure a place of influence for her son to continue the legacy she and Mordecai worked so judiciously to obtain for her people, hearkening to Bathsheba's plea for her son Solomon to inherit the throne. A review of Kings I and II and Chronicles I and II demonstrates how common and deadly the battle over an heir could become.

In the last scenario, Ahasuerus, whose age is never revealed in the Book of Esther, may have been a very old man in search of a virginal bride. We have seen this story on David's deathbed, where the aging king was warmed by the virgin Avishag (I Kings 1:3–4). If Ahasuerus was indeed an old man, the likelihood is that Esther would outlive him, especially given his hedonistic lifestyle. A new king might not be kindly disposed to Esther, Mordecai, or the Jewish people. Regime changes in the Bible and throughout Jewish history are always a time of high anxiety for the Jews, whose very existence was often at the mercy of the reigning monarch. This particular ending, which is no ending, would have been lifted straight off the pages of Exodus chapter 1.

Instead of these options, we close with a triumphant Mordecai. Introduced as an exile, we bid him farewell as a Persian leader. As readers, we are left to wonder, if the chance came, would Mordecai go back to his beloved homeland? Life was suddenly sweet in his diasporic bubble, and the position he occupied would be hard to replicate among his own. But perhaps after years as second-in-command, he would have seen the opportunity to influence Ahasuerus and achieve certain objectives for his people that would lead them and him back to the Land of Israel. That ending might read this way:

> *Darius the Great, the ruler of one hundred and twenty-seven provinces, in the first month on the fifteenth day of the first month, gave permission for the Jews to return to Judah and rebuild the Temple in Jerusalem. These are the people of Persia who came up from the captive exiles who were carried to Babylon and returned to Jerusalem, each to his own city: Mordecai, son of Jair son of Shimei son of Kish, a Benjaminite who had been exiled from Jerusalem and carried into exile with King Jeconiah of Judah by the evil King Nebuchadnezzar of Babylon, returned to his ancestral home. With him were the Levites, the singers, the gatekeepers, the Temple servants, the chiefs of the clans, them and their sons, and their households, their horses, their camels, their donkeys. On arriving at the House of the Lord in Jerusalem, they gave freewill offerings according to their means and donated to the treasury. The Temple servants took up residence in their towns and all Israel in their cities.*

These words are paraphrased from the Book of Ezra, chapter 2, with embellishments to add in our story. Mordecai, in this scenario, led the charge back to Jerusalem, where he could once again sit on the Sanhedrin in a Temple chamber. Esther, however, would have had to stay with her husband, forcing uncle and niece to part ways.

Rabbi Binyamin Lau suggests an alternative ending for Esther that aligns with the emergence of Zionism. His ending takes us to another biblical book:

> The solution the Megillah presents is not really much of a solution. The return to Zion, the establishment of an independent polity, and the attempt to construct the Third Temple require that we continue on to a "non-existent" eleventh chapter of the Megillah. In truth that chapter indeed exists, though it appears at the beginning of the book of Nehemiah. These chapters are an important addition to the Megillah, and they pick up, both chronologically and spiritually, where the Megillah leaves off. Nehemiah approaches the king who inherited the throne from Ahashverosh and asks him permission to build the ramparts of Jerusalem. This wave of *aliyah* to reinforce the second Temple serves as the corrective of the story of Diaspora Jews who forgot their homeland and obscured their identity. If the story of the Megillah is a story of chance and "the lottery," then the story of Nehemiah is the transition from chance to destiny.[2]

In this reading, it is Nehemiah who wrote the last chapter of the Book of Esther, transitioning his people back to their homeland after exile in Shushan, where any power the Jews held was merely a propaedeutic to the governmental autonomy Jews would enjoy when the shackles of exile were removed.

To this end, Rabbi Lau makes the bold suggestion that the first two chapters of Nehemiah be read on Purim afternoon to continue the story and ensure that life in the diaspora is neither the end nor the goal of the *Megilla*. Our success story in a sliver of history/fantasy in the Persian Empire may be worth retelling, but it cannot set the actual precedent for Jewish living. Even so, the story is powerful as it stands. Abraham Cohen suggests that the Jewish people's success makes Esther a religious text: "God was not overt, His word not direct, and His face not revealed, still, behind the veil of Purim, God's providence toward his people, would uphold them against adversary and ideological force alike."[3] Baldwin observes that the holiday "generates unfailing enthusi-

2. Lau, introduction to Eisenberg, *The Vanishing Jew*, 15.
3. Abraham D. Cohen, "'*Hu Ha-goral*': The Religious Significance of Esther," *Judaism* 23 (1974): 94.

asm and keeps alive Jewish belief in God's continuing providence, despite all the victimization."[4] She concludes this passage with six words that sum up the emotion Esther inspires each time it is read in public. "In Jewish eyes the book lives."[5]

It lives in Jewish hearts, but not for the reasons Baldwin assumes, namely, that the persecution it depicts and the victimization its characters suffer play themselves out in history again and again. This is true, but Esther is not the only biblical story to reflect this sad and repeated predicament. The story of Esther lives because it reflects more than a hope for the anticipated future; it portrays a community in exile unafraid to display its influence and power.

The Actual Ending

The actual ending we have consists of three unusual verses that seem, on the surface, disconnected from each other. Why end the story here? Surely there was more to say about the future of the Jews in Persia. The abrupt end may be a literary device that itself suggests an underlying message in the story. In this diaspora tale, the author chose to end on a happy note. The Jews were a protected nation. Ending the story here might allow future readers to delude themselves into believing that life would stay this way. By cutting off the story so sharply, the author suggests that such an idyllic story line cannot possibly be sustained. The book stops here for narrative purposes, but there is no real end. The historical story of the Jews will, no doubt, cycle downward again. One can only hope and pray that as the story continues it will contain less drama and suffering than before. If the ending is essentially a random demarcation, then let it be a satisfying one.

By drawing attention to itself, the book's ending invites readers to consider their own experiences in the diaspora and the future for Jews there. Many commentators throughout Jewish history did just that, reading into this ancient tale the conditions of their own expulsions. A mindful reader in the diaspora might apply the book and its sudden ending to his or her own family narrative in an exile that often did not

4. Baldwin, *Esther*, 37.
5. Ibid.

seem like exile until the cycle turned downward once more. Those living in the State of Israel, however, must read the story annually with a sense of relief. Today, there is a refuge for Jews to call home, a place for our own happy endings and a place for so many miraculous beginnings.

> They say there is a country
> A land that flows with sunlight.
> Where is that country?
> Where is that sunlight?[6]

6. Saul Tchernichovsky, "They Say There Is a Country," in *Modern Hebrew Poetry: A Bilingual Anthology*, ed. Ruth Finer Mintz (Berkeley: University of California Press, 1966), 70.

Epilogue

Dressed in a contemporary idiom, the Book of Esther could easily have been written today because what was true of yesterday will likely be true of tomorrow.

This story's surface impossibility is captured in an unusual and evocative object. I first saw a *Megillat Hitler* at the United States Holocaust Memorial Museum in Washington, D.C. Initially I was confused and thought the museum had made a mistake. In front of me was a traditional looking scroll, parchment wrapped around a wooden holder. What was a scroll of Esther doing in the Holocaust section of the museum? Moments later, I understood. A clever calligrapher replaced the Book of Esther with narratives of the Holocaust. The medium is the message. The original scroll contained a story of baseless hatred and persecution toward the Jews, and the scroll of Hitler did the same. Of course, there was one major difference in the scrolls. The Book of Esther has a happy ending, at least temporarily. Justice was eventually served, and the Jews survived and thrived. Not a single Jewish death was recorded. The same could not be said of any Holocaust narrative. *Megillat Hitler* reminds us that stories of persecution are easily interchangeable. When my children were young they often confused details of Hanukka, Purim, and Passover, particularly their villains. Haman died trying to capture the Jews when they crossed the Reed Sea. We light candles on Hanukka because a mean old king named Ahasuerus would not tolerate our religious practices.

These are easy enough mistakes to make because, in some way, all of our shared stories and collective memories center around a monstrous scoundrel and end with a devastating dimension of trauma, loss, and surprise victory. In the Holocaust scroll, someone collapsed time and saw in Haman the seeds of evil that would one day reemerge in Hitler.

Yad Vashem, Israel's national Holocaust museum, also has a *Megillat Hitler* in their collection. Theirs is only seven chapters long. According to museum archives,[1] the scroll was penned by a teacher and *sofer* (scribe) from Casablanca named Prosper Hassine. It was owned by a family who fled restrictions in Florence in 1939 and moved to Casablanca to avoid the changing status of Jews across Europe. Their copy of *Megillat Hitler* was preserved with a copy of *Megillat Esther,* binding together the message of both documents. Rather than allowing Hitler's answer to the Jewish question to remain the last word, in this version, the Book of Esther stands as the better outcome.

Hassine later retold the story of this tragic event in four chapters, highlighting Hitler's rise to power, the political changes spreading throughout Europe as a result of Nazi occupation, the murder of the Jews, and the requisitioning of Jewish property. The last three chapters feature the history of North Africa's Jews and their liberation by the Allies.[2] But the story, despite many parallels to its ancient predecessor, has a different ending. The author of *Megillat Hitler* stressed the seriousness of this scroll because it does not end with military victory and the ensuing festivities but with the tragic loss of millions. Hassine suggested that a *Purim Katan,* a holiday in miniature, be observed to honor the memory of the victims on the international day that marks the end of World War II: November 11.

Hassine's efforts suggest a continuum of regressive time and space in a world where persecution is the expected Jewish condition. With

---

1. See http://www.yadvashem.org/yv/en/exhibitions/bearing-witness/corcos.asp.
2. According to Rafael Medoff, the author of this *megilla* was likely writing his work at the same time that American authorities, credited in part with liberating Jews from Tunisia and Morocco, were trying "to keep in place the anti-Jewish legislation imposed in North Africa by the Nazis." See http://new.wymaninstitute.org/2011/03/megillat-hitler-fdr-and-the-jews/.

this in mind, one passage of Herzl's "A Solution to the Jewish Question" would not have sounded odd in the mouth of Mordecai, some thousands of years earlier. The Jewish experience of loyalty met with crushing dismissiveness at best and death at worst led Herzl to the conclusion that, metaphorically speaking, there was no future in Shushan:

> We have honestly striven everywhere to merge ourselves in the social life of surrounding communities, and to preserve only the faith of our fathers. It has not been permitted to us. In vain we are loyal patriots, in some places our loyalty running to extremes; in vain do we make the same sacrifices of life and property as our fellow citizens; in vain do we strive to increase the fame of our native land in science and art, or her wealth by trade and commerce. In countries where we have lived for centuries we are still cried down as strangers; and often by those whose ancestors were not yet domiciled in the land where Jews had already made experience of suffering. Yet, in spite of all, we are loyal subjects ... who were forced to emigrate. If we could only be left in peace ...[3]

Efforts to benefit the host culture may be met with temporary success but will never eventuate in the experience of being truly welcomed, settled, and accepted. This psychic reality experienced as a people has had a profoundly limiting effect on individual and communal self-understanding. Michael Fox notes the book's impact on him personally:

> Although I doubt the historicity of the Esther story, and as a critical reader, I must make that clear, every year at Purim when I hear the Scroll read in the synagogue, I know that it is *true,* whatever the historical accuracy of its details. Indeed, I relive its truth and know its actuality. Almost without an effort of imagination, I feel something of the anxiety that seized the Jews of Persia upon learn-

3. Theodor Herzl, "A Solution to the Jewish Question," in *The Jew in the Modern World: A Documentary History,* ed. Paul R. Mendes-Flohr and Jehuda Reinharz (New York: Oxford University Press, 1980), 423.

> ing of Haman's threat to their lives, and I join in their exhilaration at their deliverance. Except that I do not think "their," but "my."[4]

The Book of Esther is as popular as it is because it captures the way Jews have experienced the world. In this regard, the Book of Esther is not only possible, persecution and hatred of the Jews is probable.

Today, we can view both scrolls, ancient and modern, from the perch of safety and autonomy, in a museum located in Jerusalem, overlooking its surrounding, crowded hills. The sad and happy stories of the Jewish experience blend with the same message: never forget. It's best to remember in a land that is ours.

4. Fox, *Character and Ideology*, introduction, 11.

A Note on the Text

The biblical translations used throughout this book are largely but not exclusively from the Jewish Publication Society Hebrew Bible, Masoretic Text, 1999, and the Jerusalem Bible Edition of the Koren Tanakh. Sometimes I have used an alternate published translation or my own when I felt the existing translation was too archaic or did not capture the nuance of a word in context. I have also used Sefaria's translation of Rashi and other commentaries where available. Otherwise, I use my own unless specifically indicated. The many talmudic citations throughout are mostly, but not always, from the Noé edition of the *Koren Talmud Bavli,* a translation into English of the Hebrew work of Rabbi Adin Even-Israel Steinsaltz. They include the words the translators used to fill in the ellipses and obscurities of the talmudic text for greater comprehension.

Acknowledgments

This is a bigger book than I probably should have written. I couldn't help myself. In the shadow of the staggering amount of commentary on the Book of Esther, I wanted to capture pieces of it all. That supposition was inherently flawed and impossible. Although I have yet to meet a biblical book I do not admire, I have a special relationship to the Book of Esther, having written my dissertation on Eliezer Ashkenazi's *Yosef Lekaḥ*. While I was unable to use much of the material, I have inserted some passages, paraphrasings, and notes from my dissertation where relevant. This research inspired a general preoccupation with the text; for years, I have been turning its verses inside out and upside down, in the spirit of Ben Bag Bag, and often finding striking, new, and bold interpretations.

With big books, the appreciation for editors enlarges. I would like to acknowledge, first and foremost, the outstanding support and encouragement of the Koren/Maggid team, led by the wry, fearless, and tireless Matthew Miller and series editor Reuven Ziegler; Tani Bayer, Debbie Ismailoff, Ita Olesker, Akiva Schick, Yehudit Singer-Freud, and Nechama Unterman. Their contribution to the dissemination of Jewish scholarship is inspiring. I do not take for granted the long relationship we have enjoyed and the fruits of that relationship. For partnering with Maggid, I extend my appreciation to Rabbi Simon Posner, a special reader, and the folks at OU Press. A special thanks to intern Judah Guggenheim for his assistance with the references. Although many have helped me with various aspects of this manuscript, I take full responsibility for any errors contained therein.

I am deeply grateful to my parents, in-laws, extended family, close friends, and students. You have all helped me weave the tapestry of text and Jewish continuity. Thanks also go to my spectacular children, those I gave birth to and those who joined our family through marriage: Tali, Yoni, Gavi, Bec, Shai, Alison, and Ayelet. Since the start of this book, we have also been blessed with two beautiful and exceptionally wonderful grandchildren, Erez and Adi. Jeremy, I am grateful for the light you bring each day.

Working on this book gave me an opportunity to revisit earlier research and redeem it from the often difficult process of studying it at an earlier stage of my life. "Let the redeemed of the Lord tell their story," says Psalms 107:2. I am grateful, as always, to the God who redeemed this story for me. Words cannot adequately express the disbelief at my good fortune.

Bibliography

Ackroyd, Peter. "Two Hebrew Notes." *Annual of the Swedish Theological Institute* 5 (1967): 82–86.

Albright, William Foxwell. *From the Stone Age to Christianity*. Baltimore: John Hopkins Press, 1957.

Allis, Oswald T. "The Reward of the King's Favorite (Esth. 6:8)." *Princeton Theological Review* 21 (1923): 621–32.

Almosnino, Moses ben Barukh. *Yedei Moshe*. 1597. Reprint, Farnborough, England: Gregg International Publishers, Ltd., 1969.

Alter, Robert. *The Art of Biblical Narrative*. New York: Basic Books, 1981.

———. *Strong as Death Is Love: The Song of Songs, Ruth, Esther, Jonah, Daniel*. New York: W. W. Norton & Company, 2015.

———. *The World of Biblical Literature*. New York: Basic Books, 1992.

Altmann, Alexander. 1971. "Astrology." *Encyclopedia Judaica*, 790–95. Jerusalem.

Anderson, Bernard W. "The Place of the Book of Esther in the Christian Bible." *Journal of Religion* 30 (1950): 32–43.

Appiah Kwame Anthony. *The Honor Code: How Moral Revolutions Happen*. New York: W. W. Norton & Company, 2011.

Arama, Isaac ben Meir. Introduction to commentary on Esther, *Akedat Yitzchak*. Lemberg, 1868.

Aristotle. *The Poetics of Aristotle*, translated by S. H. Butcher. London: Macmillan and Co., 1904.

Ashtor, Eliyahu. *The Jews of Moslem Spain.* 2 vols. Philadelphia: Jewish Publication Society, 1992.

Auerbach, Eric. "Odysseus' Scar." In *Mimesis: The Representation of Reality in Western Literature,* 3–23. Princeton: Princeton University Press, 2013.

Baer, Yitzhak. *A History of the Jews in Christian Spain.* 2 vols. 2nd ed. Philadelphia: Jewish Publication Society, 1992.

Bakhtin, Mikhail. *Rabelais and His World,* translated by Helene Iswolsky. Bloomington, IN: Indiana University Press, 1984.

Baldwin, Joyce G. *Esther: An Introduction and Commentary.* Tyndale Old Testament Commentaries. Leicester, England: Inter-Varsity Press, 1984.

Bardtke, Hans. "Das Buch Esther." *Zeitschrift für die Alttestamentliche Wissenschaft* 17/5. Gutersloh: Gutersloher Verlagshaus Gerd Mohn, 1963.

Barrick, William D. "Old Testament Introduction." *Syllabus OT,* 796 (Summer, 2012).

Barton, John. *Oracles of God: Perceptions of Ancient Prophecy in Israel after the Exile.* New York, 1996.

Baskins, Cristelle L. "Typology, Sexuality, and the Renaissance Esther." In *Sexuality and Gender in Early Modern Europe: Institutions, Texts, Images,* edited by James Grantham Turner, 31–54. Cambridge: Cambridge University Press, 1993.

Beal, Timothy K. *The Book of Hiding: Gender, Ethnicity, Annihilation and Esther.* London: Routledge, 1997.

Berg, Sandra Beth. *The Book of Esther: Motifs, Themes and Structure.* Missoula, MT: Scholars Press, 1979.

Berger, Yitzhak. "Mordechai and Flowing Myrrh: On the Presence of God in the Book of Esther." *Tradition* 49:3 (Fall 2016): 20–24.

———."Esther and Benjamite Royalty: A Study in Inner-Biblical Allusion." *Journal of Biblical Literature* 129 (2010): 625–44.

Berkovits, Eliezer. "Exile and Redemption." *Tradition* 14, no. 4 (1974): 5–19.

Berlin, Adele. "The Book of Esther and Ancient Storytelling." *JBL* 120, no. 1 (2001): 3–14.

———. "The Book of Esther: Writing a Commentary for a Jewish Audience." In *The Book of Esther in Modern Research*, edited by Sidnie White Crawford and Leonard J. Greenspoon, 9–16. London: T & T Clark International, 2003.

———. *Mikra LeYisrael*. Tel Aviv: Am Oved, 2001.

Berman, Joshua. "Establishing Narrative Analogy in Biblical Literature: Methodological Considerations." *Beit Mikra* 53, no. 1 (2008): 31–46.

Bialik, Hayyim Nahman and Yehoshua Hana Ravnitzky. *The Book of Legends/Sefer Ha-Aggadah*. New York: Schocken Books, 1992.

Bickerman, Elias. *Four Strange Books of the Bible*. New York: Schocken Books, 1967.

Bonfil, Robert. *Jewish Life in Renaissance Italy*. Berkeley: University of California Press, 1994.

Bourdieu, Pierre. "The Sentiment of Honor in Kabyle Society." In *Honor and Shame: The Values of Mediterranean Society*, edited by J. G. Peristiany. Chicago: University of Chicago Press, 1966.

Bowman, James. *Honor: A History*. San Francisco: Encounter Books, 2007.

Brenner, A. "On the Semantic Field of Humor, Laughter and the Comic in the Old Testament." In *On Humour and the Comic in the Hebrew Bible*. Bible and Literature Series, 39–58. Sheffield: Sheffield Academic Press, 1990.

Brettler, Marc Zvi. *How to Read the Jewish Bible*. New York: Oxford University Press, 2005.

Brockington, L. H. *Ezra, Nehemiah and Esther*. Century Bible New Series. London: Thomas Nelson & Sons, 1969.

Brown, Erica. "In Death as in Life." *Bible Review* 15, no. 3 (June 1999): 40–47.

———. *Jonah: The Reluctant Prophet*. Jerusalem: Maggid/OU Press, 2017.

———. *Seder Talk: The Conversational Haggada*. Jerusalem: Maggid/OU Press, 2015.

———. "Strange Words Between Strangers." In *Torah of the Mothers: Contemporary Jewish Women Read Classical Jewish Texts*, edited by Ora Wiskind Elper and Susan Handelman, 244–61. Jerusalem: Urim Publications, 2000.

Brown, J. M. "Rabbinic Interpretations in the Characters and Plot of the Book of Esther (As Reflected in Midrash Esther Rabba)." *HUC-JIR* (1976).

Browne, L. E. "Esther." In *Peake's Commentary on the Bible*, 381–85. London: Thomas Nelson and Sons, 1962.

Broyde, Michael J. "Defilement of the Hands, Canonization of the Bible, and the Special Status of Esther, Ecclesiastes, and Song of Songs." *Judaism* 44, no. 1 (Winter 1995): 65–79.

Bryce, Glendon E. Review of Sandra Beth Berg, "The Book of Esther: Motifs, Themes and Structure." *JBL* 100, no. 2 (1981): 276.

Burrow, Millar. *More Light on the Dead Sea Scrolls*. London: Secker and Warburg, 1958.

Bush, Frederic W. "The Book of Esther: *Opus non gratum* in the Christian Canon." In *Bulletin for Biblical Research* 8 (1998): 39–54.

Cassel, Paulus. *An Explanatory Commentary on Esther*. Edinburgh: T & T Clark, 1988.

Chambers, David S. *Patrons and Artists in the Italian Renaissance*. Columbia: University of South Carolina Press, 1982.

Chevalier, Nicole. "The Discoverers of the Palace of Susa." In *The Palace of Darius at Susa: The Great Royal Residence of Achaemenid Persia*, edited by Jean Perrot. London: I. B. Taurus, 2013.

Clines, David J. A. "Esther and the Future of the Commentary." In *The Book of Esther in Modern Research*, edited by Sidnie White Crawford and Leonard J. Greenspoon, 17–30. London: T & T Clark International, 2003.

———. *The Esther Scroll: The Story of the Story*. Sheffield: JSOT Press, 1984.

———. Review of W. Hermann, *Esther im Streit der Meinungen. Society for Old Testament Study Book List* 78 (1988): 10.

Coggins, Richard J. and S. Paul Re'emi. *Israel among the Nations: A Commentary on the Books of Nahum and Obadiah*. Grand Rapids, MI: William B. Eerdmans Publishing, 1985.

Cohen, Abraham D. "'*Hu Ha-goral*': The Religious Significance of Esther." *Judaism* 23 (1974): 87–94.

Cohen, Norman J. *Masking and Unmasking Ourselves: Interpreting Biblical Texts on Clothing and Identity*. Woodstock, VT: Jewish Lights, 2012.

Collins, John J. "The Court Tales in Daniel and the Development of Apocalyptic." *JBL* 94, no. 2 (1975): 218–34.

Cornill, C. H. *Introduction to the Canonical Books of the Old Testament,* translated by G. Box. New York: Williams and Norgate, 1907.

Craig, Kenneth. *Reading Esther: A Case for a Literary Carnivalesque.* Louisville, KY: Westminster John Knox Press, 1995.

Crawford, Sidnie White. "Esther and Judith: Contrasts in Character." In *The Book of Esther in Modern Research,* edited by Sidnie White Crawford and Leonard J. Greenspoon, 61–76. London: T & T Clark International, 2003.

———. "Esther." In *The Women's Bible Commentary,* edited by Carol A. Newsom and Sharon H. Ringe, 124–29. Louisville, KY: Westminster John Knox Press, 1992.

———. "Esther: A Feminine Model for Jewish Diaspora." In *Gender and Difference in Ancient Israel,* edited by Peggy L. Day, 161–77. Minneapolis: Fortress Press, 1989.

Dalley, Stephanie. *Esther's Revenge at Susa: From Sennacherib to Ahasuerus.* London: Oxford University Press, 2007.

Didion, Joan. *The Year of Magical Thinking.* New York: Vintage, 2007.

Eisen, Robert. "Joseph Ibn Kaspi on the Secret Meaning of the Scroll of Esther." In *Revue des Etudes Juives* (July-August 2001): 379–408.

Eisenberg, Michael. *The Vanishing Jew: A Wake-Up Call from the Book of Esther.* Charleston: CreateSpace Independent Publishing Platform, 2017.

Eissfeldt, Otto. *The Old Testament.* New York: Harper and Row, 1965.

Feintuch, Yossi. "Judah and Jacob; Ahab and Ahasuerus – Comments on the Methodology of the Use of Analogy as an Exegetical Device." *Megadim* 44 (2006): 9–23.

Fokkelman, J. P. *Narrative Art in Genesis: Specimens of Stylistic and Structural Analysis.* 2nd ed. Sheffield: Sheffield Academic Press, 1991.

Fox, Marvin. "The Moral Philosophy of Maharal." In *Jewish Thought in the Sixteenth Century,* 167–83. Cambridge: Harvard University Center for Jewish Studies, 1983.

Fox, Michael V. *Character and Ideology in the Book of Esther.* Grand Rapids, MI: William B. Eerdmans Publishing, 2001.

———. "Three Esthers." In *The Book of Esther in Modern Research*, edited by Sidnie White Crawford and Leonard J. Greenspoon, 50–60. London: T & T Clark International, 2003.

Friedlander, Gerald. *Pirkei de Rebbi Eliezer*. New York: Hermon, 1965.

Friere, Paulo. *Pedagogy of the Oppressed*. New York: Continuum Publishing Company, 2000.

Fuchs, Esther. "Status and Role of Female Heroines in the Biblical Narrative." In *Women in the Hebrew Bible: A Reader*, edited by Alice Bach, 45–52. London: Routledge, 2013.

———. "Who Is Hiding the Truth? Deceptive Women and Biblical Androcentrism." In *Feminist Perspectives on Biblical Scholarship*, edited by A. Y. Collins, 149–60. Chico, California: 1985.

Fuerst, Wesley J. *The Cambridge Bible Commentary: The Books of Ruth, Esther, Ecclesiastes, the Song of Songs, Lamentations*. Cambridge: Cambridge University Press, 1975.

Gan, Moshe. "The Book of Esther in Light of the Story of Joseph in Egypt." *Tarbiz* 31 (1961–1962): 144–49.

Garsiel, M. *The First Book of Samuel: A Literary Study of Comparative Structures, Analogies and Parallels*. Ramat Gan: Revivim Publishing House, 1985.

Gaster, Theodore. "Esther 1:22." *JBL* 69, no. 4 (1950): 381.

Gindin, Thamar E. *The Book of Esther Unmasked*. Zeresh Books, 2015.

Ginzberg, Louis. *The Legends of the Jews*, translated by Henrietta Szold. 4 vols. Philadelphia: Jewish Publication Society of America, 1909.

Gleicher, Jules. "Mordecai and the Exilarch: Some Thoughts on the Book of Esther." *Interpretation* 28 (2001): 187–200.

Goitein, Solomon. "Megillat Esther." In *Iyunim BaMikra*, 59–72. Tel Aviv, 1957.

Gordis, Robert. *Megillat Esther: The Masoretic Hebrew Text with Introduction, New Translation and Commentary*. New York: Ktav, 1974.

———. "Religion, Wisdom and History in the Book of Esther." *JBL* 100, no. 3 (September 1981): 388.

———. *Purim and Hanukkah in Custom and Tradition*. New York: Henry Schuman, 1950

Green, Alexander. "Power, Deception, and Comedy: The Politics of Exile in the Book of Esther." *Jewish Political Studies Review* 23, nos. 1–2 (Spring 2011): 61–78.

Green, Arthur. *The Language of Truth: The Torah Commentary of the Sefat Emet*. Philadelphia: Jewish Publication Society, 1998.

Green, Barbara. *Mikhail Bakhtin and Biblical Scholarship: An Introduction*. Atlanta: Society of Biblical Literature, 2000.

Greenspoon, Leonard J. "From Maidens and Chamberlains to Harems and Hot Tubs: Five Hundred Years of Esther in English." In *The Book of Esther in Modern Research*, edited by Sidnie White Crawford and Leonard J. Greenspoon, 217–41. London: T & T Clark International, 2003.

Greenstein, Edward L. "The Scroll of Esther." *Fiction* 9, no. 3 (1990): 52–63.

Grossfeld, Bernard. *The First Targum to Esther*. New York: Sepher-Hermon Press, 1983.

———. *The Two Targums of Esther: Translated, with Apparatus and Notes*. Collegeville, MN: Liturgical Press, 1991.

Grossman, Jonathan. "'Dynamic Analogies' in the Book of Esther." *Vetus Testamentum* 59 (2009): 394–414.

———. "The Edicts of Haman and the Vineyard of Naboth." *Megadim* 30 (1999): 55–58.

———. *The Outer Narrative and the Hidden Reading*. Winona Lake, IN: Eisenbrauns, 2011.

———. "The Vanishing Character in Biblical Narrative: The Role of Hathach in Esther 4." *Vetus Testamentum* 62 (2012): 561–71.

Groves, Elizabeth. "Double Take: Another Look at the Second Gathering of Virgins in Esther 2.19a." In *The Book of Esther in Modern Research*, edited by Sidnie White Crawford and Leonard J. Greenspoon, 91–110. London: T & T Clark International, 2003.

Gunn, David M. and Danna Nolan Fewell. *Narrative in the Hebrew Bible*. London: Oxford University Press, 1993.

Hacham, Amos. *Ḥamesh Megillot, Daat Mikra*. Jerusalem: Mossad HaRav Kook, 1973.

Hacker, Joseph R. "HaYeiush Min HaGeula VeHaTikva HaMeshiḥit BeKhitvei Shelomo LeVeit HaLevi MiSalonika." *Tarbiz* 39 (1970): 195–213.

———. *The Ottoman-Jewish Encounter: A Social and Cultural History of the Jews in the Ottoman Empire*. Jerusalem: Hebrew University Press, 2013.

Halbertal, Moshe and Stephen Holmes. *The Beginning of Politics: Power in the Book of Samuel*. Princeton: Princeton University Press, 2017.

Hallo, W. W. "The First Purim." *The Biblical Archeologist* 46, no. 1 (1983): 19–29.

Haran, Menachem. *Olam HaTanakh*. 24 vols. Tel Aviv: Ministry of Education and Culture, 1999.

Harris, Monford. "Purim: The Celebration of Dis-Order." *Judaism* 26 (1977): 161–70.

Harvey, Dorothea. "Book of Esther." In *The Interpreter's Dictionary of the Bible*. Vol. 2, edited by George Buttrick. Nashville: Abingdon, 1962.

Hazony, Yoram. *The Dawn: Political Teachings on the Book of Esther*. Jerusalem: Shalem Press, 1995.

Herzl, Theodor. "A Solution of the Jewish Question." In *The Jew in the Modern World: A Documentary History*, edited by Paul R. Mendes-Flohr and Jehuda Reinharz, 533–37. New York: Oxford University Press, 1980.

Hiebert, Theodore. "The Tower of Babel and the Origin of the World's Cultures." *Journal of Biblical Literature* 126, no. 1 (Spring 2007): 29–58.

Holzer, Elie. "Allowing the Biblical Text to Do Its Pedagogical Work: Connecting Interpretive Activity and Moral Education." *Journal of Moral Education* 36, no. 4 (2007): 497–514.

Homer. *Herodotus*. Translated by A. D. Godley. 4 vols. Cambridge, MA: Harvard University Press, 1924.

Hoshander, Jacob. *The Book of Esther in Light of History*. 1923. Reprint, Andesite Press, 1983.

Housel, Morgan. "Ironies of Luck." *Collaborative Fund*. March 14, 2018. http://www.collaborativefund.com/blog/ironies-of-luck/.

Humphreys, W. Lee. "A Life-Style for Diaspora: A Study of the Tales of Esther and Daniel." *JBL* 92 (1973): 211–23.

Ishiguro, Kazuoa. *The Remains of the Day*. New York: Vintage, 1990.

Isserles, Moses. *Meḥir Yayin*, edited by Joel Avidor. Jerusalem: Mossad HaRav Kook, 1926.

Josephus, Flavius. *Antiquities of the Jews: The Complete Works*. Translated by William Whiston. London: Wordsworth Classics, 2006.

Kasher, H. Introduction to *Shulḥan Kesef*. [Hebrew] Jerusalem: 1996.

Keil, C. F. *Commentary of the Old Testament*. Vol. 3. Reprint, Grand Rapids, MI: William B. Eerdmans Publishing, 1971.

Kirsch, Adam. *The People and the Books*. New York: W. W. Norton & Company, 2016.

Klitsner, Judy. *Subversive Sequels: How Biblical Stories Mine and Undermine Each Other*. Philadelphia: Jewish Publication Society, 2009.

Kohen, Yosef. "Megillat Esther BaAspaklarya Shel Ḥakhmei Tzefat BaMe'a Ha-16." *She'arim* 5, no. 3 (1966).

Kohler, Andrea. *Passing Time: An Essay on Waiting*. New York: Upper West Side Philosophers, Inc., 2017.

Koller, Aaron. *Esther in Ancient Jewish Thought*. New York: Cambridge University Press, 2014.

Kugel, James L. *The Great Shift: Encountering God in Biblical Times*. Boston: Houghton Mifflin Harcourt, 2017.

LaCocque, André. *Esther Regina: A Bakhtinian Reading*. Evanston, IL: Northwestern University Press, 2007.

Laffey, Alice L. *An Introduction to the Old Testament: A Feminist Perspective*. Philadelphia: Fortress Press, 1988.

Landy, F. "Humour as a Tool for Biblical Exegesis." In *On Humour and the Comic in the Hebrew Bible,* Bible and Literature Series, 99–115. Sheffield: Sheffield Academic Press, 1990,

Langston, Scott M. "Reading a Text Backwards: The Book of Esther and Nineteenth-Century Jewish American Interpretations." In *Esther in Modern Research*, edited by Sidnie White Crawford and

Leonard J. Greenspoon, 200–16. London: T & T Clark International, 2003.

Laniak, Timothy S. "Esther's 'Volkcentrism' and the Reframing of Post-Exilic Judaism." In *The Book of Esther in Modern Research*, edited by Sidnie White Crawford and Leonard J. Greenspoon, 77–90. London: T & T Clark International, 2003.

———. *Shame and Honor in the Book of Esther*. Atlanta: Scholars Press, 1998.

Levenson, Jon D. *Esther: A Commentary*. Louisville, KY: Westminster John Knox Press, 1997.

———. "The Scroll of Esther in Ecumenical Perspective." *Journal of Ecumenical Studies* 13 (1976): 440–52.

Lewis, Bernard. *The Jews of Islam*. Princeton: Princeton University Press, 1984.

Loader, J. A. "Esther as a Novel with Different Levels of Meaning." *Zeitschrift fur die alttestamentliche Wissenschaft* 90 (1978): 417–21.

Luzzatto, Moshe Chaim. *The Path of the Just*. Jerusalem: Feldheim Publishers, 1980.

Magonet, J. "The Liberal and the Lady: Esther Revisited." *Judaism* 29 (1980): 167–76.

Malul, M. "More on *paḥad yisḥāq* and the Oath by the Thigh." *Vetus Testamentum* 35 (1985): 194–96.

McKane, W. "A Note on Esther IX and I Samuel XV." *JTS* 12 (1961): 260–61.

Medoff, Rafael. "'Megillat Hitler,' FDR, and the Jews." The David S. Wyman Institute for Holocaust Studies. Marc 2011. http://new.wymaninstitute.org/2011/03/megillat-hitler-fdr-and- the-jews/.

Meier, Samuel E. *Speaking of Speaking: Marking of Direct Discourse in the Hebrew Bible*. Netherlands: Brill, 1992.

Montefiore, Claude. *The Bible for Home Reading*. 2 vols. New York: Macmillan Company, 1899.

Moore, Carey A. "Archeology and the Book of Esther." *The Biblical Archeologist* 38 (1975): 62–79.

———. *Daniel, Esther, and Jeremiah: The Additions*. New Haven, CT: Yale University Press, 1977.

———. *Esther: A New Translation with Introduction and Notes*. Garden City, NY: Doubleday, 1971.

———. "A Greek Witness to a Different Hebrew Text of Esther." *Zeitschrift fur die Alttestamentliche Wissenschaft* 79 (1967): 351–58.

———. "On the Origins of the LXX Additions to the Book of Esther." *Journal of Biblical Literature* 92 (1973): 382–93.

———. *Studies in the Book of Esther*. New York: Ktav, 1982.

———. *Esther: The Anchor Bible*, Vol. 7B. New York: Doubleday, 1971.

Neulander, Judith S. "The Ecumenical Esther: Queen and Saint in Three Western Belief Systems." In *The Book of Esther in Modern Research*, edited by Sidnie White Crawford and Leonard J. Greenspoon, 176–99. London: T & T Clark International, 2003.

Noble, P. R. "Esau, Tamar, and Joseph: Criteria for Identifying Inner-Biblical Allusion." *Vetus Testamentum* 52 (2002): 219–52.

Okland, Jorunn. "Ancient Drinking in Modern Bible Translation." In *Stones, Bones, and the Sacred: Essays on Material Culture and Ancient Religion in Honor of Dennis E. Smith*, edited by Alan H. Cadwallader, 85–100. Society of Biblical Literature, 2016.

Oppenheim, A. L. "On Royal Gardens in Mesopotamia." *Journal of Near Eastern Studies* 24 (1965): 328–33.

Orwell, George. *1984*. New York: Signet Classic, 1981.

Paton, Lewis Bayles. *A Critical and Exegetical Commentary on the Book of Esther*. New York: Scribner, 1908.

———. *International Critical Commentary: Esther*. London: T & T Clark, 1908.

Perrot, Jean. *The Palace of Darius at Susa: The Great Royal Residence of Achaemenid Persia*. London: I. B. Taurus, 2013.

Pfeiffer, Robert. *Introduction to the Old Testament*. New York: Harper and Brothers, 1941.

Radday, Yehuda T. "Chiasm in Joshua, Judges and Others." *LB* 27/28 (September 1973): 6–13.

———. "On Missing the Humour in the Bible: An Introduction." In *On Humour and the Comic in the Hebrew Bible*. Bible and Literature Series, 21–38. Sheffield: Sheffield Academic Press, 1990.

Ratzaby, Yehuda. "MiFeirush Rav Se'adya LiMegillat Esther." In *Sefer Yovel LiKhevod...Yosef Dov HaLevi Soloveitchik*, edited by Shaul Yisraeli, Nahum Lamm, and Yitzhak Refael. Jerusalem, 1983–1984.

Roskies, David G. *Against the Apocalypse: Responses to Catastrophe in Modern Jewish Culture*. Cambridge, MA: Harvard University Press, 1984.

Roth, Cecil. *A History of the Marranos*. Philadelphia: Jewish Publication Society, 1947.

Rowland, Christopher. *The Open Heaven: A Study of Apocalyptic in Judaism and Early Christianity*. New York: Wipf and Stock Publishers, 1982.

Rubenstein, Jeffrey L. *The Culture of the Babylonian Talmud*. Baltimore: Johns Hopkins University Press, 2003.

Ruderman, David. *Jewish Thought and Scientific Discovery in Early Modern Europe*. New Haven: Yale University Press, 1995.

Safran, Bezalel. "Bahya ibn Pakuda's Attitude toward the Courtier Class." In *Studies in Medieval Jewish History and Literature*. Vol. 1, edited by Isadore Twersky, 161–65. Cambridge, MA: Harvard University Center for Jewish Studies, 1979.

Sandmel, Samuel. *The Enjoyment of Scripture*. New York: Oxford University, 1972.

Sarna, Nachum. "Excursus #2: The Abandoned Hero Motif." In *The JPS Torah Commentary: Exodus*, 268. Philadelphia: Jewish Publication Society, 1991.

———. *Understanding Genesis: The Heritage of Biblical Israel*. New York: Schocken Books, 1970.

Sasson, Jack M. "Esther." In *The Literary Guide to the Bible*, edited by Robert Alter and Frank Kermode, 335–42. Cambridge, MA: Belknap Press, 1987.

———. *Kabbalah*. New York: Meridian, 1974.

Shalev, Meir. *Four Meals*. Edinburgh: Cannongate Books, 2002.

Shmeruk, Chone. "Purim-shpil." *Encyclopedia Judaica*. Vol. 13. 1971, 1396–404.

Siegel, Monique. "Book of Esther – a Novelle." *Dor le Dor* 14 (1985): 142–51.

Simkovich, Malka Z., Zev Farber, and David Steinberg. "Ahasuerus and Vashti: The Story Megillat Esther Does Not Tell You." TheTorah.com. http://thetorah.com/ahasuerus-and-vashti-the-story-megillat-esther-does-not-tell-you/.

Simon, Moshe David. "'Many Thoughts in the Heart of Man…': Irony and Theology in the Book of Esther." *Tradition* 31, no. 4 (1997): 5–27.

Simon, Uriel. "Minor Characters in Biblical Narrative." *Journal for the Study of the Old Testament* 46 (1990): 11–19, and in *Reading Prophetic Narratives*, translated by Lenn J. Schramm. Bloomington, IN: Indiana University Press, 1997.

Soloveitchik, Joseph B. *On Repentance*, adapted and edited by Pinchas H. Peli. Jerusalem: Maggid, 2017.

———. "Redemption, Prayer and Talmud Torah." *Tradition* 17, no. 2 (1978): 55–72.

Soltes, Ori Z. "Images and the Book of Esther: From Manuscript Illumination to Midrash." In *The Book of Esther in Modern Research*, edited by Sidnie White Crawford and Leonard J. Greenspoon, 137–75. London: T & T Clark International, 2003.

Sommers, Tamler. *Why Honor Matters*. New York: Basic, 2018.

Spufford, Francis. *Golden Hill*. New York: Scribner, 2016.

Standage, Tom. *A History of the World in 6 Glasses*. New York: Walker and Company, 2005.

Stanton, Elizabeth Cady and Lucinda B. Chandler. "The Book of Esther." In *The Woman's Bible*, edited by Elizabeth Cady Stanton. Reprint, Mineola, NY: Dover Publications, 2003.

Sternberg, Meir. *The Poetics of Biblical Narrative: Ideological Literature and the Drama of Reading*. Bloomington, IN: Indiana University Press, 1987.

Stewart, Frank Henderson. *Honor*. Chicago: University of Chicago Press, 1994.

Stillman, Norman. *The Jews of Arab Lands*. Philadelphia: Jewish Publication Society, 1979.

Strickman, H. Norman. "Abraham Ibn Ezra's Non-Literal Interpretations." *HaKirah* 9 (2010): 281–96.

Talmon, Solomon. "'Wisdom' and the Book of Esther." *Vetus Testamentum* 13, no. 4 (1963): 419–55.

Tirosh-Samuelson, Hava. *Happiness in Premodern Judaism*. Cincinnati: Hebrew Union College Press, 2003.

Troyer, Kristin De. "Esther in Text – and Literary – Critical Paradise." In *The Book of Esther in Modern Research*, edited by Sidnie White Crawford and Leonard J. Greenspoon, 31–49. London: T & T Clark International, 2003.

———. "An Oriental Beauty Parlor: An Analysis of Est. 2:8–18 in the Hebrew, the Septuagint and the Second Greek Text." In *A Feminist Companion to Esther, Judith and Susanna*, edited by Athalya Brenner, 47–70. Sheffield: Sheffield Academic Press, 1995.

Walfish, Barry. *Esther in Medieval Garb*. Albany, NY: State University of New York Press, 1993.

———. "Kosher Adultery? The Mordecai-Esther-Ahasuerus Triangle in Talmudic, Medieval and Sixteenth-Century Exegesis." *The Book of Esther in Modern Research*, edited by Sidnie White Crawford and Leonard J. Greenspoon, 111–36. London: T & T Clark International, 2003.

Walton, John H. "The Mesopotamian Background of the Tower of Babel Account and Its Implications." *Bulletin for Biblical Research* 5 (1995): 155–75.

Wills, Lawrence M. *The Jew in the Court of the Foreign King*. Minneapolis: Fortress Press, 1990.

Wright, J. S. "Historicity in the Book of Esther." In *New Perspectives on the Old Testament*, edited by J. B. Payne. Waco, TX: Word, 1970.

Yehuda, A. S. "The Meaning of the Name Esther." *JRAS* 8 (1946): 174–78.

Yerushalmi, Yosef Hayim. *From Spanish Court to Italian Ghetto*. New York: Columbia University Press, 1971.

———. *The Lisbon Massacre of 1506 and the Royal Image in the Shebet Yehudah*. Cincinnati: Hebrew Union College, 1976.

Zaeske, Susan. "Unveiling Esther as a Pragmatic Radical Rhetoric." *Philosophy and Rhetoric* 33, no. 3 (2000): 194–216.

Zakovitch, Yair. *An Introduction to Inner-Biblical Interpretation*. Even-Yehuda: Kadima, 1992.

———. "The Tale of Naboth's Vineyard, I Kings 21." In *The Bible from Within: The Method of Total Interpretation,* edited by Meir Weiss, 379–405. Jerusalem: Magnes Press, Hebrew University, 1984.

Zeitlin, Solomon. "An Historical Study of the Canonization of the Hebrew Scriptures." *Proceedings of the American Academy for Jewish Research* 3 (1931–1932): 121–58.

Other books in the Maggid Studies in Tanakh series:

Genesis: From Creation to Covenant
Zvi Grumet

Joshua: The Challenge of the Promised Land
Michael Hattin

Judges: The Perils of Possession (forthcoming)
Michael Hattin

I Kings: Torn in Two
Alex Israel

II Kings: In a Whirlwind
Alex Israel

Isaiah
Yoel Bin-Nun and Binyamin Lau

Jeremiah: The Fate of a Prophet
Binyamin Lau

Ezekiel (forthcoming)
Tova Ganzel

Jonah: The Reluctant Prophet
Erica Brown

Nahum, Habakkuk, and Zephaniah
Yaakov Beasley

Haggai, Zechariah, and Malachi:
Prophecy in an Age of Uncertainty
Hayyim Angel

Ruth: From Alienation to Monarchy
Yael Ziegler

Nehemiah: Statesman and Sage
Dov S. Zakheim

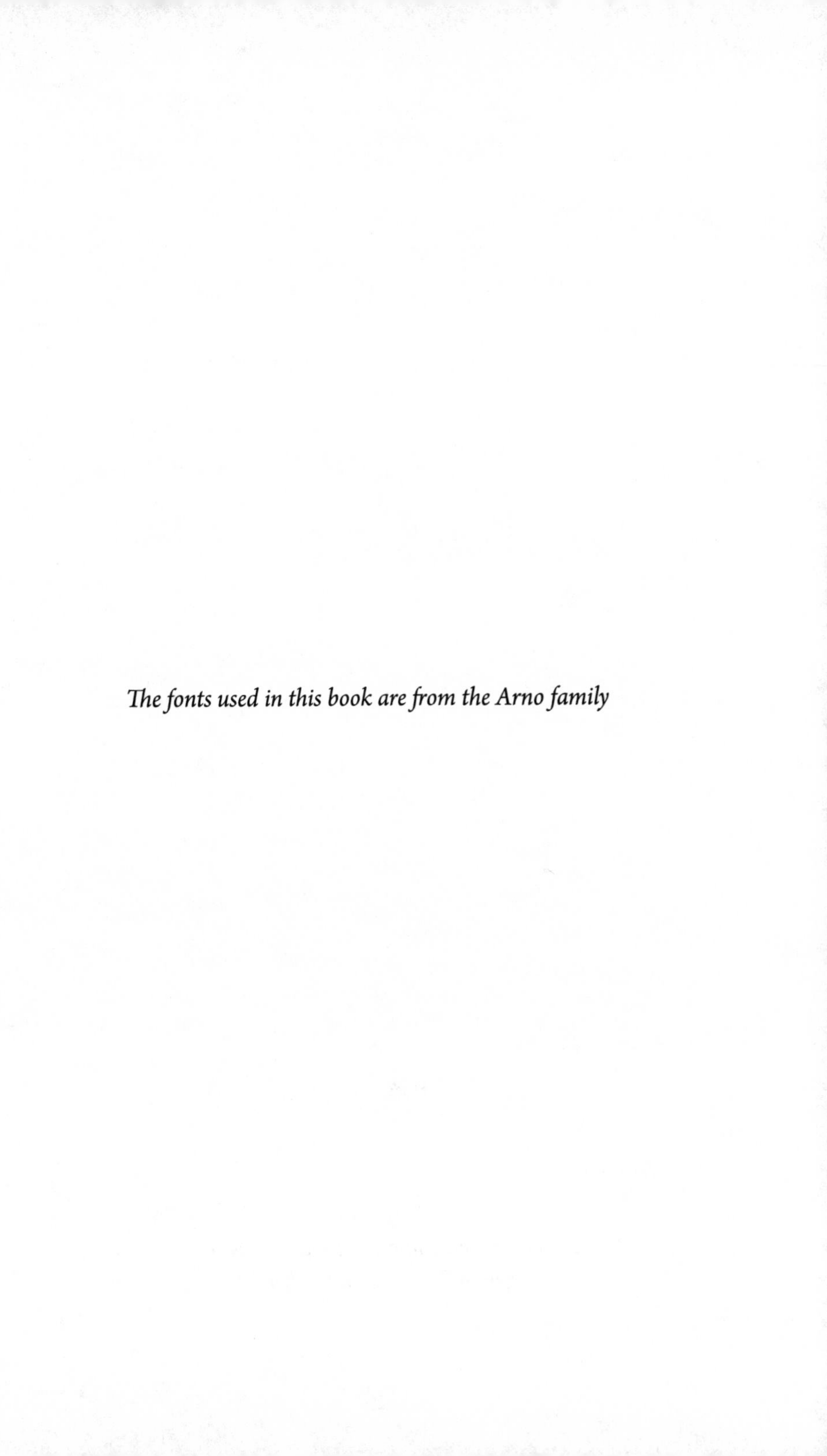

The fonts used in this book are from the Arno family

Maggid Books
The best of contemporary Jewish thought from
Koren Publishers Jerusalem Ltd.